JOURNEY TO THE HEART
OF THE CONDOR

JOURNEY TO THE HEART OF THE CONDOR

LOVE, LOSS, AND SURVIVAL IN A SOUTH AMERICAN DICTATORSHIP

For Jennifer — One of my favorite people on the planet. Dare to dream! Thanks for the many years of friendship and support ♡ Emily

Emily C. Creigh
Dr. Martín Almada

A PEACE CORPS WRITERS BOOK

JOURNEY TO THE HEART OF THE CONDOR:
LOVE, LOSS, AND SURVIVAL IN A SOUTH AMERICAN DICTATORSHIP

A Peace Corps Writers Book, an imprint of Peace Corps Worldwide

In collaboration with Casa Satori (www.casasatori.com) and the
Celestina Pérez de Almada Foundation (www.fcpa.org.py)

For more information, contact peacecorpsworldwide@gmail.com. Peace Corps Writers and the Peace
Corps Writers colophon are trademarks of PeaceCorpsWorldwide.org.

Cover design by Kathleen Koopman
Cover photo (and most interior photos) by Emily C. Creigh
Paraguay map by Wesley Fawcett Creigh
Author photo by Rochester Studios, Asunción

ISBN 10: 1935925644
ISBN 9781935925644

Library of Congress Control Number: 2015938014
Peace Corps Writers, Oakland, CA

First Peace Corps Writers Edition, February 2016; Second Edition, September 2016

The struggle of man against power is the struggle of memory against forgetting.

Milan Kundera
The Book of Laughter and Forgetting

Dedicated to the memory of Celestina Pérez de Almada,
pioneer of Paraguayan educational reform and martyr for freedom—
and to everyone engaged in the struggle for truth and justice.

Celestina Pérez de Almada, propulsora de la educación liberadora, militante del Partido Revolucionario Febrerista. Los ideales de justicia y solidaridad febreristas la llevaron a impulsar acciones de trascendencia social. Co-fundadora del Instituto "Juan Bautista Alberdi" de San Lorenzo y promotora del programa "Por un techo propio a cada maestro paraguayo". Víctima de la dictadura stronista, en el marco del OPERATIVO CONDOR, murió a causa de las torturas psicológicas a que fue sometida durante el secuestro y prisión de su esposo, Martín Almada, el día 5 de diciembre de 1974 en San Lorenzo, Paraguay.-

Museo de las Memorias: Dictadura y Derechos Humanos – Paraguay

Celestina Pérez de Almada, driving force of liberation education, militant member of the Febrerist Revolutionary Party. Febrerist ideals of justice and solidarity moved her to support movements of social significance. Co-founder of the Juan Bautista Alberdi Institute of San Lorenzo and developer of the campaign "A Roof for Every Paraguayan Educator." Victim of the Stroessner dictatorship, under Operation Condor, died as a result of the psychological torture she was subjected to during the kidnapping and imprisonment of her husband, Martín Almada, December 5, 1974, in San Lorenzo, Paraguay.

Museum of Memories: Dictatorship and Human Rights

PREFACE

To teach is not to transfer knowledge but to create the possibility for the production or construction of knowledge...The teacher is no longer merely "the one who teaches," but one who is himself taught in dialogue with students.

PAULO FREIRE (1921–97)

It is 2011, the first of July, and my life is over.

My working life, anyway. I've just been laid off from my thirteen-year dream job with Pima College Adult Education for the third and final time in two years, now that funding for the Family Literacy program has dried up for good.

It appears that an educated populace is not in the interest of our elected officials.

I scrape together a modest pension, take a deep breath, and set out on another dream: the long-awaited journey to my Peace Corps (PC) past and this much-hoped-for book.

I have no idea that what I'm about to discover will change my life.

A quick Internet search reveals a Paraguayan educator whose name I don't recognize, as I haven't followed events in that country since I left it thirty-six years ago: Dr. Martín Almada, lawyer, PhD, environmentalist...*political prisoner from 1974 to 1977?* Excuse me? Those were *my* years! I am spellbound by his story but devastated to realize that *I was in Paraguay as a PC trainee and volunteer for thirty of the thirty-four months Dr. Almada languished in prison.*

Especially heartbreaking for me is that as a professor and school administrator, Dr. Almada had been a follower of Brazilian liberation educator Paulo Freire (as had I at Pima College, having presented on Freire's "Problem Posing" technique at a conference) and was passionate about teaching critical thinking—which, along with his relentless fight for teachers' rights, was why he had been under surveillance. Finally, after he denounced the Paraguayan educational system in his August 1974 doctoral dissertation, Dr. Almada was picked up, dragged to the Office of Investigations in downtown Asunción, accused of being a communist, and tortured...only weeks before I arrived in that city as a fresh-faced PC recruit.

An educated populace was clearly not in the interest of the dictator, Alfredo Stroessner, either.

Because this type of news was censored—and Peace Corps volunteers (PCVs) are strictly prohibited from getting involved in local politics—I knew nothing of Dr. Almada at the time...although we were often just blocks away, me enjoying dinner with friends in a café as he was fighting for his life in the basement of a government building. Reading about him now overwhelms me. I know the PC often has no choice but to cooperate with host governments, but I see for the first time how from 1975 to 1977, as a PCV in agricultural extension and public health, I effectively *worked for the dictator* who imprisoned Dr. Almada without due process, appropriated his livelihood, and caused the death of his wife.

I discover Martín's book on his website and can't help but weep as I read about his ordeal. I realize I must contact this courageous man, apologize to him, and ask to include his story, in his voice, to complete my version of those years, if he will let me—the United States was, after all, complicit in his suffering. I take weeks to compose the right email, then one night screw my courage to the sticking point and click SEND, having no idea what, if anything, will become of my true confession as it disappears into cyberspace.

To my astonishment, Dr. Almada responds before I even wake up the next morning, as he is four time zones ahead. He thanks me and says he is "still struggling against impunity." He says his concept of Americans changed when, as visiting professor at Kansas State University from 2000 to 2002, he saw how "government is one thing and the people another entirely. I want you to know that I am fond of your people, who are noble and generous." He invites me to Asunción for a "delicious typical meal made in a solar oven" and, in a postscript, says I am welcome to include his story.

Since then, in my three trips back to Paraguay (I'd also taken my family there in 2004), I have spent many hours with this diminutive, soft-spoken man who sacrificed so much for freedom and human rights. I am honored and grateful to stand with him in support of his vital work, which has changed history.

On December 22, 1992, in a police station outside Asunción, Dr. Almada and a courageous young judge found several tons of documents now known as the Archives of Terror. These meticulous records of the covert kidnapping, torture, and assassination of thousands of innocent people included Martín's own file. The landmark discovery resulted in the immediate arrest of some of Martín's torturers—who for years had denied to his face that such atrocities ever occurred—and the ultimate indictment of several high-level officials throughout South America's "Southern Cone" (Argentina, Bolivia, Brazil, Chile, Paraguay, and Uruguay) including Chile's Augusto Pinochet and Argentina's Rafael Videla. (Alfredo Stroessner, on the other hand, died with impunity in Brazil in 2006.)

The archives also proved that Operation Condor, the secret campaign to carry out terrorist attacks against political opponents around the world, did in fact exist, and was supported by the United States. Estimates vary, but Condor resulted in at least fifty thousand people killed, thirty thousand "disappeared" (certainly killed), and four hundred thousand arrested. And that's just Condor, not the other country-specific "dirty wars" of state terrorism being waged at the time. It stands to reason that many more thousands of surviving family members still search desperately for information about their missing loved ones.

So many lives ruined…and the tragedy is that, according to the 1985 Trial of the Juntas, so-called "subversives" never posed a viable threat to the dictatorships in the first place.[1]

The day after Martín's discovery of the archives, the Third Precinct—a crowded prison in Asunción where he had spent four miserable months—was closed. Fittingly, the Museum of Memories, founded by Martín and his second

---

1 *"El estado de necesidad"* ("The State of Need," desaparecidos.org), documents of the Trial of the Juntas.

wife, journalist María Stella Cáceres, now sits across the street from the Third Precinct, in offices and cells formerly used by the dictatorship.

Months after being released from his 1,038 days in Stroessner's hell, in February 1978 Dr. Almada was exiled to Panama, where he finished the book he'd begun in prison, much of it written (by him) in shorthand on papers from cellmates' packs of Virginia Slims and smuggled out in his mother's clothing. Currently in its fourteenth printing in Spanish, *Paraguay: Forgotten Prison, Exiled Country* (Asunción: MARBEN, 2010) is published here in English for the first time (with my edits and some translation).

The backbone of our coincident memoir, Martín's story is a gripping account not only of his prison experience and the inner workings of the dictatorship, but also of conversations he had with prisoners from across the political spectrum about how to solve their country's problems. He writes fondly of his humble beginnings, his martyred wife, and his path to awareness, as well as that of his mother, whom he taught to overcome her fear of confronting people in power—a Paulo Freire-based skill we used to empower women in the Family Literacy program as well.

I am certain that Martín's story will touch you as it did me. We were unknown to one another but had several things in common: we were both curious, dedicated learners who loved to read the dictionary and engage in scholarly pursuits; we both believed in a more evolved, communal society; and we were both driven to observe and record the experiences that were so deeply affecting our lives, sharing a dogged need for self-expression that helped us survive our respective grief.

A few months after graduating from college, I made the decision to join the Peace Corps, a lifelong dream, and was changed forever by the opportunity I was given not only to be of service and truly valued, but also to see life from a different perspective, to learn more about the world—including myself—and discover inner strength in doing so. Since that time I have become a mother, teacher, professional musician, cancer survivor…I am sure the resilience I learned in the PC helped me get through those challenges.

But in 1975 I was sure of nothing. My father's sudden death the year before had left me shattered and adrift, the void inside me a black hole sucking me in. Of course my suffering didn't begin to compare with that of Dr. Almada, whose world had come tumbling down also, but in a most horrific way. What kept him going was his hope for a free and just Paraguay.

I had hope, too: that I might make the world a little better place and, in the process, become whole again. I was convinced the farther away from home I got, the sooner I could escape my demons and discover my purpose in life. The answer was waiting for me somewhere—I just had to go out and find it.

Forty years later, using original journals and letters, I have dug deep to create an affectionate and informative yet entertaining portrait of those often-rocky times, when Peace Corps life and work nearly consumed me, the Paraguayan people became my family, and I learned to love again.

Dr. Almada and I believe our interwoven narratives offer a unique and compelling window to the past. We hope you agree. Together we can keep the memory of those times alive, so that despite the troubling emergence of military drones—whose objectives mimic those of Operation Condor—and revelations of "extraordinary rendition" and "enhanced interrogation techniques" by the United States, such crimes against humanity will be halted forever and their perpetrators held accountable.

Congratulations on being part of the educated populace! And heartfelt thanks for joining us on our journey. We invite you to read our book in one of three ways: (1) Emily's story of personal transformation; (2) Martín's story of socio-political evolution; or (3) the two together, as they appear, for maximum impact—there are some uncanny parallels. We hope you will take the third path, of course, although the chapters are numbered to facilitate reading it any way you choose.

In peace,
Emily and Martín
September 2016 (2nd Edition)

NOTE: Names of persons in Emily's chapters have been changed except for family members, those who have passed on, and the rare exception. Conversations with native Spanish speakers presented here in English took place in Spanish or Guaraní; non-English words are defined either where they first occur or in context. There is also a glossary at the back. Guaraní words are (for the most part) spelled according to Antonio Ortíz Mayans's *New Dictionary of Spanish–Guaraní* (Buenos Aires: Librería Platero Editorial, 1973). For more information, please visit Casa Satori at www.casasatori.com.

WARNING: Dr. Almada's first two chapters contain descriptions of his torture. While it is disturbing to witness man's inhumanity to man, we believe the story must be told. As pacifists, however, we accept that some readers may choose to skip these chapters.

Dr. Almada presenting documents on Operation Condor to Pope Francis in September 2015. During a private audience with the pope on September 30, Martín requested that all Vatican archives related to the illicit pact be released.

Emily's Acknowledgments

I must first beg forgiveness from the fair city of Stockton, California, and its citizens for my somewhat disparaging remarks at the beginning of my story. It's true I was young and disaffected, but I must admit that I had come to love you both—a lot.

And many thanks to the beautiful country of Paraguay and its equally beautiful people. I treasure you and everything you have taught me.

I am forever indebted to the Peace Corps, which—despite being woefully underfunded—continues to improve lives and bring hope to people around the world. Every Peace Corps volunteer has a story. To all past, present, and future PCVs and staff: thank you for your service.

Words cannot express my gratitude to those who helped see me through this book, especially Dr. Martín Almada and his wife, María Stella Cáceres, for their courage and inspiration; my siblings, Ginny Creigh and Sam Creigh, for their understanding and support; my niece Wesley Fawcett Creigh, for showing me the way; and my husband's family, especially Connie Poley, for their ongoing encouragement.

More sincere thanks go to Peace Corps friends whose brains I picked: Alyce Tidball and family, Marjorie Becker, Bruce Brogan, Craig Wall, Loni Brönimann-Wells, Larry Hodgson, Shannon Hefler, and Mike Stake (Diego Hay would be in this list, but he succumbed to lung cancer in 2009—RIP, my friend); friends who listened, including Trish and Tom DeFilippis, Phil Ponce, Kay Kokwe, Ruby Anderson, Ed Stoltz, Bill Rost, Jean Griffin, Don Armstrong, Brian Parshall, Randi Pantera, members of the String Bean Folk Orchestra,

Carolina Turner, Pete and Kristi Everts, all the Camp Billyans from Telluride Bluegrass, and the Thayer Girls; and Theresa Cameranesi (RPCV–Paraguay) and other members of the School of Americas Watch (soaw.org) delegation to Paraguay in April 2013, along with the Paraguayan nonprofit SERPAJ (Servicio de Paz y Justicia, serpajpy.org.py).

Special thanks go to friends who were kind enough to read early versions of the manuscript: Evelyn VandenDolder, Sue Newman, Woody Hume, Dan Ferguson, and others; those who assisted once I was "finished": Rigoleto Alva, Robin Peel, Karen Smith Davenport, Chip Curry, Gregory McNamee, Beth Judd, Kathleen Koopman, Lynne Jaffe, and the Lost Hombre; and other essential advisors along the way: John Polle, Joe Sweeney and the Pima Writers' Forum of Tucson, Gail Woodard of Dudley Court Press, Renni Browne and Shannon Roberts of The Editorial Department, the team at CreateSpace, and Marian Haley Beil and John Coyne of Peace Corps Worldwide.

I am also grateful to the following: my Paraguayan friends from the time, especially Eva, Dominga, Margarita (RIP—she died in 2004, unaware that I would be visiting in a few months), 4-C club members, and their families; current Paraguayan friends Eva Martínez and family, Lilia Valdez of the Black Cat Hostel in Asunción, the Sosa family, and Antonio Dacak; my former colleagues in Family Literacy and those at Pima College Adult Education who brought Paulo Freire into our curriculum and lives; Sister Shirley and other programmers from Tucson's community radio station, KXCI 91.3 FM; and National Novel Writing Month (nanowrimo.org) for the book *No Plot? No Problem!* which I picked up with great skepticism at a Tucson Goodwill but ultimately motivated me to consider myself a writer and begin the process.

To my parents, F. Connor Creigh and Bonnie Lou Oswalt (RIP 1974 and 2000, respectively, Mom from lung cancer), I owe much gratitude and love for giving me good tools to work with and being there for me, no matter what.

Most of all, I wish to thank my family—Tom, Nicole, and Max—for loving and believing in me. You are my life.

All of you helped make this book possible. My deepest apologies and thanks to anyone I may have missed.

MARTÍN'S ACKNOWLEDGMENTS

My sincere thanks go to the following people for their contributions to my inspiration and other help in the writing of this book:

Celestina, the martyred educator, mother of my children and companion of my ideals, who died as a result of psychological torture and pain;

Amnesty International, especially the group Padrino No. 46 from Basel, Switzerland, in recognition of their humanitarian work in the defense of human rights, with special thanks to Rita and Gilbert Gervais, Pia and Urs Brogle, Margarita and Peter Saladin, and Albert von Brunn;

General Omar Torrijos Herrera, heir of the leader of the Paraguayan revolution, the Panamanian José de Antequera y Castro, and the people and government of Panamá, who welcomed me with affection;

Amanda L. Irwin and Naomi Ossar for translation coordination and editing of *Paraguay: Forgotten Prison, Exiled Country*, along with assistant translators Kit Cutler, Sonja Johnson, Jill Reifsteck, Jennifer Gallant, and Andrea Strickland;

Emily Creigh, for contacting me in 2011, for her tenacity in seeing the project through, and for her love of Paraguay and its people;

My children, Ricardo, Lincoln, and Celeste;

Above all, my beautiful and talented wife, María Stella Cáceres, whose vision and creativity—not to mention hard work—give wings to my ideas.

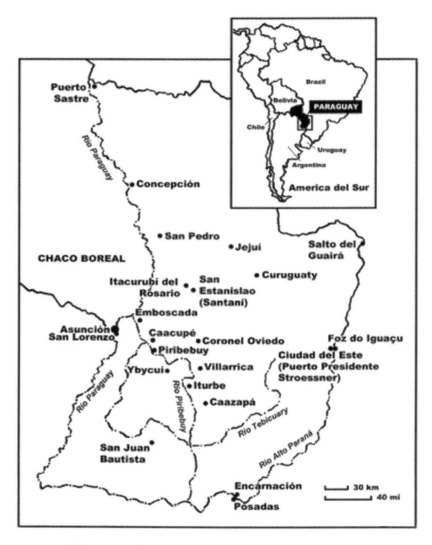

Map of the eastern half of Paraguay; the country's western half is the
Chaco Boreal. Insert shows Paraguay's location in South America,
as well as the six countries that comprise the "Southern Cone."
Cities, towns, and rivers shown here appear in the book.

CONTENTS

Emily playing her Epiphone guitar on the back stoop of her Stockton home in October 1974, before joining the Peace Corps. She is wearing her family signet ring, which she still wears on the same finger.

PART I

WILLIN'
SEPTEMBER 1974–JANUARY 1975

—✂—

EMILY AND MARTÍN

Is not this the fast that I have chosen? to loose the bands of wickedness, to undo the heavy burdens, and to let the oppressed go free…

Isaiah 58:6
American King James Bible
Paraphrased by President John F. Kennedy in his inaugural address
January 20, 1961

1

EMILY

Just before my twenty-second birthday I was single and living in Stockton, California, doing what I swore I would never do, wasting away in that hole of a town after graduating from college there simply because I had nothing, and I mean *nothing*, going for me. My only goal in life had been to get my BA—certainly not the "MRS" my parents prayed for—but now that I had one, what was I supposed to do with it?

I wanted something big, seismic even…but nothing could have prepared me for the tsunami about to break over the horizon that would rattle the cages of my soul and forever change the way I looked at the world.

It was 1974 and a lousy year to be graduating, frankly—an uncertain time in America for young people, especially women, what with the war, the pill, double-digit inflation and unemployment, gas rationing, even mandatory fifty-five miles per hour, for crissakes. I wanted, *needed*, to go home to Tucson but just couldn't without a decent job, something to show for myself after the crushing cost of my liberal arts degree. My pride wouldn't let me. I couldn't do it to Dad.

Oh, I'd had work. During college I designed posters for the University of the Pacific (UOP) Student Union and worked at Fat City Café (named for Stockton's cynical epithet), which I loved, but it wasn't a career. Besides, I never intended to stay here. Tucson—or anywhere other than Stockton—was where I wanted to be.

Somewhat ironic, given that four years earlier I was desperate to leave Tucson, too…no way was I staying home for college. You could say I was restless, like Jojo (how cool was it the Beatles actually knew about my hometown!) looking for some "California grass."[2] It had to be greener, right? Or headier anyway. But establishing roots here was out of the question—I was a tumbleweed, never to be tied down.

---

2 John Lennon and Paul McCartney, "Get Back," 1969.

Then why in the hell was I still here?

The job, mostly. Since graduating in June, I'd been working in the kitchens at St. Catherine's Hospital to explore a career in nutrition, a subject I'd found fascinating ever since I went on that crash diet in 1969 and ended up anorexic. Last year at this time I was living with a family in Japan (to graduate from Callison, a cluster college of UOP, I needed to live in a non-Western culture, and the program had recently moved to Japan from India), where the plant-based diet—and, yes, regular meals—helped me get back both my menses and my mojo.

That's when I got interested in food. I was struck by a revelation one day while standing in front of a vending machine at the language school in Kyoto, deciding what snack to get. I could choose something good for me or something bad for me (though it was hard to tell because the wrappers were in Japanese; what looked like chocolate was often bean paste, a sorry substitute). It occurred to me that if I chose something bad for me, it wouldn't be just a negative, but a *double* negative—not only would I be putting something bad into my body, I would also be *depriving* my body of something good.

Satori![3]

I knew there was a lot to be said for eating bona fide food, but here at St. Catherine's mashed-potato flakes and Jell-O reigned supreme. To me, feeding that crap to sick people seemed an ingenious way to hustle them to the hereafter.

My time was split between the kitchen, where I mostly washed dishes, and the cafeteria, where I did short order and served people in the buffet line. I also delivered meals to patients. Because most of the kitchen staff seemed suspicious of me (I was a college graduate, after all), I took my breaks with the gruff, chain-smoking Filipino cook, who was only too happy to let me share in his favorite pastime of slamming the doctors.

After a couple of months, one fine day I exercised my right—not to mention my propensity—to take foolish risks and gently teased the cafeteria

---

3 Zen Buddhist term for sudden illumination, awakening, or "seeing into one's true nature." Zen is a Japanese school of Buddhism.

manager (my boss and a tyrant) about her employees' tendency not to stick around very long. Her response came quickly.

"You know, Emily, you have a smart mouth and you're rude. I used to think you were a nice little girl, but somewhere along the line you changed, and I don't like you anymore."

I was in shock! No one had ever spoken to me like that before—and in the presence of my coworkers, no less! So in the space of a few dizzy seconds, I picked myself up and did what any red-blooded American with a shred of self-respect would do: I quit right there and then.

I felt terrific. I felt terrible. I grabbed my pack, punched my timecard, slipped out the door, cruised across the parking lot, and sank onto a grave in the cemetery behind the hospital. Looking around, I couldn't help but think how much it would *suck* to be a patient in a hospital that had its own cemetery.

Was I a quitter, or had my quick Irish ire been justified? I didn't know, but either way I was out of a job. Time for Alternate Plan B…whatever that was.

As I rode my bike home that sweaty September afternoon, I thought about President Kennedy's inaugural speech back in January 1961. I'd just turned eight, and even though I was mad because I was sick at home and the inauguration was the only thing on television *all day*, I was entranced by the words and images—mostly the flashes of steam—coming out of the president's mouth.

"We observe today not a victory of potty," he'd begun, which confused me a little, and then he talked about people living in huts and the "dahk powahs of destruction unleashed by science," which may well have been the beginning of my existential angst. But I was ultimately won over when the president said the line about asking not what your country could do for you, but what you could do for it. "Ask not"—I had no idea two words could be so powerful! I loved the phrasing, the semantic twist (called "chiasmus," I later learned), the mere sound of it.

And President Kennedy looked like my dad! As I focused on his sincere face, my purpose in life was revealed: I would serve my country.

Now suddenly it was thirteen years later and I had no other prospects. It was time to put my hard-earned degree in international studies to work and answer the call.

I drove the eighty miles to San Francisco to fill out an application at the Peace Corps office. They were looking for generalists, liberal arts grads with no special training. Though I chafed at the implication—well rounded, tinker of all trades, master of absolutely *nada*—there was no denying that was me.

I was able to apply for a specific job in any country. When Kennedy established the PC in March 1961, you applied and were sent where there was a need—you could end up in the heart of dearth. But the system had changed, so now we knew exactly where we were going and what we were getting into. The goals were to help the "people of interested countries" meet their need for trained men and women and to promote understanding between cultures. The PC would have to take responsibility for the former, but I felt I could handle the latter well enough on my own.

The country that best fit my skills and interests (nutrition, agriculture, ability to speak Spanish—*not to mention the one available the soonest*) was a country that hardly ever made the news here. It was one of those *–guays* in South America with a "benevolent" dictator, whatever that meant, where people spoke an indigenous language, the climate was subtropical, and the order of the day was apparently pretty "tranquil"—the booklet said it wouldn't be the last time we'd hear that word. The capital, Asunción [ah-soon-see-OHN], meant "assumption," a concept I didn't really get. I was a little disappointed: Ecuador or Peru would've been sexier.

But, at the end of my rope by this point, I completed the exhaustive application—the question I always hated was "Where do you want to be in five years?" Who in their right mind knew that?—and headed back to Stockton to wait. And wait. The endless weeks with little to do became unbearable. As September dissolved into October I strummed my Epiphone, hung out at Fat City, had a fling of sorts—doing anything to feel something, it seemed—and felt my spirit seep out like the air from a pooped-out party balloon.

The worst part was I'd have to come up with another plan. *Soon.*

I considered joining the navy. The idea wasn't without precedent: Dad had fought in the Pacific in World War II—I could honor his memory. It might not be too dangerous, as we weren't in a war at the moment (our troops had been pulled out of Vietnam last year by Nixon, who just resigned from office in August, the criminal—if you asked me, it was *his* fault my father was dead). I liked that the navy would pay me to train me in nutrition. Everyone knew the Peace Corps didn't pay much, so the navy was logically the better choice.

Besides, I was a warrior. I'd practiced aikido [ahee-KEE-doh] in Japan and at the dojo here in Stockton. Aikido means "the way of harmonizing with the spirit of the universe" and teaches you how to turn the flow of an aggressor's energy around and use it to bring him down or send him flying. It's all about controlling the breath and extending *ki*, cosmic energy. I practiced it more for the spiritual training than the martial, but I loved being a "samurai" and—in my mind, at least, as I'd never actually been tested—not taking shit from *no*body. Plus I liked to run and stay in shape and had secretly (perversely?) always wanted to try my skills on one of those military obstacle courses they showed in the movies.

So I went to Oakland and talked to recruiters—my bum knee presented some problems in the physical—but after I told them I didn't feel I deserved any special privileges just because I held a university degree, and furthermore I had no intention of attending officer candidate school (I didn't want to be *that* embedded in the system), they said they couldn't take me till July. *July?* I needed a job *now*.

Besides, I was having second thoughts. The navy's approach to nutrition wouldn't be any different from St. Catherine's. Not only that, I knew I couldn't possibly do the "yes, sir/no, sir" thing with a straight face—I mean, I respected my elders but had never said those words to anyone in my whole life! Plus I knew I would get deathly seasick bobbing around that mighty wavy ocean. So it was anchors aweigh to the navy...and back to sleepless nights.

It wasn't until mid-November that I got the very good news: I'd been accepted to represent the United States of America as a Peace Corps volunteer in Agricultural Extension in the Republic of Paraguay [pah-rah-gWHY], starting in January of 1975.

My elation knew no bounds! My dream come true! My ass saved!

Thanksgiving was in a couple of weeks, three days after my birthday on the twenty-fifth—I was a Sagittarius, an arrow-slinging centaur always "making distant connections" and "aiming for the truth" (or so I liked to think)—and now I had plenty to be thankful for, even though it would be the first Thanksgiving without Dad. I thought of my family. Was now the right time to leave them, yet again? When I phoned Mom, her voice sounded far away, as if it didn't come from the five-foot-nine mother I knew but the bag of bones I'd held when I got home from Japan last January after Dad died.

"You should go, honey," she said. "I know it's what you've always wanted. I have Mother here, and your brother and sister, of course. I'll be fine. We'll visit. No, I really *want* you to go."

Now, the fact that my mother and I had not had the best of relations made me wonder what she really meant by that. But I knew I had to go, so I was happy, more or less—I still couldn't shake the sadness over Dad—and celebrated with friends as I packed up and got ready to leave Stockton, finally and forever.

The aphorism about teaching a man to fish and feeding him for life became my mantra. I felt fulfilled because I was going to realize a lifelong dream of serving my country and making the world a better place.

1

MARTÍN

"By order of the chief of the Office of Investigations, we have instructions to proceed with the inspection of the Juan Bautista Alberdi Institute," declared an officer dressed in civilian clothes after barging through the front door of our school in San Lorenzo, on the outskirts of Asunción. He was accompanied by other police officers whose names I would later come to know.

I asked if he was carrying a judicial order to search the institute, where I had been director (principal) since 1959, to which the officer replied, "Don't be ridiculous. Under martial law that doesn't apply." I was well aware that the Paraguayan people had lived under a regime of martial law and terror since

May 4, 1954, when Alfredo Stroessner [STROHSSner] took power—that is to say, for the past twenty years.

It was the night of November 26, 1974. My wife, Celestina Pérez (who founded the institute in 1956 and currently worked as its office manager), my young daughter and nephew, and one of the teachers were with me in my office. While the police inspected the premises, Captain Cecilio Giménez arrived. A retired military man, he was a respected member of the community where our institute was located. From that moment on, Captain Giménez expressed his constant and determined solidarity, even in the most difficult moments of my suffering.

The police did not find the weapons they were supposedly looking for, so they requested that I accompany them for a short interview with Chief of Investigations Pastor Coronel. They shoved me into a police van (the feared red **Chevrolet Suburban police car known as** *caperucita roja*, "little red riding hood") and, leaving my frightened family and colleague behind, raced me downtown to the Department of Misdemeanors and Surveillance.

A large, fat man with a pale complexion, Pastor Coronel was seated at his desk surrounded by about twenty people, civilian and military, among whom I recognized the chief of police of Asunción and the head of the intelligence service of the armed forces. Also present were several other individuals who appeared to be foreign. They were elegantly dressed, some with dark, aviator-style sunglasses. I would later learn that one of them was the chief of police of Córdoba in Argentina and another a colonel in the Chilean air force.

A young waiter, smartly dressed in white with a black bow tie, served coffee and soft drinks to those present—everyone but me, an attorney, of course.

Pastor Coronel broke the silence, inquiring about my connection to the Armed Workers' Revolutionary Party (PORA), supposedly linked to the People's Revolutionary Army (ERP), and to Leandro Velásquez, the commander of PORA. I answered that I knew of no such organizations, but that Dr. Velásquez had been a classmate of mine at the National University of Asunción and visited me later at the University of La Plata in Argentina, where I had recently obtained my doctorate in education.

Pastor Coronel insisted on certain points, for example, my participation in the recent "subversive plot" against the president of the republic and my membership in the "armed revolutionary movement." He asked what instructions I had received from Leandro Velásquez and what my role was in the conspiracy, adding that I would be rewarded if I told what I knew about the plan. He said they were well informed of the "case" through Velásquez himself, who was already being held at this location.

I knew nothing, but my answers did not convince Pastor Coronel, who made one last attempt to persuade me. He mentioned my youth, my abilities, and my future in the government of General Stroessner. He advised me to "sing" willingly—if not, they would force me.

I insisted on my complete innocence. Infuriated, Pastor Coronel said, "This conversation is finished. We represent two irreconcilable enemies confronting each other: you, the idiotic dupes, the godless, bloodthirsty communists, and us, the defenders of order. Let the torture begin!" I was shocked to hear him call me a communist as I'd been an active member of his party, the ruling Colorado Party, my whole life.

An officer nicknamed Tatá ("fire" in Guaraní) accompanied me to the torture room in the Office of Investigations, which operated on the premises of the Department of Misdemeanors and Surveillance. While Tatá was getting ready to start "work," he suggested that I "sing" to avoid being beaten for no reason.

I felt terrified during the preparations. I was stripped naked, my hands and feet bound with electrical wire. My torturers, most of them potbellied, were dressed in black shorts. A man called Sapriza was the only one impeccably dressed; he wore dark glasses that he constantly took off and put back on.

Looking at them frightened me even more. It seemed their eyes were shooting fire and they were being transformed from humans into beasts. I knew from reading international reports that in Chile and Argentina, torturers appeared before victims with their faces hidden behind masks. But in Stroessner's Paraguay, the torturers did not need to disguise themselves—the long-lived institution of dictatorship protected them from justice.

The work was clearly divided: Tatá was in charge of the *pileta*, a bathtub filled with fetid water, excrement, and urine, into which someone threw me and put his foot on my chest to keep me down; Sapriza, the main inquisitor, kicked me and officiated as secretary; someone used karate on me; a man called Kururú Piré [koo-roo-ROO pee-RAY] ("toad skin" for the warts covering his face), viciously attacked my back with the famous *teyuruguái* ("lizard tail," a whip with metal balls at the end) in one hand and a bottle of Aristócrata (brand of *caña* [KAHN-yah], cane liquor) in the other; and Laspina beat my head with a blackjack. Off to one side, a military sergeant around thirty years old, extremely pale and gaunt, urged the torturers to "make the subversive sing."

A telephone rang incessantly, and after each call the violence increased, sometimes with the receiver pointing toward me. Flashes of lightning unleashed by a storm reached the small room—sounds of rain and fierce winds from outside joined my cries of pain inside.

Kururú Piré tore at my flesh with the *teyuruguái* while Sapriza shouted, "Talk, damn it, talk, son of a bitch, criminal, bandit." I felt like my body was on the verge of exploding. Not content with ripping my back to shreds, Kururú Piré beat the soles of my feet, and Sapriza kicked my legs with pointed shoes. Spurts of blood stained Sapriza's clothes, enraging him further. To appease Sapriza, Laspina battered my head with the blackjack.

I didn't see people—I saw mad dogs.

They were exasperated by my silence. They plunged me several more times into the *pileta*, demanding that I talk. Mercifully, I lost consciousness.

The next day a guard awakened me. I was surprised to find myself tied to a chair and handcuffed with my arms behind me. From a few feet away, a five-hundred-kilowatt spotlight shone in my eyes. I was left there all day.

Later that night Laspina arrived and, kicking and shouting, ordered me to go with him: the chief wanted to talk to me. Pastor Coronel, again surrounded by the same team, showed me a book and asked if I recognized it. It was my doctoral dissertation, *Paraguay: Education and Dependency*, which I had defended several months earlier at the National University of La Plata in Argentina—and which postulated that Paraguay's educational system served the dominant class only and caused underdevelopment. I wondered how they had obtained it. Pastor Coronel told me this was my last chance and if I didn't sing, they would tear off my scalp with a club.

They wanted to know who had ordered me to write the dissertation: Moscow, Havana, Peking, or General Torrijos of Panama? Actually, the Panamanian model of educational reform of 1971 had inspired my writing, as had the works of Paulo Freire, the progressive Brazilian educator and author of *Pedagogy of the Oppressed* (1968).

Threats quickly progressed to action. This time the target was my testicles—a strong electrical charge caused me to faint.

Sometime later I awoke to find myself lying on a metal bunk bed. My hands were tied to the upper portion, and the railing served as my pillow. Because of the *pileta,* I was suffering from intense diarrhea and vomiting. Moaning on the floor nearby lay an opposition leader named Comandante Tato, Dr. Roberto Vera Grau (an orthodontist), and the former first secretary of our diplomatic representatives in Argentina and Brazil. Enormous cockroaches crawled over our bodies, and cat-sized rats eyed us hungrily.

Around 10:00 p.m. Laspina greeted me with a kick and guided me into the torture room. There he sat me face-to-face with an older woman I had never seen before. She turned out to be Gilberta Verdum de Talavera. Her husband had been assassinated in 1961 by Antonio Campos Alum and his henchmen under orders from Patricio Colmán, commander of the infamous "Antisubversive Operation" to eliminate the opposition. She had been in prison for nine years, released, and recently arrested again.

Laspina peppered me with questions about my connection to doña Gilberta's organization. Disappointed by my answers he left, saying he would make me sing that night. A short time later, the old woman was savagely tortured. But doña Gilberta's behavior filled me with amazement and admiration: firmly, without hesitation, she denied the accusations and refused to supply names.

I thought I would be next, but the door suddenly opened and two policemen dragged in an old man, well built, with a face like Jesus Christ. I didn't know then but it was my colleague, Professor Julián Cubas. They tortured him next, but all they got were cries of rage: "Assassins, criminals, fascists, straw men of the dictatorship…cowards, *cowards!*"

The defiant conduct of doña Gilberta and Professor Cubas helped me firmly maintain my position against the torturers—I resolved that I would die before talking. That is, I would not make anything up, as I was completely innocent.

My turn came again. New accusations included my supposed connection to the "people's jail" set up in San Lorenzo. They also demanded to know the source of financing for the trade and artisan workshops (flooring, carpentry, electrical work, and the like) that we were building as an annex to the Juan Bautista Alberdi Institute; I told them I had obtained credit from the state-owned National Development Bank. I told them I had never heard of the "people's jail." The violence that ensued caused me to black out.

The torture was on a grand scale, so the torturers had to recruit common prisoners, mostly petty thieves, to keep the work going. I estimate that seven to ten people were tortured daily, and more than fifty each night. The torturers' questions were apparently supposed to make the prisoners believe that a significant political-military conspiracy had been foiled.

Dr. Almada's prison ID, issued on November 29, 1974, three days after he was picked up. Eighteen years later, on December 22, 1992, Martín discovered the ID—along with several tons of documents later known as the "Archives of Terror"—in a police station outside Asunción.

Five or six days after my arrest, four young men were taken to the torture room. I could hear their cries. The torturers left the room visibly nervous because they had not achieved their objectives. "They're tough," they said. "They won't talk. If they go on like this, we're the ones who'll take the rap with Pastor Coronel."

The air was filled with cries for help, groans, weeping, Brazilian military marches blaring out of a tape player, torturers shouting, and the telephone ringing nonstop—Pastor Coronel checking on how the interrogations were going. The Office of Investigations was in downtown Asunción, near the Parliament, the archdiocese, the post office, the Catholic University, the cathedral, the National Oratory, the Municipal Theater, the Federation of Paraguayan Educators, and the Government Palace. But our cries never penetrated the walls of that sinister place.

For the fourth time I was dragged to the torture room. The interrogation always revolved around the communists and who had incited me to write my dissertation: "Who got you to join? Which books have you read? Marx, Engels, possibly? Mao, Trotsky, or Fidel?"

They alleged that both the approach and the content I had used were communist inspired. They added that I had insulted General Bernardino Caballero himself, the founder of the Colorado Party, of which Stroessner was considered the heir. My crime was considered high treason against the country. "You call yourself a Colorado," they said, "but you are conspiring against the unshakable unity of the party."

They also claimed to have a recording of a talk I'd given at a conference on Paraguayan education at the National University of Córdoba in Argentina. They wanted to know the first and last names of the people who had organized the conference. I said nothing and soon after lost consciousness again.

I felt better when I awoke the following day, but there was a loud buzzing in my ears. My torturers' howls resounded like a tape recording in my head, as did the words shouted by Pastor Coronel: "I'll make his son read this filthy book so that he can see an example of an educator who is a traitor, traitor, *traitor!*"

A well-built blond officer who looked like a Nazi was at my side. He assured me that I had survived the storm and my body was strong, like a *quebracho* tree. Because he checked my pulse, breathing, and heart, I gathered the man was a doctor. He told me I had almost died of a heart attack. He said he knew my background through a mutual friend, a veterinarian. Either his medications or the effects of the torture transported me to an unreal world.

Two or three days of terrible suffering passed. I thought I was dying. In my lucid moments, the doctor spoke to me about our veterinarian friend. I would later learn that this man was the general director of the police department hospital.

Comandante Tato and Dr. Roberto Vera Grau remained in serious condition. I received no further news of doña Gilberta or Professor Cubas; I feared they were dead. As for me, I was sure I would not be able to bear another torture session.

The torturers' methods were scientific, their instructors having learned their US Army–taught lessons well. They knew which were the most sensitive parts of the body and attacked them mercilessly. They used every instrument necessary to destroy the prisoners, both physically and psychologically. The use of sodium pentothal ("truth serum") was common, and in some police stations they also used trained dogs and stocks. Their objective was not just to make the prisoners talk, but to break their spirits and reduce them to human wrecks. To achieve this, they also used sleep deprivation.

Each instrument of torture had a nickname. The braided cables that ended in metal balls were called "the national constitution"; the *pileta* "human rights"; a small but fearsome whip "little Paraguay"; all the different blackjacks "democracy"; the large cobblers' needles "General Stroessner"; and the smaller needles "Pastor Coronel."

The torturers often acted under the influence of drugs. They took cocaine before "work" in order to better carry out their duties. Benítez and Laspina, however, preferred Aristócrata.

Some of the torturers were semiliterate but still tried to talk politics with us political prisoners. In their minds, we were all communists who got precise orders from Moscow, Peking, or Havana. Priests, bishops, and Protestant ministers were considered communists as well. Tatá went so far as to claim that the Bible itself was of Marxist inspiration, saying "Karl Marx won Jesus over for his cause and made him into a subversive element." They maintained that Paraguay was a haven of peace and tranquility, unlike Italy, the United States, France, and "all those countries where all they do is rob banks and plant bombs."

The torturers constantly threatened me with the Mariscalito (little mariscal, or marshal), "a very vicious officer in whose hands no one can last." I later realized the Mariscalito had been a pupil in my middle-school course at the institute, a troubled and unbalanced adolescent who was able to finish his studies only because of the help he got from Celestina. The police academy had aggravated his psychopathic tendencies, and upon graduation he got a job as a torturer for Pastor Coronel.

Adding to the depravity of the situation, intense commercial activity took place in our prison underworld. The food (boiled cornmeal, salt, and rotten meat) was disgusting, so prisoners would trade personal belongings for a piece of bread. Employees of the Office of Investigations had a vast clientele.

The officials did permit prisoners to read, though they rejected most reading matter brought in from the outside. Any visitor who showed up at the prison with a periodical or book was subjected to much inconvenience. We were allowed *Patoruzú* (*Donald Duck*), *Spider-Man*, *Superman*, *Mickey Mouse*, *Telefilm*, *Claudia*; sports magazines and anything published by Spanish romance novelist Corín Tellado; *Ten Years of Progress in the Era of Stroessner* and any other panegyric of the dictator; anti-Soviet publications; all materials from the United States Information Service (USIS); pornographic magazines; and bestsellers with militaristic and racist propaganda, such as stories of exploits against Arabs, blacks, Indians, etc.

There were reservations concerning some of the newspapers; forbidden were all works of progressive inspiration. On one occasion the guard threatened the relative of a prisoner for bringing a science fiction book titled *Invasion of the Martians*. For him, "Martian" and "Marxist" were the same thing. By contrast, another prisoner encountered no problems when he received *The Holy Family*—by Karl Marx and Frederick Engels.

Paraguayan students, particularly those who had studied abroad, were targeted as well, according to their universities. The Catholic University of Asunción was viewed with suspicion. Those of La Plata and Córdoba in Argentina were classified as "hotbeds of extremism," and their graduates were treated the worst. The Brazilian universities, on the other hand, enjoyed great prestige because "there the young people really study, don't waste their time mixing in politics."

In the suitcase of a Paraguayan student returning from Argentina, the police found a book entitled *Revolution in Contemporary Architecture*, which caused him terrible torture and imprisonment for more than six months. His efforts to prove his status as a student of architecture close to graduation did nothing but make his situation worse. The book was about "revolution," and that was enough.

All reading matter seized in the prison (or outside) entered the black market and ended up resurfacing in bookstores or personal libraries. In 1973, the June issue of the magazine *Selecciones (Reader's Digest)* was confiscated because it contained an article on Paraguayan drug traffickers, including Pastor Coronel. The normal price of the magazine was fifty guaranies, but the June issue sold for up to one thousand guaranies and circulated widely throughout the country.

Noel Báez, a *pyragüe* [püh-rah-GWAY] (spy or informant for the political police) from Puerto Presidente Stroessner (Paraguay's easternmost city, now called Ciudad del Este), had fallen into disgrace and become a common prisoner, allegedly for smuggling in the border zone with Brazil. The authorities immediately appointed him foreman of the political prisoners. As such, he was the one who chose and ordered the newspapers that entered the prison.

One very hot day, December 20, 1974, Báez was reading the newspaper *ABC Color*. When he finished reading, he passed the paper to fellow prisoner Bernardo Rojas. A moment later Rojas asked me, "Do you know Señora Celestina Pérez de Almada?" I said I did. Without a word, Rojas showed me the page where the death of my wife was announced. It had occurred on December 5, more than two weeks earlier.

16

I cried out loudly in disbelief. Kururú Piré came over to me, tightened the cords around my wrists, and said, "The same thing will happen to you if you don't shut up." But I was in shock and couldn't stop wailing. How could this have happened? How could a perfectly healthy woman die so suddenly? I had no way of finding out.

A few days later, things began to change. An officer, no doubt on instructions from his superiors, visited me often, repeating words of consolation. "You have to calm down," he said. "As soon as one is gone, another always appears. In Paraguay there are seven women for every man. You've lost one, you'll meet a thousand. This might even bring you luck." They were afraid I would follow the example of other prisoners who had tried to commit suicide.

The superintendent sent me a book on resignation, which claimed that everything was preordained and no one escaped his fate. According to the superintendent, this was my fate and no one was to blame. Another officer said to me, "This is what happens when you meddle in politics." And Kururú Piré repeated his slogan: "Politics is dirty, and nothing good comes of it. Understood, Almada?"

After Celestina's death, my days passed in an environment of spiritual misery, a despair I feared I could not endure.

2

EMILY

"Still my little ragamuffin, I see," were Mom's first words to me when I showed up in Tucson at her and Dad's townhouse for Christmas a few weeks later. They'd bought it a couple of years earlier, but—like all the places they'd lived in after I left for college—it wasn't home to me. I was wearing my prized baggy black-and-white checkered chef's pants I'd just bought at the Stockton Goodwill.

Mom—who would never set foot in a secondhand store—always seemed disappointed in me, the wayward child. She'd named me Emily after an imaginary childhood friend, and I'd turned out to be somewhat of an imaginary daughter.

Naturally I got upset with her right away for getting rid of Dad's clothes. Well, it *had* been almost a year, but I wanted to touch them, smell them, and (somehow, through the cigarette smoke) feel *him*. Now I couldn't.

I'd felt the same way when she got rid of all my childhood porcelain and plastic horses. She'd asked about the trophies and ribbons, why not the horses? It was when Dad started having financial problems and they'd had to move to an apartment. I was in my first year at college and only found out about it when I came home for Christmas. When I confronted Mom, she got upset and wouldn't discuss it. I wasn't sure I ever really forgave her—or trusted her again.

Of course things might have been different if I hadn't decided at age fifteen to be *nothing like* my mother. She and my grandmother, Nanny (Irene Chapman Oswalt), had been raised to be modest Midwestern ladies, never uppity, never wanting to be a burden or put anyone out—a persona I'd resisted though in the end had become myself, to my lasting regret (deep down, however, I knew those values were born of humility and as solid as the earth). Also, my mother's "talk" had consisted of one clear warning: *If you get pregnant, don't bother coming home.* Nice. That had pissed me off to no end, in addition to imbuing me with a warped and, as it turned out, tenacious sense of shame and secrecy around sex.

But I knew it was unfair to criticize Mom for trying to move on so quickly after Dad's death, especially as she was pretty old now, having just turned fifty. I realized I had no idea how difficult it must be for her to exist without Dad here day after day, month after month—after being together more than twenty-six years, half her life.

I hadn't exactly been here for him, had I?

Mom even had a job now, to take her mind off things, the first work she'd done since marrying Dad in 1948. As a young woman she'd sold tickets at the movie theater in Garden City, Kansas, where Dad had gone from Chicago to work on the gas pipelines. He always told the story that when he first saw Bonnie Lou he bragged to friends, "That's the gal I'm going to marry." She was, and his three kids were born there, me in the middle (the cards were stacked against me from the start). I guess that irascible sailor with the crew cut and sockless penny loafers would've had to admit he was a romantic at heart, though: I was likely conceived on Valentine's Day.

On Christmas, when the whole family was at Mom's, no one seemed to want to talk much about Dad, but we didn't have to—his absence filled the place almost to bursting. That's what my heart was doing, anyway, as I realized I would never be able to have an adult relationship with him. It was hard to believe that last year at this time I was in Japan, my first Christmas away from home, from my family…and in a place my father loathed to his very core. Not only that, but Dad knew I loved it there.

I was aware of the wartime atrocities committed by the Japanese but chose to see only the artistic, spiritual side of the culture. That new perspective saved my life, though, as I'd arrived in Kyoto so depressed I didn't want to wake up in the mornings. A bad relationship the year before—along with the painful realization that I was making a mess of my college career and would be nothing but a disappointment to Dad, something I feared more than anything—had sucked the very life out of me.

Fortunately I was better now, a year later. But the day after Christmas I started feeling oppressed by all the bad memories…including the lousy ones I was currently making because I didn't want to see any of my old friends. I felt so different these days. What was there to talk about, anyway? I'd soon be out of here forever.

So I started packing for Peace Corps–Paraguay. All I had was the oversized canvas duffel I'd taken to Japan; that thing had seen some miles. Of course I would take my guitar and cassette player and tapes (including the new ones I got for Christmas, Joni Mitchell and Linda Ronstadt especially—I kept singing, loudly, defiantly, letting the world know I was "will-in'"[4]…to be moo-vin'!)

---

4 Lowell George, "Willin'," 1970.

plus extra batteries, my low-end SLR camera, 35mm film, and a few essential books: dictionary, collection of Yeats, and the *I Ching* for starters.

I was perplexed about the PC's suggestion to bring a warm hat, gloves, scarves, two jackets…and *long underwear*? Wasn't it supposed to be a jungle down there? But I threw in what I had—including the chef's pants, of course. And even though the PC said not to bring expensive jewelry, I would include my family ring, which was gold but never left my finger.

Everything felt surreal, though, without Dad in my life anymore. What was the point, anyway? My family wasn't intact, and neither was I. Everything I did to forget just ended up in the same old cul-de-sac, around and around with no escape.

How long could I take it?

2

MARTÍN

After Celestina's death, the authorities left me alone for a while. But my peace lasted a short time. One morning at dawn, an army sergeant woke me up and dragged me off to the torture room. He turned out to be extraordinarily sadistic.

This time the accusation was my link with MOPOCO.[5] They said I had connections with these exiles in Argentina and Brazil, and I had to name some names. I knew none of them. I passed out and so had no idea how long the "work session" went on.

The next morning an officer woke me up. With malicious irony in his voice, he offered his "sincerest apologies," saying he'd made a mistake the night before. The candidate for interrogation was not me but a different Almada, Valentín Almada, but because I had the same last name and was better known, I had

---

5 Movimiento Popular Colorado, a movement formed in 1959 by anti-Stroessner Colorado Party youths. MOPOCO was immediately exiled and held its first congress in Argentina in 1960.

suffered the consequences. He and the other officers looked at me and laughed, saying I had broken the record for swallowing excrement in the *pileta*. I spent the day on the floor, vomiting.

The Brazilian music, played at full volume, continued to drown out the prisoners' cries of pain, preventing neighbors from noticing what was happening in Pastor Coronel's infernal facility. That wall of music was the sign that torture was going on. Tatá again dragged me to the torture room to make me decide once and for all to sing, to reveal all that I supposedly knew.

The *teyuruguái* shook me to my fibers, and my cries were louder even than the music. I could hear an argument in the adjoining room, which escalated as my groans increased. "They are killing that innocent man," was the phrase repeated. Shortly thereafter, Captain Cecilio Giménez and another officer burst into the room. Giménez, infuriated and with a pistol in his hand, shouted, "If you have proof that Martín Almada is a communist, show me so I can kill him myself right now. If not, stop torturing this innocent man!"

After an embarrassed silence, Tatá and his cohort left. Captain Giménez embraced me, sobbing, and very tenderly freed me from the wires binding my feet and hands. In Guaraní he cursed the torturers and solemnly promised to fight for my freedom.

Because I had lost a lot of blood, convulsive tremors seized my body. I was consumed with anguish as I lay freezing on the damp, foul-smelling tile floor. I entrusted myself to God, whose infinite compassion let me lose consciousness, and the pain disappeared. Thus ended the night.

The next day, an official allowed some common prisoners—about fifty held in a twenty-five-square-meter room—to get some air in a little corridor with us political prisoners. One of them, an Argentine, heard someone call me "Doctor Almada" and came over to tell me about a problem he was having: he suffered from asthma and suspected he was going to be tortured again that night.

After I explained that I was a PhD, not a physician, the Argentine told me about the reason for his arrest. He said that, frankly, he was a crook and a smuggler of vehicles, and his last job had been to deliver fifty vehicles to leaders of the Colorado Party. He said that even though the price of the cars and trucks was extremely low, he had received only 30 percent of the agreed-upon amount. After a long argument, they promised him that after thirty days they would pay him more. But instead of paying him, they arrested him and accused him of international terrorism.

The Argentine soon regained his liberty thanks to the intervention of Dr. Alí, who had him sign a document in which he swore he had received the full amount for the vehicles. As the legal consultant and chief commissioner of the Office of Investigations, Alí would deposit large sums of money to free drug traffickers and smugglers and reap rewards from them later, all the while appearing to be a benefactor of the innocent.

One day a gangly young officer ordered me to perform an operation on a prisoner who had an enormous boil. The officer tried to give me a razor blade to use as a scalpel, but I declined, explaining that I was not a medical doctor. He took my explanation for insubordination and proceeded to punish me brutally, stressing that my conduct was "typically subversive."

I was often witness to Kafkaesque acts. One time, the neighborhood superintendent was ordered to round up everyone whose names ended in "-eiro." The order was carried out, and Carlos A. Bareiro and other innocent San Lorenzans were jailed. Also, as a result of the coerced "confession" of one of the many people tortured who described a supposed revolutionary, there was a massive arrest of all bearded young men with long hair wearing or owning red shirts who were found in the vicinity of the Asunción neighborhood Sajonia. I saw among them the son of a European diplomat who, even though he wasn't wearing a red shirt, had a beard—no less a sign of "subversion."

Tourists with beards or long hair were arrested because of their "suspicious appearance," but this was merely an excuse to rob them of money and personal effects—especially passports, which were then laundered and sold. Foreign representatives occasionally interceded on behalf of their compatriots and requested explanations. In order to justify their abuse, the police tried to implicate the victims in criminal or terrorist acts.

The Department of Misdemeanors and Surveillance was filling up with political and common prisoners, prostitutes, homosexuals, small-time drug smugglers, drug addicts, people of different nationalities—Argentines, Brazilians, Uruguayans, Spaniards, Chileans, Bolivians, Chinese, Japanese, Koreans—and numerous tourists. The environment was unbearable, but the prisoners were often reminded that in the Office of Investigations next door (where the torture took place), the situation was even worse.

Barbarism was taking over the Paraguayan capital. The young officers were proud of their sadism. The police department's goal seemed to be the systematic cultivation of repression, arbitrariness, and licentiousness. The other prisoners and I got the impression that many of the officers suffered from gonorrhea, as much of their conversation revolved around that disease.

Among the women arrested were prostitutes who had refused to share their earnings with the police. There were also rural women, former domestics in the homes of those in power, who had been accused of theft to deny them their wages. Under torture, they were forced to declare that they had been paid and had no complaints.

Some tragicomic events occurred in my presence as well. One of them was the treatment of the owner of a bull named Fidel Castro. This bull belonged to a *campesino* (rural dweller, farmer) from San Lorenzo. The animal was well known in the area for its qualities as a stud.

Pastor Coronel had bought a weekend cottage adjoining the property of this farmer. One night a heavy rainstorm knocked over a tree that served as a boundary post, and when it fell, it dragged down the barbed-wire fence that divided the properties. At dawn, Fidel Castro the bull went onto Pastor Coronel's property and damaged the flower garden and small vegetable plot. Coronel's foreman notified him of the event. There was an immediate police deployment that resulted in the arrest and execution of the "subversive animal" and the arrest and torture of its owner.

The interrogation of the campesino in the torture room went like this:

"Do you know how to read and write?"

"No, I started school but left before second grade."

"Do you know who Fidel Castro is?"

"No, I don't know him."

"So why did you give this name to your bull, you criminal?"

"Well, the bull was lusty even when young. One day a friend visited me, and seeing that the animal had very large testicles and having heard my plan to use him as a stud, he said to me, 'Congratulations, friend, on the idea of keeping this hunk of an animal as a stud—and I am sure that he will behave like Fidel Castro, king of the bulls, and there won't be a cow he won't impregnate or a bull that will compete with him.' And that's where his name came from."

"Jerk! Idiot! It's a sure thing this pal of yours is a *castrista* (supporter of Cuba's Fidel Castro)!"

"No, he's a *taxista* (taxi driver)."

"Ah, you're playing stupid. What's your pal's name, and where does he live?"

Silence.

"Let the torture begin!"

About ten days of apparent calm passed, during which I started to recover my strength and take a few steps. But I was told my situation had worsened, and once again I was called in to make a declaration. They wanted me to sign a document stating I was an active communist and an agent of the government of Argentina. It wasn't true, and I refused.

During the subsequent torture session, Sapriza shouted, "That business of 'A Roof for Every Paraguayan Educator' is a communist slogan. The measures we are taking with you are to avoid worse evils. What you want is to fool the unwary. Your plan of affordable housing for the teachers of San Lorenzo is a ploy." Sapriza was referring to the Teachers' Village of San Lorenzo, a residential complex developed through Celestina's and my initiative, with the participation of teachers and support from the local community.

Tatá reminded me—as he whipped me—of my work as a lawyer, reproaching me for having defended a young man from Trinidad in a 1969 criminal trial involving one of Pastor Coronel's close friends. He added that because of me, a climate of "mental subversion" was being created among the youth at the Alberdi Institute and that, as its director, I had been a complete failure.

I shouted in a weak voice, "Barbarians! Ideas don't kill!" This of course only made them batter me more.

The director of political affairs of the Office of Investigations and his advisor watched the whole process of my torture in silence—I assumed it was they who signaled for it to stop. It was possible that this barbarism was not to everyone's taste.

Days later, after torturing me, an official expressed that he was sure of my innocence but could do nothing because he had received orders from above. He said he could not understand the wickedness of some people from my town who had come to confirm the accusations against me, and said the informants from San Lorenzo were, more than anyone else, the ones responsible for my tragedy. I knew precisely who they were.

The psychological torture continued as well. Every time the officers saw horror in my eyes from what I was witnessing, they told me I would be the next candidate, and after that would come my family.

Every day my family sent me a container of milk. The torturers took great care not to harm the container, though this treatment did not extend to the prisoners, whom they treated as savagely as possible when delivering their food.

The dead weren't respected any more than the living. One day the guard on duty gave us a strange speech in which he expressed with the greatest of ease that he was a thief, but he stole only from the rich and the living. For that reason he had not accepted the offer made by the other torturers that he pull out Benicio López's gold teeth and take his shoes after his recent death by torture.

Each of the prisoners reacted to this news in a different way—some cried out in anger while others kept a cool head and asked for more details about the murder. The guard then told us about the entire process of the man's arrest, torture, and death. One of the prisoners was a godson of the victim and provided more information. López had been a vendor at the municipal market in Caazapá (a town in the interior) and a decorated war hero. One windy day some flyers with political propaganda were blowing around on the roof of his shop; these were supposed to be irrefutable proof of his "subversive activities." The young prisoner assured us his godfather knew nothing of the pamphlets, neither what was in them nor who had created them.

One day the torturers dragged someone out from the torture room who looked very young and was completely disfigured as a result of the beatings. They had given him up for dead and thrown him in the corridor to wait for the *perrera* ("dog catcher," a large red van with no windows), which would take him to the common grave they used for victims. The truck was late, and as we were interested in knowing if the young man was a political prisoner, we observed him closely. Suddenly, we noticed the big toe of his left foot move. One of the prisoners did CPR and brought him back to life. Without our intervention, the poor boy would have been buried alive.

One victim followed another, the sinister machine of repression working at full speed. By my count, from November 26 to December 24, more than twelve hundred people passed through that torture room. No one was safe— not children, priests, old people, or pregnant women. Not even the police and soldiers were off limits.

Detainees were subjected to subhuman conditions. The common prisoners were sent to the Hotel Guaraní, the most luxurious of the city, and the Lido Bar to scavenge leftover food intended for the pig farm of the chief of the Vigilance and Crime Section. The other political prisoners and I often had to appease our hunger with these already-spoiled leftovers.

On Christmas I thought back to Christmas and New Year's of 1973, when I was invited by a friend to attend a dinner party in the capital. The main speaker was Dr. J. Augusto Saldívar on the topic "The Stroessner System: The Final Stage of the Colorado System."

"You will all agree with me in my emphatic condemnation of the cowards that, because of some so-called 'rule of three,' did not support the immediate promotion of His Most Excellent Mr. President of the Republic and commander in chief of the nation's armed forces, Army General Don Alfredo Stroessner, to the rank of mariscal," Saldívar said. He added that there was still time to correct this historical error, as the Paraguayan people had originally and unanimously launched the campaign to award Stroessner the rank of marshal. In his opinion, Stroessner had been destined since birth to hold the highest military rank, and it would be unfair for him to remain a mere general after his memorable feats.

Saldívar assured his audience that the generalísimo [hen-ehr-ahl-EE-see-moh] (very much general) was precisely the reincarnation of the blond centaur of Ybycuí, General Bernardino Caballero, the hero of a hundred battles and founder of the Colorado Party. "Stroessner rose from the pure sources of the Colorado system in order to carry it forward to the future," he said. "The Colorado system has now fulfilled its historical phase. The present demands an ideology that will avert chaos and overcome the economic and social crises that endanger humanity. The remedy for the evils of this century is the Stroessner system, the final stage of the Colorado system."

Even at the time of this writing [1978], speeches like this issue forth every day in Paraguay. Those at the top surely give them in order to keep their positions, and those who aspire to power use them as a way to rise, or "climb," as it would be expressed in Stroessner-speak.

At the same time, the symptomatic behavior of most of the population is intriguing, including that of the Stroessner supporters themselves. Many of them prefer to turn off their radios during broadcasts of the official news channel, most likely to avoid the copious flattery and praise for the "second rebuilder, the general of steel, the Guaraní lion, the unequaled patriot, the one and only leader."

Character worship is the religion of the obsequious, and at the same time it is a business that renders abundant wealth. Therefore, in their free time, employees of the Office of Investigations sell portraits, busts, and cockades (ornamental ribbons on hats signifying office or party) of the general. They sell them door to door, and people buy them out of fear of reprisal. Or people might buy subscriptions to magazines that praise the general. As I recall, one employee promoted these sales operations, arguing that "Thanks to the sacrifices of General Stroessner, the country is enjoying an unprecedented period of peace and progress. Therefore, all its inhabitants—citizens and foreigners alike—have an obligation to contribute to the maintenance of that peace through the purchase of at least a framed photograph of the general."

On the evening of December 26, 1974, a month after my arrest, the other political prisoners and I were ordered to prepare our things: we were to be freed! We climbed into a *caperucita roja* and were transported a short distance.

In the new destination, we entered a large room and were ordered to line up. There I ran into a former professor at the Alberdi Institute, Alcides Molinas, who had become leader of the Paraguayan Teachers' Organization.

The next morning we discovered that we were in police headquarters, the First Precinct, which also housed the main office of INTERPOL (International Criminal Police Organization) in Paraguay. In the cell were some forty-three individuals: farmers, laborers, students, professors, government officials, and two police officers. At first the new location seemed to us an earthly paradise compared to the Office of Investigations…although—as we would soon find out—it was a paradise in hell.

3

EMILY

When the worst holidays *ever* were finally over, I was once again only too eager to pick up and go, my favorite thing to do it seemed (practice making perfect and all). But saying good-bye to everyone this time was harder than ever. Two years and three months in South America, thousands of miles away…that was a huge commitment. What was I thinking? Was I embracing the future or simply running away—again?

"Just follow your heart, Em," my sister, Ginny, said with strained patience as she dropped me off at the airport (I'd been obsessing again). She gave me a hug, said good-bye, got in the car, and drove off.

"Heart?" I couldn't help asking as I watched my beloved navy VW bug disappear around the bend.

"What heart?"

Our all-expense-paid Peace Corps orientation took place at a fancy downtown hotel in Miami. I was excited but nervous as I knew all the icebreakers, introductions, and group discussions would test the measure of my self-confidence, which at the moment was on a downward trend. Always a misfit, I'd had a hard time connecting with others in college—people told me I thought too much, and I'd taken it as a compliment (I considered myself a contemplative)—and wasn't sure I was any better at it now, despite my rapidly advancing age and, one would hope, wisdom.

You see, talking was not my forte. I'd spent my formative years alone, on horseback in the foothills north of Tucson. My parents, both college educated, were loving (though not exactly in an expressive way), but we ate dinner on TV trays, for crissakes, while watching such thought-provoking programs as the primetime cartoons *Huckleberry Hound* and *Yogi Bear* and sitcoms like *McHale's Navy*—true, we also watched *Combat!*, a drama about World War II that I naturally hated. Later it was *Hullabaloo* and *Laugh-In*, which were actually pretty entertaining. Unlike other families, we never used the verb "visit" to mean "talk"—*au contraire*, our motto was "no news is good news." It got to the point where none of us even *wanted* to talk. As a result, I never learned how to express myself orally, which was why I had to write.

I'd taken to heart Socrates's assertion that the unexamined life is not worth living so rigorously that I'd begun examining my own life through some damn micron lens that never failed to reveal flaws. Now I was trying to be less self-conscious.

At the initial meet and greet, questions bubbled up around the room: "Where are you from? Where did you go to college? Why did you decide to join the Peace Corps? Why Paraguay?" We all appeared to be in our twenties.

I talked to a few of the guys (there were nineteen in all), who for some reason would be doing their three-month training in Costa Rica. I discovered I had martial arts in common with Tom from Michigan (a white dude with an Afro) and music with sweet Texas cowboy Duane—the only guy with a beard—who, like me, had brought a guitar but who, unlike me, actually knew how to play it. (I wondered how "Duane" would translate to Spanish.) Ray was from the Pacific Northwest.

It seemed I had a lot in common with a few of the girls in our group of twelve, those from the Midwest anyway…I was at least born there. Petite Miriam, with her charming drawl, hailed from Georgia; she was a journalist brimming with intellect.

At one point I overheard a willowy girl with long blond hair—my idol Joni Mitchell's twin!—say something with what I recognized as a Minnesota accent. My family had been going there for generations, and I knew the accent so well I could imitate it. I went over to her and held out my hand. Chest high. And looked up. She was tall, even from my not exactly short five-foot-five-and-a-half-inch perspective.

"Hi. I'm Emmy Creigh."

She looked me over and said, "Funny, you don't look Native American." I was delighted she'd heard of the Cree Nation.

I laughed and pointed to my nametag. "It's just pronounced that way, like Janet Leigh."

"Hi. Nice to meet you. I'm Ellyn Tisdale—Ellyn with a *y*." She pointed to her nametag and winked. Firm handshakes from us both.

Just the way she said it made me blurt, using my best "Ole" impersonation, "Are you by any chance from 'dohn' in Min-nih-soh-ttha?" Everything there was "dohn" to the lakes or "dohn" to the cities. Of course I had to risk it all by adding: "Don'tcha kno-oh."

Her look told me she was nobody's fool. "Guess my accent gives me away. Ya sure, you betcha, I'm from Min-nih-soh-ttha," she said in that singsongy way Norwegians had, like a boat on waves…but was she overdoing it, mimicking *me* now?

"Hope you're not offended." I giggled, suddenly nervous. "I have connections there myself. Ever heard of Battle Lake? Western-central Minnesota? Near Fergus Falls, not far from Fargo? My great-grandfather from Indianapolis caught some fish there in 1895 and ended up…"—I added with exaggerated posh—"'summering theah.' It's still in the family."

She seemed amused by my attempt at humor. "Yes, I think I know where it is. I grew up in Plainview, ninety miles southeast of Minneapolis."

Never heard of it. "What brings you to Paraguay?"

"Good question." She laughed, exuding a self-assurance I could only envy. "I've been wondering that myself. I was teaching in Scotland and this seemed like a good thing to do next. But why Paraguay? It's definitely warmer. I guess it was just the luck of the draw."

O happy day—she shared my passion for irony! Ellyn told me she'd done a lot of acting, something I'd secretly wanted to do in high school but was too chicken. We hit it off pretty well, especially over dinner that night, when I discovered she also shared my passion for pilsner.

My roommate, Polly, was, as she said, "African-American." The first night in our room, she played my guitar using a fingerpicking style I still hadn't learned and sang a song I'd never heard before, an old Jewish number called "Dona Dona."[6] Now, why a black girl would be singing a Jewish song was beyond me, but the words created a disturbing image. As a farmer takes a calf to market, the calf complains he isn't free, but the farmer chastises him: Then why don't you have wings? Stay in your place. The last line says whoever treasures freedom will learn to fly like the swallow. *Would that it were that simple!* A tremor shot through me thinking about that ill-fated calf—there'd be no way out for him. The word "die" in the chorus was unsettling, too.

But I definitely got the message about the expediency of flight.

Polly had a beautiful voice. I couldn't play guitar or sing like that and felt discouraged. We started out well enough, but I overdid my attempts at not being shy and she soon became distant.

The next day we attended presentations, filled out forms, and got vaccinations up the wazoo. The shots just kept coming, and a couple of guys fainted. I had to laugh: *The stronger sex? Yeah, right.* Needless to say, the pain didn't stop some of us from partying all night and watching the sunrise on the beach.

Miami was seductive with its warm January weather and Latino influence. You couldn't help but move to the rumba in Little Cuba—it filled the air as I stood at a counter and tossed back an espresso straight, no sugar. *Hyaah!*

I was good to go.

---

6 Sholom Secunda, "Dana Dana," 1940; the song became a popular children's camp song in the US after Joan Baez's recording of it in 1960.

And on January 8 we went—shuttled to the airport and boarded our evening Braniff flight for the nine-hour journey south. That afternoon I'd mailed a postcard home, a night view of Miami's skyline, the moon bright behind a palm tree and a blimp hovering over the waterfront. "Poor gals," I'd written, "worrying about becoming 'baby blimps' (note front)." Then: "Adiós, amores!" I was missing my family already.

I had a window seat so I wouldn't have to talk to anyone. When a stewardess came around with coffee I gave in to my weakness for it, and as a result not even the last few days' sleep deprivation could calm my hyperactive brain. I was relieved that everyone else was snoozing so they wouldn't see me looking "out" the closed window shade, seeing only the moving pictures in my head.

Leaving the family again *had* to be the right thing. Mom *told* me I should go. I wanted to cry but just didn't have it in me.

It was still dark when the stewardess woke me up for breakfast. The butterflies in my stomach were causing such turbulence I could barely get my eggs down.

3

MARTÍN

At police headquarters the food improved, a small consolation. For breakfast we had *cocido* (sweet *mate* [MAH-tay]) with powdered milk sent by the Committee of Churches of Paraguay or the International Red Cross. For lunch there was boiled corn with plenty of bones, and at night the usual *saporó* (boiled beans). Family visits lasted only thirty minutes a week, though the police presence was discreet.

The forced coming together of people from different social backgrounds was an enriching experience for me and the other political prisoners. Exemplary spirit and camaraderie reigned in this little subworld. The prisoners made an effort to avoid issues that would cause tension. Most of them still had open wounds, and their attitude was that of a great brotherhood. I had the impression we were in one of those Christian catacombs of Roman times. On Sunday afternoons a community mass was held in which believers and nonbelievers participated respectfully.

My fellow prisoners and I admired the campesinos—most of whom were activists from the Farmers' (or Christian) Agrarian Leagues[7]—for their discipline, and were impressed by the level of their ideology.

I made friends with a former director of the Colorado Party. We were like-minded and spent hours discussing our hopes and concerns. The man told me of his experience in prison and talked about the desperate struggle of our people against oppression. He had a surprising memory and could recall the names of dozens of torturers and their respective victims. He even claimed that the Spanish ambassador to Paraguay enjoyed attending torture sessions.

Corazón Benítez, a farmer and member of the Colorado Party, was also with us. He'd been arrested as a result of the intrigues of a Stroessner supporter who wanted to take over Benítez's land. Like the political prisoners, Benítez had suffered frightening humiliations. He was arrested under the pretext of

---

7 The Ligas Agrarias were rural organizations founded in cooperation with Catholic clergy in 1960 (in Paraguay) and based on the principle of the *minga* (from Guaraní and the Andean language Quechua), the ancient indigenous custom in which people worked in each other's fields both to lighten the work and to strengthen friendship. Proceeds were shared among the members. The leagues also emphasized *jopói*, or "sharing," and the idea of helping people became a fundamental principle. The *jopói* was often held on Saturdays and consisted primarily of building or repairing houses.

Schools founded by the Agrarian Leagues were known as *escuelitas campesinas*. Begun in 1971, they welcomed children whose families couldn't afford the books, shoes, and uniforms required by the public schools, or who were labeled "problem kids" because, as children of league members, they often asked the teachers awkward questions, such as why they had to learn Spanish—and learn *in* Spanish—when no one spoke it at home.

The leagues opened twenty-eight schools run by campesino teachers who used the pedagogy of Brazilian liberation educator Paulo Freire. Freire emphasized valuing one's own culture and speaking one's own language. Children didn't wear uniforms but came to school as they were, often barefoot and with patched clothes. They were taught in Guaraní how to solve problems using vocabulary and examples familiar to them. Adults were taught to read as well, and to look at their lives in a different way, as something they could change for the better.

Stroessner considered the leagues to be communist-inspired and condemned them. (See www.santamariadefe.com.)

possessing a decrepit 1932 rifle from the Chaco War.[8] During the interrogations, Benítez defied the torturers with fury.

In my cell I met a group of nine Brazilian citizens and one Chilean, all drug traffickers. The group had cold-bloodedly murdered a young soldier and raped and killed his date, then thrown the victims' bodies into a ditch along the highway and turned the car over to their leader, who waited on the Paraguayan side. I was terrified by the matter-of-fact way they told the details of their story. There was not the slightest remorse, as if it were simply one more bit of mischief among many.

Sharing a cell with these criminals was a new form of torture for me.

---

8 The Chaco is the semi-arid and inhospitable northwestern half of Paraguay. The war (1932–35), fought between Paraguay and Bolivia over supposed oil reserves and/or access to the sea (Chile had annexed Bolivia's entire coastal region in 1884), ended in a truce with Paraguay winning two-thirds of the disputed territory—which has no oil—and Bolivia gaining access to the Paraguay River. One hundred thousand men lost their lives.

PART II

THE DEVIL'S CAULDRON
JANUARY–APRIL 1975

—⚏—

MARTÍN AND EMILY

Life shrinks or expands in proportion to one's courage.

Anaïs Nin

4

MARTÍN

My cohorts and I at the First Precinct were awakened one morning by desperate cries for help in the patio of the building. We looked out and saw an elegantly dressed woman on the ground, shaking. Farther back were ten more. The guards immediately ordered us away from the window. We later found out the women were prostitutes who had "refused to obey the police department's rules."

Spectacles like this, and the cries that accompanied them, became everyday events. Every week an estimated fifty to sixty young women began the day at headquarters, most of them from the rural areas. The women washed police uniforms as part of their punishment and later, like a harem, handkerchiefs in hand, chased away the flies that landed on the potbellied defenders of public order during their refreshing summer naps. Those women who were repeat offenders were taken to the police-run "Ancients' Home" located in Capiatá, twenty-two kilometers from Asunción.

Prostitution is a prosperous business in Paraguay.[9] High-ranking police and military officers, in complicity with pro-Stroessner leaders of local Colorado Party factions, participate in the exploitation of brothels that are teeming in the capital and its surrounding areas. So-called "madams" are the proprietors and share their profits with the authorities. In other words, the guardians of the nation's sovereignty, along with those of civil order, exploit the madams, who in turn exploit the defenseless women. Police repression is made immediately apparent when prostitutes try to deal directly with clients, particularly tourists. Madams are instructed by the authorities to intervene. The zone of each officer's "franchise" is carefully defined; that is, in each neighborhood, the officer running the business is handpicked by his superior.

Prostitution is supported as well by the "presidential seedbeds" run by Eduvigis Amarilla de Benítez, a well-known obstetrician who is also president

---

9 Dr. Almada is writing in 1978.

for life of the Pro-Stroessner Women's Civic Movement. Her nickname is "Ña Matute [mah-TOO-tay] the Indefatigable," and she owns brothels and casinos. She travels throughout the country promoting the Women's Civic Movement and at the same time recruiting rural adolescent girls from low-income families to work in her brothels. Parents are assured that the girls will receive food, clothes, a good education, and above all, a promising future. Both ña Matute and a colonel known derisively as "Popol Perrier" bring these girls to the city to live in regal estates with all the creature comforts, where they are fed a special diet. When they turn fifteen, they are offered as gifts to the president of the republic.

The business of sexual exploitation is not limited to the police—interestingly, it is also part of the political-training tours led by the president's personal secretary, Mario Abdo Benítez, the "benefactor of university students." The following is from the program of one of the famous political-party tours, according to the official newspaper, *Patria*:

1. Organization in charge: Government Committee on Student and University Affairs
2. Lecturers: Mario Abdo Benítez, Leandro Prieto Yegros, Martín Chiola, J. Eugenio Jacquet
3. Participants: Presidents of local party factions and subfactions of Puerto Presidente Stroessner
4. Special guests: Journalists
   Note: In order to participate in these tours, one must be a pro-Stroessner party member and attend the event unaccompanied by a woman.

The requirement to attend alone allowed participants to enjoy the companionship of the "journalists," all of them female. These were mainly young women who worked in government offices or decentralized government organizations. To keep their jobs, they had to comply with the often-outrageous whims of the pro-Stroessner faction leaders.

It appears the first to come up with the policy of using female civil servants for the enjoyment of Stroessner loyalists was General Ramón Duarte Vera, while he was chief of police. At one time Duarte Vera had the privilege of crowning Miss Paraguay, as well as the beauty queens of social and athletic clubs, who were then offered high salaries as secretaries in government offices. Those who accepted were not required to show up at the office, but they were forbidden to miss an appointment to accompany a loyalist party leader on a leisure trip, usually to one of Duarte Vera's ranches in the Chaco.

During the height of Duarte Vera's power, diplomatic relations with Uruguay were strained—not for political reasons but because this head of the Paraguayan police had assaulted a flight attendant who worked for the Uruguayan airline Pluna. (Although known for being a rapist and for crimes committed as a torturer, Duarte Vera was later appointed ambassador to Bolivia.)

We heard about another incident involving diplomats in Asunción, which had to do with a group of female artists from Argentina who were part of an exchange program in Paraguay. The group was invited expressly by General Duarte Vera to dine at the Centenario Club, popular among the social elite of Asunción, located on Avenida Mariscal López a few blocks from the president's residence.

The details were carefully planned. Invitations were sent through the head of public relations, with gifts for each guest: boxes of whiskey, American cigarettes, Paraguayan folk art, and exotic bathing suits. After consuming copious amounts of food and drink, the guests were invited to jump into the pool to escape the summer heat. Suddenly, the women realized they were completely naked—their imported suits were made of paper that disintegrated in the water.[10] The anguish of the Argentine "Venuses" delighted the police chief, who ordered his friends to "attack," and the women were "subjected to the firing squad," in the jargon of the Stroessner regime.

The attendees tried to seek redress, but the Argentine ambassador took it upon himself to intervene, keeping the matter behind closed doors and among friends. More gifts were distributed to ensure silence and maintain positive relations among the military governments of the Southern Cone.

---

10 Advertising claims to the contrary, this was the major drawback of paper swimsuits (see photo from 1967 at http://www.reddit.com/r/ImagesOfHistory/comments/2jc27s/).

Another surprising aspect of the dictatorship that I learned about in the First Precinct was the system used by Stroessner's government to recruit junior officers. We observed that some young males, incarcerated for common crimes and between the ages of twenty and thirty, were periodically removed from their cells and taken to the barber. After they were cleaned up, they received a new corporal's or sergeant's uniform. The rank appeared to depend on the delinquent's abilities to read and write.

The physical bath was followed by an intense "mental bath" (brainwashing) called the "academy." This consisted of a daily sermon teaching that Stroessner had brought peace, tranquility, and progress to the country, and that the communists were trying to wreak havoc. The world was divided into good and evil, the former of which was represented by the United States of America and the latter by the Soviet Union. Within this design, Paraguay was on the side of the righteous, and Stroessner was their prophet.[11] The anticommunist classes were followed by karate classes taught by a famous specialist known as a "breeder of torturers."

One inspector tirelessly repeated a strange theory: "Progress is a breeding ground for delinquency, and more education and culture bring more subversion." This was why everyone should distrust intellectuals and, above all, keep an eye on them. We political prisoners were his favorite example. He would say, "Look at who is in that cell. Most of them are lawyers, doctors, engineers, teachers—and some are even Colorado Party members who, thanks to General Stroessner, were given scholarships to study abroad, and they came back subversives, an inexplicable and unforgivable fact."

As I said earlier, there were forty-three political prisoners in my cell: three university professors, one recently graduated physician, four lawyers, one economist, one labor leader, one diplomat who had been first secretary of the Paraguayan Embassy in Buenos Aires, and six students who had received scholarships to study in Argentina at the Universities of La Plata and Córdoba. The rest were farmers from the Agrarian Leagues who, the inspector claimed,

---

11   On the tyrant's birthday, greetings were published in the media and also read and discussed during sessions at the "academy." Birthday greetings from the president of the United States were the cause of special pride, as were those from dictators like Pinochet, Duvalier, and the president of South Africa.

"had been stupidly deceived by Spanish communist priests, particularly Jesuits." "Academy" instructors always concluded that the other political prisoners and I were simply "naive dreamers who wanted to right wrongs and had been won over by Havana, Peking, and Moscow, the ones responsible for our being anti-social, unsavory, and malleable dupes."

After the junior officer recruits passed the anticommunist and karate courses, those who could read and write were guaranteed candidates for the Carlos Antonio López Technical School of Middle Management. Here they learned electricity, plumbing, bricklaying, and carpentry. At the General Eduvigis Díaz Police School, they completed their studies in police investigation, the subversive cause, and other lessons in repression.

The *acä-në* junior officers (those with zero intelligence) were sent to the Police Department School of Physical Education for lessons from the director. Graduates became bodyguards for Stroessner's higher-ups or torturers at Pastor Coronel's Office of Investigations.

Those who passed the tests from Antonio Campos Alum's Office of Anticommunist Technical Management could either register as regular police academy students, receive scholarships to study at Augusto Pinochet's police academy in Chile, or go directly to the specialized US Army school in Panama, where antisubversive teams were trained.[12]

Junior officers of acceptable intellectual ability who received certificates from the vocational-technical school were often sent to police stations, and from there to the homes of government officials to work in construction or maintenance of their palatial mansions. These officers received very low wages, like farmers and laborers, but enjoyed the great advantage of having access to the "remainders" of the month—the right to payment in kind, such as whiskey, American cigarettes, sacks of flour or potatoes, and such, which had been confiscated from unauthorized smugglers. The "remainders" were in turn placed on the black market by the junior officers' wives and children.

---

12 The School of the Americas is now located in Fort Benning, GA, and called WHINSEC—Western Hemisphere Institute for Security Cooperation.

Thus, official commercial activity became a family business, and corruption involved all family members. Pawnshops—owned exclusively by the police—sprouted up like mushrooms during the military dictatorship. Spoils of the many lootings and murders ended up being sold in these shops.

These lower-level custodians of civil order also benefited from the custom known as "personal initiatives" promoted by their superiors. An example of this was the famous institution under Stroessner known as "driver-license kidnapping," whereby a traffic violation was fabricated, the vehicle pulled over, and the victim's license confiscated—only to be ransomed back to the frightened driver. The "fine" was determined based on the driver's appearance, with the money ending up in the officer's pocket. Another "personal initiative" task reserved for junior officers was the collection of a "tax" imposed on small businesses like grocers, magazine vendors, shoe shiners, and small-time brothel keepers.

Acä-në junior officers who joined Pastor Coronel's political police agents *(pyragüés)* became notorious for their ability to snatch billfolds and briefcases on public transportation and in public spaces. According to "orders from above," the victims were to be anti-Stroessner party members and foreign tourists. Documents and personal papers obtained in this manner were turned over to Pastor Coronel, but the officers could keep the cash. This practice was supposedly to keep the opposition in line and help detect guerrilla fighters disguised as tourists.

When junior officers were denounced by public opinion, they were punished in exemplary fashion—not for committing a crime but for getting caught. This was known in Stroessner jargon as "punishment for being weak."

This unique method of recruiting junior officers was apparently devised by the former minister of the interior, assisted by his chief of police. Others, including Chief of Investigations Pastor Coronel, helped perfect the reprehensible institution. All of them acted, naturally, with the approval of the "first worker, first journalist, and champion of anticommunism," Generalísimo Alfredo Stroessner.

4

EMILY

Flying over Paraguay in the morning, I was mesmerized by the intense emerald landscape, flatter than Kansas, a crazy quilt of fields tucked among dark patches of woods and the occasional overgrown outcrop.

Green turned to red—or Crayola's "burnt sienna," a name I'd always found curious—as we cruised over Asunción, the majority of houses roofed with terracotta tile. Home to a few tall buildings, one of them oddly triangular, the city sat on the edge of a glassy river.

We landed at Aeropuerto Presidente Stroessner (the president's father had apparently been a German immigrant) and taxied to the terminal, stopping in front of a huge sign: Bienvenidos a La Muy Noble y Leal Ciudad de Nuestra Señora Santa María de la Asunción—Welcome to The Very Noble and Loyal City of Our Lady Saint Mary of the Assumption. Whew, we were in Catholiclandia, all right! I was thankful the name had been abbreviated as I knew no one would write me if they had to spell it all out like that.

As I stepped out of the plane onto the stairs, the humidity made me catch my breath; it was like trying to breathe under water. Now I knew what people meant about Arizona's being a "dry" heat. That was tolerable—but this?

High-pitched insect voices swelled, died down, and then built up again in a kind of slow-motion siren that seemed to be coming from inside my head. I descended to the spongy tarmac, where a tall, lanky man with dark hair and sunglasses stood waiting.

When we were all accounted for, he smiled and said, "Hi. I'm Todd Logan, the agricultural extension program manager for Peace Corps–Paraguay." We shook hands and repaired to the relative cool of the airport. Our visas and other requirements had been taken care of, so all we had to do was clear customs, which took a while.

I had to laugh when I saw the reason for the delay: Miriam's portable typewriter! She must be serious about writing. Maybe I should've brought mine; on the electric ones in high school I'd hit sixty words per minute—*Now is the time for all good men to come to the aid of their country,* ad infinitum *et* nauseam. But I honestly couldn't imagine clacking away into the night on one out in the *campo* and keeping everyone awake, including the roosters.

No, I'd stick with the old-fashioned method of scratching away into the night on paper with pen and ink (black)...and perhaps a little blood thrown in as well, as I was wont to do in college. But no banal "Dear Diary" for me—no, my journal would be lyrical, inspired, like Emerson and Thoreau, with a little Anaïs Nin thrown in to spice things up. That was the plan, anyway. I'd brought a spiral notebook from UOP but planned to get a proper journal here as soon as I could.

On the road to town, we passed a boxy *carreta* with wooden wheels nearly as tall as a man, drawn by two oxen with pointy horns and obsidian eyes. The chassis was piled high with what Todd said was sugarcane, its bamboo-like stalks extending several yards out the back. The driver tapped the animals with a thin branch as several women and children sat on the *caña*, their heads still as their bodies jerked back and forth with each plodding step.

Soon we were on a broad, leafy street called Avenida Mariscal López. "That's the president's home," Todd said as we passed a surprisingly flat white building with columns. Armed guards patrolled the wrought-iron gate. "In Guaraní it's called Mburuvichá Roga, 'chief's house.'" He paused: "And Stroessner really *is* the big kahuna." Not everyone laughed.

All of a sudden we were downtown and jostled by taxis, buses, cars, scooters, all manner of internal combustion going one way down a hemmed-in street, tooting and passing within inches of one another (Lord have mercy!) as there were no lanes per se. It was obvious the same traffic rule applied here as in Mexico—whoever got there first had the right of way. The buildings were Spanish colonial, thick and curvy with columns and arches painted mostly in pastels. From their facades hung jumbles of electric wire, just waiting to catch fire.

Did I mention it was hot?

We were perspiring (as Gidget would say) our asses off by the time we arrived at Peace Corps "headquarters." It was crammed into a charming two-story house with an imposing front and serene inner courtyard filled with flora and bordered by rooms—soothing respite from the helter-skelter outside. We were greeted by Country Director Barry Coucher, who had a thick, dark beard and seemed friendly, though the bags under his eyes were veritable hammocks.

"Welcome to Paraguay, the liver of South America," he said, smiling. I for one appreciated his joke and laughed out loud—Paraguay was usually portrayed as the "heart" of the continent. (Either way, it *did* have the shape of an internal organ.) "As you probably know by now," he went on, "Paraguay is one of only two land-locked countries on the continent, a dubious distinction it shares with Bolivia."

Barry introduced us to everyone in the office and several volunteers who happened to be floating around. "PCVs"! I loved the sound of it. I located the library right away, where I knew I'd be spending lots of time, as I had in college. There was also a darkroom—I was thrilled to be able to pick up where I'd left off in Japan.

As we walked, Barry gave us a short history of the Peace Corps in Paraguay. The program had been here since 1967 and would have ninety volunteers this year, half of whom worked in the agricultural sector like us and the others in education, nursing, or finance. "The completion rate for volunteers here is around 90 percent," he said, "and 82 percent for trainees." Good—it sounded stable.

He reminded us we were not Peace Corps *volunteers* until we completed our training and were sworn in. Until then we *trainees* could use the PC office as needed, which probably wouldn't be much because we would be busy with our language and technical training and spending time in cultural immersion with our families.

We entered Barry's office and sat down. "One more thing," he said. Our collective eyes rolled, jet lagged as we were, and a few girls couldn't help yawning. He smiled and said, "Don't worry, I'll keep this short." Then he got serious.

"It's been a bit tense around here with all the terrorist activity going on," he said. "But I want to make it perfectly clear that President Stroessner is an *ally* of the United States." Barry looked around to see if anyone had a problem with this statement, but no one registered anything, so he went on.

"Yes, Stroessner is a dictator. He's been in power for twenty years and keeps changing the constitution so he can be, quote, 'reelected.' But he has brought stability to this country; it's hard to imagine, but there had been twenty-two presidents here in the twenty-seven years before he took over. His party, the

Colorado or 'Red' Party, is firmly in control. Not that there haven't been attempts to undermine his power...and not just his. All throughout the Southern Cone, insurgents have been blowing things up and killing people. Groups like the Tupamaros from Uruguay...you've heard about Dan Mitrione, the US operative who was killed by the Tupamaros in 1970."[13]

Was it a question or a statement? I'd certainly never heard of Mitrione. I was just astounded that *colorado* meant "red" and not "colored," as I'd always thought. *Oh yeah, that would be "colorEado."* That meant Arizona had its own "Red River Valley"—no less than the friggin' Grand Canyon! (Of course these days the Colorado River was green, now that it came from the bottom of Lake Powell at Glen Canyon Dam, that travesty of environmental justice.)

I snapped out of my reverie when Barry said, "And of course there are the Montoneros from Argentina, who are, quite frankly, out of control. Did you know last year alone they assassinated dozens of people? They kidnap for ransom—and often kill—wealthy executives from Ford, General Motors, Chrysler...just last September they set off forty bombs throughout Argentina—imagine, forty!—in American places of business like Goodyear, Chase Manhattan, Xerox, even Coca-Cola, for Pete's sake..."

Our mouths hung open. It *was* a little close to home, so to speak, even though I myself eschewed Coke—it gave me zits.

"I don't mean to scare you, I just want you to be aware," he continued, looking as exhausted as we felt. "Last September the Montoneros were discovered training with weapons here in Asunción, and several of the leaders were gunned down by police, right on the street; they were apparently involved with some agrarian groups in Paraguay's interior. There are other factions, all of which want to get rid of the president. In fact, a car-bomb plot against Stroessner was foiled only a few months ago."

We all just stared at him.

"Be that as it may," Barry continued with a sigh, "the dissidents have their *reasons*, it's just their *techniques* we can't accept. Now, you may be thinking,

---

13 For more information, read the outstanding book *Hidden Terrors: The Truth about U.S. Police Operations in Latin America* by A. J. Langguth (New York: Pantheon Books, 1978). The book was the subject of the brilliant Costa Gavras film *State of Siege* (1972).

'One man's terrorist is another man's freedom fighter.' So be it. But let me repeat: The United States is helping President Stroessner rid his country, this country—*your* country now—of communists. So…you must promise not to get mixed up in any groups not sanctioned by the Colorado Party. Better yet, no groups at all." He didn't quite manage to control the tremor in his voice.

No one moved. Finally Polly said, "Are volunteers in danger here?"

Barry blinked for so long I thought he'd nodded off. Then he sprang back to life, leaning forward in his seat: "No, they're—*you're*—not. PCVs who follow the rules stay out of harm's way. The government and people here are extremely pro-US, and no PCV has ever been mistreated. We will make sure it stays that way. With your diplomatic immunity you'll be safe…to some extent. But if you buck the rules and get in serious trouble, we can't guarantee we'll be able to help you. So, please, you *must not antagonize* this administration, which kindly allows *us*—*you*—to be here in the first place."

His stern look and words troubled me, but not as much as his behavior. I certainly didn't intend to cross the corps. After Barry's sobering message, I realized what a huge responsibility he had to keep us safe. No wonder he looked so fried.

"It's ironic that here," I said, "the 'Reds' are the *anti*communists."

Miriam looked intrigued and said, "Yes. Also ironic is how fascists and communists vilify and annihilate one another yet seek the same end—subjugation of the masses through totalitarian control." I shuddered: "totalitarian" was arguably the scariest word in the English language.

"I guess you could say that," Barry conceded. Then he paused and smiled, looking at us one at a time and emphasizing each word. "Now, go out there and *do some good*. Just promise me, ladies, you will not get politically involved. We don't want any Patty Hearsts[14] here."

---

14 The granddaughter of publishing magnate William Randolph Hearst, Patty Hearst was abducted from her Berkeley, California, apartment in February 1974 by the Symbionese Liberation Army (SLA). She began supporting the cause of the SLA by committing armed robbery, shooting at a shop owner to defend other SLA members, and making improvised explosive devices. She'd managed to avoid arrest, however, and was still on the lam.

Was that supposed to be a joke? We nodded again and promised we wouldn't, so he let us go. I knew I'd have no problem as I didn't care for politics anyway, having failed miserably at it my sophomore year of high school. I'd managed to get elected to the student council—heaven help me, I even gave a speech in front of the student body!—but was terrified to open my mouth during the infernal meetings in the dean's office (the price I had to pay for getting out of class). I'd steered clear of politics ever since.

We filed back into the van, turned a corner, and drove down the street, stopping after a few blocks at the official PC resting place: the Hotel Stella D'Italia de Fernando Graziani, Cerro Corá 945, which had three floors and bathrooms down the hall. PCVs—including us wannabes—got a special discount.

Ellyn and I were roommates. As soon as we put our bags down, she collapsed onto the flattest bed I'd ever seen, and I headed to the bathroom down the hall. The tub was an old-fashioned one with claw feet. I noticed there was a second "toilet" that shot water straight up.

"What's that thing in the bathroom—you know, with the fountain in it?" I asked as I returned to our room and lay down on the other bed, also flat. Fatigue was draining the life out of me.

"Emmy, dear, it's called a *bidet*, and you use it to wash yourself, you know, after you *go*." She said it in a motherly way, as if she had something tremendous to teach me—which she did, when it came to bidets anyway. But I couldn't believe they had bathroom fixtures here that I'd never even heard of...and from France, no less.

"Seems like a waste of water to me," I murmured, ever the desert rat, before passing out.

A few hours later we awoke and, still groggy, went to the Parrillada La Preferida, where we ate grilled steaks served with mandioca, the national staple. When I bit into the whitish piece that looked sort of like a potato, I was stunned to discover it had the consistency, not to mention the flavor (I imagined) of a wax candle. As I cut the mandioca and examined it, I was even more amazed to see it broke naturally into three pieces around a central "string"—the wick! *Hmm...looks like a candle...tastes like a candle...probably has as many nutrients as a candle...*

Why anyone would want to eat these empty calories was beyond me. (I wasn't picky—I just had discriminating tastes.) I ate a couple bites and then gently pushed it aside, deciding to focus instead on the steak, which was a little tough but not bad...though I really could have gone for a baked potato with butter and sour cream.

We sat on the terrace drinking beer and sweating as we watched young barefoot women perform folkloric dances while balancing empty wine bottles on their heads. Men climbed ladders and made a great show of placing one bottle atop another, getting up to eight or so. It was an interesting skill, but what was the point? It seemed demeaning. Besides, the bottles *had* to be stuck together somehow.

The music I found enchanting, though, with its harps and guitars and percussive strumming. Someone said the national music was called the *guarania* [gwah-RAH-nyah]. I couldn't wait to try out the new Yamaha nylon-string guitar I'd bought in San Francisco before I left California.

In the morning I nearly cried with joy when I beheld breakfast, always my favorite meal: fresh fruits, juices, cheeses, breads, *dulce de guayaba* (guava jam). And the crowning glory, the magically restorative *café con leche*, the coffee thick and black, the milk hot and foamy in its own little pitcher.

The Stella truly was a patch of heaven—according to PCVs, the best place in town to rest between trips to the campo. And it was literally just up the street, "only" nine blocks from the hallowed PCV meeting grounds, the Hotel Guaraní, which, as it turned out, was the triangular building I'd seen when we flew in...only yesterday? Hard to believe.

After morning meetings at the PC office we visited the American Embassy, a blocky and uninspiring two-story building with scalloped roof and huge arched portico. We later tossed back a few *chopps* [chohps] (a term I'd never heard for draft beer) at the Bar San Roque and explored some local eating establishments.

A company called Monitor had been contracted to teach us Guaraní and other necessary skills for working in Paraguay. The school was a house in Villa Morra, the neighborhood just northeast of the embassy, where the host families lived.

The first words we learned in Guaraní were "small" and "large," as our two primary Peace Corps trainers were "Anna-í" [ah-nah-EE] and "Anna-guazú" [ah-nah-gwah-SOO] Big Anna was terminating soon. One of our other trainers was local PC legend Diego Hay. We'd heard about him from some PCVs at the Stella. Diego was soft spoken and the favorite go-to guy for everything Paraguayan. He was famous for telling stories and embellishing them with a little high-pitched laugh. You couldn't help but like him.

I was fairly fluent in *español* (four years in high school, two semesters of Spanish literature in college, and spring semester of my sophomore year in the Yucatán) and loved speaking it but was surprised to learn Paraguayan Spanish used *vos* instead of *tú*, the familiar "you." The verb changed, too; instead of saying *Tú eres*, "you are," people said *Vos sos*. That cracked me up—after all my years studying the language, I never knew anyone spoke Spanish like that. The commands were easy, though: *vení* was "come here," a lot easier than the regular command forms I'd managed to never quite learn. *Vení* was usually followed by *un poco*: "Come here a little."

I also heard *al pelo, che*, which literally meant "to the hair" but translated as "far out, man." The Argentine *che* at the end (with a hard "ch") meant "friend." Che Guevara was called that because he himself—being Argentine—was often heard saying it. (I saw how deeply Che Guevara was revered here for his courage and conviction.) *Ciao, che* was a favorite expression of PCVs.

When it was my turn to meet my family, Todd packed my belongings in the PC Suburban and drove me to my new home in Villa Morra. I was a little apprehensive because I didn't really like living with families—there were too many expectations and awkward moments, like the time my Japanese mother started feeding me cold rice because I was spending too much time with my Callison friends.

We drove up to a modest brick house. A redhead came out with open arms, her three little kids affixed firmly to her body and not about to let go. She kissed me on both cheeks Paraguayan style (I'd seen others do it) and said her name was Teresa. Her husband, a supervisor in the interior, would be home tomorrow. Teresa couldn't stop mooning over my blue eyes, and I realized that's how it would be here, as it had been in Mexico and Japan. I got a kick out of how she pronounced "Emily" like "Emmy-lee."

Satisfied that all was well, Todd drove off. It was up to me now—I was on my own. Hopefully this would all work out. I took a deep breath and followed my new family inside.

The house was comfy with tile floors and plastic-covered furniture. Christian images abounded, and on the living-room wall hung a portrait of Stroessner next to one of JFK—unlike many Americans, Latinos had certainly never held Kennedy's Catholicism against him (ironic that JFK was the reason I was here in the first place). The den, which looked like it had been added on, held the television and Tere's mechanized knitting machine; she taught classes at a vocational school. The family wasn't rich but lived well enough.

My room was in back, a storage closet really but large enough for my Spartan needs, despite having to share it with the family's stuff. The walls were green and the floor a rough brick. Sitting under an open window—which fortunately had a screen—was the bed, a wood cot with a thick cotton pallet covered by a white chenille bedspread. An armoire, what they called a *ropero*, had been crammed into the room for my clothes. On the table next to the bed, a small fan blew valiantly from side to side but succeeded merely in redistributing the hot air.

It was perfect.

Outside in the yard shimmered a genuine Eden of bananas, grapes, grapefruit, limes, guava, corn, tomatoes, onions, and who knew what else. Plus countless birds and insects…chirping, tweeting, and buzzing so loudly I wondered (jokingly) if I'd be able to hear my cassettes playing over all the racket. I unpacked and then napped until Teresa called me for dinner.

We all sat down and said a prayer, me mumbling until the "ah-MEN." I had no idea how to pray in Spanish.

Tere served me a steak and then asked if I'd like some Paraguayan soup.

"Yes, thank you," I said. I didn't see any bowls or spoons.

She handed me a plate with cornbread on it. "Here you go."

"That's *sopa paraguaya?*" I said, starting to laugh.

She nodded, confused at what was so funny.

"In the Castilian Spanish I learned in high school, *sopa* is a liquid you eat with a spoon." I held up a piece and inspected its dense texture. My mouth started to water just as an invisible force propelled the sopa in that very direction.

Teresa nodded and said, "Here in Paraguay, soup is *caldo*." No longer able to hold back, I sank my teeth into a corny, cheesy, oniony delight not unlike our own cornbread but much more flavorful. This solid form of soup was fine with me.

The meat, on the other hand, presented some problems, not the least of which was *I couldn't chew it*. I mean, my father had been in the cattle-feeding business (that is until March 1973, when Nixon froze the price of beef but not the price of feed, causing Dad and others to go out of business), and we'd always eaten the "finest" cuts, always medium rare—a pox on steak sauce—though I'd never been crazy about eating animals.

Now here I was, chewing and chewing but making no progress, ending up with a wad of gristle in my mouth that I wasn't about to swallow and didn't know what to do with. I couldn't spit it out—I might offend Teresa. Besides, where would I put it? So, feeling rather bovine, I calmly moved my mouth around and around in a faux masticating motion as I tried to come up with a plan.

After some thought I realized if I worked fast and created a diversion, I could spit it into my hand. By this time I was desperate just to get it the hell out of my mouth.

"What's that?" I asked, pointing to a colorful embroidered rooster that was hanging on the wall. As the family turned their heads I smoothly ran my hand by my mouth and retrieved the gristle.

"It's called *ñandutí* [nyahn-doo-TEE]," Tere said. "In Guaraní it means 'spiderweb.' It's a typical form of embroidery here...my aunt makes it."

"I'll have to take a closer look at it later," I said, giddy now. My ploy had worked! The only problem was, now the gristle was in my right hand. How was I going to eat? I transferred it to my left hand under the table. But I couldn't just let it sit there...I would need my left hand to cut more meat. What to do?

Genius, like lightning, strikes at random. I reached down, rolled up my pants leg, and deposited the gristle there. That would have to do for now—I'd come up with a better plan later.

As it turned out, I could barely finish the steak because my jaws were getting sore. Of course Teresa offered me more and when I politely refused, she started to give me some anyway. I protested that I really couldn't possibly eat any more, so she applied the guilt trip: "You don't like it?"

"Yes, of course I like it," I said, but before I could say I just didn't *want* any, here came another hunk of cowflesh onto my plate. *So this is how it's going to be,*

I fumed. I hated it when people decided things for me. I would have to put my foot down…eventually.

The next day my "father," Rafael, came home, and I liked him right away. Tall and handsome with a fair complexion, he was affectionate with Tere and the kids. He even played the guitar and promised to teach me some guaranias. He explained how his work, installing electricity in rural areas, took him out of town a lot and, with Teresa nodding in agreement, acknowledged how difficult this was for the family.

I can only imagine how "difficult" it is for you out on your own like that, I thought. I was no newcomer to Latin men.

But I quickly became fond of my boisterous, loving family. They prided themselves on being Italian-Paraguayan, which made no difference to me so long as my mother could cook—and she definitely could. That night she showed me how to make *"ñokeess,"* her signature Italian dish. She mixed mashed potatoes (not from flakes) and flour and formed it into balls, which she somehow rubbed off the end of a fork with a flick of the wrist, and presto—little gnocchis were born. At dinner I was relieved she didn't try to make me eat too much.

I was excited to start class on Monday. I'd always loved studying languages—Spanish, Hebrew my sophomore year to get on the morning session at my overcrowded high school (what a coup *that* had been), Japanese during my semester there—and was looking forward to adding Guaraní to the list.

That night, though, some of the charm of being there wore off. I couldn't sleep because of the heat and mosquitoes, let alone the sheer exhaustion. In the corner a green coil smoked away, its noxious byproducts failing to dissuade the mosquitoes. *How did the little bastards get in, anyway? I told the kids to close the damn door!*

It was hard to believe this time last year I was in Japan—and Dad was still alive. The date he died, January 16, was fast approaching. What were his final thoughts? Was he calm or in anguish? Did he secretly hope Mom had found the letters? She said she'd seen them on his desk but hadn't been nosy enough to read them. God, I wished she had. But we weren't that kind of family, were we? Privacy mattered more than anything to people like us.

The hardest question was *Where was I when Dad needed me?*

Which of course always led to *What am I doing here, now that Mom needs me?*

I was being torn apart, but I fell asleep before I could wonder why I still couldn't cry.

5

MARTÍN

During my thousand days in prison, there were many nights that I lay awake. It seemed as if, in that den of suffering that was our cell, the hours would not pass, as if time had been divided into two opposing halves—one a few meters from our iron door, leading toward the future and its inevitable changes, and the other inside the cell, leading back to the past and medieval treatment, back toward the time of the birth of Jesus Christ.

In the Office of Investigations, torturers had placed destroyed bodies by my side, made me witness torture, or threatened me with more torture. I tried to convince myself it was just a bad dream, especially when I heard the ringing of the old bells of the Cathedral of the Assumption from my cell in the First Precinct.

Mental escape was my way of tolerating the psychological torture. Thinking about the present and remembering the past made me feel worse, so I tried to imagine myself in the future. I dreamed about the UNIBANCOOP,[15] a strategy for fighting poverty (through employee ownership) and protecting the environment, which would succeed the Alberdi Institute. It would put into practice the self-management of learning. I imagined feverish activity, with the full participation of students, professors, and parents—an incubator for cooperatives, mutual-benefit societies, any organizations resulting from work in solidarity.

I also spent hours watching the activities of the ants and cockroaches that shared our cell. One day I even convinced myself that I, too, was an ant—I imagined myself a part of the troop, crossing through the iron bars, walking around on the sergeant's boot, reaching the other side of the wall and finding freedom at last!

---

15 This vision is being realized through the Celestina Pérez de Almada Foundation.

The midnight changing of the guards gave me a terrible feeling. I couldn't stand the voices and footsteps of the arrogant superintendents, much less the sound of their swords, the locks, the chains, the orders they shouted. The head guard would stick his nose into the cell and count, "One, two, three, four…" When it was my turn I held my breath, without really knowing why. This all happened in an atmosphere of tension and anxiety that didn't last more than five minutes. To me, though, it seemed like centuries.

Lying faceup on the ground, I thought I saw clowns hugging each other, but it was just our clothes hanging from the ceiling and walls. Glancing sideways, I could see beyond the bars to the movement of black boots. The shiniest ones belonged to the superintendents. I closed my eyes and felt as though the hanging clowns, the black bars, and the police boots were spying on me to see if I was asleep. The guards made the prisoners sleep whether we wanted to or not because they didn't trust us, and they feared even our weary sleeplessness. One night I decided to resist and not follow the orders of the pudgy superintendent. Realizing that my thoughts, unlike my body, had not succumbed to Stroessner's prisons or his dictatorship made me immensely happy.

Then I felt the temptation to provoke the jailers—in my imagination, of course, the only weapon I had for resisting the psychological torture in the dungeon-tomb-cage-cell-hell. And from that sprang these lines of verse:

Aquí está mi cuerpo, encadenado
Sobre frías baldosas carcelarias,
Pero mi pensamiento vaga libre,
Filigrana de voces libertarias…

[Here is my body, chained
On cold prison tiles,
But my mind wanders free,
A filigree of libertarian voices…]

Conversation among political prisoners was not prohibited, so the forty-three prisoners sharing the cell had stimulating exchanges about our experiences from both before and after imprisonment.

One cellmate told of his trip to Buenos Aires to see a Paraguay-Argentina *fútbol* (soccer) match. He said more than fifteen thousand Paraguayans descended on the capital to cheer on the players in the red-and-white jerseys. On their return to Asunción, after a 3–1 defeat, the Paraguayan fans met with police violence at the port of entry, Itá Enramada. They were subjected to a meticulous search, and those who had picked up reading material in the Argentine capital were mistreated. Right there, before the defeated Paraguayan fans, the police proceeded "à la Pinochet" to burn books, pamphlets, magazines, and any other printed matter. Travelers who were carrying flyers or publications from Paraguayan political parties organized abroad were taken to the Office of Investigations.

Our cellmate remarked that all of those materials had been distributed throughout the match. There had been other signs of resistance as well: the Paraguayan political police, hired to observe the crowd during the sporting event, could do nothing to prevent TV cameras from focusing on the huge banners with anti-Stroessner slogans like "Reject the Itaipú Treaty," "Freedom for Political Prisoners," and "General Amnesty."

Another cellmate told about one of the many crimes committed by two officers at the Office of Investigations. They had proceeded, naturally without a court order, to search the house of a student whose last name was Blanco Cáceres, where they found a sociology book of suspected Marxist inspiration. They hauled the victim directly to the torture chamber. After whipping him and applying electric shocks to his testicles, they put a hole in his ear, through which they tied the end of a cord and then lifted him to the ceiling with a pulley. Later they tied his legs together, hoisted him to the ceiling again, and repeatedly bashed his head against the wall. Cáceres was buried in the Santa Elena cemetery, and his mother, upon finding out what happened, went mad with grief.

A cellmate belonging to the Paraguayan Confederation of Workers told us the history of the union. Established in 1951, its mission was to fight for the effective enforcement of the right to unionize and bargain collectively. This topic led my cellmates to ask me about the union situation with Paraguayan teachers. I told them about the Federation of Paraguayan Educators (FEP), which comprised both primary and secondary schoolteachers. I said I had considered the actions of the FEP and concluded that it was urgent to reorganize the union around the professional interests of teachers in the new society that would be built after the old regime was toppled.

The prisoners felt that in the process of reorganization, educators should create a union of education and science workers, with the full participation not only of those who taught for a living, but also researchers and scientists. They thought Paraguayan teachers should develop a labor consciousness capable of extending militant solidarity to all the teachers and scientific and cultural workers of our nation, and then to those throughout Latin America. They felt that only from that perspective could the problems of Paraguay and the region be resolved. We discussed the teachers' labor organization often, and everyone agreed that labor problems should be under the jurisdiction of the Ministry of Labor and not the Ministry of Education, as they had been until then.

Someone took up the soccer conversation again and told the tragicomic story of Antonio Ayala, a Paraguayan citizen residing in Argentina. The Argentine champions, Boca Juniors, were scheduled to play against the Paraguayan champions, Cerro Porteño, in Asunción. Many Paraguayans living in Formosa (Argentina) as economic exiles came to Paraguay with the Boca team to see the game. At Itá Enramada Paraguayan police were checking documents, and when it was his turn, Ayala was detained and led immediately to the interrogation room next door. There he was greeted with punches and kicks. He was later transferred to Investigations in Asunción, where he was tortured for three weeks.

He appeared later at a police headquarters on the outskirts of town, where he met our cellmate. One day Ayala was visited by one of his torturers, who had been a boxer and was the father of a well-known pro-Stroessner lawyer. This man explained that an error had been made, and everything was due to there being two Antonio Ayalas. The authorities had confused him with the notorious subversive by the same name. But instead of offering his apologies, the torturer offered to represent Ayala's defense to his superiors for $3,000.

After much effort, Ayala's family and friends living in Formosa managed to pull together the price put on his head, and he was freed after three months in captivity. An ambulance registered in Argentina was used to transfer him from the Paraguayan capital to Formosa because the man was unable to walk.

Another prisoner recalled the case of Dr. Quirno Codas Thompson, an internationally renowned radiologist who, for having criticized a few deficiencies he had observed in the management of the Social Security Institute, was expelled from the country. The political police rousted him out of bed in his pajamas and dropped him off at the Argentine border, for the serious offense of having spoken critically about the accomplishments of General Stroessner—at a benefit dinner, no less.

Then the case of Angel Moglia came up. He had been given twenty-four hours to leave the country with his family for producing Dürrenmatt's *Romulus the Great: An Ahistorical Historical Comedy in Four Acts* in a theater in Asunción. The Presidential Office of Information and Culture, as well as the Ministry of Education, surmised that the play contained an ideological message threatening the peace and progress of the republic and was, therefore, subversive.

Someone told the story of Gumersindo Gamarra, a humble father of seven who lived near Capiatá. An active member of the local Colorado faction in his town, Gumersindo worked in a brick factory and cultivated a little plot on the outskirts of town. He was well respected in his community for being friendly and helpful.

On February 4, 1969, Gumersindo had gone to collect money from the sale of his bricks. Afterward he went with his coworkers to have some drinks at a neighborhood bar. Around 10:00 that night, the group decided to accompany Gumersindo home, given his state of inebriation. As they walked, Gumersindo cheerfully sang songs in Guaraní and shouted hurrahs to the Colorado Party and his beloved fútbol team, Cerro Porteño. The group soon became a chorus of voices that broke the silence of the small-town night. Gumersindo insisted on delivering a serenade to his wife and called for his guitar.

Not far off, a few shotgun blasts sounded and Gumersindo, without knowing it was the police and drunk as he was, drew his .22-caliber revolver and fired two shots into the air. He was arrested on the spot and taken directly to the Third Precinct, where he was tortured. For two and a half years he moved through the jail cells of the city as a "potential subversive." His wife presented a writ of habeas corpus before the courts and received the well-known, twenty-year-old response: "The detainee is being held under executive power, by order of the president of the republic"—which meant imprisonment without a set jail term.

Gumersindo began a hunger strike to protest his detention. His wife and children pleaded in vain before the chief of police and the interior minister to be allowed to visit him. The hunger strike lasted sixty-four days and ended with the cold notification of Gumersindo's death. His corpse was delivered to his widow with the threat that she would suffer the same punishment if she ever told what had happened to her husband. The instructions were precise: his body was to travel from the Rigoberto Caballero police hospital directly to the Capiatá cemetery, without stopping for religious services.

The people of Capiatá, who knew Gumersindo and the cause of his detention, loudly expressed their indignation. Word spread that the punishment was meant to set an example: an individual outside the circle of power could not playfully fire a shot—not even straight up into the air—to show his happiness, as this act was immediately considered "an affront to the authority constituted in the person of His Supreme Excellency Mr. President of the Republic and Commander in Chief of the Armed Forces of the Nation Alfredo Stroessner."

Another prisoner mentioned that he had recently shared a cell with an English tourist who had been robbed of his wallet in Puerto Presidente Stroessner and made the mistake of reporting it to the police—when it was in fact the police who had taken it. He was accused of being an international terrorist and transferred to the infantry regiment in Villarrica, where everything he owned was stolen and he was left with only the shirt and trousers he was wearing.

The Englishman was put in a suffocatingly small cell with Doroteo Grandel, a farmer who had been held and tortured there for more than eight months for refusing to sell his land to the barracks commander, a general. Grandel had studied only up to the third grade, but he had participated actively in the Agrarian Leagues. Land problems took up most of his conversation. He stressed the need to demand a fair price for agricultural products and talked about the people's resistance to the violent evacuations forced by the police and military. He also spoke of the creation of self-defense groups and the role of the farmers' movement in the struggle for freedom. The Englishman

learned through Doroteo that more than 60 percent of the Paraguayan population is made up of farmers and almost 80 percent of the nation's activity is
in agricultural production, yet the farmer belongs to the most repressed and
marginalized class in the country.

At that moment Doroteo was on the disappeared list, and of course the
government denied all responsibility for his disappearance. The Catholic
Church had taken on his defense and ceaselessly demanded his freedom, but in
truth, as long as Doroteo refused to give in to the general's pressure, he was
condemned to more torture.

For his part, Her Majesty the queen of England's subject was transferred
to Asunción, to "purgatory" under Pastor Coronel, the chief of political repression. There he shared a cell with twenty other prisoners—including several campesinos who were beaten the worst for having committed the offense
of belonging to the Farmers' Agrarian Leagues—where he was forced to witness countless acts of abuse.

Someone told the story of the well-known anarchist leader of Paraguay,
Ciriaco Duarte, who was arrested by the political police and arrived at
Investigations carrying a bag full of anarchist books over his shoulder. Before
being taken to the interrogation room for the serious "offense" of owning
subversive materials, he was forced to remain standing for 48 hours, facing
the wall with his hands cuffed behind him. As part of the pretorture strategy,
the guard in charge did not allow him to lean against the wall or make even the
slightest bodily movement.

Duarte, who was around seventy years old, suffered from varicose veins;
his legs soon became swollen, and his hands turned blue. But he never lost his
calm or his sense of humor. This was around his hundredth arrest for the same
"offense." The room was full of political detainees, and Duarte tried to communicate with the one next to him, also standing but facing another wall. The
guard intervened, prohibiting him from talking to anyone.

A while later Duarte asked for one of his books so he could distract
himself by reading, or at least have the guard read to him; this request was
also denied. Finally, with an air of seriousness and grandiloquence, Duarte
asked if he could think. The officer, already on edge, lost his patience. He

threw himself on Duarte and punched his face, knocking him down, and then kicked him and beat him with a club. While Duarte whimpered in pain, the guard shrieked that in a police institution, it was "prohibited to read evil literature and, above all, to think."

5

EMILY

"Emi, time to get up for school!" Teresa called at 6:30, and after *café con leche* and bread I stumbled up the sharp cobblestone street—basalt, surely, but who'd had the unenviable task of cutting and laying all these rocks?—to Monitor, eight blocks away. I appreciated that I was being given this amazing opportunity and wanted to at least show up on time; 7:30 didn't seem too early, given the heat.

We greeted the staff and got ready to start our first Guaraní class with our teacher, Carmen, who wore a T-shirt with "Make Love" in huge letters on the front. She didn't speak English so had no clue what it meant, but she smiled a lot at our friendly teasing. I was fascinated by the cavity taking root between her two top front teeth and wondered why she didn't go to the dentist.

Two girls I didn't know well, Jessica and Vicki, who were sharing a family, strolled in around 7:45, complaining that the food wasn't good, the beds were uncomfortable, the children insufferable. They were among those who had protested when Anna-í suggested we wear bras and dresses (not too short) if we didn't want to be harassed by men here. It sounded like they'd spent their weekend not with their families but at the embassy pool. Their lack of cooperation annoyed me.

It turned out that most of the girls in our group had been a little too optimistic about their Spanish ability and needed a refresher course, so our Guaraní class had a whopping enrollment of three: me, Polly, and Miriam.

"*Che che rera Carmen* [shay shay RAY-rah Carmen]."

We snapped to attention. Carmen pointed to herself. When she wrote it on the board I could see that the *r* was an alveolar flap, as in Spanish, which made it easy—the tongue touched lightly on the roof of the mouth just behind but not touching the teeth (kind of like the *d* in English though that's an alveolar *stop*). She said it a couple more times and then pointed to me.

I said, *"Che che rera Carmen,"* looking for a laugh, which I got. We were all a little nervous. Carmen smiled but didn't look quite as amused, so I tried again. *"Che che rera Emilia."*

Carmen nodded and we went around. The syntax was similar to English and Spanish, unlike Japanese, where the verb comes last.

Carmen: *"Che a-ñe-ë la Guaraní-me* [shay ah-nyay-AY la gwah-rah-NEE-may]." I speak Guaraní.

Us: *"Che a-ñe-ë la Guaraní-me." (Yeah, right, I speak it fluently!)*

She gave us examples of words in Guaraní. The shortest word of all, *y* [üh, the vowel sound in "good"], was the most difficult to pronounce...and about the most important word in the whole language, apparently. Carmen demonstrated: *"Y, y, y."* The sound was unlike anything I'd ever heard, primeval almost, a noise you'd make involuntarily if someone gave you the Heimlich.

"Uh, uh, uh," we chanted, trying unsuccessfully not to laugh.

"No, you have to say it in your throat with your tongue back and down against the epiglottis," Carmen insisted. She was serious now. *"Y* means 'water' and is the very foundation of the Paraguayan people and culture. In fact, our country lies over the largest freshwater aquifer in South America.[16] The last 'y' in *Paraguay* should be pronounced like *y.*" We tried our best but just couldn't get it right.

After a few hours and a couple of breaks, Carmen wiped her brow theatrically and said, *"Che a-jha oga pe* [shay ah-HAH OH-gah pay]. *Ja-jha py* [dja-HAH püh]." I'm going home. Let's go then. It was 11:30, time for lunch. Guaraní floated out of the kitchen radio as we walked through but I couldn't understand a word of it, and judging by the others' faces they couldn't either. It took me

---

16   In 2005–06, former US President George W. Bush purchased 121,000 hectares (just under 300,000 acres) in Paraguay's Chaco, scrubland that sits directly over a rich source of "blue gold"—the Guaraní Aquifer. The aquifer is estimated to contain some 8,900 cubic miles of water, roughly equivalent to a swimming pool three times the size of California. There have also been reports of a US army base being built in the Chaco.

years to learn Spanish and now we were expected to learn Guaraní in twelve weeks? I had my doubts.

We had three hours for lunch and a *siesta*, but I never could fall asleep on demand like that. Besides, my body was still on California time, five hours earlier—I would just be getting out of bed there now. At 2:30 I returned to Monitor in a sleepless fog. Diego was there to fill us in on what we'd be doing as volunteers.

"You'll be working for the Ministerio de Agricultura y Ganadería, with SEAG [SAY-ahg], Servicio Agrícola. The ministry is in San Lorenzo, just outside Asunción, where the School of Agriculture is also located. We'll do some training there. You'll be going into the countryside and forming girls' clubs a lot like our 4-H clubs in the States. Each club will elect its own officers and decide which projects they want to have, such as gardening, manual arts, or nutrition. The ultimate goal is to build raised-brick stoves called *fogones* [foh-GOHN-ayss] so the people don't have to cook with a fire on the floor, which as you can imagine is both unsanitary and dangerous. The clubs will need to raise money to buy *planchas*, the metal plates that go on top of the fogones for cooking."

He laughed at our doubt-ridden faces and said, "Don't worry! We'll train you to do all of it. By the end of three months, you'll have a really solid idea of what you want to accomplish in the campo. You'll be working with Paraguayan counterparts who are also SEAG employees, so you won't be completely alone out there. And your attempts will be appreciated, even if they're not successes…right away. Any questions?"

Ellyn and I looked at each other and shrugged our shoulders. It sounded feasible. But some of the girls didn't look convinced. I was starting to resent their cultivated, "What's in it for me?" expressions of boredom. In my less secure moments I'd wondered what I was doing here, but now I wondered why some of them were here—they just didn't seem particularly service oriented (or if they were, it was service *for* and not *by* them).

But they had questions, all right: "Why do we have to live with a family?" (You don't, it's just easier at first.) "How often can we come to Asunción?" (It's up to you, but we expect you'll stay in your towns most of the time.) "What if I don't like my town?" (Just communicate with us and we'll see what we can work out.) "My family here doesn't speak Guaraní. Why do we have to learn it?" (Yes, here in Asunción people have often been away from Guaraní for generations and don't speak it, but in the campo everyone speaks it, and many speak no Spanish.) Et cetera.

These girls also had *requirements*: "I prefer to be near Asunción. I'm not living in a hut. I want electricity. I need a real bathroom. I'm a vegetarian and have to make sure I get the right kind of food." It went on and on until Diego's patience wore them out.

"Is that it?" he said with a grin. "Okay, good. Now we're going to prepare a bed."

Oh, he means gardening! Al pelo, che.

"Raised beds, called *tablones* [tah-BLOHN-ayss], are best here, for drainage. This afternoon we want to dig three beds about a meter wide and five meters long. When we finish that, we'll sterilize the soil with boiling water to get rid of fungus." He raised his eyebrows to let us know he thought we were capable of all this. "And then tomorrow we'll plant."

I for one was thinking *What do you mean "we," kemo sabe?* It sounded like an awful lot of work, but we started digging. And sweating. And digging some more. When we were finished digging, we raked and sweated some more.

After a couple of hours Diego invited us to stop and rest. We pulled up some plastic garden chairs and sat in a semicircle around him as he finished a cigarette.

"*Ja-tereré* [djah-teh-reh-RAY]! Let's drink *tereré*." He sat forward and looked around expectantly, as if about to share a great secret with us, and held up a shiny white paper bag plastered with red and blue Paraguayan flag motifs (interesting that our countries shared the same colors).

"This is yerba *mate*," he explained as he opened the bag and displayed its contents. "In Guaraní it's *ka'a-y* [kah-ah-ÜH], which is a combination of *ka'a*, 'yerba,' and *y*, 'water.' It's a mild stimulant consumed by Argentines and Brazilians as well, but only the *paraguayos* drink it cold. That's called 'tereré' because that's the sound it makes when you're done sucking on the *bombilla*

Emily preparing a *tablón* during training. Diego
Hay is just visible on the right.

[bohm-BEE-yah]"—he held up a metal straw with a spoon-shaped strainer at the bottom—"like when you finish a milkshake…only better."

"I seriously doubt that," a few girls said at the same time and then laughed. I peered into the yerba bag and laughed myself: it was bright green and, complete with small stems, looked a lot like marijuana.

Diego smiled as he poured less than a cup of the powder into a cow's horn (with a bottom) he called a *guampa* [GWAHM-pah]. A nice poof of yerba floated up and away in the breeze. He then stuck in the bombilla, adjusted it a little, put a little iced water from a pitcher in it, and let it sit.

"This first drink is for Santo Tomás." Sure enough, the water disappeared. Diego poured in some more.

"I put some mint in the water. People here always add fresh medicinal plants, or *yuyos* [JOO-johss], which are first mashed. Now, you don't want to move the bombilla around. In fact, you don't even want to touch it because the server— usually someone who is inferior or wants to show deference—is in charge."

Because my family was Italian-Paraguayan—that was the reason they gave—they didn't drink *mate*, so, unlike some of the girls, I hadn't tried any since arriving last week.

Diego continued, "Yerba *mate* is made from leaves of the *Ilex paraguariensis* tree, which are smoked over a fire and then ground up. Once you've tried it, you'll have to drink it every day for the rest of your life. You'll be addicted, like me." He got a goofy expression on his face and held up the guampa as if toasting something.

"Well, Diego, we know how much willpower *you* have," Miriam teased. He did smoke a lot of cigarettes. But he just smiled and shrugged as he reached for the pitcher. By this time our tongues were thick with thirst.

"Now, I'm going to pour some water in the guampa, about a mouthful, and take the first drink. The server needs to test the temperature—only when it's hot, of course—and make sure the *yuyos* are ju-u-ust right."

He took a giant drag and drained it. "Aaahh!" he said melodramatically, refilling it. "I pass the guampa to the first person on my right…like dealing cards only backwards." He passed it to Ellyn. She took a couple of tentative sips, looking like it was hard to swallow, until it was finished. "Not bad," she said stoically. *"Gracias."*

Diego motioned for her to pass it back and poured in more water. "Now, you only say thanks when you've had enough and don't want any more. Vicki's next in line."

Vicki sipped a tiny bit and grimaced. "It needs sugar," she said, handing it back unfinished. Diego laughed.

"Sorry, you have to finish it. And—sorry—no sugar. That's for kids, in cocido." Vicki reluctantly finished her *trago* and handed it back.

As he refilled the guampa, Diego said, "I hope you all get to try cocido sometime. To make it, you burn sugar over a hot coal, along with the yerba, and then pour water over everything. It's a cool procedure."

Excuse me? You pour water over a burning coal and then drink it?

"You have to strain it first, of course," Diego added, laughing. *Ooh-kaay.*

It was Polly's turn, but her hand shot out, palm forward. "No, thanks. What about all the germs?" I had to agree: sharing a straw with strangers could give you the willies, not to mention other things you couldn't see without a microscope.

Diego laughed. "Everyone feels the same way at first. But it's just what people do here, morning, noon, and night. It's a national pastime, really, and I think it contributes to the close-knit society. You'll form strong bonds with people if you drink yerba with them in the campo. But if you really don't want to, you can say you haven't eaten or you just drank a glass of milk or ate some fruit... for some reason they won't drink yerba after any of those. Or you can just say you're sick."

It was my turn to taste the tereré. I took the guampa from Diego, aimed the bombilla at my lips, and sucked. I must have been holding my breath because when I filled my mouth with the cold liquid and bits, I didn't taste anything right away. When I let out my breath, though, I could taste it...but my gag reflex kicked in and I started coughing like crazy. At least I was able to swallow it before it all came spewing back out again.

Hyaah! It was the bitterest thing I'd ever tasted, even more so than Japanese ceremonial tea, or espresso for that matter. All I could taste was the smoke. Like Scotch.

"I think it's going to be an acquired taste," I offered in a squinty voice. Then, to get a laugh, I did my Jack Nicholson routine from *Easy Rider* and crowed like a rooster, putting my hand in my armpit and flapping my elbow, lifting my leg a little in turn.

Diego and a few of the girls chuckled. "Hey, it's not a microphone," he said in mock offense. "That's what the *paraguayos* say when you take too long." I laughed and gave him back the guampa.

"Speaking of this 'close-knit society,'" Miriam said as she looked around. "What about the abuses being carried out by the Stroessner regime *even as we speak?*"

Diego paused as he poured the next serving and handed it to Jessica. Everyone was focused on his bearded face, his sky-blue eyes clouded now, serious. He'd been here a long time, first as a volunteer in San Estanislau—"Santaní" for short—and now as a trainer. Lowering his voice he leaned in a little, and we unconsciously did the same.

"It's true there's a lot of repression here right now. I don't know much, but I have heard that throughout the country, people who openly oppose the dictatorship have been sort of…dropping off the face of the earth…and no one knows if they've been arrested or gone into hiding or exile or what. You'll be fine, of course. Just don't arouse suspicion in your towns. This regime has been known to get rough." He took the guampa from Jessica, poured another shot, and handed it to the next girl.

This was disturbing. I mean, we figured Stroessner wasn't the "benevolent" dictator we'd been told he was, but that he was "rough" was another matter. Yet we had to trust our government to gauge the danger and ensure our safety. The details of what was happening here really weren't my concern—I just wanted to go out and help rural Paraguayan families better their lives.

But I believed passionately in human rights and power to the people. In college I'd attended demonstrations, some in Stockton and the largest rally to date on the West Coast, the San Francisco contingent of the national "Out of Vietnam Now" march in April 1971, where many Vietnam vets had joined the 156,000 protestors walking peacefully from the Civic Center to Golden Gate Park. I'd always thought being "dissident"—that is, engaging in civil disobedience when necessary—was part of our legacy as Americans. Hell, our country was *founded* on resisting oppression! We were *supposed* to criticize the government.

I also thought (not seriously, of course) that every college student should major in sociology, so they could understand people better and learn to tolerate differences—Lord knew there were going to be enough of us crammed on the planet soon enough, and we'd better learn to live together. I might have even called myself a socialist, though I'd never joined any political parties...to me they were as bad as organized religions. My father, the diehard conservative, even asked me once if I was a communist, no doubt in response to my saying something like everyone should have the same opportunities, there should be no more rich and poor, we needed to redistribute wealth in the world by organizing and educating people.

Wasn't that what we would be doing here? Working in community? Forming collectives? Empowering the poor? Communism by any other name...but I'd better keep my mouth shut. That was the easy part—I'd learned in college it was better to keep quiet and appear ignorant than to open my mouth and remove all doubt, as the saying went.

We finished the tereré and went back to digging, raking, and mixing for a couple more hours. Diego let us go early, so we said goodbye and with aching muscles went our separate ways home. I decided to take a different route this time and stumbled on a basketball club, Felix Pérez Cardozo (FPC), where some girls were playing two-on-two. I told them I loved the game, and they said I could stop by and play anytime.

That night after dinner I wrote letters and listened to tapes. My brother, Sam, had given me *Heart Like a Wheel* for Christmas. I loved Linda's voice, but some of the songs on this album pissed me off—the victim thing was not my scene. I mean, if the guy's no good, leave him. Why be so strung out on something that doesn't matter anymore, and then on love that is faithless, whatever that means? I would never go out with anyone who demanded to be loved, and I certainly hoped I would never fall in love with someone I had to meet at the dark end of a street.

The song "Heart Like a Wheel,"[17] though, really hit home, the part about love being the only thing that could turn a person inside out. *Tell me about it!* Was it really better to have loved and lost? I wasn't convinced.

---

17 Anna McGarrigle, 1972.

"Willin'" was great, of course—it mentioned Tucson, and the "three Ws" spoke to my own weakness for those very things. And the song I knew just had to be written about me: "Keep Me from Blowing Away."[18] I, too, lived in a world without sunshine, squandered everything on the slightest of nothings, saw lines showing in my face already…the song said it all. Well, that and "Desperado,"[19] from an earlier album of Linda's, about the proud cowboy a lot like me whose prison is riding the range all alone.

So it was side A for anger, side B for the blues. Music really was my salvation, from listening to singing and playing it.

I decided to play *Blue* and—after grooving on Joni's exhilarating sixteen-bar guitar vamp intro—began singing along about traveling down that lonely road, "searching for something,"[20] what could it be? Now, Joni was the consummate musician: singer, songwriter (poet: her ode to "blue" was sheer genius), player, producer. Even more important: *she knew my soul*. Her songs, both the melancholy and the joyful, were about *me*…like Joni, too damn "busy bein' free"[21] for my own good. But oh how I longed for a dizzying relationship like the ones she sang about, with see-saw kisses from rain walkers and singers in the park, no we won't need no silly paper from the city hall, Carey, come on, grab your cane and we'll dance our socks off to some jukebox jive!

Where was Kerouac's supreme dharma bum, Japhy Ryder—Gary Snyder in real life? I'd been waiting a long time for fellow Zen lunatic Japhy to appear and carry me off to Japan, to the misted woods of Oregon and northern California, to yabyum[22] and satori and completion. I'd brought *Earth House Hold*[23] to keep me going until he showed up.

---

18 Paul Craft, 1973.

19 Glenn Frey and Don Henley, 1973.

20 Joni Mitchell, "All I Want," 1970.

21 Joni Mitchell, "Cactus Tree," 1968.

22 Himalayan Buddhist term for the primordial union of compassion and wisdom, male and female; a sex ritual/game in Jack Kerouac's *The Dharma Bums* (New York: Viking Press, 1958).

23 Gary Snyder, *Earth House Hold: Technical Notes & Queries to Fellow Dharma Revolutionaries* (New York City: New Directions Publishing, 1969).

One might have said I had unrealistic relationship expectations, which was probably true. I wasn't inexperienced, but I hadn't achieved that mystical union I knew was awaiting me with the right man…if only I could find him.

Of course I'd never understood why guys were attracted to me in the first place. I wasn't feminine. I hated girlie things like makeup and manicures. My hands and skin were ruddy, not delicate. My legs were too long and heavy (I had muscular thighs), and I had nothing even approaching a twenty-four-inch waist—or a thirty-six-inch bust, for that matter.

So why did they keep falling for me? It was probably my lack of interest in them. I was a jock at heart and just wanted to be friends with most guys, having more in common with them than girls. As a rule, girls didn't care for me much—and I had to admit I felt the same about a lot of them. I didn't like to sit around and talk about other people…or sit around *period*.

No, I preferred riding horses, playing sports (three college intramural championships, one with basketball greats the Frivolous Five and two with the Home-run Honeys), diving (one-and-a-halfs and backflips and gainers off the high dive), waterskiing on one ski, and schussing down dangerous snow-ski runs. Okay, maybe not that dangerous after I tore the ligaments in my knee on Mount Lemmon in eighth grade. When I was five, my granddaddy paid me a nickel to walk across his living room floor on my hands. A year later, I displayed great derring-do by riding my brother's two-wheeler down the street with my hands not on the handlebars but on the hem of my T-shirt as I deftly removed it over my head…tadaah! In junior high I seldom took a bath, though I spent six days a week at the stables nuzzling with horses. In fact, I still bathed only when necessary.

Let's face it, I had few womanly qualities.

I went to the bathroom to brush my teeth and scrutinized myself in the mirror.

Why would anyone I liked be interested in me, anyway? It certainly hadn't happened in college—the guys I'd fancied had found me wanting. One even said I was "childlike," and though he was careful to distinguish it from "child*ish*," I got the point. To this day I was a loner, incomplete, *de todo un poco y de nada mucho*, a waif in an angry emotional state that I suppressed.

In my view, happiness was overrated; I even agreed with Montaigne that it was a "singular incentive to mediocrity." I mean, how could anyone be truly happy, knowing all the suffering life had to offer (its transitoriness, for one)? It was sad to see how people deluded themselves into thinking they could buy happiness, an impossible dream—not to mention hoax. No, I subscribed more to Unamuno's "tragic sense of life" (I'd studied Unamuno in the Yucatán), which was in effect the "consciousness of death."[24]

Who said I hadn't learned anything in college?

Therefore, like Groucho Marx and the club he wouldn't be a member of if they let in people like him, I figured if someone liked me, he must have a serious problem. It followed—naturally—that the kiss of death for any boy was to act too interested in me. Of course my priority at the moment was to be the best PCV I could be, so that other stuff would just have to wait. I would remain the artful dodger with a "lean and hungry look" for now.

I got in bed. A few mosquitoes were naturally waiting in ambush for me when I turned out the light. When one keened in for a landing on my face, I smacked myself hard and must've got him, because it was quiet after that.

6

MARTÍN

Austerity measures were an immediate indication to us of the presence of Pinochet, Uruguayan president/dictator Bordaberry, or some big fish from South Africa. Whenever one of them was visiting, our already small ration of food diminished even more. We hoped the fat cats were "enjoying" the food that otherwise would have gone to us.

The sergeants on guard outside our cells often talked about what was going on in and around the department. They would discuss visits from important people, or how much the superintendent's profits were. Or they would talk

---

24 Miguel de Unamuno, *Del sentimiento trágico de la vida* (Madrid: Renacimiento, 1912).

about some "private" business of their superiors (usually a brothel), or about their superiors' family lives in general—including infidelities, which the officers related in minute detail.

Superior officers generally avoided having conversations that could be overheard from behind bars. In the First Precinct, however, we could hear the "academy" classes. We followed them with interest, listening as the sergeants and troops received lessons on "communist subversion." The classes included long lists of General Stroessner's patriotic government's achievements, which were mainly "the dignity and complete discipline of the army and police, running water, the weekly opening of new schools, colleges, bridges, and barracks…" Naturally, the "atheist communists and traitors" were trying to destroy everything Stroessner had accomplished.

Career officers of lower rank talked about their fellow officers' scholarships at the Police College of Chile or the National Police Institute of Bolivia or other places, and about distinctions awarded by Pinochet, Bolivian president/dictator Banzer, and others. They also recalled their friends with scholarships in Guatemala, Nicaragua, El Salvador, Honduras, and Uruguay—countries like ours, with highly "democratic" governments. The one topic that officers and subordinates always discussed was karate. They knew who had what color belt and couldn't hide their admiration for those who had black belts.

The troops spoke mostly of fiestas and sports events; echoes of magnificent palace parties and even of neighborhood dances reached our cells. A favorite topic of conversation was the minister of defense, who tended to make mischief when he got drunk. This is how we learned that the minister's strange behavior had caused a stir at Cerro Corá, in front of the Mariscal Francisco Solano López monument, during a commemoration of the anniversary of the mariscal's death, with national and foreign authorities present. The troops told us that during the opening speech, a "totally drunk" defense minister told all the Brazilian dignitaries present to "go to hell" for having assassinated Paraguay's greatest hero. This happened on the first of March—at the same spot where hordes of Brazilians had assassinated Mariscal López.

The story of Gustavo Stroessner, the dictator's older son, also came up. During a fit of madness, Gustavo had fired his pistol at a young officer named Báez, one of his father's personal guards, at the presidential residence, Mburuvichá Roga. The bullet had struck Báez's spine, likely leaving him paraplegic. What was interesting was that the sergeants didn't blame the one responsible for the deed—they attributed it to Báez's bad luck, explaining in a resigned tone that he had simply "met his fate."[25]

The officers were generally not very communicative, as if deep down they too were afraid and, like us, were being watched. I remember one who always had a grave expression on his face but was very proper toward us. He was being punished by Stroessner and had no possibility of being promoted as long as the regime lasted. His offense had been attempting to stop the driver of a vehicle breaking the speed limit at kilometer thirteen of the San Lorenzo Highway. The officer had used his whistle and then his gun to shoot into the air and at the car's tire. The car crashed and the driver was killed. At the site of the crash, smuggled merchandise from Brazil littered the pavement. The driver turned out to be a relative of the dictator's.

The soldiers often discussed their labor, much of which they donated, in the repair and construction of their superiors' residences. Police and military officers of certain rank were "entitled" to have one or two full-time conscripts at their home cleaning, caring for children, running errands, and sometimes acting as the wife's chauffeur. There was much rivalry among low-ranking soldiers to be commissioned as assistants to construction workers and maids, and they were popularly known as *tambo verá* (lit. "sparkling-clean milking stall"). Their work was far removed from what would be considered national defense. If a *tambo verá* ever committed an offense or fell into disgrace, he was punished by being sent to the barracks or precinct where he had been originally assigned. At the precinct, a *tambo verá* was the object of ridicule and scorn by officials and superintendents, as well as by soldiers.

---

25 Gustavo Stroessner met his own fate in February 2011, when he died of complications from treatment for lung cancer at age sixty-six. A sister, the surviving sibling (Alfredo Jr. died in 1993—see footnote 76), needn't have worried for company—her father is reported to have left behind at least fifteen illegitimate children.

The lower-ranking soldiers also commented on the police food rations that were given to members of the private sector—goods sent to individuals who had started out as police officers and moved into careers in law, banking, government ministries, Parliament, and other positions. I was surprised the first time I saw shoe shiners and magazine sellers in the police cafeteria, receiving preferential treatment. It wasn't easy to get used to the idea that they, too, were "police," as were bartenders, canoe rowers, prostitutes, taxi drivers, and domestic servants—an enormous number of people from very diverse fields.

The regime of terror was sustained by the services of countless employed spies—so many that it was joked they often had to invent any "new" information they gave the authorities.[26]

The law of ruthlessness reigned in all aspects: the economy, society, education, culture, even religion. The villains in power appropriated the means of administering the life, honor, and property of the defenseless population. It was the "price of peace," to quote officials from the US State Department and the Pentagon, as well as from multinational corporations, when they visited Paraguay for a few hours or days.

The political system in place as of May 4, 1954, had produced a unique phenomenon at this stage of the process—the "senile titular plutocracy"—in flagrant contradiction with what the Declaration of Colorado Party Principles postulates in its Fourth Article. The following is from the Colorado Party Convention of February 23, 1947:

> The Colorado Party declares itself opposed to all dictatorship of individuals or groups and considers that democracy, in that it assures the people a growing participation in the benefits of wealth and culture, guarantees evolution toward an egalitarian society, without privileges or exploited classes.

---

26   One in ten citizens was a paid informant, according to Alan Whicker's extraordinary documentary, *The Last Dictator* (https://www.youtube.com/watch?v=JUhgYj_ywCw), made in 1970. The film's title is eerily prophetic, as Stroessner would in fact become—when finally deposed nineteen years and several fellow dictators later—the last one standing (see footnote 94). The film also states that at the time, 600,000 Paraguayans—*nearly one-quarter of the population*—were living abroad.

The dictatorship had obviously been dazzled by the spotlight of power, so it had covered the country with a mantle of darkness where brutes were held in esteem and the virtuous persecuted. Intelligence was suppressed or systematically ignored, and mediocrity was promoted in every way. Mediocrity and support for Stroessner were the necessary conditions for moving high up in the government.

The moral decadence of the dictatorship was reflected in the following image, in the words of Paraguayan statesman Dr. Eligio Ayala (member of the Liberal Party and president of Paraguay twice, from 1923–24 and 1924–28):

> The political end is to occupy an administrative position and then strive only to hold on to the position, earn more and work less. Everything is subordinated to self-interest; personal interest is the assumed criterion of good and evil. Science, patriotism, everything is feigned, sometimes even disinterestedness. No one trusts anyone; everyone slanders, betrays, and spies on the others…They hate each other like courtiers because each one seeks nothing but greater political advantage. They consider one another as obstacles or instruments, and they can't stand each other except when one is the instrument of the other. They are either enemies or accomplices.

It is interesting to note that despite twenty years of the vertical imposition of "peace and progress," Stroessner's government never managed to obtain the disinterested and spontaneous adherence of a single honest Paraguayan or foreigner. However, during those two decades, the military-political dictatorship did convert the country into a haven for Nazi criminals, international mafia druglords, prostitutes, and of course the "traveling sales-general" Tachito Somoza. Also, no domestic or foreign supporter of Stroessner was ever bold enough to present him as a candidate for the Nobel Peace Prize, even though he proclaimed himself "peacemaker," "premier soldier of peace," and "champion of peace," among other titles.

It is also worth noting that this supposed "champion of peace" allowed José Asunción Flores, the great composer and father of Guaraní culture, and Teodoro S. Mongelós, the Colorado poet of peace and harmony among Paraguayans, to die in exile.

6

Emily

"*Buen día* [bwen DEE-ah]," chirped Carmen the next morning in class, using the Paraguayan form of *buenos días*. How could she be so bloody cheerful at 7:30 a.m.? I was fighting delirium as I hadn't slept well after waking up every few hours drenched in sweat.

"*Mba-eichapá* [mbah-AY-shah-pah]?" How's it going? We did pretty well repeating.

"*I porä eterei* [ee-poh-RAH eh-teh-reh-EE]." Very well (literally "good very"). The "rah" was nasally and hard to get right—I felt a little like Tammy Wynette. Class was fun, as always.

During the break, Carmen taught us possibly the most valuable skill we would learn at Monitor: making instant coffee not just plain and ordinary, but *frothy*. We watched as our guru put some Nescafé and way too much sugar in a cup, added a few drops of water, and patiently went around and around with a spoon, around and around until a chestnut-colored foam appeared, a rich meringue whose peaks rose with each stroke of the spoon and awaited, quivering, the deluge of hot water soon to engulf it. Carmen was master of her craft, and we were so impressed we clapped.

It took time to achieve perfection, but the effort was worth it. I, however, was doomed to failure as I couldn't stand to use that much sugar—my peaks ended up more like plateaus. Of course it had nothing to do with the fact that patience was not one of my virtues.

After lunch we planted black-eyed peas, spinach, radishes, and squash. We were like kids playing in the rich-smelling soil, and everyone was getting along great.

When at last it was time to go, I said to Diego, "See you tomorrow. *Ja-jhechúta ko'êro.*"

He smiled. "Here's a version you'll hear out in the campo: *Ja-JUE-chúta ko'êro.*" He paused and then laughed. "We'll see each other *if* tomorrow comes." I chuckled at the irony…and the absurdity of trying to learn a language in which one tiny shift in sound resulted in a complete change in meaning.

I played basketball for a while at FPC but didn't want to get home late because it was Tuesday, a very special night, Tere had told me that morning. After putting the children to bed, the adults crowded around the small color TV and watched a new *telenovela* called *La Caldera del Diablo*, "The Devil's Cauldron." I thought I'd better check it out even though I hadn't watched soap operas since high school.

When I saw the telltale belfry and recognized the music (that much had been impossible to avoid all those years ago), I couldn't believe it: *Peyton Place?*[27] *You've got to be kidding me.* I seemed to recall the show had come out when I was in junior high, so it must be over ten years old. It had been off the air for a long time in the States. What could the good Paraguayan people possibly feel they had in common with *norteamericanos* in a small town in New England, of all places?

Ah, the pillory...such an "inhumane" form of punishment, so cruel and unusual. I was amused by my own wit. Tell you the truth, though, Ryan O'Neal didn't look too bad cruising around in his white convertible.

But once the show got going, I just wanted to laugh. The dubbing, always a hoot, was done in Colombia they told me, which was one reason why I couldn't understand it well. The voices seemed all wrong, too, Allison Mackenzie sounding like a grown woman. It took a Herculean effort not to snigger in all the wrong places.

I was enjoying myself immensely but, as I never could stand too much of a good thing, said good night during a commercial and retired to my pallet, flabbergasted that *Peyton Place*, something I'd ridiculed all my life, was being televised here in South America, of all places, and actually watched by millions of educated people. Surely the predicaments would be nothing new to them, but such a voyeuristic look at the worst aspects of my own culture made me a little uncomfortable.

One morning a gentleman was waiting for us at Monitor, señor Alberto Arzamendia. He had a guitar and was pretty old, probably in his fifties. He

---

27 From the novel by the same name by Grace Metalious (New York: Julian Messner, Inc., 1956).

gave us some legal-sized pages turned horizontal that had Paraguayan songs in both Spanish and Guaraní, other songs in Spanish that weren't Paraguayan (with English translations), and songs in English translated into Spanish.

A couple of the English songs were ones I'd loved as a kid, "When the Saints Go Marching In" and "You Are My Sunshine." But now they seemed quaint, out of place, the Spanish versions cumbersome. I didn't think I'd be playing and singing them. I wondered who had chosen them.

Don Alberto began to play, and I was captivated by the percussive rhythm he was creating. In a loud baritone he sang "Mis Noches sin Ti"[28] ("My Nights without You"), a song so full of longing and remorse that I decided to ask Rafael to teach it to me: "I suffer to think how destiny has managed to separate us / I have such beautiful memories, which I'll never forget." I flashed on Dad and got a catch in my throat.

"The next song, 'Recuerdos de Ypacaraí'[29] ('Memories of Ypacaraí') is a classic," don Alberto said. "People all over the world know it. Ypacaraí is the biggest lake in Paraguay…a very *romantic* place," he added with a smile so dazzling we all leaned back a little. The song was about love, of course, a guy wondering "Where are you now, *cuñataï* (young, unmarried woman), that your gentle song no longer reaches me?" As in the first song, there was that word *frenesí* again, frenzy—well, everyone knew how passionate the Latin lover was supposed to be (not that I knew firsthand or anything).

Don Alberto then sang a couple of songs in Guaraní only. Because I couldn't understand the words, I had to suppress a laugh because they sounded downright comical. I mean, I loved singing in Spanish but couldn't imagine doing it in Guaraní—the language just didn't seem meant to be put to music.

"The first number I did for you," don Alberto said, "was 'Nde Rendape A-ju,' or 'I Come by Your Side.' It was written by one of Paraguay's most famous composers, José Asunción Flores. He was born in 1904 here in Asunción, in La Chacarita, and invented Paraguay's unique musical genre, the 'guarania,' saying it was 'from my people, written for and by my people.' The Paraguayan government even declared his song 'India'—also written out for you here on this

---

28 Demetrio Ortíz and María Teresa Márquez, 1943.
29 Demetrio Ortíz and Zulema de Mirkin, 1950.

sheet—our national song, even though Flores had been living in Buenos Aires since the 1930s. In 1949 he was awarded the National Order of Merit. Things were going well for him until…"

Don Alberto cleared his throat and looked around to make sure we were still listening. I for one couldn't take my eyes off him.

"Until a student was killed in an antigovernment rally here in Asunción. Flores felt compelled to protest the killing, so he refused the award—and for that was branded a traitor. When Stroessner came to power, he forbade Flores ever to return to Paraguay, even later in Flores's life, when he was ill and wished to visit his homeland one last time. Don José died in Buenos Aires three years ago this May. His songs are officially banned here, but radio stations play them anyway, and people aren't about to stop singing them."

God, what a schmuck I was for thinking the songs sounded funny. This exile business was some serious shit. How sad that artists and musicians had to suffer so much for their integrity. We applauded when don Alberto finished and served him frothy coffee (how his face lit up!) before he left.

For lunch we'd agreed to meet at the Hotel Guaraní—where I supposed no PCV had ever spent the night—and take a tour of the municipal buildings in the *centro*. The heat drove a few girls to the embassy pool instead. *To each her own*, I figured.

A small bus appeared out of a cloud of diesel, with several men hanging out the doors, barely holding on—such a common sight. The *micro* [MEE-kroh] stopped and we squeezed on. The fare collector was in a hurry, as always, guaraní bills sticking out from between his fingers like Ninja knives. *Tranquilo [trahn-KEE-loh], man!* The driver was constantly stopping to let people off, then stopping to let people on, with no actual bus stops. Crazy. Paraguay.

We stood next to the open door the whole way. As we approached our destination, I grabbed the handle and began to swing off. "Emilia, no!" Miriam cried, but I couldn't help it: I loved getting on and off buses while they were still moving. What could I say…danger was my business! I was just grateful I had the agility.

Two lanky blonds wearing black slacks and long-sleeved white shirts with black ties spun in and out of traffic on bicycles. "Mormons," Ellyn said. They were good looking but seemed so out of place here.

We crossed the street to the hotel, where Diego and Anna-í were waiting for us. Diego suggested we try the *milanesa*. I had no idea what *milanesa* was, but I ordered some because Teresa had mentioned it once, making sure I knew it was "Italiano, from Milano" (I'd already figured that out). It turned out to be chicken-fried steak—and a Paraguayan staple. Who could've guessed? I had to admit it was tasty and a good way to turn a tough piece of beef—which they all seemed to be here—into something edible.

Diego warned us not to use the verb *coger* in reference to "catching" the bus. Although that's what it meant in other Spanish-speaking countries, he told us if we said *"Voy a coger el bus"* in South America, we'd be saying (in his words), "I'm going to…pardon my French…fuck ze bus." He turned bright red. "I can't believe I just said that…and to a flock of feminists, no less!"

Ay, Diego! All we could do was laugh.

After lunch we crossed the street to the Plaza de la Independencia, a square park with sidewalks in geometric patterns and shade trees that had a slight cooling effect.

"What's that tree over there?" I asked Diego. I'd noticed some when we drove in from the airport. They were tall and willowy and had crimson flowers with bright yellow centers. The large, oval leaf-shapes were made up of many tiny leaves. I loved how they came together to create a whole, *e pluribus unum* and all. The small leaves reminded me of the mesquite, my favorite tree in Arizona.

"The Paraguayans call it a *chivato*. I don't know what it is in English."

I decided to adopt the *chivato* as my official tree in Paraguay. Not that I needed one or anything, it just gave me comfort.

"Over there is a *quebracho* tree," Diego pointed out. "They say it takes a hundred twenty years to reach maturity. It's an extremely hard wood—the name means 'axe breaker,' *quebra hacha*—and is one of Paraguay's main exports. It's also used for tanning leather." I marveled at how humans could figure these things out.

"Of course the tree is threatened now," he said. Terrific.

We crossed Palma. Crossing streets here was fun! You walked down the street in the direction of traffic until you saw an opening and could dash across before someone ran you over.

We turned right at Calle Chile, passing the bustling Lido Bar on the corner. As we walked toward the Paraguay River, a group of guys emitted an annoying "Sst sst sst." Diego just shrugged his shoulders and grinned sheepishly. There wasn't anything he could do about it...though he obviously enjoyed being surrounded by so many *chicas bonitas. Secret macho man, busted!* I knew Diego wasn't really like that but figured it must be irresistible for an otherwise reasonable man to become intoxicated with the power he acquired in Latin America just by being male.

The first thing visible as we approached the plaza was a neon sign flashing "Stroessner: Peace, Work and Well-being."

"What a crock," said Miriam. "The only reason there's 'peace' is that everyone is afraid to talk." How did she *know* these things? All of a sudden JFK's "ask not" took on an ominous new meaning...though I had to admit, life here in downtown Asunción seemed normal enough.

When we got to Avenida Mariscal López, Diego stopped and pointed. "That's the Plaza Constitución, the original plaza of Asunción. In front of us is the Congress, or Palacio Legislativo. Over there on the left is the post office, to the right of course is the cathedral, and that lovely building across the street is the National Police Headquarters, where the Department of Investigations is. Trust me, from what I've heard, you don't want to end up in there."

Grim police officers—or were they soldiers?—stood around what seemed more of a fortress than a building, cradling machine guns and keeping people at bay. Many were mere adolescents. Conscription was obviously a requirement in this "democracy"—as it had been in our own until a couple of years ago—and the younger the better. It dawned on me that armed "children" patrolled nearly every street corner in the city.

"Down there by the river is a slum called La Chacarita," Diego said as we walked toward the cathedral. I recognized the name from don Alberto's concert...that was where José Asunción Flores was born! It certainly was bleak, with people literally holding on by a thread—hard to believe the composer of some of Paraguay's most beautiful music had come from such squalor.

"And over there," Diego continued, "across from the Customs Building, is the Parfina Building, where the US Agency for International Development, or USAID, has its offices." I nodded and thought of my college roommate Nancy from Pakistan, whose father had been in the US Information Service. She told me the USIS loaned out books, movies, and such to promote understanding among cultures, and it had sounded pretty cool. Thinking about Nancy made me remember how grateful I was to her for finding that guitar on the beach in northern California (or so she'd said) freshman year and bringing it to our dorm room. Learning to play it changed my life, but talk about random—I may never have picked one up otherwise. I'd always thought other people played guitar, not me.

Not true. We arrived at the cathedral, Our Lady of the Assumption (I got it now—the "assumption" was how Mary went to heaven), which of course loomed large in its mission to make worshippers feel inspired…or insignificant, depending on how you looked at it. It had columns and two bell towers on either side of three massive arched doorways, whose coolness drew us in like flies. We walked slowly, each step echoing through the cavernous space as our eyes adjusted to the familiar tragedy unfolding around us of Christ's agony and Mary's benign helplessness, scenes guaranteed to fan the flames of guilt.

Some in our group headed toward the altar while Miriam and I ducked into a rear pew, unsure of what to do (I knew to do a quick genuflect and cross, up-down-left-right). She was Jewish and I was…what was I?

I was a WASP by birth but would never be caught dead consuming Marx's "opium of the masses"—free will, baby, that was the ticket! To my mind, religion was a conspiracy to usurp people's power by instilling fear and making them unable to think or act for themselves, like those poor folks in *The Poseidon Adventure* who, rather than trying to save their own souls, stayed put and prayed to their Heavenly Father for salvation…but were forsaken in the end.

One of God's children myself—weren't we all?—I believed God was inside us, not "out there" in the heavens dealing out destinies and manipulating us like some celestial marionettist with a sick sense of humor. I knew that view sounded blasphemous to some, especially here, but in Asia it was simply a way of life.

Even as a child I'd been skeptical. I mean, they lied to us about Santa Claus and the Easter Bunny, what else were they capable of? Studying advertising in high school confirmed it: first they told you what your "needs" were—deliberately confusing them with "wants"—and then they sold them to you.

It was the same with religion. I had a lot of questions but didn't want anyone giving me the answers. My generation hadn't coined the phrase "Question authority" for nothing. Besides, wasn't the purpose of life to *search* for the truth, not necessarily to *find* it? I never understood how people could just give up their freedom, their autonomy, for so-called "security"...clearly an illusion to begin with.

Studying comparative religion in college confirmed my doubts about my own Christian upbringing—too much suspension of disbelief. (The idea of immortality of the soul appealed to me, though, as it seemed a prerequisite for karma and reincarnation, concepts I could get behind.) But I didn't begrudge people the church experience; I knew churches did good work in the community and helped in times of need.

I was a big fan of Jesus, of course. I thought everyone should look at the world through the carpenter's eyes, do things to make him proud; I tried to do that in my own life, flawed as it was. To me, though, he was just one of several prophets, like the Buddha (five hundred years before Jesus) and Muhammad (five hundred years after Jesus), who happened to show up around the time mankind needed a good moral kick in the ass. Of course some of the prophets (not the Buddha) began preaching the idea of a single God—*theirs*—and it was pretty much "my way or the highway" after that. It was frightening to think of the atrocities committed *to this very day* in the name of religion.

Fundamentally, though, Jesus taught simple compassion, as did the Buddha. (I loved how the Buddha had been born a prince but renounced that life to become a spiritual seeker once he realized the world was full of suffering.) I felt bad that Jesus was martyred, but I just couldn't understand how he died for *my* sins, mere misdemeanors, surely, in the overall scheme of things. I suspected there were some real sinners around here, starting with Stroessner himself, supposedly a "God-fearing" Catholic. *Does Stroessner go to church and pray?* I wondered.

I did think prayer was important, the humility it required…so long as you were expressing gratitude and not just asking God for things like good fortune or forgiveness—surely even priests (and dictators) who terrorized people believed they were doing God's will somehow and would be absolved in the end.

Of course I knew better than anyone that there were times when God was the only "person" you could talk to…but I didn't think God talked back, or called us to commit acts, or even loved us or wanted us to be happy. To me God was simply the energy that created the universe and as such flowed through our bodies as *ki*. Morality came from honoring that notion and the respect for life it entailed.

I never understood how people who prayed to God could forgive him when he "betrayed" them and let bad things happen. So, to avoid the crisis of faith that Job and Arjuna[30] and countless others—even Jesus, for that matter—suffered, I chose to pray to, and have faith in, the universe. No one to blame but the cosmos…and myself.

Speaking of blame, I could never figure out why the Ten Commandments had to be so punitive, like some puffed-up parent threatening a little child: *"Thou shalt not!"* Maybe in Moses's day it worked, but wasn't it obvious by now that telling someone *not* to do something only made him more determined to *do* it? I certainly didn't need to be told not to kill people. Whatever happened to good old "Love thy neighbor" and "Do unto others"—the damn Golden Rule?

Oh well, whatever people needed to keep on the straight and narrow was fine with me, so long as they didn't burn me at the stake or chop my head off over it. Why couldn't people just get along, anyway, not judge each other, work together toward a common goal—the "Greater Good," as it were? Was that so impossible? But of course there was that little problem with the word "good"—even dictators thought they were "good" people, just trying to "do the right thing." To me, that was why the concept of good and evil was so dangerous—and counterproductive—in the first place.

Over the past couple of years I'd studied Zen, with its focus on "waking up" and "being here now." I loved the koans, those cryptic tales of monks who

---

30 From *The Bhagavad Gita*, a sacred Hindu text composed sometime between the fifth and second centuries BCE (Before the Common/Christian/Current Era).

achieve satori simply by sweeping their cells…or being whacked over the head by their masters. In the end I proclaimed myself a maverick Buddhist with agnostic tendencies and took my vow of poverty—which helped explain why I was here in the first place.

The lyrics to "Guantanamera"[31] were as true for me now as they were when Mr. López taught them to us in third-year Spanish at Sahuaro High: I still wished to cast my lot with the poor of the earth. When Nanny took me to Jalisco (Guadalajara and Melaque) after graduation in 1970, I saw how people there had *nothing* compared to what my seventeen-year-old self had. (It's true I was born into privilege, but I would discover in college just how near the bottom of the heap my family really was.) Americans obviously had way too much, I concluded, more than we needed…surely it could all be balanced out somehow. From that moment I couldn't help it—I was simply incapable of desiring wealth.

And still desperately seeking answers.

Everyone stood to go. As we emerged from the cathedral, the sun was a spotlight, blinding us.

We ended our tour by walking to the Government Palace. Diego said it had been built by the first president, Carlos Antonio López, for his son, Francisco Solano, later known as Mariscal López, who got Paraguay into its first devastating war, the Triple Alliance, against Brazil, Argentina, and Uruguay, from 1865 to 1870, but came out a hero because Paraguay defied the odds and lasted longer than expected, due to the "courage and determination" of the Paraguayan people. Whew! It took your breath away.

"It's estimated that out of a Paraguayan population of somewhere around 800,000, only 221,000 survived the war, of whom only 28,000 were adult males," Diego continued, sounding very professorial.

"And the guy was a *hero*?" I said, doing a quick estimation and figuring less than 15 percent, around one in seven, of the population had been male after that. "How could he have let so many of his countrymen die?"

Diego shrugged. "I guess he didn't want to surrender."

Miriam laughed and said in a perfect Scarlett O'Hara, "Those 28,000 adult males must have been very much in demand. I'll bet they were simply *mortified*

31 José Fernández Díaz, 1929.

to have to continue serving their country by spreading their precious seed throughout the land." I laughed but had to wonder if Paraguayan men still felt "entitled," as it were.

On the way back, we passed a large metal statue of Mariscal López atop his rearing horse, charging bravely into battle with sword drawn and thrust forward, looking very heroic indeed.

That night after dinner, Rafael offered me caña with *jugo de pomelo* [HOO-goh day poh-MEH-loh]—an offer I couldn't refuse—and went out to get the last ones off his tree. I sat in the living room with the music I'd gotten at Monitor.

Of the five songs in English, I realized three could be considered "protest" songs: Dylan's "Blowing in the Wind" and Pete Seeger's "Where Have All the Flowers Gone" and "If I Had a Hammer." Both men's music had been vital to counterculture movements in the States and around the world—if I remembered correctly, Seeger had even been blacklisted in the fifties. Were we to teach these "subversive" songs to our clubs?

Rafael brought in the drinks. "Caña is our national liquor," he said. "The best brand is Aristócrata." We clinked *¡Salud!* and drank. It had a different flavor from rum in the States but tasted pretty good with grapefruit juice.

"There's also a whiskey made from caña," he said, "which is superb, like Irish whiskey." Who could imagine sugarcane was so versatile?

When I showed Rafael the Paraguayan songs, he nodded. "They're all pretty old," he said, "but they're good guaranias."

"I didn't know there were so many songs in Guaraní," I said.

Rafael laughed. "Oh, absolutely! I don't speak it much myself, but I understand it. I think in a way Guaraní is what helps keep Paraguayan society together, the ability to speak in a secret code, as it were. You know, Guaraní was used to send secret messages in all our wars."

The cocktail was a little too good; I ended up drinking three as Rafael tried to show me how to play "Mis Noches sin Ti." He and don Alberto made it look easy, but my attempts to master the strum just got more and more ludicrous—and I never even made it to the lyrics.

We were like schoolgirls on a fieldtrip the following Friday as we boarded the midnight bus to Yguazú [üh-gwah-SOO] (Big Water) Falls. We would be passing through Puerto Presidente Stroessner and then crossing the border into Brazil and Argentina.

The mood changed, however, when we got into a discussion about Chile and its former president, Salvador Allende. When some of the girls started bad-mouthing the United States, saying "we" (the CIA) had caused the coup that ousted the democratically elected Allende and so forth, I got mad and forgot my rule about not speaking up.

"Oh, come on," I said. "We would never do a thing like that."

About six pairs of eyes turned on me and I felt like I was being executed in front of a firing squad.

"Emily," said Jessica, who clearly didn't like me, "everybody knows the US was *determined* to get rid of Allende...he was a *socialist*, remember? 'Super bad guy'...to *us*. *We* first helped destabilize Chilean society, and then *we* proceeded to assist the Chilean air force in bombing the Presidential Palace...where Allende was *assassinated*, in case you forgot."

Ouch! She paused, ready for the kill: "You're not one of *them*, are you? A spy?"

"NO! Of course not," I sputtered. "That's ridiculous! Don't be absurd. I'm not a spy. And I'm not one of *them*," I added with the most repugnance I could muster.

Then I sat back in my seat and it was over.

I was shocked. Where had *that* come from? It reminded me of college, when a history professor tried to radicalize me but I resisted...even though I knew he was right about some things. But to suggest I was a spy for the US government? Never. These girls had no idea how anti-establishment I really was (let's face it, our parents' generation had totally screwed things up).

I wanted to shout *Okay, so it's true, everybody on the planet, every country, every corporation, everybody who is anybody is greedy and corrupt. So what else is new? Jeez.* But I didn't.

Of course I was humiliated by my public pillorying. I'd felt a wave of disgust from some of the girls and knew whatever credibility I may have had with them was lost forever.

Way to go, Creigh! Why did I have to be such a damn patriot? And what did I know about Latin American politics, anyway? I'd been in Japan at the time, hostage to the coup raging inside my head.

Naturally, I didn't sleep a wink as I stared into the darkness outside my window.

Arriving around 7:00 a.m. on the Argentine side of the falls—roughly 80 percent of the national park, the bus driver said—we disembarked and went our separate ways in little groups. I stuck with Ellyn but was withdrawn, unable to let it go, despite the breathtaking beauty of the place.

For some reason the most impressive cataract, Devil's Throat, with its massive drawing power and mist so thick you couldn't see the bottom, made me think of Holden Caulfield's cliff, and I was one of the kids Holden couldn't catch before I fell over the edge, plunging headfirst into the abyss of adulthood.

Was I the only one who wondered what it would be like?

The longest day of my life ended at midnight, when we got back on the bus for home. Yguazú Falls—taller by half and with hundreds more cataracts than Niagara—had thrilled in every way, but for me the trip was sheer torture.

7

MARTÍN

For the dictatorship, the truth is always revolutionary and therefore dangerous. To repress it, the only recourse is brute force—against farmers, workers, professors, students, journalists, artists, and intellectuals. This is the daily bread in the era of "Pax Stronista": the peace of the cemetery.

The tyrant's first attack was against the press. Systematic persecution began in 1968, when many journalists were arrested. In 1969, programs broadcast on Radio Guaraní by the Radical Liberal Party and its spokesman, "The Dwarf," were forbidden, and many radio-station owners were arrested, exiled, or forced to shut down. This oppression continues today [1978]. In its fight against "subversive journalists," the regime has repeatedly tried to corrupt them. The Paraguayan Journalists Union denounced the dictator for his policy of offering national journalists and accredited foreign news correspondents free rein to import luxury items and discretionary credit to buy lavish mansions.

The second attack was against education. Private schools beyond the government's control have been accused of being seedbeds of opposition and of subverting students' minds. The authorities behind these efforts at repression report to Pastor Coronel. The roundups and arrests are conducted while school is in session. In the midst of general panic, civilians from the Office of Investigations and military personnel on antiterrorist assignment go about detaining students and professors...like me.

This fascist aspect of the regime can also be seen in its organization—the unmovable dome of perpetual officeholders at the top, with the base made up of the populace, which is in turn composed of local pro-Stroessner Colorado factions mobilized through fixed internal elections. During these "elections," the contradictions inherent in Stroessnerism are demonstrated right out in the open.

The salaries of the leaders of Stroessner's government do not exceed $500 per month, but their daily expenditures are as much as $700. Their bank accounts are in the local currency, the guaraní, for everyday use, and in dollars for their "private" matters, in American or Swiss banks. It is estimated that the one hundred newly rich members of Stroessner's civil and military corps would be able to pay for half the construction of the Itaipú hydroelectric dam.

Ninety percent of the members of the government hold university degrees. For promotion within the Stroessner regime, it is not enough to be rich—one also has to conceal one's mediocrity by holding a degree. Mediocrity is cultivated, and after twenty years the dictatorship is reaping the desired fruits: mediocrity with diplomas. Most of my torturers held bachelor's degrees or were lawyers.

Moreover, the Stroessner regime has made it fashionable to use military and/or police rank along with one's university title—for example, "commissioner doctor" or "general doctor"—even after adding a parliamentary title, as in "Commissioner Doctor National Deputy Martín Chiola."

During the nineteenth century, the National University took responsibility for educating the ruling elite. University graduates could fill the highest bureaucratic positions, but they could never enter the inner circle of political power. This was essentially reserved for the landowners (the *latifundistas*) and the commercial-industrial-agricultural bourgeoisie.

Currently, however, under Stroessner, university graduates easily acquire political power after passing through the military university or finishing a special course in political warfare in Taiwan or Israel. The rector and secretary general of the National University are very preferential toward their police academy students who are pro-Stroessner faction leaders. Therefore, the majority of today's commissioners and faction presidents also hold university degrees.

While Dr. Mario López Escobar was dean of the law school (and known for his close connection with the anticommunist office run by Antonio Campos Alum), it was decided that the title of "doctor in law and social sciences" from the National University should be bestowed upon Mario Abdo Benítez, the private secretary of the president of the republic and "benefactor" of up-and-coming Colorado university students.

The father figure of those doctors, engineers, and teachers needed a title corresponding to his rank—hence the idea of creating "Doctor" Mario Abdo Benítez and thereby elevating the too-common image suggested by the unimpressive title "don" Mario. Another desired objective was to put an end, once and for all, to the many rumors and jokes about Mario's intelligence, and show that his suspicious IQ was in fact higher than the average for members of the national and international ruling class.

It seems the initiative originated with López Escobar himself, who aspired at that moment to the post of ambassador to Washington and wanted to earn the support of the all-powerful private secretary of "his excellency." To lay the groundwork and sway national and international public opinion, a pro-Stroessner journalist made reference to "don Mario, the intellectual" in a series of articles in the official newspaper *Patria*. The first article included a photo of Mario reading about politics in his luxurious private library; the next day he appeared lying by the pool, mulling over economic problems; later he was shown walking in Caballero Park with a philosophy book in hand, and so on. The writer wanted to sell the image of a disciplined, self-taught individual who only lacked a diploma.

After the media charade, the academic formalities were arranged: the examination board was called together, and a date and time were set. Finally, Mario Abdo the student had the opportunity to prove himself. He appeared for his first university exam, received at the door by the dean himself and the board of examiners.

The bashful Mario was nervous in front of Stroessner's minions, members of the opposition, and onlookers, all crowded in the doorways and windows of the room, and he gave the wrong answer to his indulgent examiners' first question: "Who discovered Paraguay by land and in what year?" He responded, "Stroessner, on May 4, 1954. He came by land from Paraguarí with his triumphant troops."

The answer provoked laughter from the audience and made the examiners tense. Embarrassed, they asked Mario to calm down, and they silenced the spectators. "We were referring to the time of the Spanish colonies," said the examiner in a paternal voice.

The president of the board decided to ask a different question: "Who discovered Paraguay by sea?" And Mario could not respond. He fixed his gaze on the ceiling as if looking for something in the cobwebs of the ancient building. The examiners could not get another word out of him, but neither could they silence the ill-mannered crowd. The dean had to tell those trying to whisper the answer to leave—unheeded, he closed the doors and windows. The examinee, though, remained mute, and the board had to suspend the examination.

So it was that Mario Abdo, "the informer," lost his grand opportunity to earn the degree of doctor. But the other Mario—López Escobar—did get the position in Washington he so desired.

7

EMILY

I had to admit, though, when I didn't think too much I was happier than I'd been in years. I had free room and board and a stipend, and was in effect being paid to study. And I didn't have any real responsibilities yet, which made it perfect.

We attended class Monday through Friday at Monitor and wherever the Peace Corps had us go in the afternoons for technical training, often at the Ministry of Agriculture in San Lorenzo. After that I'd play basketball for an hour or so, sometimes with Ellyn. The girls at Pérez Cardozo said they'd like me to be on the team if I didn't have to leave, which was flattering—I doubted they were serious but liked hearing it.

The PC had a stake in keeping us healthy, so the injections kept coming; I had to laugh wondering how the guys were faring. One time I was first in line, and the two doctors were so well prepared that I got a stunningly painful gamma globulin shot (for hepatitis) in my *gluteus maximus* at the same instant a rabies vaccine burned its way into my arm. I wouldn't make that mistake again.

Taking a nap in the afternoons was becoming so routine I started getting good at it—in fact, my body began to expect it. I simply couldn't resist those leaden eyelids after the midday meal. Well, it *was* hot…*still*. In the evenings, against my better judgment, I often got roped into watching TV, including *Caldera*. I loved hearing the church bells chime and marveled at how Dorothy Malone's eyelashes could flutter so without falling off.

Basically I was free to do whatever I wanted. Weekends found me with my family or PC friends. One Saturday Ellyn invited me to a party at the home of two guys she'd met who were foreign service officers. It was a spacious, tiled house with a pool and live-in "domestic" (*must be nice*). Embassy personnel did very well, I could see, but I knew this wasn't what I wanted. I was itching to get out to the campo and live simply, without electricity or running water, just me and the land.

One Sunday I made oatmeal cookies with raisins and peanuts and invited the kids to help. But I was blown away when they would eat neither the raw dough nor any cookies hot out of the oven. They were convinced it would give them a stomachache, and nothing I did (including eating one myself, of course, with no ill effects) could change their minds. I thought about kids in the States—you couldn't hold them back from that stuff! I'd also noticed that Paraguayans didn't eat savory food after sweet (which actually made sense). No doubt about it: culture was powerful.

The kids had been starting to annoy me a little, so I hadn't been as "friendly" lately, closing my door a lot and keeping to myself. That afternoon I wrote some poems in my journal. The first was from Yakamochi out of my Japanese poetry book, which described how I'd been feeling lately:

My love thoughts these days come thick like the summer grass
Which soon as cut and raked grows wild again.

Then one of my own:

I feel like a cadaver in this dead heat
Thirty flies in my room
*   on my body*
*   getting stuck in my sweat*
Flies flying flies screwing
Flies rubbing front legs together
*   in that horrible little gesture*
*   of satisfaction.*

I read some Kerouac, my literary hero. I loved his stream of consciousness—I thought of it as "verbal impressionism"—and how he reportedly typed on shelf paper. Talk about drive...well, that and amphetamines.

I wrote to "Mom and Everyone" on a Paraguayan aerogram, a full-color folded-up sheet showing scenes from Paraguay. The postage was a huge stamp of Augusto Pinochet—my nemesis, after the fateful bus trip—that read "Commemoration of the Official Visit to the Repubic of Paraguay of the Excellent Mister President of the Republic of Chile General Augusto Pinochet—May 1974." What a ridiculous string of titles! Pinochet looked a lot like Stroessner, little mustache and all, though darker and more sinister.

I was starting to be able to play "Mis Noches sin Ti." The rhythm was thruuum-chuck-thrum-chuck-chuck, using the tops of the fingernails starting with the pinky. You stroked down across all the strings on the first "thruuum," the highest strings only on the "chuck," the lowest strings on the second "thrum," and the high strings on the next two "chuck-chucks." It was challenging playing that along with the song's 4:4 time signature. "My

Nights without You." It was way over the top sentimentally, but I liked how it was in Spanish except for two Guaraní words comparing the longed-for person's kisses to a delicious fruit, *yvapurü* [üh-bah-poo-ROO], and her/his tenderness, *cunu-ú* [coo-noo-OO], to a soft lullaby.

I liked it even better than "Your Cheatin' Heart," one of my standards—or would have been if I hadn't needed prodding to actually play and sing it. Of course Rafael asked me to teach it to him. I had to write out the words phonetically as he didn't speak a word of English.

Then he taught me "Bésame Mucho,"[32] a bolero, a rhythm I could actually play. It felt odd telling someone to kiss me a lot, however, as the urgency in the words was not something I wanted any *paraguayos* to think I felt.

Paraguayan males could be annoying, no doubt about it. It seemed the girls and I couldn't walk anywhere without being whistled at or ogled. I didn't know if the Paraguayan girls liked it or simply tolerated it, but it turned us *americanas* off completely. How infuriating that we'd been portrayed in films and magazines as sex mavens! The impudent macho men would even stare at our breasts when speaking to us. We felt dirty knowing they'd just undressed and fondled us with their eyes.

The sexual revolution obviously hadn't made it this far south.

Speaking of which, I had to admit I myself was awaiting its arrival, as I still couldn't seem to separate sex from love. It was around that time that I took a shine to a volunteer I'd met in the darkroom at the PC office. We'd had lunch together, then a few nights later dinner and drinks, and before you knew it we'd hopped in the sack. It must mean love, right? I was starting to think we had potential when he told me there was someone else. Oh well, so much for that idea.

Damn if history wasn't repeating itself! The same thing had happened in college, when I was desperate to lose my virginity to blond surfer Michael from Oceanside (he would always be "Michael from Mountains"[33] to me). I got rid of my roommate and lured Mike to my room with cocoa I'd nicked from the cafeteria. I even had "Moondance"[34] playing on my record player

---

32 Consuelo Velázquez, 1940.

33 Joni Mitchell, 1968.

34 Van Morrison, 1969.

to set the mood: *Do you want to make love to me to-night?* But Mike politely declined, saying he had—you guessed it—a girlfriend back home. (Though disappointed, not to mention mortified beyond belief, I'd always respected him for his decision.)

Screw love, I'd decided. It didn't matter now anyway. I was here to work, not waste my time on some stupid relationship.

It was the first week in March and finally cooling off—a little. We were preparing to go into the campo for three weeks of technical training. We'd been divided into three groups and would spend one week in each of three towns. Guaraní classes—which everyone was attending now—would stop, but we'd have no shortage of opportunities to use what we'd learned so far…which, sadly, failed to exceed expectations. I was glad Miriam was in my group, which also included Polly and Jessica (heaven help me).

Our first town was Ybycuí, where there was a model PCV whose model clubs we'd be visiting. I was excited to see firsthand what we'd be doing in a few more weeks in our own sites as *educadoras del hogar*. Honestly, I could have educated you on what I knew about the home in a minute and a half, but there we were—nearly trained paraprofessionals.

Ybycuí was about an hour southeast of Asunción. On the drive there, shading his eyes from the nascent sun, Diego said the name meant "fine sand" in Guaraní. Of course we'd been set up with families, which we met when we arrived. My glamorous "mother" was single and child-free, even though she had to be in her thirties—unusual, to say the least. Her name was ña Karina. That was another thing about Paraguay: instead of saying "doña," as I'd been taught, people here just said "ña." For some reason I found that hilarious.

Karina said she was part Arab, which I didn't doubt because I knew Paraguay was itself a melting pot. Diego had described how former Nazis, German Mennonites, Japanese, Italian, and other colonists ran slick agricultural operations here and managed to get wealthy while Paraguayan farmers just got deeper in debt. Still, I hadn't heard of Arabs being in Paraguay.

Karina's house (two rectangular rooms) was sturdy, made of cement. She showed me my room off the patio out back. It was more of a cell: six concrete surfaces, painted green, stained by time, echoing. The door resonated with its own weight, and the window was too high to look out. It was a room Karina rented out—cot with thin mattress, small table and chair, ornate but shabby *ropero* to hang and stack things. The bed was away from the wall so no bugs could reach it.

Good. Bugs were God's creatures too, for sure, but if they so much as touched me I'd have to play God and smite them.

Our training this first week would be on nutrition and take place in the SEAG office nearby. Walking there in the morning, I was amused to hear people saying "good-bye" instead of "hello" when they passed each other on the street… just like in that Beatles tune where "you say" one and "I say" the other.[35] I took a picture of a boy riding a burro on the flat part of its behind, wisely sparing his gonads—I knew all too well how skinny withers could wreck you.

The office was bare except for two metal desks and filing cabinets and lacked any charm whatsoever—certainly no wasteful spending going on here. We chatted about our families, did some warm-up activities, and were then introduced to the basic food groups. I stifled a groan: *Puh-lease…I've been studying this for years already!* But I decided to just go with the flow and absorb as much as I could.

Susana, the PCV here, said, "We'll be preparing a lot of food this week… and eating it." Her eyes twinkled—she clearly relished the idea.

"We'll start with the national dish, sopa paraguaya. Now, I already chopped and boiled three onions in three cups of salt water so they'd be cool when we started. Because you pour the onions in with the water, it has to be cool so the *grasa* won't melt." She held out a bowl with a large, ominous-looking white blob in it. We peered in.

Good lard almighty! I recoiled in horror. Pig fat certainly did not fit into my definition of healthy eating.

"Couldn't we use butter or something?" I asked, thinking of all the grasa that must've been in Teresa's sopa…which, come to think of it, was probably why it tasted so good. Susana gave me a scornful look that told me she knew I wasn't serious.

---

35 Paul McCartney, "Hello, Good-bye," 1967.

"In case you haven't noticed," she said with mock condescension, "the Paraguayan people love all things animal. And they eat the whole enchilada, whether it's cow's brains or blood sausage—which is basically blood boiled in intestines—or fried pigskin...with little hairs sticking out of it."

We sucked in our breath, and she was loving it. "They certainly wouldn't be able to survive without grasa," she said. "But don't worry, there's only three-fourths of a cup here, which will make enough sopa for ten to twelve people."

I felt queasy as I estimated how much that would be per person. I remembered from somewhere—seventh-grade Foods class?—there were about forty-two teaspoons in a cup. So three-quarters of that would be...a little over thirty, divided by ten people would be...three teaspoons! That much grasa in one measly piece of sopa paraguaya? And of course nobody could eat just one.

Outside, the sky was getting dark and the smell of rain drifted in through the open window. The sudden coolness brought me back. Autumn was approaching, and a few extra calories might be a good thing. This wouldn't be easy, but I'd have to suck it up. Literally.

"What do you use to beat it with?" I asked.

Susana handed me a whisk, and we were off: grasa, eggs, farmer's cheese, onion with water, all beaten together, and then cornmeal and curdled milk, alternated. We made two batches, one regular and one with soybeans Susana had already boiled and ground up. We then poured the two *masas* into well-greased pans—oh boy!—and put them into a 200°C oven (400°F) for an hour.

I didn't think sopa was the best dish to add soy to as it already had protein in the form of eggs and cheese, but I held my tongue. I'd just have to be patient and see how things turned out.

Susana announced, "Tomorrow we're heading out to the campo, but on Wednesday we'll make chipa [CHEE-pah], which I'm sure you've all seen sold out on the streets." *Seen* it? You couldn't miss it. People hawked the mostly donut-shaped breads on buses, in parks, outside the Hotel Guaraní—"¡*Chipa caliente, que quema los dientes!*"—but I hadn't really wanted to try any, even if it *was* hot enough to burn my teeth, which I doubted.

"It's made with mandioca flour," Susana continued. "Well, not the flour, but the *almidón*, the starch." Ugh, not mandioca again! Was there no escaping the stuff?

I turned to Diego. "What *is* mandioca, anyway, Diego?" I asked, not trying to hide my revulsion. "And what in the world is it for?"

He laughed and seemed only too happy to set me straight. "Well, in English it's 'manioc root'; it's also called 'cassava'—'yucca' in Central America—and is a tuber, which, as I'm sure you know, grows in the ground. Potatoes and yams are also tubers. Mandioca is native to South America, but it's now the main staple in Africa because it can withstand tough growing conditions like poor soil and sporadic rainfall. It's not the most nourishing of foods, but it keeps people fed."

He flashed his winsome smile and looked down at the *cigarillo* between his yellow-tipped fingers. Was he embarrassed to be the center of attention? He took a drag and looked back up, exhaling white smoke out the side of his mouth to avoid our faces.

"And USAID is doing research to make it more healthful. In the meantime, soy—they call it *soja* [SOH-hah] here—is a pretty good alternative...it's just that it hasn't caught on yet, not as much as we'd like. We'll be promoting soybeans in our projects with the farmers, and the goal is to teach the women how to cook with it."

Great idea—the Japanese did just fine with soy as their main source of protein. It sure beat the pants off mandioca. And if the farmers could make money on it, even better.

As we finished cleaning, the mouth-watering smell of baking corn, cheese, and, yes, lard, was somehow reassuring. We drank *mate*, the hot form of tereré. People spent a lot of time drinking yerba here, didn't they? Especially PCVs, I'd noticed.

When the sopa was ready, we had a large piece of both the control and the experiment. All agreed the traditional sopa was better than the soy version, but the latter was good nonetheless. I realized living off the land meant eating whatever you could, whatever you needed to stay alive...especially if it came from animals and you were lucky enough to have some. At least people here didn't seem to starve.

Back at ña Karina's afterward, I had a stomachache from eating three pieces of hot sopa—nine teaspoons of grasa, good grief! I could feel my arteries clogging up already. I started writing a letter home but fell asleep until suppertime.

Later that night, lying in the clammy cell, I reviewed my battle plan for the mosquitoes. A coil smoldered in the corner, singeing my nose hairs but not even fazing the little suckers. I couldn't let them bite me—we were constantly being warned about "the dengue." I decided I would simply *will* them away this time. "Mosquitoes away, mosquitoes away," I chanted over and over. "Mosquitoes away..."

The next thing I knew, I was being hoisted up to the ceiling, up and up, and then dropped down and dashed against the wall, only to be hauled up and dashed into the wall again, back up to the ceiling and down hard, my body limp, my head rolling, rolling, threatening to snap off my neck. What was happening?

I woke up in a sweat, rigid under the covers, my heart about to explode out of my chest. That had felt so real. *I was actually there, flying through the air!*

A flash of lightning lit up the room, followed by a loud thunderclap that zapped me out of the fetal position, onto the floor, and into panic mode. I reached for my flashlight on the table—I had to light the lamp, mosquitoes or no. The pages of my journal ruffled in the sudden breeze, and the temperature dropped. I broke out in goose bumps as I touched the match to the wick.

What was that all about? Someone must have been tortured here...during the Triple Alliance War, perhaps?

An hour later I was still trembling. I had entered a paranormal state, true terror, in which all my senses were engaged at once...and now all I could do was lie there, spent. At least the mosquitoes were gone.

I had to get some sleep, so I blew out the lamp as the rains came at last.

Showers continued throughout the morning. Naturally, because the "fine sand" of Ybycuí was in fact clay, the roads to the outlying communities, or *compañías*, were closed—¡*Ruta clausurada!* [ROO-tah clow-soo-RAH-dah]—and would stay that way until further notice. It was back to the kitchen, then, where we made chipa with mandioca starch (sigh, but resistance was futile) and other Paraguayan dishes, substituting soy in more recipes where it didn't belong.

Oh well, that was part of our mission here, and I fully embraced it. I loved soybeans, except they made me a little nostalgic for Japan. I'd been ripped way too soon from that Zen paradise and still fantasized about going back. I thought about the morning I learned of Dad's death, the phone call from Sam during ceramics class in Kyoto. I'd bolted out of there and walked across the whole city to program director Horace Dutton's house, stopping at every shrine and temple along the way, crying my heart out and trying to understand what happened—and inadvertently scaring the wits out of poor Horace and his wife, who'd waited all day to hear from me. On the flight home I listened to "Rainy Night in Georgia"[36] for ten hours straight, over and over, as I looked out the window and wept. Dad, too, had left a life he'd come to know, gone back to a simpler time and place...could I possibly live without him in my world?

I'd never been able to listen to that song since.

The roads connecting Ybycuí to the rest of civilization opened the next morning, and we went out to visit Susana's clubs, excellent examples of organization and functioning. The girls presented themselves and their projects with humility and grace. I was struck by how people in these compañías lived without electricity or running water, and farm animals roamed around at will, as in the Yucatán. Houses were made of mud and lath, with palm fronds laced together for roofs—hardly more than basic shelter.

Yet the girls, smiling and teasing the whole time, wore nice clothes, always ironed (how did they do it?), and seemed as up to date on styles as their counterparts in town. They definitely loved color—as long as it was colorful, they didn't care if they wore stripes with polka dots, patterns with polka dots, plaids with polka dots, or any combination of the above. And combine they did. I had to admit it did brighten up the place.

---

36 Tony Joe White, 1962.

8

MARTÍN

Labor leader Odón Oviedo was serving time in the First Precinct under suspicion of having painted murals on the walls of the main streets of Asunción saying "Down with the Dictatorship," "Freedom for the Political Prisoners," "We Demand the End of the State of Siege," and others.

One day Oviedo was inspired to compose a few lines of poetry for his beloved wife. As he didn't have access to such "subversive" means as a pencil and paper, he devised them in an original manner—he used the inside wrapper from a pack of cigarettes, the wood of a matchstick, and his own blood extracted from his big toe. Naturally the police found the poetry, which provoked a lightning storm. The head guard put us forty-three political prisoners in a corner at gunpoint and threatened Oviedo.

"Declare immediately who gave you the pen and ink to write this worthless propaganda. Otherwise, you menace to society, we will make an example of you." Oviedo explained the method he used to write down his thoughts, which, he said, were not propaganda but romantic poetry with just a touch of protest. With his foot in the air, he pointed to where he had drawn the blood.

"If this is not proof enough, I take full responsibility, as my cellmates are innocent. On the other hand, I categorically reject your claim that reading and writing are the attributes of a menace to society—they are the patrimony of all civil societies." This of course only inflamed the guard.

Everyone knew Oviedo would not hold up to a new torture session, given his advanced age and weak physical state (one of his lungs had been punctured during torture). Our attempts to intervene on Oviedo's behalf did not improve the situation. For the police, the poetry was proof that Oviedo was in fact the creator of the murals that had threatened the "peace and progress enjoyed by the republic."

The outraged officers calmed down when we political prisoners collectively threatened to go on a hunger strike if Oviedo was taken back to the torture room.

A new prisoner smuggled into our cell a tiny, folded-up article published by one of the shut-down newspapers, *El Radical*, on May 31, 1972 (No. 195), "Culture: The Sinister Virus of Paraguay." Here is an excerpt:

> The policy of the Paraguayan government on cultural matters has too much in common with what the obese Nazi General Herman Goering once said: "When I hear the word culture, I reach for my revolver." Let us consider some examples:
>
> All of our most important writers and musicians live (or have now died) abroad. The case of José Asunción Flores is a patent example of this, as are Felix Pérez Cardozo, Pablo Max Insfrán, Hérib Campos Cervera, Eusebio Ayala, Elvio Romero and many others.
>
> We have only cited some of the more illustrious men. It is not necessary to name one by one the dozens of university professors—expelled from their teaching positions in Paraguay—who must share their knowledge with university students in other parts of the world. And to make up for them, Mario Abdo Benítez is the philosopher of training courses for Colorado student leaders.
>
> It seems that culture is a sinister virus, capable of infiltrating the minds of youth through hidden passageways and later—abracadabra—converting them into sordid killing machines at the service of the Kremlin.
>
> Everything related to freedom of thought is abominable to the government authorities. It is even considered seditious to read forbidden authors, see famous award-winning films, such as *Z* by Costa-Gavras, or listen to radio stations from other countries that have not been officially approved. These are horrible crimes, capable of inciting righteous indignation in even the most peaceful minds.

8

EMILY

After a week in Ybycuí, we regretfully (because we were five pounds heavier) bid adiós to our families and headed back to Asunción. In a town called Capiatá, we saw women boarding buses while balancing huge baskets of chipa on their heads. Diego explained that the *chiperas* would ride to the next stop, selling their goods to passengers, and then return the same way, free of charge. It sounded like a cozy little business deal—surely the bus companies took a cut, or perhaps the drivers just got free chipa.

Tomorrow we would head north to San Pedro to learn more about gardening. San Pedro was halfway to Concepción on the Paraguay River, quite a distance. The best way to get there was by small plane, and ours was awaiting us at the airport in the morning.

Now, for all my so-called strength and daring, my Achilles's heel was motion sickness. I was notorious in my family for barfing in all the wrong places, like the rental car at Disneyland, the plane to Minneapolis, my uncle's sailboat outside Boston...I couldn't help it. Call it genetic weakness—my grandmother was the same way. I hated Dramamine: it put me to sleep for an hour and I'd wake up cranky. I dreaded going up in this flimsy contraption so asked to sit in the front seat; it worked in cars, maybe it would in small planes as well.

Our Paraguayan pilot in his Ray-Ban aviators was all business as we taxied down the runway, faster and faster, his fingers flipping switches and then pulling back on the joystick, until we left the earth and wobbled into the sky like a badly thrown Frisbee, me with a frozen smile looking down at my dear, disappearing mother, tilt right, tilt left, stable now in the middle...okay, we made it—we were airborne.

Now we just jerked up and down a little, was all. I did a half-hearted thumbs-up to the pilot, which he reciprocated. *Ndaipori problema.* No problem, indeed.

I turned around and looked at the others. They looked at me. No one seemed particularly relaxed. Let's face it: we were crammed into a sardine tin being buffeted through space miles high and at the mercy of every current we encountered. No free will was possible here—we were smack in the hands of fate. Or the pilot. Or God. Call it faith in the universe or faith in God, it was being sorely tested.

Look out the window, fool!

I still couldn't get over how green—and flat—Paraguay was. We followed the river for the most part, where a few small communities had sprung up. I kept my eyes on the landscape and didn't feel too bad. The pilot even let me steer for a while. I had to admit it was magical being up here—I'd always wanted to be a bird. I wondered if I shouldn't learn to fly, like Uncle Ozzie in Kansas, who liked to take his plane to the Baja and fish. But could I trust myself in an emergency? I had my doubts.

The forty-five minutes whizzed by, and before we knew it the bottom felt like it dropped out and we were descending. I could see no landing strip as the earth rapidly approached us, just a grassy field with cows on it. We got down close to the cows and then jerked up again. I looked at the pilot, who was peering out the side window as he banked left. We circled around and did the same thing: swoop down, swoop up, circle around, dive, climb. I really didn't appreciate this little game the pilot was playing, this roller coaster of death.

One by one the bovines began to mosey, and then it hit me: this field *was* our landing strip! And we were using the plane to scatter the herd. Peachy. At this point I was more worried about my heart than my stomach.

After a couple more loops, a space finally opened up and we landed with a big-ass bump, followed by several smaller bumps as we bounced over ruts and cow pies and finally, *gracias a dios*, jerked to a halt. Welcome to San Pedro! I jumped out of the plane determined to kiss the ground, but the stench deterred me—my cookies were still intact, and I wanted to keep them that way.

San Pedro had a different feel from Ybycuí, more open, less like a town. It turned out the family I got this time was the one Ellyn had just stayed with. At dinner the first night they told me Ellyn had sung "Old MacDonald Had a Farm" and said it was our national anthem. Now why would she go and do a thing like that? I'd have to set that girl straight.

I sang the correct anthem for them but forgot to start low and couldn't hit the one high note—"in the la-and of the *freeeee*." It made me homesick and tearful even as we all laughed together, each of us finding the humor in our own way.

This family was a lot poorer than ña Karina. They had a flimsy house with no electricity and fed me mostly soup whose only evidence of meat was a thin layer of grease on top and a well-picked bone. (There was, however, plenty of mandioca, whose usefulness in staving off hunger I was beginning to appreciate.) The latrine out back was in bad shape. Yet I was touched by how everyone went out of their way to accommodate me. For one, they gave me the only mosquito net—who'd had to go without? And I couldn't help but notice my mother gave me more food than anyone else, as if I needed it.

Nevertheless, my attempts at Guaraní were, if not effectively communicated, at least a means for them to pity me. Imagine a grown-up talking like a three-year-old: *"Che a-ñe-ë la Guaraní-me mishimínte* [mee-shee-MEEN-tay]." I speak Guaraní just a little bit. Ha! Not even close. People here spoke mostly Guaraní, and many of the older people didn't speak Spanish at all. I saw how important it would be to learn as much as I could. Still, as with learning any new language, it was amusing to hear strange sounds coming out of my mouth and see that they actually made sense to people.

For training we drove around the campo to see different agricultural projects, including soy and tobacco. Huge tracts of land were being cultivated, giving the area a different look from what we'd seen farther south, where farming was generally on a smaller scale.

We passed some men sawing a log into planks—by hand, no less! One stood at the bottom of a pit while the other sawed from above. I couldn't believe the drudgery that must be involved…though at the moment these guys were drinking tereré and having a good old time trying to get us *chicas* to turn our heads their way. They took particular notice of Polly's dark skin, which made me uncomfortable but gave me a sense of what she must have to deal with here.

I decided to make myself less noticeable and that evening had my "sister" cut off my dishwater-blond locks, which had been down to my shoulder blades. Unused to short hair, I then worried about getting a cold neck come winter. Oh well…such is life.

One afternoon we saw a dead monkey lying stretched out by the road, its front paw reaching for something beyond its grasp…that rock there? It looked so out-of-place—what was a monkey doing in a soybean field, anyway? I couldn't get it off my mind.

We learned more about SEAG and the 4-C clubs we'd be forming. The four Cs were *cabeza*, *corazón*, *capacidad*, and *cooperación* (head, heart, capacity, and cooperation).[37] I loved how the words held so much meaning. Each club would elect its own officers, thereby teaching the girls about representative government. They would learn parliamentary procedure. Ah, nothing like democracy in the midst of dictatorship.

We also learned more about gardening and what would be happening on the guys' end of things (they were still in Costa Rica but would arrive in a couple of weeks). They'd be working with the farmers themselves, helping them adopt modern farming practices—such as the correct application of pesticides—and form cooperatives to get higher prices. Among other things, we would all be expected to write monthly reports and submit them to our SEAG counterparts.

The government was pushing soy because of its profitability, though a few farmers told us they didn't want to grow it because it had been overproduced and lost its value. Inflation was also a problem—the government couldn't provide money to put roofs on unfinished schools, much less pay for books. San Pedro itself had power, but only recently…imagine it's 1975 and your town just got electricity! So much for the "benevolent" dictator who supposedly cared about the well-being of his people.

Only one more week of training in the campo, and then it would be back to Asunción. I was starting to miss "civilization," though I knew this was how it would be when we got to our sites. We'd be choosing them when we returned to Asunción. I couldn't wait to see where we'd all end up.

---

37 To compare, 4-H in the United States stands for "head, heart, hands, and health."

In our last town, Itacurubí del Rosario, a few hours northeast of Asunción, we learned about group leadership and how to actually form the clubs and train the *socias* [SOH-see-ahss] to do the rest: plan and conduct meetings, do cooking demonstrations, create and maintain gardens, hold fundraising events, etc. I was starting to get a sense of what I would be doing in the campo and feeling more confident.

This was Anna-í's site. She'd done a lot to decorate her home, where she lived alone, so we too built shelves by drilling holes in planks, knotting ropes above and below, and suspending them from the ceiling. I looked forward to hanging mine in my own little house on the prairie.

At one point Miriam asked Anna what she thought about PCVs dating locals, and Anna admitted she had a boyfriend.

"Do you sleep with him?" Everyone shot me a look. Well, we were all wondering...*someone* had to ask.

"Yes," she said, blushing. "We meet in Asunción from time to time for that, though."

So it *did* happen. Good to know, though I couldn't imagine ever engaging in such a practice.

One day when returning to Itacurubí from the campo, we heard someone screaming, followed by an eerie silence, and soon after stopped at a house where we were invited for *mate*. The woman could have been in her forties but it was hard to tell; she was missing a few teeth and looked wrung out. Several children ran around, including a toddling girl with nothing on but a shirt. Good idea, I thought—no need for diapers here. I looked around, wondering where all the shrieks had come from.

Then I saw it: from a tree in the yard hung a huge *chancho*, upside down, its throat slit, blood dripping into a pail. Two men were in the process of removing its guts. Shaken, I thought *Every kid in America should see this so they can understand bacon doesn't come from the supermarket or McDonald's but from a living, breathing...Wilbur!* As the "sacrifice" had only just been performed, it seemed like the thing's spirit was still there. I felt like a voyeur, witness to an execution almost, and had to look away.

All in a day's work, I knew. But the idea of vegetarianism was starting to grow on me, especially when I saw the *chicharrones* frying over a fire in a cauldron of pig fat—the family hadn't wasted any time hacking off some pork rinds. They offered me some, complete with little hairs, just as Susana had said. What could I do? *Oh well, "When in Paraguay..."* Down the hatch they went. I had to admit they were pretty tasty.

The woman was also in the process of making a dish she called *soyo* [SOH-djoh]. "The name is a combination of *so'o*, 'meat,' and *josopy*, 'crushed,'" she said. We each took a turn at the *angu-á*, the hollowed-out tree trunk with a "pestle" the size of a baseball bat that they used to mash things together like corn and mandioca and now meat and rice to make the *soyo*. The woman fried some onions and tomatoes in grasa and then added the rice/meat mixture and water to make a thick soup that didn't look half bad.

The family invited us to stay, but we couldn't because we were going to a *cóctel* in Santaní, forty-seven kilometers away, Diego's old site. (He was off somewhere training one of the other groups.) The cocktail party—the name cracked me up because only my parents went to those—was being thrown by some bigwig politico in the town, a guy with the incongruous name of Pastor Coronel. *Preacher Colonel?*

As we walked up to his stately home, I couldn't help but notice all the men working the barbecue pit. They'd whacked Y-topped stakes into the ground at each end of a long fire and attached a cross beam to the Ys. Then they'd taken smaller pieces of wood that had been sharpened and threaded through great-Jesus slabs of beef and leaned them on both sides of the crossbeams over the fire. I'd never even imagined you could cook meat that way.

Beyond the portico was a party going on, all right. Laughter billowed up from under the lights as waiters scurried around with trays of empanadas and beverages for the local elite—police chief, mayor, Colorado head, their wives, everyone of importance, the "beautiful" people of Santaní. Pastor Coronel, by contrast, was dreadful, obese, his skin like uncooked pizza dough. A total boor, he strutted around with his extra-large laugh, lording it over his guests and basking in the deference they showered upon him like rose petals, while never missing an opportunity to snap orders at his domestics.

I honestly thought I might die laughing when our esteemed host, *muy borracho* by this point, grabbed a guitar and started serenading us *güeras lindas de los estados unidos*. God, did he reek of caña! We clapped politely, but I hated having to pander to him, especially having to shake his sweaty palm—twice! Gross. It was obvious he was a "well-respected man" in this town, meaning he most likely didn't hesitate to throw his weight around, considerable as it was.

I didn't think I could be a PCV here. We left soon after, and like a child I fell asleep on the way back to Itacurubí.

The next day we returned to Asunción. It was a *Caldera* night, and I popped into the TV room to see how things were going in good old Peyton Place. It didn't look too swell. Betty was living in the Harringtons' luxurious home after forcing Rodney to marry her, though she'd admitted lying to him about being pregnant. He was rejecting her. There were too many lies and secrets for me, so I went to bed.

In class the next morning I marched over to Ellyn and said, "Ellyn, why in the world did you tell those good people in San Pedro that 'Old MacDonald' was our national anthem?"

She blushed. "I didn't tell them that. They asked to hear a song, so I sang that one. The problem is, I can't sing to save my soul, so I had to think of an easy one. But I never told them it was our national anthem!"

My eyebrows shot up—I couldn't understand how anyone could *not* be able to sing, which to me was like breathing—and I realized either Ellyn didn't speak Spanish well enough to understand that they were asking for the national anthem, or more likely they were shrewder than we thought and had been messing with us big time. There was nothing to do but laugh about it, so we did.

It was now the moment we'd all been waiting for—time to select where we would spend the next two years of our lives. We were at Monitor one morning, and the girls were poring over a map of Paraguay, flush with excitement. We were, however, one short: a mousy girl I didn't know well had decided to terminate for unspecified reasons and was on her way home. It seemed strange to carry on without her, but we did. One down, eleven to go.

"I want to live in Villeta, along the river," Polly said. I thought that sounded appealing myself, but after Polly "claimed" it I didn't feel I could say I wanted it, too. One by one the girls called out where they wanted to go…names of places I'd never even heard of. They must have been contemplating this for a while, unbeknownst to me. They had clearly gotten the jump on me somehow, which I thought unfair, but I didn't want to compete with them over it. I would just let them choose and take whatever was left. What difference did it make, anyway?

Ellyn chose Concepción, way up the river past San Pedro, very isolated, which I wouldn't have wanted anyway and thought was a courageous choice… she would either have to fly there or go by boat, which took a whole day. She certainly wouldn't be coming to Asunción much. Most of the others chose towns fairly close to Asunción. Miriam put in for General Aquino, a small hamlet to the northeast that had never had a volunteer and wasn't too far from Itacurubí, where we'd just done our training.

When all the dust settled, there were two towns that hadn't been chosen, like kids picked last for kickball. I felt kind of sorry for them. One had had PCVs, though not currently, and the other had never had a volunteer but boasted a head agent (*ingeniero agrónomo*—it seemed everyone here was an "engineer" of something) who was reportedly very smart, had a lot on the ball, was eager to get 4-C clubs going, etc., etc.

I didn't want to "show up" any volunteers from the past, or so I let on—it was actually because I was afraid I wouldn't measure up. So, after thinking how great it would be to have a head agent who was really motivated, I chose the town with the "amazing" agronomist and prepared to spend the next twenty-four months in the small town of Iturbe, Guairá Department, central Paraguay, right there on the Don Carlos Antonio López railway line.

The railroad was a bit of a disappointment in that it meant the town had electricity, which I didn't want. I'd have to give up my dream of living like Gary Snyder, out in the mountains with a lamp and a well and lots of books on shelves all around.

But I had a feeling Iturbe would be primitive enough.

The guys from our group (fifteen of the original nineteen) arrived the Thursday after Easter. Leaving the Hotel Guaraní one night after a late beer, we noticed some boys rummaging for food in the trash bins under the hotel. They must have been homeless or perhaps from La Chacarita. It was sad to think they had to eat scraps off the plates of the rich.

I wrote my grandmother that we'd begun showing the guys around Asunción, taking them to all the scenic areas "such as the bar in the Hotel Guaraní, the Lido Bar, the Preferido Bar, etc. Tonight after we're sworn in we'll probably hit Happy Hour at the Marine House, US Embassy; tomorrow we have an 'ASADO' (cookout, Paraguayan style) and later a big smash bash. Well, now you know what Peace Corps life is like!"

Of course, we weren't actual volunteers until the swearing in, as we'd been constantly reminded. I wrote home that I was so excited "I even shaved my legs for the occasion." I also mentioned my hope of buying a horse to ride around the campo so I wouldn't have to depend on unreliable SEAG transportation (we'd heard stories) or closed roads whenever it rained.

Later, at the embassy, I raised my right hand and repeated after Ambassador George Landau:

> I, Emily Creigh, do solemnly swear that I will support and defend the Constitution of the United States of America against all enemies, domestic or foreign, that I take this obligation freely, and without any mental reservation or purpose of evasion, and that I will well and faithfully discharge my duties in the Peace Corps, so help me God.

It was official—destiny, here I come![38]

The next night, Jessica and Vicki were throwing a little party. I felt like celebrating and decided to go. It was at Ian's, an ant guy from England who lived in the neighborhood (and whom Vicki was rumored to be shacking up with). As I got ready, I thought about what was coming up. We were shipping out to the

---

38 Sixteen months later, on July 27, 1976, Ambassador Landau stopped two suspicious-looking passports from being issued at the American Embassy. The applicants eventually got their fake passports in Chile...and two months later (on September 21) orchestrated the car-bomb assassination of Chilean opposition leader Orlando Letelier in Washington, D.C., as part of Operation Condor. The wife of Letelier's American assistant at the Institute for Policy Studies, Ronni Moffitt, was also killed. The assassination was one of many carried out worldwide under Operation Condor.

campo in three days. Tomorrow would be an official reception downtown, and one by one we would disappear into the currently very soggy interior.

I got dressed singing with Linda Ronstadt. Man, what a voice—no other singer could touch her talent. Linda was from my hometown. Her father's family came from Sonora, and she apparently excelled at mariachi as well; how anybody could sing those complex operatic songs was beyond me. I'd never seen Linda perform; she moved to Los Angeles in 1965, when I was only twelve and knew little about music beyond the carols we sang in the Christmas pageant at Fort Lowell Elementary and the show tunes Mom played on her shiny black Steinway. But now, singing with Linda, even adding the third part now and then to create that celestial orb of harmony, was pure joy—though I of course lacked her range.

Still, life was good.

When I got to the party, a friend of Ian's was carrying around a bowl and offering people something from it. He came up to me and introduced himself as Pepe. The bowl contained blue-and-green capsules. "Want some 'ludes?" he said.

Now even though I liked to smoke pot, I'd never taken sedatives or even seen a Quaalude before. I knew what they were but never had the urge to try them, unlike the speed I'd taken once or twice in college when I pulled all-nighters to finish a paper. I mean, who would want to take *downers*?

Vicki came up and said something to Pepe, after which he handed her the bowl and headed toward the kitchen. Vicki really wasn't so bad, I thought. It was just a pity she'd allied herself with Jessica, who was obviously using her. Maybe there was still a chance for some kind of friendship between us—after all, we ended up here together for a reason, didn't we?

"Well?" she said, smiling.

"I don't know," I said, looking into her friendly eyes. "It would be the first time."

"It'll help you feel relaxed, loosen your tongue a little." I'd confided in her once about my discomfort around people. "Take a couple. It's no big deal, I do them all the time. Prescription, of course."

That explained a lot!

I'd always been one to take risks. What could be the harm in it? It was time I let loose a little. So I grabbed two and down the hatch they went. Voilà! Vicki winked and walked away.

I started feeling loopy right away. A cute guy from Australia was in town for a while; I'd met him at Ian's before. He was a bit of a rogue, which I liked—I had a wild streak and was attracted to dangerous guys. We sat and chatted each other up.

The next thing I knew, the party was over. I was sitting on the curb outside Ian's house, just sitting there by myself and realizing, as painful images started to surface, that something terrible had just happened...that sometime earlier, I had no idea how long before, I'd been lying on a horizontal surface (couch? bed?) and...*I was having sex! The Australian was having sex with me! And people were passing by!* But I'd been powerless to stop it—I hadn't been able to comprehend what was happening. I was functioning somehow but actually blacked out. I wasn't putting up any resistance, to be sure, so I must've appeared to be having a gay old time.

Certainly no one had tried to intervene.

I sat there for a long time putting it all together before picking myself—or the pieces that now constituted me—up and stumbling home. Horrifying thoughts forced their way into my mind: Who had seen it happen? I was morbidly shy and would never do anything like that in front of anybody. No one would think well of me now.

Pregnancy wasn't a concern because of the IUD I'd gotten in college. But what if the bastard gave me some disease?

It was when I finally climbed into bed that I realized why my feet had dragged—they were red, swollen, and screaming with ant bites! Still under the influence of the narcotic, sitting outside Ian's and coming to, I hadn't even noticed the hordes of *hormigas* crawling all over my feet and stinging the hell out of them.

I felt like an insect myself, Kafka's Gregor, but the comparison stopped there: Gregor at least had some dignity. Pain and self-recrimination ripped through my body as I struggled to breathe. Finally, I passed out.

In the morning I stayed in bed a long time, assuring Teresa from behind my closed door that I was fine, just a little stomach upset. I couldn't let her see my tear-swollen face. I was supposed to be packing, but how could I possibly carry on? How could I possibly show my face around those people again? Surely they thought I was nothing but a slut.

I couldn't report it because I was convinced it was my own fault—in fact, I hoped to God the PC would never find out. The deepest shame I had ever known suffused my whole being, along with a merciless inner thrashing: *You idiot! Why did you believe Vicki and take those pills? You should have known better. You deserve everything you got.* And so on.

What was I going to do? I couldn't quit now. I couldn't be weak. How could I go through life saying I joined the Peace Corps but didn't finish? My pride, for better or worse—like Dad's—was too great. Finally, after Teresa and the kids left, I got up and shuffled to the bathroom, wincing each time a foot touched the floor. The swelling had finally gone down so I could count them: forty ant bites. *Forty!*

Whatever self-confidence I had disappeared down the drain as I showered and sobbed over my pitiful existence. I wanted to disappear down the drain, too. But I had to somehow find a way to keep going and hold my head up—even though my heart was sinking fast.

It was unbearable.

At the reception that night, Ellyn was extra kind, so I figured she'd seen what happened but didn't hold it against me. Someone took a picture of us on a balcony in the colonial building downtown where the event was held. I'd never felt lower in my life but knew she was a friend, so I did my best to smile.

Jessica and Vicki, on the other hand, acted like I didn't exist. Was it my imagination, or were they positively gloating over my spectacular fall from grace? Why did they hate me, anyway? Because I followed the rules and didn't complain? Because of my ignorance? My need to be liked?

I hated myself—wasn't that enough?

Rationally I knew I shouldn't care what they thought, and I didn't really, but it still rankled. I swore I would have nothing to do with them, would instead focus on my future life out in the campo in my own little house, little town, little world—where no one would know anything about me and I could start over. Who was it said dignity is in your bearing and can't be taken from you? I thought about my aikido training and its focus on conquering fear.

Finally I decided *I'm a warrior. Giving up is not an option.*

I could survive this—I'd just stuff it so deep inside you'd have to pump light to it, as Dad would say. Thank God he would never know.

PART III

MIS NOCHES SIN TI
MAY–JULY 1975

—∞—

EMILY

You'd say to the wind when it took you away:
"That's where I wanted to go today!"

A. A. Milne
When We Were Very Young

Thus began the most challenging period of my life as I struggled to bury the past and do what I'd joined the Peace Corps to do. But my trials were far from over: Iturbe turned out to be a total bust.

As I wrote my mother, the head agent there—young, handsome, and incredibly cocky—"wanted to plant a seed and it wasn't tobacco." Ramón liked being seen with me, especially driving me around in the SEAG vehicle and sparking rumors. He did not, however, like being spurned by me. What, was I supposed to be following some script or something? "Peace Corps Volunteer goes to foreign country, falls in love with native coworker, lives happily ever after." Sorry, that just wasn't going to happen.

Especially as Ramón was certain it was.

Not only that, but Mr. Know-It-All—he made sure I knew he had a degree in forestry—got a lewd expression on his face when I told him I liked the *chivato*. In a mocking tone he called it the "flamboyant" tree and, heedless of my personal space, practically pinned me to a wall as he informed me I couldn't possibly like the *chivato* because it was "nonnative, an invasive species, nothing more than a weed." Imagine being told what you can and cannot like! I wanted to defend it *just because*.

He wasn't really a bad sort—I just couldn't take being around him.

It certainly didn't help that the dentist, of all people, used the room next to the SEAG office to do nothing but pull teeth…clearly the favored alternative to fillings via the terror-inducing "drill" that, dare I say it, was operated by foot, as in *pumping*! (It turned out there was no electricity in Iturbe.) His unanesthetized patients—who, God help them, lined up through our office—had to sit in the antique dentist's chair and spit into an uncovered metal bin (as there was no running water, either). I made the mistake of looking into the bin my first day and nearly gagged: it was a tangle of blood-and-spit-soaked gauze that was starting to smell!

I knew I was coming unglued when even the stoicism of the patients got on my nerves. I myself hated going to the dentist (after fibbing about brushing my teeth as a child and suffering the consequences) and couldn't understand how everyone could be so annoyingly *tranquilo*.

Worst of all, the rain simply wouldn't stop, for hours that turned into days, and Iturbe became one giant mudhole. The ceiling of my room leaked on everything, even my bed. It was too wet for Ramón and me to get out and do any work, so we just sat around the office drinking *mate* and driving each other crazy—he even sucked on the bombilla in a suggestive way. It soon became obvious the "gung-ho" *ingeniero* and I were not suited for partnership on a professional level.

The constant gloom threw me into a deep funk. Flashbacks of the party still haunted me, of course, were in fact destroying me…as were thoughts of Dad. I got depressed and could think of nothing, day and night, but going home.

So when my "father" there took a belt to his teenage daughter for hiding a stack of love letters (which she had just shown me!), I hightailed it out of Iturbe on the first train to Asunción. I'd always loved trains, but not even this wood-burning relic from the 1800s that went twenty-five miles an hour and had a high-pitched "tooweeeeet" like a toy could cheer me up.

Just out of the gate and already flat on my face. Termination seemed the only option as I walked the streets of Asunción, looking for an answer. Then I looked for the answer in the arms of a PCV, a liaison I immediately regretted (and broke off). What was happening to me? Why was I veering out of control like this, not only unmoored but rudderless to boot?

I thought of the dozens of times I'd been bucked off horses, had the air knocked out of me and thought I was going to die…and then gotten right back on. Why couldn't I do that now? I was falling apart, as evidenced by some poems I wrote while lunching alone one day:

Napkin Poems—Bar San Roque, 30 April
Good-bye sounds:
> *train whistles*
> *sniffles*
> *slamming doors*
Please: no more.

—⁊⁊—

The promise made,
the heart sad;

the promise broken,
madness.

—⁓—

Love, love, is loving
and not falling in.

Nevertheless, some PCVs talked me into giving it another try, and Gary and Todd took pity on me by letting me move. I only hoped I could get my life—which was starting to resemble the shifting floor in the fun house—back on track here in my new town, Caazapá [kah-ah-sah-PAH].

Caazapá was pretty, a little run down, just twenty kilometers south and east of Iturbe, "on the other side of the *monte* (mountains, forest)," its name in Guaraní. It had a couple thousand people and was on Route 8, a dirt road, fifty-five kilometers south of Villarrica. I'd come here for a meeting and fallen in love with the place. It had a main street and sturdy block houses with two-toned columns. As in every town (so far), dogs chased *carretas* while ruminants grazed untethered. The word "bucolic" came to mind, even though I'd always thought that sounded more like a stomach affliction than life on *Green Acres*.

As the capital of the department, or state, Caazapá had a SEAG department head, Sr. Vargas, as well as a head agent, Sr. Velázquez, both older, married… and, I could tell, no threat whatsoever. Velázquez was a little goofy and Vargas seemed friendly enough. A cheerful, pretty young woman in her late twenties named Elena lived behind the office—a compound of sorts surrounding an inner courtyard—with her old aunt Vicenta, who was sweet but must've been a hundred and spoke in a toothless Guaraní I couldn't begin to comprehend.

With no vehicle at the office (a major concern of the PC though SEAG had promised one), on my first day Vargas suggested I make a map of the town's compañías. They had exotic-sounding names: Tayy-í [tah-djüh-EE], Boquerón, Rojas Silva, Arroyo Guazú, San José, San José-mí, Cabajú Retä (homeland of the horse)—I would *have* to go there as I'd been half horse since I could remember. Where did they come up with all these names, and for such small communities? I couldn't wait to get out there and meet the people.

What I'd really fallen in love with in Caazapá was the Hotel Díaz, located a few blocks from the center of town near the cathedral. I was staying in one of the bright and airy rooms off the dining room. Everything smelled like gardenias, and outside my window a bird kept singing "Pete away, Pete away," which made me think of my friend in Battle Lake. "Pete away, where?" I answered it. I later learned the bird was a *pitogüe* [PEE-toh-gway]. Small wonder!

The *pensión* was a lively place. The owner, ña Sara, also called "Tía Sarita," her husband, don Pedro, and a woman named Margarita ran it and lived in the house next door. I wondered if Margarita and Sara were sisters but didn't think so. I was introduced to a young woman named Chelo (short for Consuelo, one of those weird girl's names ending in *o*), who lived next door as well and was a primary school teacher, and to a teenager named Alejandro, who also seemed to belong to the place somehow. Plus there was an adolescent girl, Perla, who helped Aurelia, the cook.

Tía Sarita was a little fireball with dark, curly hair—it was probably dyed, as she had to be in her fifties. Margarita seemed around ten years younger. Don Pedro drifted in and out doing things of importance, no doubt.

The topper was the bathroom. It had a flushing toilet—the tank was overhead on the wall, utilizing the miraculous property of gravity—and a shower. As in other bathrooms I'd seen in Paraguay, the shower had no curtain and was next to the toilet, so you didn't really know if the toilet was in the shower or the shower in the "toilet"...not that it mattered, of course. Margarita showed me the tank on the roof where you could heat water if you pumped it up there early enough on a sunny day.

The pensión also had a refrigerator, fueled by kerosene—I never even knew there *was* such a thing. Best of all, it held cold beer! I was impressed. These people had no electricity or running water but were totally on the ball, so unlike my family in Iturbe, who'd had no amenities whatsoever. That family, in addition to serving me gallons of cocido—which I had to admit was delicious but way too sweet—had also fed me these grotesque spherical "crackers" that were nothing but white flour and so hard they resembled golf balls (my not-so-affectionate term for them)...whereas here at the Hotel Díaz they served *real bread*.

Margarita (l.) and "Tía" Sarita in front of the Hotel Díaz with a young ward/errand boy.

Best of all, the pensión generated electricity from 7:00 to 10:00 every night. I could read and write to my heart's content. I was staying here until I could find a house, and was even told I could borrow a bed and armoire for two years. Their generosity knew no bounds.

On the bureau in my room sat a large flowered ceramic bowl with a pitcher in it, just like the ones from the olden days back home. Margarita instructed me on the finer points of taking a "BAHN-yoh tree-ahng-goo-LAHR"—*Oh, "baño triangular"!*—in my room, a concept that was new to me. I mean, I knew the bowl and pitcher were for washing your face, but I didn't know about the other parts.

Two men who boarded here worked at the bank. Montoya was an *ingeniero agrónomo*—naturally—tall and slim with kinky hair and in his early thirties. Dávila was older, in his forties, a little paunchy but funny and kind. They of course held university degrees and were fun to talk to (though they were careful, I'd noticed, to skirt the subject of politics). Their families lived in Asunción, where they often went on weekends.

I would see them during meals and at night, of course, and whenever I went to the bank to get money. Wired there electronically from the PC office in Asunción, my ninety-eight dollars per month—which, at 126 guaranies to the dollar, came to 12,348 Gs—would be more than enough to live on, according to the corps. I would also get a stipend for vacations and a "readjustment" allowance accrued at seventy-five dollars monthly for when I returned home—another reason to stick it out for the whole two years.

I couldn't believe my sudden good fortune, and felt the clouds lifting a little.

A PCV was terminating just as I arrived. He invited me on a serenade. I had a great time being "one of the guys" and especially loved being on the giving end of the *serenata*—I didn't know how I'd feel about being awakened in the middle of the night by a bunch of caña-swilling *cabrones*. Male PCVs definitely had it made here: they could go anywhere they wanted at any time, including bars or even houses of ill-repute if they chose…a privilege obviously denied us *chicas*.

I'd been in Caazapá about a week when someone mentioned a house for rent. It was eight blocks from the pensión in an unfamiliar neighborhood. The over-friendly landlord, Narciso (the perfect name for him), couldn't get the gas stove to work, and I discovered I couldn't even start a bloody fire. It was cheese and crackers for supper that night…though the shock on the store owner's face when I asked for half a kilo of cheese (it was Parmesan and usually purchased by the gram) made it almost worthwhile.

Then some kids snuck into my kitchen and stole a sack of flour and my Nido powdered milk (made by Nestlé[39]), followed by my camera—requiring an unpleasant visit to the police, army, whatever they were—and I just didn't feel safe there. I'd had to return to the pensión with my tail between my legs and endure merciless teasing.

It seemed I couldn't catch a break to save my life.

A few days later I was sitting outside the pensión drinking tereré with some guests when a youngish woman carrying a toddler came out of the house across the "street"—it *was* a street but looked more like a soccer field. She had shoulder-length hair and a sort of impish grin that went up on one side and appeared to be accompanied by an invisible wink.

We introduced ourselves. Her name was Zunilda and her son was Elton. She, too, was a primary school teacher and lived around the corner with her husband, Epifanio. Her mother lived across the street from the pensión and ran a small store called a *despensa*. I wondered why I hadn't met Zunilda yet.

"I just got back from Asunción and hear you're looking for a house," she said. "We have one available. It's just past ours." Just around the corner? Super! I could come to the pensión anytime I wanted, unlike with the first house. This sounded ideal—maybe Caazapá really *was* Shangri-La.

"Thank you very much," I said. "I'll look at it after lunch." It was Sunday and the meal was special: *asado*, with good old grass-fed Paraguayan beef. It may have been tough but at least it was natural, not like the beeves my dad fattened in the feedlots he leased near Casa Grande.

Luckily for me, getting rid of the gristle was easy here. I just spat it into a paper napkin—or the square piece of paper that served as a napkin—in a brilliant feint disguised as wiping my mouth. Some of the men just used the cotton

---

39   At the time, Nestlé was under fire for unethical marketing of infant formula to mothers in developing countries. An international boycott against the company was launched in 1977.

tablecloth to wipe theirs. Gross! Did they feel it was their right? Well, there *were* a lot of women around to clean up after them.

I went to look at the one-room house, freshly painted Barbie pink, agreed on three thousand guaranies (twenty-four dollars) a month, and that afternoon started moving into my *casita rosada* with brick floor, small front porch, kitchen out back with two-burner kerosene stove on a wooden table, well with bucket (no pulley), and outhouse in the back corner of the huge backyard. Vacant lots surrounded me, even on the other side of the street, so except for Zunilda and Epifanio's place ten or so yards to the east, I would have plenty of privacy.

I noticed my latrine had no seat, which was fine—if the Japanese could do it, so could I. My Japanese mother had laughingly claimed their legs were short and sturdy from centuries of squatting. Of course their latrines were indoors, but I was tough enough to handle it—how cold could it get here, anyway? I was just relieved I didn't have to share the thing like I did in Iturbe—although that *was* a sitter. In fact the daughter sat on it a lot while I waited for her outside, in the mud. She refused to go out there without me in tow—for protection, I supposed, but from what, exactly? It wasn't even that far from the house. In my journal I called her "Shit and Spit" because the whole time she sat there, she refused to swallow a single gob of saliva.

I took out my tape player and put on some Allmann Brothers, singing "Lord, I was born a ramblin' wo-man"[40] as loud as I could, filling my lungs and getting high on the oxygen. I started decorating the house, stacking crates for shelves, outfitting the kitchen with the shelves I'd made, putting pictures and maps on the walls. I loved maps. My favorite was the upside-down one of the Western Hemisphere that pointed out the arbitrariness of "north" and "south" and the negative psychological effects of the concept "down there."

The house's only window was next to the front door and looked north onto the street, making it a little dark inside, but it would be all right—I could leave the back door open most of the time. Like most houses in the campo, the window had no glass or screen. A small *chivato* grew in front, which made me laugh: *Take that, Ramón.* I was disappointed there were no fruit trees, but my

---

40   Richard Betts, "Ramblin' Man," 1973.

new landlords promised to help me prepare the large plot between our houses for a garden, which seemed fair enough.

Zunilda loaned me a three-segment partition like those in Japan only made of cloth, which helped divide the space. Epifanio helped me put the armoire behind the partition across from the cot that was already there, and of course he had to make lewd comments about the bed. *¡Idiota!* But I knew he'd never try anything because it was obvious Zunilda, the more formidable of the two, would be only too happy to hand him his head—or some other body part—on a platter.

I would bathe in the kitchen, where I could heat water in the winter. Cooking with only the two-burner stove would be challenging but fun. My roommate Marilyn and I had come up with some creative recipes on one in the Yucatán—well, creative so long as you liked bananas and rice. At least I wouldn't have to start a wood fire every time I wanted to cook—even if I could—like the campesinas using the "modern" stoves we so generously procured for them here.

The first thing I planned to do was hire a local carpenter to make a round table. It sounded so *Camelot*.[41] I laughed at how I'd cried my eyes out over that film at age fifteen. No doubt about it, King Arthur was the man for me: "Not might *is* right, Jennie, but might *for* right." I'd read later that JFK loved it as well (the musical). He would listen to it on his record player before bed, especially the last scene, when a defeated Arthur tells the boy not to forget there once was a spot that for "one brief shining moment" was known as Camelot. I teared up just thinking about JFK's "Camelot." It hadn't lasted long, either—just over a thousand days, as I recalled.

That evening Margarita came over, saw me sweeping, and told me how *guapa* I was. I swore under my breath…people said that when I swept the office, too. "Why are you saying I'm 'pretty' just because I'm sweeping the floor?" I snapped.

"What do you mean?" she said, looking at me incredulously. "*Guapa* means 'hardworking.'" I almost choked. Everything had a different meaning here!

She'd brought me a *miramenotoca* (pyracantha), which she said could grow in the flower box on my porch and the cows wouldn't eat it. Its pretty red berries and needle-like thorns told me instantly why it was called "look at me don't touch."

---

41 Alan Jay Lerner and Frederick Loewe, 1960.

I thanked her and said, *"Ja-tereré?"*

She nodded, and we went inside to share some yerba "gringa" style. I'd added mint and lemon juice—not exactly kosher, but it was refreshing. Margarita didn't seem to mind. We sat down on chairs Zunilda had loaned me.

I needed to know who was who at the pensión. "Margarita, tell me more about Chelo."

"Ah, Chelo." She sighed and smiled, pausing for a moment. Then she looked at me. "Consuelo's my daughter." I nearly dropped the guampa. My face turned red at all the questions I wanted to ask but just couldn't.

She read my mind and said, "Her father was Sarita's brother." Oh. My. God! And here I'd thought Margarita "the spinster" was so innocent.

"We weren't married. I had come from the campo to work for Sarita's family, and her brother...well, he had his way with me." She shrugged her shoulders and said it so matter-of-factly I was taken aback. "When I got pregnant, Sarita was kind enough to take me in, and Chelo and I have been with her and don Pedro ever since. Consuelo is the light of my life and the reason for my existence," she said quietly.

No wonder she'd named her daughter "Consolation"!

"Do you ever see...the father?" I finally asked.

She shook her head. "No, he left and hasn't been seen since." *Poor, dear Chelo.* At least she'd been raised in a loving home and was accepted by society, as evidenced by her good job as a teacher. I'd watched her do lesson plans in bound notebooks and complete them by drawing flowers and leafy vines around the margins in colored pencil. She was also being courted by a man who was a lot older than she, an upstanding citizen though a bit sickly, but now I could see how she must have considered herself lucky to have him.

To lighten the mood, I asked about Alejandro.

Margarita gave a little laugh. "Alejandro is Aurelia's son." Pause. "His father is Beto, Sarita and Pedro's oldest son."

No! I'd met Beto. He came to the pensión once, with his wife and children. I talked to him for a while. From the things he said, I got the impression he considered his mother a saint and his wife a whore...*Why? Because she likes sex?* What a dog!

I couldn't believe Alejandro was Sarita's grandson. She treated him like everyone else. Beto and Alejandro were friendly, but father and son? Never. So

Beto "came of age" with the cook—this was definitely more *One Hundred Years of Solitude*[42] than *Peyton Place*!

I didn't know what to say, and a few quiet moments passed. That's when Margarita asked the question I'd been successfully avoiding up to now: "Emi, if you don't mind my asking, how did your *papi* die?"

"Poppy"! I had never called him that, but now it sounded so sweet. Once again I felt the ground give way beneath me. Of course everyone knew he had died, they just didn't know how. Where to start? I could think of only one way to say it in Spanish, though I avoided the English equivalent.

I sighed and looked at her. *"Se suicidó."* Her eyes welled up and I began to lose it, so I tilted my head back and looked at the ceiling for reassurance—the surest way to keep my own tears from falling.

But it didn't work. Margarita scooted her chair over next to mine and held me, and we both cried for a few minutes. Well, she cried while I bawled. Uncontrollably. I'd never done that in anyone's arms before. Once I realized how good it felt, I just stayed there sniffling and blowing my nose with the tissue Margarita gave me until I could talk again. She waited until I was ready.

"His main business was failing," I began, "through no fault of his own...and he couldn't afford the premiums on his life insurance anymore. Dishonest men robbed him of real estate investments. His orange trees froze. The economy was terrible, there was an oil crisis, and his man Nixon—President Nixon, you remember?—let him down. My father was fifty-six and didn't think anyone would hire him, as he'd always been in business for himself."

Margarita poured me some tereré, and I accepted it gratefully. I wondered what this must sound like to her. *Life insurance? Investments?* And just about everyone in this place was in business for himself. I took a deep, shaky breath and let it out slowly.

"He wanted his family to continue living in the manner we were accustomed to—according to him, anyway—and didn't want to drag us down with

---

42 Gabriel García Márquez (Buenos Aires: Editorial Sudamericana, S.A., 1967); first English translation © 1970 by Harper & Row, Publishers, Inc.

him. I guess he just figured he was worth more to us dead than alive. Of course we didn't believe that. But no one knew what he was thinking—and I was far away, studying in Japan. My father always said my college expenses weren't the reason for his financial problems, but they *must* have been. 'None so blind as those who will not see,' huh, Margarita?"

She didn't take her eyes off me, and I felt safe. Not many people knew how to listen.

"My father planned everything out, wrote letters to us, suggested steps to take, asked us to think of it as an accident. An *accident*, Margarita! But I understood, and I consider him a hero, a true Samurai, which in Japan is a warrior, a man of honor and courage who would sooner take his own life than dishonor himself or his family." She looked troubled but nodded—I knew her Catholicism prevented her from seeing it that way.

I decided not to mention how angry I'd been with Dad at first. How could he have pulled the rug out from under me like that? Who was I going to turn to now? But I'd gotten over it when everything started to sink in.

"My father sacrificed his life for his family," I finally said. Thoughts of him pulling the trigger still tormented me. What hurt most was that, at the time, in Japan, I was starting to heal while he was sinking deeper and deeper into a despair that his letters to me had never revealed...just as my letters home had concealed my own.

"Emi, I'm so sorry." She looked down and held both my hands in hers. "Did you give yourself time to grieve?"

Grieve? Never. After Dad's funeral I'd gone straight to Stockton to finish my degree, not letting myself feel anything. Maybe that was my problem. I shook my head.

A few minutes later Margarita said softly, "I never even knew my father, Emi. He moved away, left his wife and children for another woman. I don't even know who he is." She sighed and looked at me. "The ache never goes away completely, believe me. We carry it with us wherever we go. We can never forget it...we just have to learn to live with it, invite it in, sit down and have *mate* with it"—she smiled—"make peace with it."

I didn't know if that would be possible. Nonattachment had to be the most difficult—though surely the most important—of the Buddhist tenets. Besides,

God knew I had more than my share of suffering to "learn to live with"...
though Margarita's *mate* image did almost make me laugh. But of course she
was right: you had to go straight to the pain and surrender to it. I couldn't
imagine never knowing my father but saw how even though Margarita's and my
problems were different, they affected us to the same degree: we'd both been
abandoned.

A few minutes later she started to get up. *"A-jhavarã ógape,"* she said. I understood! She had to go home. It was getting dark.

"Where are you from, Margarita?" I asked, also rising and walking her to
the door. I was glad I didn't have any mirrors as my face must have looked a
fright.

"A small town southwest of here in Misiones, near San Juan Bautista and
the Río Tebicuary. It's poor but very beautiful."

"Is it true that if you swim in the Tebicuary River you'll stay in Paraguay
forever?" I asked, trying for a little levity. "Our trainer Diego told us that."

"That's what they say," she replied. "So you'd better get your butt
cheeks down there as soon as possible." We laughed and she started up the
street.

"Margarita!" I called after her. She stopped and looked back. "Would it be
okay if I came over for *mate* in the morning?"

"Nambréna, Emilia, claro que sí," she said as if annoyed with me, but I knew she
wasn't really—that was just how you expressed affection here. She continued
on her way, and I went back into my home, feeling empty yet serene.

I pumped up my lantern, poured alcohol into the trough, lit it, waited a few
minutes, then turned the valve to hear the welcome *WHOOSH* as the mantles
started glowing like tiny suns. The only light in the house was what I carried
with me; when I walked around, it cast fiendish shadows on the walls while
everything else stayed pitch black. I wasn't exactly afraid of the dark but had to
admit it made me a little jumpy.

Later I stood outside and marveled at the sky. I'd never imagined there
were so many galaxies that the whiteness between stars would be thick as a
comforter and incredibly bright, even with no moon. Although upside down
here, Orion the hunter was easy to spot, thanks to his ammo belt and sheath
(it would always be a schlong to me), and the Southern Cross hung on the

horizon, guiding in the sailors like its counterpart in the north that Joni sang about.[43]

I watched as a meteor streaked across the cosmos, exploded in a ball of light, and vanished. That's how I wanted to go out.

Like Dad.

Things were starting to pick up at the office. Working gave me great satisfaction and took my mind off things. I did work plans and drew posters to support my efforts to "educate" the campesinos. Of course it still remained to be seen who would be educating whom.

I'd been doing as much as I could: drawing my map, creating talks with visuals, testing recipes (soy milk, soy croquettes, soy cake, soy sopa, peanut croquettes, cream of squash soup, mayonnaise with Nido—that one didn't turn out too well). I also completed my first *informe mensual*, a report we had to do every month to let the Ministry of Agriculture and Peace Corps know what we'd accomplished. As in sushi school in Japan, I had to make a little bit look like a lot because we hadn't exactly been out to the campo.

We really needed a vehicle.

One night a cold rain fell—and fell. All night. I was thankful my roof didn't leak, but boy was it chilly; I needed more blankets. The only time my kerosene heater worked was when I was sitting directly in front of it—not the most convenient place to be. The deluge turned out to be a disaster because it was May 15, Paraguay's Independence Day, and a ton of festivities had been planned, not the least of which was a dance. But forget having a fiesta in this rain.

The sun finally came out a few days later, and when I showed up at the pensión for lunch, Margarita grabbed my arm and led me through the arch, down the steps, and onto the patio, pointing to the tank on the bathroom roof. "I pumped some water up there for you this morning. Because it's so sunny today, it should be warm enough for you to take a shower soon." I gave her a hug and thanked her. Sweet, thoughtful Margarita. She also gave me two blankets to take home to add to the one I'd gotten from Zunilda.

---

43 "This Flight Tonight," 1971.

At lunch I announced I was looking for a *bike* and about an hour later someone brought a pretty blue girl's model by my house. The tires were good and the chain was oiled, so I paid cash for it and rode it the eight blocks back to work. Wheels—what an amazing invention, so freeing! I'd always taken them for granted—didn't everyone? I arrived in a flash and decided in the future I'd take side streets to know my town better.

Emily's house and bicycle in Caazapá; the kitchen is in back.

That afternoon Velázquez and I wrote letters to parents in San José who had shown interest in their daughters' being in a club. San José was on Route 8 just north of Caazapá...in the past Velázquez had taken the bus, which was subject to inconsistent departure and arrival times and, of course, *ruta clausurada*. But as San José was "only" fifteen kilometers away, we could bike there fairly easily and catch the bus home if we needed to, so that's what we decided to do. Velázquez said he could borrow his cousin's *bici*. I couldn't wait to see him ride one, knowing how nutty he could be.

The next morning the two of us set out, as much to escape the office and Vargas's eye as to feel we were actually getting something done. The ride wasn't easy. Some places were nothing but sand, and we had to go up a lot of hills. But what goes up must come down, and even though Velázquez could normally be a pain—he was disorganized and thought sweeping the office was *my* job—for entertainment purposes he was second to none. And that day he did not disappoint. He put on his best clown act, taking his feet off the pedals, pantomiming losing control of the handlebars and looking deranged.

"*Nde tavy* [tah-VÜH]," I teased him, hoping he took it as "crazy" and not "ignorant," its other meaning. We both laughed and pedaled on.

I never realized how far nine miles was until that day.

After what seemed like hours, we finally arrived. Velázquez of course knew everyone here as he'd been working with the farmers for years, advising them about planting crops and how to get the best yields and prices, and providing seeds. He smiled and waved to them as we rode by, getting a kick out of their reactions to his riding a bicycle in the first place and especially to his being accompanied by a *cuñataï rubia e i porä* [pretty little blond señorita], a phrase I heard over and over.

We went to the house of Silvio and Antonia. Tall and slender, Silvio had the aura of a natural-born leader, focused and unflappable; Antonia was intelligent and pretty. They were recently married with no children. They lived in a thatched house next to her parents', both of which had mortar on the outside painted in two colors—reddish brown from the bottom to about two feet from the ground, white over that—which distinguished the family as having some disposable income.

Unlike in the Yucatán, people here slept on beds rather than hammocks. I figured it was because winters were colder here…the iceberg I'd only recently felt the tip of. Beds seemed more practical, anyway. I couldn't figure out how people in the Yucatán had sex in a hammock—had never tried it myself—but judging by the average family size there, it was a skill they'd mastered with flying colors.

Velázquez introduced me to a growing number of spectators, both children and adults. With his encouragement I spoke in Guaraní, telling them a little about myself and explaining the 4-C clubs. Everyone suppressed laughter but seemed to understand. I gave Antonia the letters we'd written; she said she was interested in having a club and definitely wanted a fogón.

"No one likes to cook over an open fire," she said, crinkling her nose. I was glad she was young and willing to break with the past.

We drank tereré, talked about cotton and tobacco, and arranged to meet back here next Tuesday afternoon at three o'clock. Antonia said she would invite some girls from the compañía to attend. I was ecstatic—my first club!

We mostly walked the bikes back because getting to San José had been more downhill than we'd remembered. Fortunately, we were able to flag down the bus, throw the bikes on top, and make it to Caazapá in time for lunch. We spent the afternoon planning for the fogón-building demonstration we were hosting the weekend after next.

That night at home I copied some passages from Carlos Castaneda's *Tales of Power* into my new journal, an inch-thick, hardcover Paraguayan number with vertical black-and-white stripes and two concentric red circles on the front, which I'd purchased at Vargas's *despensa*:

> *A warrior takes his lot, whatever it may be, and accepts it in ultimate humbleness. He accepts in humbleness what he is, not as grounds for regret but as a living challenge... The warrior lowers his head to no one, but at the same time, he doesn't permit anyone to lower his head to him... A warrior considers himself already dead, so there is nothing for him to lose.*

That sounded like Bushido, the philosophy behind aikido (and all Japanese martial arts). It really spoke to me. My Stockton instructor, Sensei John Smartt, had told me that in this book he'd found the culmination of what he'd endeavored to express. I revered John and could now glimpse what he'd been trying to teach me... even if it *was* fiction, as some alleged.

I especially loved the story Castaneda told about the two cats soon to be euthanized by their owner, who was moving to a new city and couldn't take them with her. She had asked for Castaneda's help in getting them to the vet's. The cat who was "indulgent" or "obsessed" licked the hand of its owner all the way to the "deadly needle."

But the other one, called Max, got away after a brief struggle with Castaneda and leapt through a grate into the city's sewer. What happened to Max isn't known, but the important thing was he sensed danger and decided to choose his own fate. That cat Max was me, for better or worse. In such a situation I would also trust no one and do whatever I could to get away.

I would never go quietly.

That Friday I got on Epifanio's case about promising but never quite getting around to tilling the garden, so he found a guy with two oxen (I learned an ox was simply a castrated bull) and a plow, who spent Saturday afternoon turning over the richest soil I'd ever seen or smelled. I was astonished at how the man could rig up a yoke out of a piece of wood lashed to the beasts' horns. The wood was chained directly to the "plow," actually just a giant metal hook with handles that the man kept upright as he walked—barefoot, of course—behind the docile *bueyes*, shouting instructions at them. What an operation! I wouldn't have even known where to begin.

Epifanio and I planted lettuce, cabbage, tomatoes, potatoes, and beets. I wasn't sure what could be planted at the beginning of winter, but he seemed to know, so I just followed his direction. He said we'd plant squash, cucumber, and watermelon in August. I also bought some chickens from him that would stay in his yard but I could collect the eggs. I couldn't bear to give them names, knowing I'd be eating them someday.

The carpenter delivered my round table, and I proudly placed it in the "front room" near the door. Sunday morning I got up early and did yoga for forty-five minutes, vowing afterward to do it as long as I could before it got too cold. I went to the pensión to get two more chairs Margarita had promised, and we drank *mate*, with *yuyos* for the digestion, she said. My digestion seemed fine, but I was sure it would be improved after the herbs.

That afternoon I built a walkway between my house and the kitchen with some bricks I found next to the latrine. I planted a purple jade plant in a gourd and hung it next to the kitchen door, and then prepared a vegetable omelet I devoured with joy...and tears.

It seemed the hole in my heart would never heal.

When it got dark I read Castaneda by lantern light and had multiple epiphanies. Later I slipped under the mountain of blankets on my bed and assumed my cold-weather, pre-snooze posture—lying on my back with hands in armpits and feet behind folded knees until they thawed out enough for me to turn over and go to sleep. But before that could happen, I felt a gnawing in my belly. Drat! I'd have to go to bed hungry again—no way was I going out to the kitchen now.

Monday dawned frigid, so I rushed through yoga and jogged to the pensión for *mate* with Margarita—it was becoming routine. It was nice to sit there in the little foyer on the plastic chairs and talk about stuff. Or not talk. She didn't push me, which I liked, and she made me feel like a human rather than some curiosity from another planet.

When I got to the office at eight, the place was jumping. Velázquez had invited the families in San José to the fogón-building course, and several farmers were there with hats in hand and questions. The course would include building demonstration fogones in the homes of four former socias with the understanding that the recipients would teach other families how to build their fogones when the time came.

I shuddered to think how long that could take. We were completing the project of the previous *educadora*. Her clubs had just received the *planchas* from Argentina they'd purchased over a year ago with the funds they'd raised. With such long turnaround times, no wonder it was difficult to keep projects going in the campo.

At least we were here now, finally, planning the course and demonstration. That is, a woman from SEAG named Naomi was planning and executing the whole shebang (thank God). Naomi would be arriving in Caazapá on Thursday. Our job was to get the supplies (tools, bricks, mortar) and labor (the families themselves). I felt everyone's excitement as I tried to understand the flood of Guaraní.

After a while I left the men talking on the stoop and went inside to try and get some work done, but the office was so cold my fingers could barely budge the keys on the medieval typewriter—that thing could have belonged to Gutenberg himself! When *mate* time finally rolled around, Elena (who I noticed was getting a little chubby) brought out her pink thermos and a small gourd with the yerba and bombilla already in place. I got warmer just thinking about wrapping my fingers around that *matero*.

Velázquez poured, and my world was complete. During those twenty minutes, as we shared the *mate* and the goodwill it engendered, all my earthly needs were taken care of. I didn't even mind sharing a little spit with the campesinos—you just had to believe everything would be all right. It sure beat the pants off working.

After lunch—which I was still "taking" at the pensión to save time—we climbed into Montoya's red Jeep and headed to Boquerón, twelve or so kilometers away, where Montoya said someone would be demonstrating the use of a new piece of equipment. Velázquez and I planned to talk to the girls there about forming a club. We drove first through a lowland area and then into the hills of the nearby mountains, or what they called "mountains" here.

"It's the Yvytyrusu, 'big mountain,' the range on your right when you go north from Caazapá to Villarrica," Montoya said as we bounced over the rutted road that was actually little more than a cow path. By the look and smell of it, a lot of cows passed by here. Every now and then we'd go by a *carreta* or someone riding a bicycle or *moto*. Of course most people walked. Their feet were huge, probably because they went barefoot so much—I couldn't imagine how they did it, but then they didn't have the prickly things we had in the desert.

"That's Tayy-í," said Velázquez, pointing in the direction of some houses set fairly far apart around a natural drainage area. I was beginning to see how a *compañía* was really little more than a few households. "The girls here insist they don't want a club, but we're going to talk to them and see if we can change their minds." I nodded. We should at least try.

We passed in front of one particularly bare-looking house with whitewash peeling off the walls of red clay—no shortage of iron oxide here (like northern Arizona). A tall young woman with curly hair came out and waved to Velázquez, who waved back. "¡Adiós!" I raised my hand as well.

"That's Olimpia," he said. "She was the former president, before the problem. We'll come back as soon as we can, and I'll introduce you to her."

There was something about Olimpia's gaze that set her apart from other girls in the campo, a mixture of seriousness and mirth that indicated a keen intelligence. She brazenly checked me out from head to toe, then broke into a tentative smile and, with one last wave, turned back toward her house, bending over and shaking her head as she entered the low doorway. She looked like someone you didn't want to mess with.

"Problem?" I wondered aloud.

"Yes...some money disappeared and there was a big flap," he said. "They worked it out in the end, but it almost destroyed the community. I think they blamed us somehow."

I wondered why they would blame SEAG but didn't have time to ask—we were arriving in Boquerón.

A Japanese-Brazilian man was there in his green Yanmar ("'dragonfly' in Japanese," he said) jacket carrying his green Yanmar insecticide sprayer on his shoulders like a backpack. It ran on gasoline and sounded like a lawn mower, making an obscene racket in the pristine Paraguayan countryside.

Around twenty farmers stood around, talking to one another about the insect eater.

I immediately hated that abomination, not wanting to think about what must be inside it. I remembered reading that after the United States banned DDT for use at home, we went ahead and exported it to so-called "third-world" (I hated that term, too) countries like Paraguay. It just wasn't right.

The campesinos seemed curious about me as well, so when the time came, Velázquez introduced me to them. I started out in Guaraní—by now I could get the basic information across. They got a big kick out of it and said I spoke the language better than they did.

"How can they say that?" I asked Velázquez.

"Well, you studied Guaraní in school, but they never did because it's prohibited."

It was irony with a touch of truth to it, but how absurd to think I could ever speak Guaraní as well as they did. And why was it prohibited, anyway? Maybe it was like Tucson earlier in the century, when people weren't allowed to speak Spanish in school—with the devastating effect that many second-generation Mexican-Americans lost their language, the connection to their culture.

After I explained who I was and what we were doing, Velázquez relieved me and started filling in the details. Some young boys gathered at the edge of the group, holding what looked like white tennis balls up to their faces and squeezing them. I couldn't imagine what they were doing and decided to ask Velázquez when I got a chance.

The farmers promised to talk to their daughters, and we made a date to return to form a club. As the afternoon shadows grew longer we got chilly, so someone built a fire and conjured up some *mate*.

We left at sunset. Velázquez said, "Too bad Boquerón is so far from town. We won't be able to have a club here without a vehicle."

"When are we supposed to get one?" I asked.

"They promised it in July or August."

"Then there's nothing to worry about," I said cheerfully. "It'll be here if they promised it." Velázquez and Montoya looked at each other with raised eyebrows.

"What?"

They each put their fingers to their lips and "zipped" their mouths closed.

"I know, don't get my hopes up," I said. "Believe me, they're not. But how are we supposed to do our job without a vehicle?"

Velázquez just shrugged. It wasn't *his* fault he couldn't get any work done. There was nothing he could do about it, so he wasn't going to let it bother him. But it bothered me a lot that we'd gone out there and given people hope without intending to return, just so we could say we'd done something.

On Tuesday I prepared materials on the basic food groups, swept the office, finished my map, wrote to Todd and Anna-í to fill them in on my activities, swept the office again, and arranged some classes with a group of women from town who had a sewing club. In the afternoon I experimented on a recipe with Elena, cookies with toasted and ground *soy*beans, which turned out well.

That's when she told me she was pregnant.

I, of course, was flabbergasted—I'd never even seen a man around. (But then again I wouldn't, would I?) She said her "husband"—*Oh, so you're married now!*—lived in Boquerón. I figured they probably weren't officially married, but then again, what did it really matter?

"Then again." You definitely had to keep an open mind here.

I was excited because I'd never known anyone who got pregnant before, and of course Elena was absolutely gushing and blushing. I had to laugh: *Aunt Vicenta must be one sound sleeper!*

On Wednesday Velázquez and I rode our bikes to Cabajú Retä. There had been a club in this compañía before as well, and we were meeting in the home of the former president. It was nicer than many, white plastered walls with a green band around the bottom. What really set it apart was its covered porch, at least ten feet wide. The surface of the raised dirt floor was so worn it was hard as rock. Around the perimeter sat some benches made of rough planks. A small wooden table and chairs sat on the porch as well, telling me the shade made for some fairly cool dining in the summer.

Which of course translated to *freezing* in the winter, but the people were used to that, so we sat *freezing* on the porch in jackets and hats or scarves of one sort or another. I couldn't believe the girls were wearing skirts and either the flimsiest of shoes or none at all. My tennies and long pants didn't even begin to keep out the chill.

There were about eight or nine teenage girls and numerous family members. The few fathers who showed up stayed in the background and talked.

Velázquez and I welcomed everyone and I did my little intro in Guaraní, which I had to admit was improving.

We then reverted to Spanish and discussed the protocol of forming the clubs: the girls would elect officers and basically run the meetings themselves; the goal was to work together to raise money and then purchase *planchas* for the stoves we would construct; the socias would develop their abilities as women to be productive members of the community. The girls, of course, already knew all this but listened politely to our little speech. Later they impressed us by remembering and reciting the 4-C pledge:

> I promise to use
> - my head to think better,
> - my heart to feel better,
> - my capacity to produce more,
> - my cooperation to better serve my club, my family, my country, and God.

They wanted to resume the meetings, so I asked everyone to sign the membership sheet I'd made. I suggested we start with nutrition, which they agreed to. Velázquez suggested we meet on Tuesdays at 3:00 p.m., which they agreed to. I said we would have elections in two weeks, and they agreed to that, too. They were most agreeable.

Riding back to town wasn't as difficult as on previous trips, partly because I was pumped up about finally accomplishing something…*and* because it was colder than hell. I could tell that Velázquez was happy, too—he needed these clubs for his reports as much as I did. We fairly flew home, wrapped in a dazzling sunset.

That night I finished *Tales of Power* before going to bed. Later I had a waking dream so real I thought I might die. Once again, as that night in Ybycuí, I felt I was being lifted out of my bed and banged against the wall—up again, down again, whack! whack!—over and over. I knew I was making noises. I was outside it yet inside, helpless. The people outside must have heard me screaming…I *was* screaming, wasn't I?

Then it was over. Why had that happened again? No clue. No sleep, either, as I lay in the dark trying to rein in my runaway heart.

The next morning we cleaned the office and waited for Naomi. Vargas said she had a degree in agronomy—unusual for a woman—and had been with

SEAG for years, in San Lorenzo, often making trips to the campo for special courses like this. She pulled up in a SEAG vehicle just before noon. One look told me she did not suffer fools lightly. Her shoulder-length hair set her apart as a freethinker, and her facial features were sharp, a bit imposing, masculine almost.

She obviously commanded a lot of respect, and it was amusing to watch Velázquez and Vargas fall all over themselves sucking up to her. I thought she was terrific. We had *mate*, of course, ate lunch at the pensión (where Naomi would be staying), then spent the afternoon planning. She was happy to hear that fifteen farmers had signed up.

Ten farmers were there the next morning when the meeting finally started on "Paraguayan time," an hour late. But Naomi didn't seem to mind as she began explaining how fogones worked, how they were constructed, what materials and tools were necessary, what alterations would have to be made to the houses to accommodate a chimney, etc. It was gratifying to see how such a relatively simple device could make cooking so much safer and healthier for families. By the time the morning session was over, the other five farmers had arrived. *Más vale tarde que nunca.* Or was it? At least they made the effort.

The plan had been to go out to San José in the afternoon but naturally it rained, *ruta clausurada*, so we sat in the office and tried to outguess the weather. I was coming down with a sore throat and begged leave, sloshing home in the mud just in time for the rain to stop. However, by this time it was too late to go out to the campo, so I gargled with hot salt water and fell dead asleep before I knew what hit me.

Sure enough, the next morning my sore throat was gone (gargling worked every time), but it was wet and cloudy, the ground a bog. For some reason, though, the road was open. I knew it was going to be messy, so I wore my rubber boots and grungiest clothes—including the chef's pants, of course.

Silvio had done a good job preparing for the "oven raising": the bricks, thinner than those back home, sat dry inside his house alongside the heavy iron slabs with two holes for pots. Shovels, trowels, and other tools stood against the wall. Women were killing chickens and peeling mandioca to feed the laborers. I couldn't get over how well everyone wielded a machete, especially the women.

Naomi seemed pleased and, just as the sun broke free of the clouds, started telling everyone what to do. She excelled at it. Paraguayan women could definitely be authoritarian. Perhaps they had to be—they seemed to be the ones running the show around here.

Building a fogón. A new kitchen will be constructed around it.

By the next Friday we had built four fogones, two under the direction of Naomi and crew (Velázquez, Silvio, Antonia, and me) and two by the farmers themselves, who demonstrated the technique to a decent number of community members. We used mud for mortar, which I found curious, though it must've had enough clay in it because Naomi obviously knew what she was doing. (That red dirt truly was the "blood and guts" of the people.) We used string to determine distance—no tape measures need apply—and bottles of water to determine level, which I thought ingenious. To avoid an inferno in the summer, the heat was vented through a newly gouged hole in the wall and up a round metal pipe on the outside.

The finished fogones were about two and a half feet wide, five feet long, and four feet high, or as high as the señoras wanted, many of whom were petite. One woman wanted hers built outside the house so she could build a new kitchen around it. Sounded good to me as long as it didn't rain before then—which we all knew it would. Oh well, it wasn't my place to question it.

As I had never laid a brick in my life, my skills were less than impressive. Naomi was charitable and let me try for a while, but I was too much of a perfectionist. Never liking to do what I wasn't good at, I soon found my forte was mixing the mud and transporting it to the bricklayers in a wheelbarrow.

When we were finally finished, everyone seemed satisfied, and Naomi deemed the workshop a success. I felt proud of what we had accomplished and was eager to see how the families' lives would be improved—they lived so simply as it was, I thought they deserved a few so-called "creature comforts."

Their homes were constructed in basically the same way and differed only in whether or not plaster had been spread over the sticks and mud and then painted or whitewashed. Thatch from the ubiquitous palms was used for roofs, whose underside—the ceiling—seemed to quiver with invisible life. Still, constructing a roof out of palm fronds took expertise—I certainly wouldn't be able do it.

I'd been in a few such homes now and was humbled at what I saw. Of course none had electricity, or even a generator. Most had only one room, though several had additions, for kitchens and extra bedrooms. The floors were dirt but always immaculate. Very little, if anything, hung on the walls, though most had at least one crucifix and a picture of the president. Some families boasted hand-colored photos of ancestors staring grimly into infinity through the curved glass of their oval frames.

Furniture consisted of a wooden table and straight-back chairs and a *ropero*—the only closet they had—plus boxes for shelves and other items the family had fashioned. The fire pits in the kitchens, equipped to hang a pot over them, were an obvious danger to children. There were beds to sleep on, but seemingly fewer than the number of family members. Privacy didn't seem to be a concern…especially as there was none in the first place. I hated being watched by people and knew I could never live so "exposed" like that.

In short, though some had more than others, the campesinos had virtually nothing beyond the fundamentals: food, shelter, clothing…and family. It was all they (or anyone for that matter) really needed. Life for them was clearly not about material possessions. And of course their lives were every bit as full and important and legitimate as anyone else's. I felt immense respect for them because I knew I could never survive in the campo like that. It took courage to live as they did, with no safety net whatsoever.

So much for my so-called vow of poverty.

It occurred to me we can't blame people for how they're born, rich or poor—it's not as if anyone asks to be dragged kicking and screaming into the world. What matters is what they do with it.

We were ready to leave the last fogón site when I saw a young man sitting on the back of an oxcart with his infant daughter. I asked if I could take their picture, and he said yes. As I focused the lens he suddenly thrust the girl skyward, his hand gripping both her feet, and with his outstretched arm balanced her as she swayed high in the air, her tongue sticking out and a tentative smile on her face. I snapped the shutter. I had a feeling it was going to be a good shot and started rewinding the finished roll of color slides.

We waved our final good-byes and headed down the road. *Click.* I smiled to hear that welcome sound telling me the film was safe in its canister…and that I'd loaded it into the camera correctly in the first place. *The amazing balancing baby will be immortalized—yippee!*

Now I just hoped I had the right aperture, shutter speed, and focus. (With so many things that could go wrong, it was a wonder pictures *ever* turned out.) I would mail the roll from Asunción to be developed in the States. It was the

PCVs' choice even though it cost a lot to send, more than five dollars. The best outfit sent a new roll back. Film was expensive, which was why I could never take as many shots as I wanted. I preferred slide film but also liked black and white and couldn't wait to use the darkroom at the PC office.

I spent a relaxing weekend doing chores around the house and washing my underwear. I'd always thought I would do my own laundry here (didn't want to "hire" the locals to do my dirty work), but after taking an insanely long time once just to wash my sheets, I realized at that rate I wouldn't wash them—or anything else—nearly often enough. So I swallowed my pride and started sending my large items out to a woman down the street who had of-fered her services from day one. I had to admit, everyone here had domestic help of some kind.

While I couldn't figure out why she insisted on ironing everything, I watched her do it one day and was amazed. She put some glowing coals into what looked like a small cruise ship with a handle, closed it, and then tested it the same way we would at home, by licking her finger and touching it to the hot surface: *sssst*. Man, that had to hurt! Without a dial to tell me the correct temperature for cotton, I knew I would burn myself—not to mention my clothes—many times over.

At home in the evenings I'd been throwing the I Ching a lot, but all it ever said was "don't cross the great stream," so I switched to tarot, where anything was possible and your future could change with the flip of a card. (I had a book to explain everything.) My favorite was the fool, who's about to step off a cliff because he's so absorbed in the "now." It reminded me of my favorite Buddhist story, about the Zen master being chased by a tiger. To escape, the master grabs hold of a vine and swings over the side of a cliff, only to see more tigers below. Not only that, but several mice start gnawing on the vine. At that moment the master sees a strawberry growing on the vine. He picks it and pops it into his mouth.

How sweet it is!

Reading *Slaughterhouse-Five*, though, was anything but sweet—how could the Allies bomb Dresden like that? But I loved Vonnegut's black humor and had picked up a couple of his books at the PC office the last time I was there... almost six weeks ago. Wow—hard to believe so much time had passed.

The "Amazing Balancing Baby."

For the next two weeks the office was a madhouse. I didn't stop for a minute, keeping track of everything in my spiffy new work notebook. It was a cardboard-bound one much like my journal (and also from Vargas's *despensa*) but about one-fourth as thick and with black polka dots instead of stripes. In a red box on the cover were the words "AVON Industria Paraguaya."

I recorded what I did in the mornings and afternoons, where the work took place, the project and activity names, numbers that corresponded with tasks on the monthly report form, and a brief description of the activity. I was determined to be prepared for Anna-í's site visit next month—for all I knew, I was on some kind of "watch list" for having created so much drama back in April.

The mornings were getting too nippy to do yoga—it was as cold inside my house as out—but I still met with Margarita for *mate* before breakfast. Dressed in her fraying baby-blue nylon robe, she'd brought out a small charcoal brazier to warm us a little as we sat in the foyer and savored the hot liquid. It tasted of bark.

"What *yuyos* are in the water today?" I asked, yawning and watching my breath become steam—I half expected it to freeze and shatter on the floor. Scrunched down into my upturned coat collar, my knit cap covering my eyebrows, I could barely see the guampa and bombilla in my right hand. (I had to be careful because on more than one occasion I'd nearly poked out my eye with the blasted silver straw.)

"I'll go look. I have to ask Josefina about something anyway." I thought about how healthy I was going to be when I got back home, my entrails in excellent running condition from all the medicinal plants I'd consumed.

Only four more weeks till the in-service! I'd been crossing the days off my calendar with a giant red slash like the proverbial prisoner. My two months in the campo had been rich and rewarding, but now I had a need to be around people who looked like me and talked like me, who didn't stare at me and ask so many infernal questions. I was more than ready to kick up my heels in a place where I wasn't such a freakin'...*freak*. I was also practically drooling over my upcoming shower at the Stella, which would be long and steamy—not lukewarm like at the pensión (though those days were long gone with the cold), but as hot as I could stand.

"It's *uña de gato*," Margarita said as she returned and startled me out of my reverie. "For the prostate. It's for don Pedro, you know."

No, I didn't know...or want to, for that matter. "Cat's fingernail." Nice—I wondered what it would do to *me*.

Just then some schoolboys passed by and caught my eye—they were sucking on those round white things I'd seen in Boquerón but forgotten to ask Velázquez about.

"What are those boys eating?" I asked. Margarita laughed.

"Be right back," she said and, despite my protestations, got up again and headed toward the kitchen. She returned with three oranges and the funniest-looking knife I'd ever seen—it was only an eighth of an inch wide at the tip but had a familiar-looking handle. I finally realized it was a butter knife that had been sharpened practically out of existence.

She sat down, got comfy, and without a word cut the top off a *naranja*, to the pith only, not all the way to the flesh. She then started peeling it from the top in a circular motion. The strips were about half an inch wide and peel only, no pith. She went around and around, keeping the orange portion in one piece that spiraled down, and reached the bottom after five or six turns. She cut off the long piece but left a tiny bit of peel.

The orange was now white. She held it up: "*¡Dale [DAH-lay]!*"

What an amazing concept! I'd never thought of eating an orange like that.

Margarita then sliced off the top, into the flesh, and handed the fruit to me. "Just suck and squeeze a little, but don't squeeze too hard or it will rupture," she warned.

So I sucked and squeezed just a little, and it immediately ruptured near the bottom. Margarita laughed and feigned a sad face. I had to scramble not to drip juice all over myself, now that I'd busted the thing.

"It's a skill you'll need to develop," she said, "eating as well as peeling it. Do you want to try?"

How hard could it be? I indicated I'd try after I finished the orange.

"When you're done sucking the juice, just throw the rest away," she said.

I objected: "But that's where most of the nutrients are."

She looked at me with mock disdain and said, "Don't worry. We have lots of oranges in Paraguay...you'll eat so many you won't know what to do with all the nutrients." There was no arguing with her, so I put the now crushed and sucked-dry white blob on the plate. She handed me the knife and a new *naranja*.

Despite my frozen fingers, I imitated her the best I could but barely got around once before cutting into the flesh. Feeling the challenge, I tried again on the same orange and cut through again. I reached for the last orange with a bit of frustration, determined to do better. But no sooner had I cut into the peel than the blade went through to the flesh, and juice squirted all over my shirt.

"Damn it!" I said loudly in English, startling Margarita. I had no patience for things I couldn't do well. It was obvious this "simple" skill would prove to be impossibly complex, like the others. I had to hand it to the Paraguayans—they were resourceful and proficient in their solutions to everyday problems.

I got up to go, and Margarita tried to console me with a smile. "You can practice on grapefruit—they have thicker skins."

She seemed to put a certain emphasis on the last two words. Was she saying my skin wasn't thick enough because I gave up so easily? I had to wonder about her sometimes—she was a practical joker. But I knew she had my best interests at heart. And of course she was right: my skin was so thin you could read a newspaper through it.

"Thanks, Margarita," I called in a cheerful tone to let her know I wasn't angry. "Hope your day goes well."

As the middle of June approached, Caazapá was abuzz with the upcoming fiestas, all being held the same weekend. On Friday the fútbol team 25 de Enero was celebrating winning the championship; I'd been to a few of the games so naturally felt obliged to attend. Saturday night was the famed Día de San Juan festival celebrating the town's patron saint. I was thrilled when Margarita told me Saint John was the saint of fire, my element—I was a fire sign born in the Chinese year of the dragon, which I thought was pretty cool. (Interesting that in Tucson, San Juan was feted for bringing on the monsoons.)

Don Pedro's saint day—also his birthday, of course—was a week later, June 29, but the party would be held the Sunday before, the day after the fiesta. I was stoked: I'd worked hard and now it was time to play hard...all in the line of duty, of course.

"Why are we having don Pedro's party a week early?" I asked Margarita one morning over *mate*.

"Because everyone will be here for the fiesta. Sarita's daughter Beba lives in Iturbe and is coming, as well as other people from out of town." The mention of Iturbe filled me with the usual heartache, but this time it was mixed with tenderness, not regret. I was relieved.

The first 4-C meeting in San José was well attended, though it started a couple of hours late...like everything else, it seemed. This "Paraguayan time" crap was getting old—I didn't want to hang around for hours and wait for people to show up. I had better things to do with my time.

Well, didn't I? Or was I just supposed to go along with how things were done here and, basically, accomplish nothing whatsoever? I was agitated by the time the meeting finally got under way but was able to get over it...the girls just made me laugh. Maybe I was becoming *tranquila, nomás* after all.

They elected officers, including Antonia as president, no surprise—like Silvio, she had leadership in her veins. I handed out membership certificates and proposed my idea to bring notebooks to the next meeting so the socias could write the 4-C pledge and song, as well as the soybean recipes we would be developing.

I was looking forward to teaching about cooking with *soja*, as I truly believed in its near-magical properties: the unbelievably high protein content with no cholesterol—no more need for unchewable, heart-killing beef—and the fact that the plants actually returned nitrogen to the soil. Plus, soy was versatile: you could eat the beans themselves, toast and grind them, make "milk" from them, use the residue from making the milk...the possibilities were endless. And of course we were encouraging the farmers to grow soy as a cash crop. What was not to love about it?

Well, the taste, for one. It was true people weren't too fond of it, not even most PCVs. I'd learned to like it in Japan. Now the challenge was to think of ways to masquerade the taste so Paraguayans would actually eat the stuff... which admittedly had even less flavor than mandioca.

The socias liked the notebook idea and were enthusiastic about studying nutrition. The meeting ended on a lively note as we ate the soy cookies I'd made and everyone found them "interesting." Well, it was a start.

The air in Caazapá was becoming positively charged: people were giddy, quick to laugh even more than usual and chatty as hell. Everyone wanted to know if I was going to the dance, which of course I was, with Margarita and the *chicas* from the pensión. (Chelo's beau didn't dance, apparently.)

"I'll be the *tomasita*," Margarita had told me the day before. I didn't feel I needed a chaperone, but that was okay—at least I wouldn't be going alone. Of course no local boy had invited me because I didn't know any, except for Dávila and Montoya from the pensión, who were, for all intents and purposes, "family." I was glad they'd left for the weekend; I couldn't imagine dancing with them, holding hands, our bodies touching…I mean, we were *friends*, I didn't want to ruin that. I did like to dance and was good at it, having been lucky to inherit rhythm from my parents, but I also knew of its seductive potential and was determined to avoid any contact that might seem encouraging.

The truth was I still had no love to give…and I feared my current state of solitude was only making me more reclusive.

People began arriving in Caazapá at the end of the week, and the place started feeling crowded. The pensión was a beehive, from serving customers to slaughtering the goat and chickens that would feed party guests on Sunday. Sacks of mandioca appeared, and Margarita ran around getting rooms ready. Sarita gave orders like an army officer, her small frame springing up everywhere, a hand-rolled *cigarro* either hanging from her lips or pinned between thumb and forefinger. (I loved how women of "a certain age" went around smoking cigars, a rite of passage I supposed—along with becoming downright bawdy, Lord have mercy!) Don Pedro came and went as usual.

A variety of gaily painted booths sprang up near the volleyball *cancha*, where the dance would be held. I could see we'd be enjoying arcade games, a greased-pole-climbing contest, and of course lots of fair food. (Margarita said there would be no firewalking this year for some reason, and I had to admit I was relieved.) For this special occasion, power would be generated until 1:00 a.m. The dance was at 9:00—*Paraguayan time?* I wasn't sure I could stay up if it started any later.

The soccer club party on Friday was pretty lame; it reminded me of junior high, with girls sitting on one side of the room and boys on the other. Being between two girls like that made it impossible to talk to one without turning your back to the other. I begged off early because Vargas was making us work Saturday mornings now.

It was actually fun at the office the next day as a steady stream of farmers passed through. I went home for lunch and took a nap.

Later that afternoon the band, a young group from Caazapá, started setting up their drums and amps and speakers. When they did the sound check, we could hear the *EEEEEE* of feedback from the pensión, just a few blocks away. The screech made us jump and filled us with excitement as we drank *mate*.

"What should I wear to the dance?" I asked Margarita.

"A dress," she replied immediately, knowing I preferred pants. "You want to dance the *polca*, don't you? You have to lift the sides of your skirts, like this." She got up and did a little dance right there in the foyer, holding the sides of her dress and, one side at a time, swishing the fabric in front of her with an up-and-down arc of her hand.

I stood up and imitated her actions as best I could with jeans on, holding an imaginary skirt and hopping from one foot to the other, one-two-three, one-two-three. We continued dancing for a few minutes and then sat down, a little winded but laughing. "You've got it," she said between breaths.

I went home to get ready and, yes, put on a skirt.

Before going to the pensión, I wandered around the booths and played for cheap prizes by trying to throw bean bags through small holes, knock down heavy objects with light balls, toss floating objects into moving bowls of water—just like at home—all to no avail. The musicians started tuning their guitars, my cue to pick up the girls. Off to my first dance! Margarita raised her eyebrows and nodded approvingly when she saw me. "Your *pollera colorada* is *i porã etereí*," she said with a wink.

We found seats at the edge of the *cancha*, which was lit up with strings of bare bulbs as if for a volleyball game. People were arriving, greeting one another, deciding where to sit, girls giggling nervously as boys talked in small groups and looked serious. Finally the music started, a slow song.

No one danced.

The band played another slow tune as married couples began shuffling to the floor. Boys started asking girls to dance, and I started dreading this a little. I knew all eyes were on me.

Finally a boy from the high school strode over. I stood up and, holding him at arm's length, started around the floor in the counterclockwise direction already established by the dancers. Dancing in a giant circle was different from anything I'd experienced, but it was amusing to pass, time and again, the same people sitting on the perimeter.

All of a sudden through the loudspeakers I heard "Feelings…"[44] (over that telltale descending fifth) and couldn't believe my ears: the guy was singing in English! I'd always hated that song with a passion, but in this context it was fantastic. I assumed the singer must know my language and decided to ask him after the dance. It would be great to have someone around who spoke *inglés*. A lot of people wanted to try theirs on me but were inevitably worse at it than I was at Guaraní. (Teachers here taught only *about* English, not how to speak it…you couldn't teach what you didn't know.)

The music started getting a little faster now, with guaranias and waltzes that sounded Mexican. Dancers began gliding around, many of the older couples so smooth they looked like one body. One man danced with his left arm stretched out toward the ground; Margarita said it was called the "chicken choke" in Guaraní, and I had to laugh—the image was exactly right! I'd seen Sarita kill chickens that way, twisting the neck as she pulled the head down.

The tempo got faster and faster, and now the band was playing polkas in Guaraní. They didn't stop between songs and the pace was wearing some folks out, including me. I danced with different guys but had to stop and rest a time or two. I tried to get Margarita to dance, but she refused.

"Mburicá," I teased her in a low voice. Chelo and Perla giggled. Margarita was pleased I'd remembered the word for "mule," her fondest term for me. She thought I was stubborn because I insisted on living by myself. She knew I mostly slept with my back door open—otherwise I would suffocate, as there was no ventilation.

"Aren't you afraid of snakes?" she'd asked me once, which I knew actually meant men. "Or Yacaré, the caiman who sneaks into a woman's bedroom to gain her favors? Or Pombéro?"

I'd tried not to laugh out loud; as far as I knew, there were no caimans anywhere near here. "Who's Pombéro?"

"He's a short, ugly man who messes up your yard. He lives in the forest and can make himself invisible. He also comes in your house and can impregnate you just by touching you."

---

44 Louis Gasté and Morris Albert, 1973.

Jesus H. Roosevelt Christ! Margarita couldn't be serious…though I had to admit it was a pretty convenient excuse for "miracle" pregnancies. "Don't worry, I'm not afraid," I'd assured her, and it was the gods' truth.

The polkas played on, and pairs of all types began prancing around the floor.

The *baile* had been going for about half an hour when the band kicked it up another notch and started playing merengue and Brazilian samba. Everyone, even Margarita, was dancing now. It was impossible not to move to this music—going around in a giant circle, dancing with no one in particular, with *todo el mundo*, shedding outer garments, stopping for a drink and to catch your breath, moving, shaking, around and around. I was in a trance.

One of the liveliest songs was a cumbia called "La Pollera Colorada," about a guy crazy for a girl with a red skirt, which struck me as hilarious since I happened to be wearing one. It seemed all the guys wanted to dance that one with me and kept tapping each other off, in what turned out to be somewhat of a spectacle. You couldn't go wrong wearing red around here.

At last it was over, and the band stopped for a break. Folks milled about while some kids played soccer with a burning ball. Chelo called it *"pelota tatá"* and said it was a tradition. The girls and I headed to the pensión to powder our noses. When we returned, the band was striking up again. The second half of the dance was just like the first, starting slowly, building, and then culminating in frenzy and abandon.

"Oh, my aching feet," said Margarita, still catching her breath after the last dance. I never even imagined she could move like that!

We decided to get something to eat before calling it a night. At one of the booths we bought some *mbejú*, which was like a pancake but with cheese and, of course, good old *almidón*. You just couldn't get away from mandioca in all its nefarious guises. I had to admit, though, mandioca was not only versatile, it also kept people from starving. There always seemed to be a piece of *mandi-ó* around to satisfy a hungry child. I just wished the stuff had more nutrients, was all.

Contrary to my expectations, however, the *mbejú* was delicious, hot and gooey.

Margarita got some *chipa kururú*, "toad," she said. I was relieved when I figured out it wasn't made with the meat of a toad, it just *looked* like one—it was hand formed and baked in a banana leaf in the coals, coming out covered with dark "warts." She said the word was composed of *kuru*, "tongue," and *rú*, "swollen." That could have described a frog as well, so I asked her what the word for that was: *yu-í*, completely different. Cool. Didn't someone say there were forty words in Guaraní for "sunset" or something? This language was definitely fun to learn.

I talked Chelo into going with me over to the *cancha*, where the band was breaking down. We introduced ourselves (they knew Chelo, of course) and shook hands. They said they knew who I was. I told them I liked their music, especially "Feelings."

"Do you speak English by any chance?" I asked the lead singer, Ernesto, who was actually pretty cute.

"No, I don't speak a word. I just learned the song phonetically, after listening to the record over and over. Did I convince you?" He grinned, openly seeking a compliment. He had nice teeth and looked to be around twenty.

"Yeah, it sounded great, just like the original," I lied, remembering with a smile how I used to turn off the song in disgust whenever it came on the radio.

"Everyone calls me Tito. I work in the local government office and am studying to be a lawyer."

Tito. Wasn't that the name of a dictator in Yugoslavia or something?

"Nice to meet you," I said, wondering why I hadn't seen him around. I was disappointed he wouldn't be serving as my English-speaking buddy.

Don Pedro's party on Sunday was fun, but I was too tired to stay long. It wasn't easy always being on display. I could hear the revelry from my house well into the night, so I knew he'd had a good time.

The afternoon before I was leaving for the in-service, Velázquez and I rode our bikes to Tayy-í to talk to Olimpia and some of the other former socias. I could see why the compañía was called "little *lapacho*"—the trees were becoming giant bouquets of pink or yellow. I felt minuscule, like Alice in Wonderland. I had to admit I was a little nervous—Olimpia had looked so fierce when I saw her from the Jeep that time, and the previous club had ended on bad terms. Would she be the Queen of Hearts, out to get me?

Outside Olimpia's gate, Velázquez and I clapped loudly—the Paraguayan doorbell—and she emerged from her home with a smile and welcoming arms. *Ndaipori problema!* She introduced me to her mother, two sisters (the older of whom had a new baby girl but no husband that I could see), and a brother; they all lived here together. The father had died some years before. Their home consisted of three separate structures joined in the center by a thatched dining area, all of which needed repair.

"It's been difficult since Papá died," Olimpia said.

I could relate to that, of course, though on a totally different level. Without a primary worker and provider, her family had to do everything themselves, a daunting task. People here in the campo didn't have jobs to go to—their only "job" was staying alive. They worked in the *chacra*, their home garden where they grew mandioca, corn, potatoes, and other edibles. If they were fortunate, they had a few other hectares (one hectare is 2.47 acres) to plant cotton or tobacco—or soy—for cash. Most had chickens and other animals that could be eaten but were better used to produce more animals to sell. Many families sold their milk and eggs, food they could certainly use themselves.

The word "subsistence" summed it all up. I wondered how they could ever get ahead. Yet people here seemed so upbeat—they must have had some hope for the future.[45] Olimpia was amiable and talkative, constantly smiling, full of life. And she took to me right away like an old friend, on a gut level, laughing and joking around.

By now people had started gathering. I saw several little girls, eight or nine years old and thin, carrying younger children on their hips, which they thrust out to the side just enough to prop up the toddlers with minimal effort. The weight must have been substantial, yet the girls transported their little charges—casually switching hips when necessary—as if they'd been doing it all their lives…which in a sense they had, through generations of women before them.

Of course the questions came fast and furious, and I saw how they tended to follow a pattern. The first, of course—after "Where did you get such blue

---

45 Gallup polls consistently rank Paraguayans the happiest, most positive people in the world.

eyes?"—was "Where are you from?" I got the by-now-predictable shooting-cowboy routine from some of the men when I told them I was from Arizona. Then everyone started shooting pretend pistols, shouting *"¡Los cowboys!"* and laughing hysterically. It was a reliable way to break the ice.

Then: "Do you like Paraguay?"

"Oh, yes, very much, it's beautiful, and the people are all very friendly." I meant that, of course.

They wanted to know how long I would be here, and when I said two years, they looked concerned and asked about my family. I assured them I stayed in close touch with my family, which of course wasn't true as I only heard from them several weeks after something had happened, and vice versa.

"Do you know how to drink *mate?*" This was a new one. I nodded. *Well, yeah, you just suck on it and give it back to the server.* "Do you know how to eat mandioca?" *Yeah, you just masticate it over and over until you can swallow it without gagging.* Why were they asking if I knew "how" to do these things?

I looked at Velázquez for help. He leaned over and said in a low voice, "They're asking if you *like* it." I laughed out loud. What a funny way to ask!

One of the men asked how much money I made. We'd been warned about this question in training, so I was prepared: "Not much!" (Laughs.) "I make enough to live and work here with you." That was the end of that.

They wanted to know how I could leave a perfectly good life in the United States to come here and be with them. *I often ask myself the same question!* I thought with a smile. "Life there is hardly 'perfectly good' right now," I told them, knowing full well that if they had a fraction of what people had in the States, they might think their lives were perfect enough.

"Are you Catholic?" someone asked. This of course always got tricky. How could I explain to them my belief that we were all God? I did believe in a higher power, but Catholic dogma and rituals meant nothing to me. I'd figured out I could tell people I was baptized—always amused to see the ripple of relief flowing through them—but then confess that, in truth, I was a Buddhist. End of conversation. Needless to say, I received few invitations to mass and could only hope that didn't get any tongues wagging.

Finally—it never failed—someone asked what everyone was really burning to know: "Do you have a boyfriend?"

"Yes," I said immediately, but they were undeterred.

"Is he Paraguayan?"

"No."

"Well, then, you need a Paraguayan one." It became clear that any *novio* who wasn't Paraguayan didn't count.

This discussion inevitably led to the big bang, whether or not I knew how to say "I love you" in Guaraní. The girls giggled and all said at once, *"Ro jhai jhú,"* and giggled some more. People always got a kick out of hearing me repeat "roh hah-ee HOO" after them, numerous times to get it right, to no one in particular—in their minds practicing for the real event, I supposed. I didn't have the heart to tell them the last thing in the world I wanted was a *novio paraguayo*.

This usually marked the end of the interrogation.

The girls had decided they wanted to have a club again and build fogones. Perfect. They were also willing to start with nutrition. *Excelente.* Velázquez and I nodded at each other, pleased with the day's work. The shadows were lengthening and people started to leave. Velázquez and I got up to go as well, when Olimpia's mother turned to me and said out of the blue, *"¿Te gusta leche?"*

Did I like milk? I didn't really drink milk a lot but I liked it well enough. *"Sí,"* I said. *"Me gusta."* It seemed a strange thing to ask, but I supposed it was just another question, something else they were dying to know about me for some reason.

Some Guaraní was exchanged that I didn't understand. They motioned us inside and I became a little edgy because, among other things, it was getting cold. *Why are they doing this?* I desperately wanted to go home and get ready for my trip to Asunción tomorrow. Then I remembered we were riding our bikes, which would take at least half an hour and seem like forever. Frustration began to percolate through me as we ducked our heads and stepped inside. *Come on, Velázquez, tell them we have to leave, please!* But he was as powerless as I.

They had me sit down at the table while Olimpia went into the kitchen. A boy around two with dirty shirt and no pants had followed us in; I wasn't sure whose he was and sat there staring at him staring at me. I kept trying not to look at his penis, which fascinated me—I'd never seen an uncircumcised one before. (Truth be told, I'd not seen much of the other kind, either.)

Olimpia suddenly appeared with the biggest glass I ever saw, which she placed on the table in front of me, beaming. The glass was full of a pearly liquid topped by a solid, inch-thick layer of white. I was speechless.

"Here's some fresh *kamby* [kahm-BÜH] for you. Look at all that cream." She winked. "Our cow gives the best milk around."

Everyone laughed and stood there watching me: Velázquez, Olimpia, her mother, her siblings, others at the door. The kid. I looked at Velázquez—he was smiling and nodding a little as if to say, "Go ahead and drink it so we can get out of here."

But how could I, when the person who *should* be drinking it, the *criatura* whose dark eyelashes were so thick and long they must have interlocked every time he blinked, stood there gazing first at me and then at the milk, impassively, as if bewildered by the sight of all that *kamby* just sitting there waiting for someone to drink it?

On the other hand, how could I offend my hosts by *not* drinking it? And why did they think I wanted it, anyway? I only said I *liked* milk, not that I wanted some. I certainly didn't want—or need—any right now. I hated to think about what they'd given up just to offer me all this…milk…damn it!

"This is for the *nata*." Olimpia handed me a large metal spoon. I had to admit I wanted to try the cream, as I'd never had it fresh like this before.

It was an agonizing few seconds, but all of a sudden I couldn't resist—I started spooning some of the *nata* into my mouth. The texture was otherworldly, like whipped cream at home only better, thicker, fresher tasting. When I broke through to the milk below, I took a swallow and was surprised how light it was. It had a faint grassy smell that wasn't unpleasant. To think it had recently come out of a cow!

I had a few more sips and spoonfuls and then, the path suddenly clear, handed the glass to the boy and helped him hold it as he took forever to drain it. I had decided it would be better to risk doing that and apologize for it later than to ask permission and be denied. I didn't know if it was right or wrong, I just knew I couldn't drink the whole glass in front of that little kid.

They looked a bit surprised but no one objected, and we said our good-byes. Pedaling up the road back to town, I asked Velázquez, "Why did they ask me if I liked milk and then bring me some? I didn't say I wanted any, just that I liked it."

He was out of shape and out of breath. "They don't mean *'Do* you like it?'" he wheezed. "They mean *'Would* you like it?'"

"But that's grammatically incorrect," I protested. "If they ask me whether I would like something they should say *'¿Te gustaría?'* not *'¿Te gusta?'* And I purposely said *'Me gusta,'* not *'Me gustaría,'* so they wouldn't think I wanted any."

I looked at him expectantly, but he just smiled and shrugged—there wasn't anything he could do about it. It was tearing me up, though. The contrast between feeling so peeved upon entering their home and then being shamed into humility at the magnitude of their gift was unsettling. To think I could've avoided the situation altogether if I'd only known.

If I'd only known. Well, I did now. From now on I would tell people I didn't like things. I wondered what else I needed to know about this place to avoid feeling inept. I hated creating awkward situations but seemed to excel at it. I was touched, though, by how the Paraguayans would go to any extreme, go without if necessary, to be able to offer a guest something worthy.

In bed that night I wanted to kick myself when I realized Olimpia and her family might not even speak Spanish that well. For the first time I truly understood how vital Guaraní was to people in the campo—and how isolating it would be for those who spoke nothing else.

The next morning, Thursday, I hopped the 10:30 Caazapeña and sat back in my springy seat to savor the six-hour ride to deliverance. I was starting to like being here but couldn't wait to see my compatriots. Tomorrow was the Fourth of July, and I would be partying with them like never before at the good ol' American Embassy. The week-long in-service would begin Monday.

Celebrating Independence Day in the winter seemed strange, but it certainly was cold enough. Over *mate* that morning Margarita had said it was five degrees Celsius, which when I went through the formula I was trying to memorize ("multiply by nine, divide by five, add thirty-two") came to a whopping forty-one degrees Fahrenheit. With no central heat, that was cold.

The bus left Caazapá behind in a cloud of red dust and headed north through Villarrica toward Coronel Oviedo, which had become a hub with restaurants and stores springing up along the highway. From there it was four hours to Asunción. I bought some chipa in Capiatá and it was okay. I realized the only thing I really liked about chipa was the anise—and the little "squeak" a fresh one made when you bit into it.

All the bus lines coming to Asunción from the interior had an office/terminal on downtown streets; it was handy to be let off so close to the Stella. I walked up the gentle grade, happy to be back in the bustle again. I ran into Ellyn checking in and we got a room together. She'd just come from the PC office.

"Did you hear about Vicki?" she said as we unpacked.

I looked at her. "No. What happened?"

"She just got kicked out."

My jaw dropped. I was filled with a mixture of shock and relief. "Why?"

"I guess she moved in with another volunteer in her site, a guy, as in 'relationship,' and Todd hit the ceiling. He almost kicked them both out, apparently. But Vicki offered to go so the guy could stay."

Wait—something wasn't right. Volunteers lived with each other, didn't they? Come to think of it, we *had* been told not to. But it wasn't surprising that Vicki couldn't live on her own; everyone knew she was helpless. Why would Todd react so...explosively? I was aghast and actually a little sad for her.

"What about Jessica?" I asked. "Will they possibly be able to live apart?"

"I think she's staying." Then: "You know, there are only eight of us now."

This time I had to sit down. What a blow—PCVs were disappearing left and right.

"Who else?"

She mentioned two girls and I wasn't surprised. I'd wondered from the start if they would make it—they just didn't seem very hardy. Let's face it, anyone who wasn't physically strong wouldn't be able to last long here. You had to ride a bike or horse into the campo. People here were constantly on their feet, sweeping, cooking, washing, laboring in the fields. And walking, always walking.

The job itself was taxing: gardening, putting on workshops, doing cooking demonstrations, forming clubs, creating leaders. And there were constant dangers, from snakes real or metaphorical to adolescents with Uzis. We were far from any medical service of the quality we were used to. How could anyone who wasn't robust survive it? For this reason I'd always worried about Miriam—she seemed so delicate. I didn't know how tough she was but was glad she was still holding her own.

"I'm sorry to see them go, but it ticks me off that they were first ones to choose the best sites and now there's no one in those places," I pointed out. "Some dedication."

"Well, everyone reacts differently, my dear," Ellyn said. "I believe you expressed an interest in going home a time or two."

She was right, I had. But I wasn't about to do that now, no matter how hard it got. Besides, if I went home, what would I do? There was nothing for me there. I'd be back where I started, agonizing over what to do with my life— might as well agonize over it here.

"I wonder why Todd was so hard on Vicki but not me," I said, "after all the grief I caused him a few months ago."

"Well, you *were* more cooperative during training," she reminded me.

That didn't seem like a compelling reason, but at the moment all I could think about was my long-awaited—not to mention overdue—hot shower, which at the moment seemed like an invention worthy of the Nobel Prize. When I stepped in, the hot water running down my body was so comforting that before I knew it I broke into tears, just let it all out, the joy, the sorrow, the whole spectrum of pent-up emotions I'd felt since being here, so far from home, from all things familiar. It was a release I needed badly.

Ellyn showered next. Thus renewed, we walked down to the Hotel Guaraní for a Pilsen Paraguaya.

I'd never seen so many PCVs gathered in one place as were at the embassy the next night—there must have been more than forty present to celebrate the birth of our nation, our *patria*, our *retâ*.

Even though it was winter, everything was outside so we could watch the fireworks. We ate burgers, brats, and dogs and then, because it was spritzing rain, squeezed under the entryway for the display. Despite the clouds we could see the sparkling red, white, and blue proclaiming dominance over the sky and drawing gasps from the crowd. America. So proud, so powerful...so potentially dangerous. I felt pride and mistrust in equal measure. Did we Americans really mean it when we pledged "liberty and justice *for all*"? Sure—until the price of bananas went up. I just hoped our country had the integrity I'd always wanted to believe it did.

I wondered what questionable activities we could be up to here.[46] "We." I knew what *I* was doing here. I also knew more than I wanted about "our" involvement in international conspiracies. What did "we" want from tiny, isolated Paraguay, anyway, other than to have our finger in every pie around the globe, telling every government what to do? What kind of despots were "we"? I mean, I valued good ol' Yankee ingenuity and all, but did we really have to be so self-righteous and control *everything*?

The more I thought about it, I couldn't help but ask myself who was more to be feared in the long run, Alfredo Stroessner or the US..."us"? I looked up at the windows of the Embajada Americana and wondered what really went on inside those smoke-filled offices. I loved my country and had to believe it meant well in the long run.

The term "meant well" rang hollow, though. What did it mean, if anything? It implied good intentions—though everyone knew where those could lead—but also an inability to carry them out, an impotence...a sign you were a non-contender. Now I understood what Dad meant when he told me he hoped no one would ever say about him, "Connor Creigh? Oh, he means well." He would rather have died.

You could also "mean well" but not really care. I believed Americans "cared" but were often afraid to see what was really happening in the world because of

---

46 At that moment, the State Department's Roger Channel was transmitting periodic top-secret messages from the top floor of the US Embassy. In 1976 the CIA began installing "Condortel," a "computerized intelligence database and telecommunications system" run by the US Army in the Panama Canal Zone, which helped Operation Condor affiliates more efficiently "coordinate transnational intelligence and operations"—that is, find and kill more suspected "subversives" (quoted from *When States Kill: Latin America, the U.S., and Technologies of Terror*, edited by Cecilia Menjívar and Néstor Rodríguez, Austin: University of Texas Press, 2005, p. 40). Other excellent sources are *The Condor Years* by John Dinges (New York: The New Press, 2004) and *Predatory States: Operation Condor and Covert War in Latin America* by J. Patrice McSherry (Maryland: Rowman and Littlefield, 2005).

the cushy lifestyles we'd come to expect, thanks in large part to "cheap labor" overseas. I was beginning to understand the implications of that term.

After an "aah"-inspiring grand finale that just wouldn't quit (amazing what a mixture of black powder and pyromania could do), a bunch of PCVs went to Diego's for a party. I got up the courage to play guitar and sing some numbers with the Texans and other musicians, who were into Jimmy Buffet and Jerry Jeff Walker. It was fun and better than talking about the Peace Corps and its short-comings—the favorite topic, it seemed, of many volunteers. A few were upset about Vicki's termination. When someone said Vicki might sue the PC, I knew it wasn't a conversation I wanted to get involved in.

What a disappointment—I'd expected a lot more "esprit de corps," so to speak. I loved being a PCV and was becoming more Paraguayan by the minute. In fact, just being in the city around so many gringos was starting to bum me out...and I still had the whole week to go. Talk about *Peyton Place*!

It was good to speak English, though. People talked fast, as if they were afraid they couldn't get it all out—about the end of the war in Vietnam, the horrific geno-cide by Pol Pot and the Khmer Rouge, and, on a happier note, Brazilian soccer star Pelé's signing with the New York Cosmos for the unheard-of sum of $7 million. Oh, and some nineteen-year-old college dropout named Bill Gates had started a computer software company. I had no idea what "computer software" even was.

Diego, solo as always, seemed to be enjoying himself. At one point I sat in a group listening to him describe a few variations in Spanish of *Cuerpo de Paz* (the *z* in Spanish is a hard *s*), which means "Corps of Peace" but could also mean "Body of Peace." The new interpretations were *Cuerpo sin Paz* ("Body without Peace") and *Cuerpo de Paseo* ("Body of a Leisurely Stroll"). After a few cervezas, the new names sounded hysterical and definitely described most of the PCVs I'd met—including myself at times.

Saturday morning I ran errands and discovered three treasures in a book-store: a Guaraní dictionary, a book on medicinal plants of Paraguay, and a pa-perback called *Land of Lace and Legend: An Informal Guide to Paraguay* published by Las Amigas Norteamericanas del Paraguay in 1965 and revised in 1969. It seemed quaint but was full of useful information about the country, geared to the American expat, with photos and drawings, suggestions for walking tours and excursions to the interior, forms of address, Paraguayan history and culture, arts, a primer of social usage…you name it. Rich.

Back at the Stella, I thumbed through *Lace and Legend* and learned that the streets here were named not only after patriots, countries, and dates— that much was obvious—but also famous battles, like Cerro Corá, where Mariscal Francisco Solano López died—the ultimate surrender—in 1870. And it turned out that Palma, Estrella, and Oliva, the three main streets in the downtown shopping district, were named for the three symbols on the Paraguayan flag.

There were several pages on *ñandutí*, the artwork I'd first seen at Teresa's, which had been introduced here by the Spanish hundreds of years ago. The delicate lace was embroidered over fabric in ornate and creative ways, using one of the more than one hundred motifs representing plants, animals, the sun… "forms symbolic of the agrarian life of the campesino." The fabric was then cut off. I decided I'd have to buy a large white *ñandutí* and have it mounted on black velvet, like I'd seen hanging on the wall at Ellyn's embassy friends' house.

Later that night I went with some PCVs to the Media Luna. Now, I'd always ridiculed discotheques and agreed with Tucson crooner Chuck Wagon that disco music *sucked*…but that night I had more fun dancing than I'd ever had in my life. Hypnotic black lights bent our minds as we drank caña and chanted "Rock the Boat"[47] like our lives depended on it. I was transported to a different world, one pulsating with bliss and infinite possibility.

We awoke in the morning to both our finitude and the ringing of bells from the cathedral. It seemed they just wouldn't stop as they pealed out a proclamation of glory and hope, sending it up past the clouds to the heavens and delivering it directly to the Almighty *Patrón* Up Above Himself. I loved those bells. Their mission aside, they lifted the soul…even as they split my head right down the middle.

At breakfast Ellyn said she'd met a guy from England named Steve who taught English here, and he'd invited us over for dinner on Wednesday. That seemed fine, as I'd already made plans to go to Teresa's on Thursday to catch

---

47 Waldo Holmes, 1973.

up with *Peyton Place* (it was broadcast twice a week now). I didn't really know why I wanted to watch it, probably because it was "home," *nomás*.

"Guaraní comes from the great linguistic family Tupí-Guaraní, whose fifty or so languages were spoken centuries ago throughout South America," Carmen began at 8:30 the next morning. "Today Guaraní has the distinction of being the only indigenous language in the world that is spoken by a majority of the population. It is not a written language, and there is much disagreement on the best way to write it."

We were at Monitor again, in Villa Morra. It had taken Carmen half an hour to get everyone settled. I was amused to see so many of the guys carrying around their own *mate* paraphernalia, much of it covered in leather with intricate tooling. Well, for Paraguayans it was definitely an addiction—benign of course, except for all the time lost drinking it—so why wouldn't gringos succumb to its charms as well? I pretty much had, though I couldn't imagine ever being that dependent on it.

Carmen continued. "In fact, Paraguay is the only nation where the language of the conquered not only survived, but became the language of the conquerors. Most Paraguayans, around 90 percent, speak Guaraní. We can thank the Jesuits for preserving Guaraní in their reductions in the 1700s, and our first great president, José Gaspar Rodríguez de Francia, for rejecting the Spanish colonizers and closing our borders in the nineteenth century, which allowed us to keep our language and culture protected from foreign imperialism."

So Paraguay really was an "island surrounded by land," as Diego had said his favorite Paraguayan author, Augusto Roa Bastos—who'd apparently spent his childhood in Iturbe—once wrote. Roa Bastos, whose 1974 novel *I, the Supreme* parodied Francia (and, by extension, Stroessner), had been exiled in Argentina for the last twenty-eight years.[48]

Polly looked around and said, "Don't forget, *Dictator* Francia also prohibited light-skinned colonials from marrying one another—they were only

---

48   Roa Bastos returned to Paraguay after Stroessner's overthrow in 1989 and was highly esteemed until his death in April 2005 at age eighty-seven.

allowed to marry blacks, mulattos, or natives." What a wild tale of reverse racism! I couldn't imagine a country in Latin America where having European blood didn't give you bragging rights.

"Yes, that was the situation for twenty-six years, from 1814 until his death in 1840," said Carmen. "I don't know how he enforced it other than by using his spies, which we call *pyragüés*, or 'hairy feet.'" Everyone laughed.

"Here's something interesting," she interjected. "The word 'tapioca' comes from the Tupí word for mandioca starch, *tipi'óka*. And the word 'jaguar,' *jaguareté*, comes from *jaguara*, which means 'beast' but is sometimes translated as 'dog.'"

Wait—weren't jaguars *cats*? Oh well, dog, cat, same difference…especially if one was planning to have you for lunch. (Was it true cats ate your entrails first?)

"'Dog' is really *jaguá*, though." It was incredible how similar they sounded.

"Guaraní has not stayed pure, though," Carmen continued. "It gets contaminated more and more by Spanish. We call the Guaraní that most people speak *jopará*, or 'mixture.' *Jopará* is also a traditional bean-and-corn soup."

It felt strange with only eight of us girls left. (The guys were down to fourteen.) We went around introducing ourselves in Guaraní and telling everyone as much as we could about our experiences. The exercise was over quickly, however, as we fumbled to express ourselves using only the present tense and the vocabulary of a five-year-old (at least we were moving up in the world).

"Gino"—funny how no one called him Duane any more—seemed to have learned the most. He said it was because of his Paraguayan girlfriend, which of course made us laugh. Well, he *was* adorable, with his shaggy brown hair, infectious smile, and endearing Texas drawl. (I noticed he'd shaved his beard.) It was just a wonder he'd narrowed down all his presumed prospects to one so quickly. He'd told us the funniest story before class, about a PCV who asked his Paraguayan family if they wanted to see his tattoo…and couldn't understand why they nearly died laughing until they told him that, in Guaraní, *tatú* meant "vulva." Good to know. I had no intention of ever getting a tattoo, especially now.

Carmen outlined the curriculum for the week: verb tenses and conversational Guaraní. She told us how Guaraní was like a train, with different time and space markers like rail cars that were simply added on. More difficult were the words that changed pronunciation based on surrounding words and their sounds. For example, "hot" was *jhakú* [hah-KOO] for I and you, and *rakú* for he, she, it. "But," she warned, "never, and I mean *never*, say *'Che jhakú'* if you're hot. You must say *'Nda che ro-yi.'*"

She blushed. "If you say, you know, what I said before…" She started giggling so much she almost couldn't continue. "If you say that, what you're actually saying is…well, let's just say you're…'ready for a good time.'"

Everyone hooted. So you couldn't just say "I'm hot," you had to say "I'm not cold," or else people would think you were "hot to trot." It was like not being able to say "I'm excited" in Spanish. All that pussyfooting around seemed ridiculous. But I had to admit, the last thing I wanted was for a *paraguayo* to think I was ready for a good time.

Or anyone else, for that matter. Thoughts about "the" party still sent waves of shame through me. Who here at the in-service thought *I* was *jhakú*? But I couldn't let it torment me—I just had to let it go. I immersed myself in the lesson.

At the end of the day Carmen said, *"Opáma.* It's over already," and we repeated it like a mantra as we headed out into the icy clear Asunción dusk. After seven hours of class and who knew how many rounds of *mate*, it was definitely cerveza-thirty.

"His name is Pastor Coronel, and he's head of the friggin' Office of Investigations here in Asunción," Ray—who had replaced Diego in Santaní—was saying the next morning at breakfast. Only a few of us were in the dining room as it was early, seven o'clock. "Emmy, you and Miriam met him at that party in Santaní."

I groaned. Who could forget *that* jerk?

Another PCV said, "Diego told us that Pastor Coronel once gave a bunch of new machetes to some men in Santaní who started going around brandishing them in public 'parades' to intimidate people."

Ray spoke in a low voice. "It may be—I've never seen them. But when I first got there, a guy told me he'd had to hide his cousin in a van and drive him to the Brazilian border because they'd heard that Pastor Coronel was out to get him."

Ray looked around the table. "I tell you, these people are *nuts*. It's said that shortly after Stroessner took power, in 1954, he held a dinner in Paraguarí, you know, on the road to Ybycuí. The dinner was for officials of the former regime, the opposition, to come together to form a new coalition. After the dinner Stroessner left, and his assassins moved in—and shot every last one of them. Dead."

I'd been spreading *dulce de guayaba* on some french bread and cheese when Ray's words sank in. I shuddered. *And they got away with it?*

Ray finished his coffee and stood up. "I'm just happy to say—and I know this is a minor accomplishment—but once, when I had the chance to shake the so-called generalísimo's hand, I declined. I couldn't do it. It wasn't much, but I felt good about it." Everyone was quiet as Ray excused himself and left the room.

My appetite left the room, too.

In class that day I learned how to ask people in the campo if they'd be able to come to our reunion (meeting, from *reunión* [ray-oon-ee-OHN]): "*Ikatú?* Is it possible? Will you be able to?"

I knew I'd get a lot of use out of "It's going to rain," and "It's raining already." But the determiners drove me batty: three words for "that," two for "those," two for "all," two for "other," all depending on whether you could see the objects or not... *Aaaggh...Help, Mr. Wizard!* (I hated to admit it, but the hapless cartoon character Tooter Turtle from *King Leonardo and His Short Subjects* was one of my earliest role models. "Twizzle, twazzle, twozzle, twome; time for this one to come home." Sigh.)

It was a lot to memorize, and I doubted I'd ever get really good at it, like Diego and a few other PCVs. I liked being in class, though. It was good having the guys around. Now we had the right balance of hormones...even if it *was* a little tilted toward the testosterone zone. What a shame they'd had to train in Costa Rica. Forget bonding with them; we barely even knew them. Training would've been so much better with them here to neutralize the acidity of the girls' group—no hope of solidarity there. *E pluribus...pluribus.* I wondered if the PC realized what a huge mistake they had made.

That evening Ellyn and I went to her friend Steve's. He was older and had a nice house in a neighborhood not unlike Villa Morra. He'd come from London to teach "proper" English, he joked, and was engaged to marry a *paraguaya* from a wealthy family, so he had to "beHIVE." He said we could stay at his house anytime we were in town—until he was married, of course—which was kind even though I loved the Stella.

After dinner—"Don't worry, the *chica* will clean up in the morning" (Did everyone here have a *"chica"*?)—we went into the living room for brandy in little round snifters. Steve put on a record. The initial guitar notes, melodic and strong, had me hooked. The first song lamented about the night leaving the singer without a soul and said something about throwing the horse in front and the soul in back.[49] I had no idea what it meant, but it was powerful. And it had a horse in it!

The second was a wrenching eulogy for a Bolivian miner who had died in vain, the third a song of love, albeit unrequited. I asked to see the album cover: Jorge Cafrune. Hmm, never heard of him. The album was titled *Siempre se vuelve*. I wondered where you always returned to.

Steve said Cafrune was a popular folksinger from the province of "Hoohooey" and got out a map to show us. Tucked into the far northwestern corner of Argentina, the province jutted into Bolivia and Chile. I studied the relief map, noting that around 80 percent of the province sat at three thousand meters, or (quick calculation) just under ten thousand feet! That was taller than Mount Lemmon back home, and we skied there in the winter. That must be one frigid place. "Jujuy" sounded like the noise you'd make if you were shivering and blowing into your hands, trying to warm them up.

Cafrune's album had been released earlier in the year. The head-and-shoulders photo on the front showed him sitting in leafy shade, wearing a loose white shirt and flat-brimmed white hat with black trim. He was looking off to his right and up at the sky with a slight scowl, his hand in a huge fist on his chest below his beard, which was thick and black with white filaments jumping out in relief. His countenance was angular, his eyes so dark there was no discerning iris from pupil. Cafrune was definitely old, probably in his fifties. I said as much to Steve.

---

49 Atahualpa Yupanqui (1908–92) and Nabor Córdoba (?), "La Añera" ("Ancient, Enduring," referring to longing, "la pena buena" [the good pain], the wandering narrator's only true companion); date unknown.

"No, I think he's only in his late thirties," he replied, "hard as it is to believe." Steve was turning out to be one of those human encyclopedias, something I was not. But how much of it was true? I raised my eyebrows and looked at him askance.

"Hey, research is my thing! Anyway, I think he was born in 1937, of Syrian-Lebanese descent, but he's known as 'El Turco.'"

I harrumphed. It figured that here in Latin America, where ignorance and racism ran rampant (from lack of education), someone from Syria or Lebanon would be called "The Turk." Still, it explained his prodigious eyebrows and long, straight nose, the right nostril of which seemed to be pulled back into a slight sneer.

He did look much older than thirty-eight, though it hardly mattered—he must have seen a lot in his day. His guitar playing was thrilling, how he mixed percussive Latin rhythms with individual notes like classical guitar. His voice was evocative, too, as he sang of people and places and love. It was the first time I'd heard the Argentine accent, the *zzhh* of the double *l* (saying "kah-BAHee-zzhhoh" for *caballo* [kah-BAHee-yoh] was just plain fun) and the dropping of the final *s* in many words, like the Paraguayans.

"Cafrune is famous in Argentina," Steve continued. "In 1967 he went around the country on horseback to celebrate Argentine culture and traditions. Oh, and in 1965 he introduced *this* lady"—he pulled out another album—"Mercedes Sosa, to the world at the Cosquín Festival, where he was performing. She was sitting in the audience."

Steve got up and turned the record over, carefully placing the stylus on the outside groove. The sound of the needle scratching silence was oddly comforting: sweet anticipation. Cafrune came in singing in three-quarter time about a guy named José Antonio riding a horse (the second song about a horse—you had to love it), and then I heard something that made me laugh.

"'Hippy HAHpa'?" I asked. Ellyn was nodding off on the couch.

"Yes, *jipijapa*! It does sound comical, doesn't it? It's the name of the palm-like plant used to make, quote, 'Panama' hats, which in truth are made in—you guessed it—Jipijapa, Peru. The hats became known as Panamas because years ago they were shipped there before sailing to destinations around the world.

This song is about the *Paso Peruano*, a Peruvian gaited horse that had been reintroduced after nearly disappearing."

I didn't know how I'd be able to handle all this new knowledge. But it didn't take long for me to fall in love with Cafrune and his music. The song "Fences: Lament of the Patagonian Indians"[50] was especially gripping, as was another poem Jorge recited, the anti-imperialist "To Roosevelt" by Rubén Darío, the fervor of which about knocked me out. It was either that or the brandy, which seemed to flow from a magical bottle with no bottom.

"Cafrune spent several years in Spain," Steve said, "some say in a kind of self-imposed exile—like who knows how many hundreds, probably thousands, of others. I think he may still be there."

It made me think of Flores, Roa Bastos, and the others. Exile, whether self-imposed or not, sounded devastating. With so many artists in that situation, where would it end? At least Cafrune's songs weren't outright protest songs, on this album anyway. They were also about love…and horses.

My favorite song was "Paisaje de Catamarca,"[51] which described in loving detail the landscape of a province southeast of Jujuy (I found it on the map) that was only 50 percent in the mountains and boasted a thousand distinct shades of green. I decided someday I'd just have to go to this paradise with little towns here and there, where a long road dropped down and got lost, where goat cheeses hung on ropes and the *chalchalero*—the rufous-bellied thrush, Steve informed me—practiced its song in a century-old walnut tree *(nogal)*. I was amused by the idea of a bird having to rehearse its song.

The last song was "A Jujuy Siempre Se Vuelve."[52] So *that's* where you always returned to, Jorge's birthplace. The first line, which he sang in the saddest voice ever, was "Jujuy, when will I return?…Life put me in chains, of the distance I'm a prisoner." I could certainly relate to that and started to tear up—music did that to me. Cafrune even sang about *lapachos* in bloom, and then in the refrain said if he died without seeing Jujuy again, he would ask the heavens to throw him down like rain and become flowers in her hills. A chill ran up my spine and lodged in the hairs at the back of my neck.

---

50   Marcelo Berbel (1925–2003), "Los Alambrados," date unknown.

51   Polo Giménez (1904–69), date unknown.

52   J. H. Chagras, date unknown.

When translated into English, Spanish can be sappy, but when understood viscerally, it's a direct conduit to emotion.

"I hope that's not prophetic," Steve said solemnly. He changed records, handing me the new cover: *Traigo un pueblo en mi voz.* Imitating an emcee he said, "And now, please give it up for...Miss Mercedes Sosa!" The cover photo, a black-and-white closeup of the singer, reminded me of my favorite album in college, Laura Nyro's *Eli and the Thirteenth Confession.*

Mercedes Sosa's singing was strong and defiant yet heartrending, her songs of outright protest. She really did carry a town, a whole people, in her voice (as the album title said), especially when she sang *"Cantaré, cantaré"* in response to the song's premise: "When the laborers have the land...I will sing."

I noticed one of her songs, "El Alazán," was written by A. Yupanqui, a name I thought I recognized from Jorge's album, which lay on the coffee table. I reached for it and checked: yes! A. Yupanqui wrote the first song, "La Añera," the one that had originally drawn me in.

"Who is 'A. Yoopankee'?" I asked.

Steve smiled at me as he would a child. "It's pronounced 'djoo-PAHN-kee.' Like 'DJAHN-kee'—what people here say for 'yankee,' by the way...and not in a flattering context, I might add."

Ellyn opened her eyes and looked at me; we had discussed this. As all PCVs, we truly believed we did not represent the "ugly" American. We were locals, not tourists, and as such did not expect things to happen like we were used to at home (or tried not to, anyway); we'd never make it here if we did. But all she said as she stood up was that she was going to the "loo."

"Anyway, the songwriter's name is Atahualpa Jupanqui, though that's a pseudonym—it's actually the names of two Incan emperors. He's indigenous, from Tucumán. 'Don Ata,' as he's called, performs too, of course—I understand he plays guitar left-handed, something you don't see much here. He was exiled for a few years in the thirties for being a communist and suffered under Perón's first administration—his songs were censored, and he was jailed a few times. I'm pretty sure he lives in Paris, but he returns regularly to Argentina."

It was starting to be too much information, and the possibility that I might remember any of it diminished with each *trago* of brandy. When Ellyn came back stifling a yawn, Steve started talking faster.

"Like don Ata, Mercedes Sosa was born in Tucumán; she's indigenous as well, so naturally she's called 'La Negra.'" I rolled my eyes. "She and Cafrune are part of what's called *nueva canción*, which is said to have originated with Violeta Parra, a Chilean singer-songwriter who sang about political issues but was driven to suicide in 1967 because the government sabotaged her ability to make a living."

That sounded all too familiar.

"These 'new song' members believe they can change the world through their music, which of course champions the poor and downtrodden…like your folk music in the States. The problem is, in Latin America they're still at it, while the rest of the Western world has pretty much moved on. Violeta wrote a song that's become fairly famous. Maybe you know it: 'Gracias a la Vida.'"

"Wait," I said. "Yes, of course! I heard Joan Baez sing it at the Greek Theater in Berkeley a few years ago. It's a beautiful song, so full of hope…how sad that Violeta could write a song thanking life for giving her so much and then not be able to endure it in the end."

Remembering the concert made me think of another song from that night, one that had haunted me all these years. "Joan sang something else in Spanish that I didn't understand completely," I said. "It was about Manuel…"

"Yes!" Steve jumped up, excited. "That's a song by Chilean Victor Jara, 'Te Recuerdo, Amanda' ('I Remember You, Amanda'), from 1968 I think, a powerful ballad about the death of a laborer by his unjust *patrón*. Very touching love story. It's become an anthem for class struggle." He poured himself more brandy and offered us some, but we declined. Ellyn went to the kitchen to call a cab.

"Ah, Victor Jara." Steve sighed as he sat back down. He sipped his drink and then leaned forward, his pale Anglo-Saxon face suddenly crimson.

"Victor Jara…a talented, cultured singer-songwriter, playwright, college professor—Victor Jara was invited by England to visit fucking Stratford-on-Avon, for crissakes! He was also part of the *nueva canción* movement with

Violeta Parra…that is, until he was assassinated by Pinochet, grand puppet of the United States of Hypocrisy."

That hurt, but I couldn't deny it: I knew it all too well now.

"Victor Jara," Steve continued, choking up. He took a gulp of brandy. "I can't even say it. Witnesses said an officer—after torturing Victor in one of the fútbol stadiums in Santiago where, as I'm sure you know, thousands of innocent people had been taken and hundreds executed—actually took the butt of his pistol and *broke* Victor's hands and then taunted him, saying 'Go and play and sing for your people *now*, filthy communist!' And do you know what Victor did? He started singing 'We Shall Overcome,' can you believe it, 'Venceremos,' for which he was thrown into the street and shot…forty-four times."[53]

Steve turned to me, his eyes as red as his face. "Forty-four fucking times. He would've been buried in a common grave if someone hadn't recognized his body three days later and notified his wife, Joan, to come claim it." Steve got up and went to the kitchen.

And just for being a folksinger! God, I hated this. It was so difficult to open your eyes to the truth. Blinking back tears, I began studying Mercedes Sosa's album cover. Two of the other songs were "Brother, Give Me Your Hand" and "Agrarian Triumph." She was definitely putting herself on the line with these.

One thing for sure: the stakes for getting involved in politics here were prohibitively high. And just for being a musician or writer—of course, the pen being mightier than the sword and all—but what would happen to Jorge and Mercedes? I worried more about Mercedes because her songs more openly protested the way things were, unlike Jorge's, which seemed more "folksy," extolling the virtues of the land and such, relatively safe material.

Ellyn returned with Steve, who was blowing his nose. He said he wanted to play one more album while we waited: *Los Chalchaleros*.

---

53 In 2012, Chilean judge Miguel Vásquez charged several officials in the murder, including Pedro Pablo Barrientos Nuñez, a graduate of the School of the Americas in Panama, who has been fighting extradition from his home in Florida ever since. On June 27, 2016—forty-three years after the fact—a Florida jury found Barrientos Nuñez guilty in a civil case brought by Victor's widow and family; the verdict could pave the way for his extradition.

"Ah," I said, "the songbirds!" He nodded. The first song was "De Mi Esperanza"[54] ("Of My Hope"), a *zamba*, a term I'd noticed on the other two albums. I asked Steve what it meant.

"It's not the same as the Brazilian samba with an *s*. The zamba with a *z* is the national dance form in Argentina. This song is an homage to the zamba, which may or may not be a metaphor for a woman...and perhaps even for *la patria*, the fatherland."

I turned the album over and read the song list, impressed to see that two of the zambas were written by none other than A. Yupanqui. These Argentine folksingers really stuck together. I would definitely listen to this album the next time I came over to Steve's.

By the time the taxi arrived, my head was throbbing, and the zigzaggy ride home didn't help. At the Stella I took two aspirin with plenty of water to ward off a hangover—a trick I'd learned in Battle Lake—and fell into bed, the ceiling doing loop-de-loops as I lay there thinking how I liked staying at the hotel but would easily give it up to hear those albums again, especially Jorge's. I was truly smitten with the man, his talent and courage.

Surely his fame will protect him, I thought, as sleep overtook me.[55]

It was cold the next night as I walked from the bus stop to Teresa's, and it seemed colder still inside the house. Rafael was out of town, the kids sleeping. Tere was flush with excitement because tonight was the season finale of *La Caldera del Diablo*. She sat on the couch covered with a blanket, her eyes glued to the screen.

The opening showed a snowy, moonlit night with storm clouds brewing, looking kind of like how it felt here. The first scene took place in a prison—some guy named Elliot Carson who had murdered his wife (though he claimed innocence) was trying to get parole. Weird. Then it turned out he was Allison's father! *Constance, what were you thinking? The guy isn't even good*

---

54 Luis Morales, date unknown.

55 Two and a half years later, on February 1, 1978, Jorge Cafrune was assassinated by Argentine military police after singing "De Mi Esperanza" (by then a banned song) by request at a music festival; he was forty years old. His remains are rumored to be buried in Jujuy. Mercedes Sosa died of semi-natural causes (organ failure) in 2009 at age seventy-four.

looking! And might you by any chance know who killed his wife? Pretty heady stuff, but way too gloomy.

Everything else in Peyton Place seemed to be falling apart as well. I figured this would be the last episode I'd watch. Who needed all those extra problems? It *was* like real life, though, in that the problems never went away—they just kept piling up until they buried you alive.

Late Friday afternoon, the last day of the in-service, Diego showed up at Monitor at last, his soft laugh and interminable cigarettes a kind of welcome consistency. Revered by the guys as much as the girls, Diego continued to enjoy near rock-star status.

A bunch of us decided to go out to dinner, which was of course a fiasco just deciding where to go—ten heads were definitely not better than one. I sat back knowing someone would eventually take charge; I just didn't feel the need to force my opinion on anyone. Finally it was settled: Chinese. I realized I didn't particularly want Chinese but was obliged to accept it, as I hadn't bothered to put in my own two cents.

We'd finished ordering and were nose deep in our *chopps* when Diego got everyone's attention. "Say, I don't suppose anyone has told you how to tell how long someone has been in the Peace Corps…?" He looked around, eyebrows raised over his black plastic glasses, and we all shrugged. Just then his soup arrived, fragrant and steaming.

"All right. Now, if you have just started in the Peace Corps and you find a fly in your soup, what do you do? Yes, quite right, you send your soup back and order a new one. Now, once you've been a PCV a little longer and you find a fly in your soup, what do you do? Correct, you simply remove the fly and eat the soup. However, you know you've been a PCV too long when you get your soup"—he paused for maximum effect—"and you *ask* for a fly to go with it!" We all groaned and chided him a little for that silly joke.

He continued. "I just want to congratulate all of you for completing three months of service…" Wild applause and clinking of glasses. "*And* your first in-service." More cheers. "The staff and I wish you the best of luck, and remember, we're always available if you need us."

It felt really good to be here with everyone. But there was discord, too, people still talking about the early terminators and Vicki's possible lawsuit. There was too much drama in Asunción, I realized, too much noise period, and I was suddenly overcome with a desire to get back to the quiet of the campo... well, the barking dogs and crowing roosters of the campo (which I'd discovered crowed any damn time of night or day, not just at dawn like we'd been tricked into believing at school). For the first time I felt a sharp longing for my home in Caazapá and my life there.

I'd be on the bus tomorrow.

As we were leaving, Ellyn suggested we all take the ferry to Concepción after the next in-service for Thanksgiving and my birthday. I couldn't think of a reason not to—surely there was no way I could get seasick on that thing.

PART IV

MY MOTHER'S DESPERATE STRUGGLE

—⟊—

MARTÍN

It changes your life, the search for truth.

Ben Bradlee (1921–2014)
Executive editor of *The Washington Post*, 1968–91

My arrest, the death of my wife, the dispersion of my family, and the looting and confiscation of my belongings came as a shock to my mother in Buenos Aires. She was there with my brothers, Asunción ("Papi") and Rutilio, both economic exiles.

I was being held at the First Precinct when my mother returned to Paraguay. From the moment she arrived, the authorities tried to break her spirit every chance they got—asking her to give up, telling her nothing could be achieved by her coming and going, assuring her she was fighting a losing battle. And they nearly succeeded.

On one occasion, an influential military man told her that, unfortunately, it wasn't a case of a criminal offense, homicide, robbery, or smuggling, matters that could be easily settled. It had to do with something much worse: Martín Almada was a communist, and not only that but a guerilla commander as well, who had ties to Argentine terrorists. My mother, who came from a strong Catholic background and traditional Colorado family, could not understand why the government was being so hard on her son, whom she knew to be incapable of involvement in such activities.

Nevertheless, the authorities succeeded in planting doubt in her mind. They were aware of this and put pressure on her to convince me to write a letter to Pastor Coronel in which I expressed remorse about having been active in communist affairs. They convinced her that if I sent the note, I would recover my freedom, my belongings, and the directorship of the Juan Bautista Alberdi Institute.

"I would rather die than take part in that farce," I told her. "I have nothing to feel remorseful about."

"Does that mean you're a communist, as they say?"

"He who sows wind reaps tempests, and the winds that are coming will sweep away Stroessner and all his henchmen," I said. "The phantom of communism doesn't fool anyone anymore—it's nothing more than a smokescreen they use to commit their crimes. The night of my arrest, on the pretext of looking for weapons and subversive books, the police seized the wages of the institute staff, due to be paid the next day, as well as the children's harp, household appliances, my encyclopedias and law books, typewriters, and some of my clothing. That was the first step. And you know, Mamá, how this looting continued: they also appropriated the plot of land that Celestina and I bought near the road to Asunción. And this is what the lowly *pyragüés* are doing. Among the leaders, things are much worse."

My mother went back and forth like a pendulum. "You may be right, Martín. That's how they treated the campesinos of the Agrarian League in Jejuí. They not only injured Father Maciel and killed several farmers, but they also stole the league's funds."

"Furthermore," I said, "my personal experience with the communists here has convinced me we have more in common than not..."

She interrupted violently: "Communists are atheists and traitors! They are against family values and want to sow confusion."

"But Mamá, you're just repeating what they say every day on *La Voz del Coloradismo* (The Voice of Coloradism) on Radio Nacional. Those are arguments Stroessner has used since 1954, but no one takes them seriously anymore."

She looked at me with a dubious expression.

I continued. "Think of what is happening in Europe. The communist, socialist, and Christian democratic parties participate in the political life of the countries. All these parties fight for the demands of the people and to defend human rights. You should also know that these countries maintain diplomatic ties with the socialist world. Stroessner is going the wrong way by isolating himself from the newly emerging societies. Think for a minute about the countries he has visited on 'goodwill missions'—South Africa, Chile, Uruguay, Argentina, Nationalist China. In all these places, people are muzzled and gagged, prisoners of terror and tyranny."

"Poor Martín, you seem very fanatic. You don't think of your mother."

"Please, Mamá, look at these mothers in mourning, these orphaned children in prison with us.[56] Do you know why their parents were murdered? Simply because they dreamed of a climate of national reconciliation and social justice, because they wanted to put an end to corruption and assassination."

The minutes passed quickly, and the guard reminded us our visit was over.

---

56 The practice of imprisoning children with their parents, while reprehensible, was not uncommon at the time.

The authorities told me repeatedly that I needed to change my "antisocial behavior," and my mother suffered from the accusations they brought against me. According to them, I was a typical *kupi-i* (termite). That pained her, and I saw that she was starting to be influenced by the official propaganda, whose diatribes she repeated in our conversations. My first task was to convince her that the real extremists, the provokers, were not us but the ones in power.

"Mamá, you know I became a member of the Colorado Party because of my democratic vocation, because I thought it represented the best way to put an end to injustice in our country. I have always opposed violence, and if I am here, it is not because I have harmed anyone, but because I envisioned an educational system in which everyone would have the same opportunities."

My mother still looked doubtful but listened with apparent interest.

"I have full confidence in the Colorado nation, *in the people*, those just like us who have been betrayed and put in chains. Until now we've been subjected to the caprices of a tyrant who calls himself a Colorado, but that won't last forever. You lived in Buenos Aires, you've seen for yourself the thousands of Paraguayan exiles there. That is true state terrorism."

The firmness of my convictions began to inspire confidence in my mother, but this process was not constant. During one of her visits to the Third Precinct (also known as the "Tomb of the Living," where I would be taken in May 1976), she asked who was with me in the visitors' room. I told her it was Professor Julio Rojas.

My mother began to cry. "Merciful Jesus! You're sharing a cell with communists! There's no hope for you." The general opinion was that sharing a cell with communists was the same as a life sentence, so my mother assumed I would remain there for the rest of my life—and that was why she had insisted that I sign the infamous letter of remorse.

On another of her visits, my mother told me I was in the Tomb of the Living because of my late wife. "My dear son, you must convince yourself that she led you down the wrong path. I know you are not a communist, but they tell me she was *puro, puro* ("pure, pure," a popular expression synonymous with "militant communist"), that she was a key member of an extremist group." My mother had fallen into a trap the police set for her. I begged her to trust the words of her own son and respect the memory of my wife.

The police also did everything they could to sow hatred between my wife's and my families. When a relative from my wife's family came to visit me, an official would approach and say behind my back, "Celestina died because of this terrorist. She was a good woman. He killed her with the grief he caused her." And when my mother came, they would say to her, "Dr. Almada is a highly respectable man, but his wife was up to no good, getting involved with the communists. That's why they've locked him up."

So great was the pressure on my mother to convince me to write the letter that one day she arrived and told me, between sobs, "We are so alone. Everyone closes the door in my face. We are going hungry. No one wants to take on your defense. Just yesterday Dr. Latorre threw me out of his office. I don't know if I will be able to come visit you anymore because I don't have enough money for the bus."

"No," I said. "We are not alone. We share the fate of an entire country. What seems to you like the neighbors' indifference is not that but fear—fear institutionalized by the dictator. In the end, the poor people will recognize who is on their side. If I signed this letter I would be lying, and you always taught me to tell the truth."

It was an opportune moment for me to explain to her that all change entailed sacrifice and ours would bear fruit, that the evil and suffering of the country were temporary because the contradictions within the regime were so apparent. After tears and hopeful smiles, we hugged good-bye and I went back to my cell.

My words turned out to be prophetic. A few days later, I learned that a group of my former pupils' relatives and friends had gotten together to provide for my family's and my basic needs. It started with visits from the mothers of former pupils, which raised my morale. To be admitted, they made up some relationship to me, which was not without risks. I remember with fondness my "aunts" Isabel, China, Modesta, and Esther.

Because of the miserable prison food, my health was very poor, my stomach and eyes particularly affected. Fortunately, the Committee of Churches joined with the community of San Lorenzo to provide better food for me and take the first steps toward restoring my freedom. I began to receive food sent by the retailers of the municipal market in my town. This gesture gave my mother new energy, and she told me of the activities surrounding this small popular mobilization.

Throughout this difficult struggle, my mother acquired a better understanding of the social problems of Paraguay. Her daily contact with the parish and frequent encounters with relatives of other citizens who shared my fate contributed significantly to her political evolution.

One day I entrusted my mother with the mission of determining the legal status of the Alberdi Institute, and she carried out her task with distinction. I emphasize this accomplishment because, until that time, my mother had been utterly incapable of approaching an authority to ask a question.

She discovered that our institute had been taken over by the Ministry of Education and Culture. The persecution by Stroessner and his cohorts had translated into a resolution to do so (No. 1316, December 19, 1974), decreed thirteen days after the death of my wife—who had not only founded the school but was its general manager. Even more surprising was the reason given: the "total abandonment" of the institute. (I had also lost my job as secretary general of the School of Agronomy and Veterinary Science at the National University—a post I'd held for twelve years—with no explanation or compensation.) The ministry had assigned the positions of director, administrator, and secretary to various professors, and the new administrative secretary appeared as "owner-director" of the institute.

The new director took drastic measures to show San Lorenzo that a new and different period was beginning, under the indulgent gaze of the Ministry of Education and Culture and the director of secondary instruction. These initial measures included (1) the eviction of my relatives and some scholarship recipients who lived in one area of the institute; (2) the dismissal of teachers who had remained loyal to me, at least one of whom had to go into exile; (3) the termination of numerous scholarships we had awarded over many years to children of deserving employees; and (4) the obligation that my daughter,

Celeste, pay monthly tuition if she wanted to continue her studies at the institute. Obviously, our tragic family situation made this impossible, and she was left with no school.

The National Development Bank, for its part, took legal action to demand repayment of the line of credit I had obtained to build the artisan workshops. (Nevertheless, the Committee of Churches of Paraguay took several steps to avoid this damage, which would have had social consequences beyond hurting me because it would have prevented many young people from learning a trade.) At the same time, most likely to stay in good standing with the police, the Adventist schools in Misiones and Puiggari closed their doors to my sons, Ricardo and Lincoln, for falling behind in their monthly tuition payments.

I also asked my mother to investigate the death of my wife. The authorities had told me she committed suicide, but I was not convinced.

"She did not commit suicide," my mother said. "She died of grief as a result of the psychological torture she was subjected to. Every night they telephoned her to tell her the details of your torture. The calls came directly from the torture room. They made her listen to your voice, your desperate screams."

My mother stopped and swallowed. "The stress was worsened by the 'anonymous' calls the poor dear received from at least five people, who said they had cut off your fingers, gouged out your eyes…torn off your testicles… and other such things. At midnight on December fifth, they called to tell her the 'subversive educator' was dead, and to come pick up your body. The shock of this affected her heart, and she collapsed. Her family called Dr. Weiss, who promised to come at once, but he didn't keep his promise. The public is aware of the crime that has been committed."

We spoke of it no more.

I subsequently found out about events that had occurred immediately after Celestina's death, which pained me terribly. Former coworkers who took over as new owners of the institute had not treated her or our family well. In addition, I discovered that Celestina had asked a student from the institute to bring me food in prison. One day the student brought back my blood-soaked clothes with several enormous needles stuck in them. For Celestina, this was proof of what the people on the phone had been telling her—she was convinced these were the needles they had used to pull out all my nails.

I was moved to the Emboscada concentration camp in September of 1976. After a few weeks of calm, the police attacked me on another front. The fact that some programs of Radio Moscow and Radio Havana had mentioned me and demanded my freedom constituted for them the strongest proof of my "involvement in international communism." In addition, Amnesty International and Colorado exiles in Buenos Aires were carrying out an intense campaign on my behalf, which exasperated the officials even more.

Prison commander Colonel Grau accused me of a new crime, that of indoctrinating Celeste—who was eight years old at the time and out of necessity staying with me in Emboscada for two months—into Marxist-Leninist thought. As a result, the food and water sent by my friends disappeared, and my mother was routinely held up at the gate for two or three hours.

Around 4:00 one very hot summer afternoon in 1977, my mother visited me in an extremely nervous state. She told me she had spent the night near the prison camp in hopes of visiting me early. She'd appeared before the guards at 6:00 a.m. but was denied entry. Without getting discouraged, she went back every fifteen minutes, but the guards turned her away, saying "The one to blame is your son and no one else," until she finally wore them out and was allowed to see me.

Later, I found out why the police had punished her so. She'd been informed that I'd received neither the ten-liter cans of water nor the food that had been sent to me. This infuriated my mother, and she reacted strongly to the officer in charge, whom she called a "torturer and crook" to his face. The officer did not miss the opportunity to explain things to her in these terms: "It seems the communists have finally won you over to their cause and enlisted you in the ranks of their dupes." And out of revenge he subjected her to more than nine hours of waiting under the burning sun.

None of these humiliations daunted her.

From comments she made about events in the world outside, I could see the stages of her evolving awareness. But one day she surprised me when she said, "Stroessner is not aware of the living conditions you are suffering under here in Emboscada, nor does he know that the officers are helping themselves to the little food and water sent to you. The bad men are the ones surrounding him."

I tried not to lose my patience. "Mamá, it's time you opened your eyes once and for all. In Paraguay, nothing is done without Stroessner's consent. He is informed about everything here in Emboscada, and he is the one who gives the orders to add to our suffering and that of our relatives. Since 1954, Stroessner has been buying and bribing those officers who are not submissive enough to him, and rewarding those most loyal, particularly those who excel at the work of repression. The dictator has yet to learn the lesson of history, which is that repression is useless and cannot be used to impede the people's progress." My mother listened attentively despite the noise in the family visiting area.

"Take Commander Grau, for example," I continued, "the owner of many properties including, lately, a modern ranch in the San Pedro district. Señora Juana de Soler, who used to own that ranch, now shares this miserable place with us. She may still hold title to the land, but Grau is the one who has the animals." There were many instances of this kind of land expropriation.

I sensed that my mother was beginning to identify with our struggle.

The prison authorities accosted my mother one day to tell her that I was completely crazy (or acting as though I were), my behavior was aggravating my situation, and, as a result, I would never regain my freedom. "Your son has a good chance to go free," they told her, "but instead of cooperating with us, he's doing the opposite."

"What do you want?" she asked.

"You have to convince your son there's nothing to be gained by defending the campesinos. We have received orders that the farmers are to work in the quarry and contribute to the clearing and harvesting of the prison's sugarcane field. Your son has allied himself with the communists, who are against this work."

"It's a matter of forced labor, isn't it?" she asked.

"No, señora, the farmers want to work but, incited by the communists, your son among them, they are now resisting. We don't want to use violence—do you understand?"

My mother explained the problem to me and said, "I want you to tell me one thing: What exactly are you trying to do? Don't you realize you are harming yourself and dragging us all into an awful ordeal? It's time you calmed down once and for all. Why do you let yourself be manipulated this way by the communists and oppose the farmers' working?"

"Mamá, the authorities are trying to confuse you so you will tire out and abandon me. They are lying to you. The truth is that Colonel Grau and his fellow repressors are making a profit off the farmers' work. Did you know that all the stones from the Emboscada quarry are sold to the Spanish company building the bridge over the river in Remanso Castillo? All of us have been physically destroyed by repeated torture, and our situation is made worse by the bad food and lack of water. For these reasons, and also out of principle, we cannot accept that anyone work in the quarry or Colonel Grau's sugarcane fields."

She was indomitable. "If you continue like this, no one is going to help you. I believe what you're saying, but there's something else bothering me. If the authorities moved you from the First Precinct to the 'Tomb,' where you shared a cell with the communists, there must have been a reason. And the same thing is happening here in Emboscada. First you were in a cell with people who did not cause trouble, and now you are with the communists again. And all because of your bad conduct."

This conversation took place in the shade of a stunted mango tree in the middle of a sad and desolate landscape. A barbed-wire fence divided the large dirt courtyard into two parts, one for the men and the other for the women and children. A few meters away, "political prisoners" from eight months to fourteen years old were playing in the hot sand.

"You say you are a Colorado," she said, looking me over.

"Mamá, I assure you I am a Colorado, just as I can assure you Stroessner is *not* a Colorado. He built his own branch of the party that today is in crisis and, in its agony, is trying to drag us all down into immorality. To oppose or criticize this regime of corruption is a mortal sin. Stroessner's ideology is a form of fascism and opposes the principles of freedom and equality upheld by *my* party, the National Republican Association. Those who follow Stroessner do it either out of political blindness or because they are afraid of losing their privileges."

She got tired of this and left.

On one occasion, the prison director's chauffeur told my mother that he knew a competent lawyer who could secure my freedom for a small fee, only 100,000 guaranies (about $800). In the days that followed, other offers poured in. A famous "prosecutor" who worked with one of Stroessner's nieces promised my mother she would get me released if I deposited the sum of 300,000 guaranies into that niece's bank account. Another lawyer, a man reputed to work with one of Stroessner's mistresses, offered me my freedom for the sum of 500,000 guaranies.

It was obvious the "presidential family" did not have the slightest idea of our dire financial situation. But collusion in the freedom of prisoners—both political and common—by those in power had become an institution in Paraguay. I responded to the offers with a categorical "no," which brought on new repressive acts intended to break my mother's spirit.

The prospect of my freedom suffered many ups and downs, but one day it all came to a head. My mother had begun appearing every day at the Ministry of the Interior. She would arrive at 5:00 a.m. and ask to be received by the minister, and would not move from that spot until the guard took her away. Tired of her insistence, the minister finally received her. Following his usual policy, he tried to frighten her with shouts and violent gestures. Months later, my son Ricardo, who was present at the interview, told me what the minister had said.

"Martín Almada is a traitor, a communist infiltrator in the ranks of the Colorado Party. Look here, señora, at the reports I get from Emboscada. Your son is incorrigible. Together with the communists, he has stirred up disorder and anarchy. And you, señora, will not work with the authorities to get him to stop making things worse for himself. We are being very patient with him. But he has no appreciation for the humane treatment offered him at Emboscada, and we will have no choice but to send him back to the Third Precinct to learn his lesson once and for all."

That afternoon my mother went to see a lawyer who had made promises to her. During the conversation the lawyer said, "I have done everything possible to help you, señora, but it has all fallen through, and it's your son's fault. The police chief told the interior minister that your son is a rabid communist and nothing can be done about him. The case of Martín Almada is closed. His behavior compromises everyone, you, his children—and it can even harm me in my professional career. I must ask you not to come back here."

When my mother saw me again, she berated me. "Why do you let yourself be manipulated by the communists? You are stubborn. You won't gain anything by confronting the authorities—they are fed up with you."

I tried to remain firm in spite of her tears. "Mamá, you educated me in the principles of the Gospel, and I have done nothing more than try to apply them. Do you think it's a crime to demand a minimum amount of humanity in our prison conditions? Stroessner wants to prevent us, the political prisoners, from uniting, and calls anyone who resists a communist. But we are not going to get caught in that trap because we know very well the foundation of our action is unity, solidarity among Colorados, communists, Liberals, and Christians. That is the best guarantee for victory."

"Martín, if you go on talking like this to these people, they will lose patience with you. How long will you continue to suffer?"

"Mamá, you mustn't be blinded by my personal situation or intimidated by the authorities' threats. The military dictatorship is punishing us now, but tomorrow the people will be rewarded. And what's more, consider this: while Stroessner accuses us in every possible way of being assassins, communists, disruptive, and unpatriotic, the Committee of Churches of Paraguay shows its solidarity with us and our families through its assistance. Who do you think is right? Bishops, monks, and Protestant ministers come to see us every week without fail. Would they be with us if our cause were unjust?"

I held her in my gaze and continued. "Not one of us has been excommunicated, yet the minister of the interior, the chief of police, and the chief of investigations have *all* been excommunicated for committing terrorist acts against the person of Monsignor Rubio, from Montevideo, during his visit to Asunción in 1971. You know the monsignor came to negotiate the freedom of the Uruguayan priest whom Stroessner had ordered to be brutally tortured. The Paraguayan authorities who accuse us of being assassins and antisocial elements have received an exemplary punishment from the Catholic Church, whose pastoral letters never cease to draw attention to the abuses committed by the authorities every day."

This confused my mother. "I no longer know what to think, my son. I want you to be out of prison, and for that I must keep quiet, but much of what you say is true. It is true the doctors at the university hospital and some diplomats here have made common cause with political prisoners and their relatives for your liberation, and have defended you unconditionally."

Our conversations gave my mother a better understanding of the problems in Paraguay. In 1974, when she first started working to get me freed, she shook with fear and embarrassment if she had to address the "authorities." In 1977, she showed high moral character and was proud to be the mother of an educator who, in his fight, used no weapons other than reason and law.

And from her individual experience, she started to draw general conclusions. She came to see that she was working not only for her son's freedom, but also for the freedom of all victims of the dictatorship. Like her, other mothers grew stronger and discovered the justice of our fight. They came to understand that at the core of the autocratic regime, the seed of a new society was beginning to grow.

PART V

BÉSAME MUCHO

JULY–DECEMBER 1975

—ᴡ—

EMILY

Everybody, soon or late, sits down to a banquet of consequences.

Robert Louis Stevenson

I returned to Caazapá determined to settle into a healthy balance of work and play, reminding myself that "play" (spending time with Paraguayans) was just as much a part of my mission here as work. It was full steam ahead now, and nothing would stand in my way.

On Monday morning the office was an icebox, with no sign of Velázquez or Vargas, or even Elena or Aunt Vicenta, so after sweeping the floor I just sat at the typewriter and typed in stream of consciousness—*don't know what to do, lost myself to loving you / i'm afraid it's the same old story / two hearts together then enter another / maybe you should have told me*—pounding out the tragedy of my life on the keys with frozen fingers, trying to get those heavy metal levers to move, slowly, painfully, every thwap echoing off the bare cement walls.

Just before noon a car pulled up, and I walked stiff legged out to see a beige Volkswagen with a military look to it. Blessed be! It was Vargas, grinning like a madman and driving what I could only surmise was our new vehicle.

"Emilia, look! We have wheels!" he called through the open passenger window. "Be right back."

Yippee! No more catching rides with leering truck drivers—I'd already decided to punch the next one who said *¡Qué curvas, y yo sin freno!*—or hopping the Caazapeña or riding bikes. Nope, now we could leave the office when we needed to and arrive prepared to do our jobs instead of panting and sweating our asses off.

Actually, at the moment I couldn't imagine ever sweating again. When would this cold spell break? I'd almost forgotten how to use my kerosene heater in the ten days I'd been gone and nearly froze to death my first night back. There was simply no respite, and all I could think about was how tough these people were. They barely even had jackets, and the young girls wore those cotton dresses with maybe a thin sweater…and of course continued to go barefoot. No wonder they were always sweeping, sweeping—anything to stay warm.

I started sweeping again.

Suddenly Vargas was back with Velázquez, and over *mate* we discussed the rules. The vehicle was for Vargas to use as head agent, but whenever he didn't need it, Velázquez and I could use it for our meetings in the campo. Velázquez then drove us around town a little, to prove his driving skills…and to show off a little, of course, like Ramón in Iturbe. But I understood how important a vehicle was in being taken seriously by the locals—and how we now had to act the part.

That afternoon Velázquez and I drove to San José to take Antonia the receipts for the *planchas* used in the fogón project there. I felt like royalty sitting in the jaunty VW with the window down (the afternoon was sunny and warmer), waving and practically singing *"ah-dee-OHSS!"* as we passed wide-eyed onlookers. We rolled up to Antonia's parents' house and cut the engine.

Antonia's older sister Rosa was visiting. She worked in a factory in Buenos Aires and shared an apartment with six other women. She'd brought the family's antique sewing machine outside into the sunlight (now muted by thin clouds) to garner even the tiniest bit of warmth as she sat making a dress.

I was struck watching Rosa sew with both feet working the treadle and getting up to high speeds. She didn't need no stinkin' electricity! I stared as she began a stitch without wasting one centimeter of thread...and it all fell perfectly into place. I reflected on my own sewing days (I'd made a lot of dresses for myself in high school) when I would leave at least three inches of thread at each end to be trimmed and thrown away. Now I could see what a waste that was...and how hard it would be to have to conserve every little thing.

"Do you like living in Buenos Aires?" I asked. City life was so different from campo life. I could imagine Rosa and her friends going to parks, dances, cafés, the occasional film perhaps...in addition to enjoying a few amenities like electricity and running water and perhaps a soft couch, things definitely missing in her life here.

"No, not at all," she answered right away. "I'd much rather be out here with my family where I can see the stars at night and don't feel so...trapped. We don't get to see much of the city because we have to work all the time and save our money to send home. And can you imagine eight women in an apartment with one bathroom? But it's all we can afford. The only consolation is all the Paraguayans living there now...we can speak Guaraní and feel a little less homesick. I don't really want to go back, but I have to—my family depends on what I send them."

I couldn't help but notice that, for all her hard work and sacrifice, Rosa's family still lived in relative poverty. How sad that so many young people had to leave their homes and families just to make money and then couldn't spend any on themselves because it was never enough.

It occurred to me that Rosa lived in a kind of exile, too—even though she could cross the border at will, unlike those who'd been forced to leave. But could she ever *really* come back? Could she marry and have a family of her own? Not if she continued supporting her parents, who were still pretty young. She had no other choice. The resignation in her bearing made me sad.

We gave Antonia the receipts and asked if she'd been using her fogón. She said she had and liked it, but didn't think her aunt was using hers because it still needed to be whitewashed. That seemed an odd reason, seeing as how white-washing wasn't necessary.

After *mate* it was time to head back. I was ecstatic that we could actually leave when we wanted. How civilized. I smiled and waved like the queen of England as we pulled away, this time with the window up as it was starting to sprinkle. I should've known! Lately I'd noticed that when the weather got warmer and there were high clouds, it tended to be followed by rain. Good thing we left when we did because we got to the office just as the downpour hit.

The next day was clear and cold, but it was *ruta clausurada* of course—I still couldn't get over how much work was lost here just because of unpaved roads—so I tested soy recipes in Zunilda's kitchen. After cooking and grinding the beans, I used the residue in chili and some savory fritters called *buñuelos*, and with the "milk" I tried to make *budín* but it turned out a little runny. It tasted good, though, with all that sugar and the golden yolks bestowed upon us by our chickens, plus my secret ingredient: ground nutmeg I'd found in Asunción.

Being in the warm kitchen all day listening to classical music on the radio was heavenly except that Zunilda was away teaching and Epifanio kept coming on to me—that is, when not indulging Elton's every whim, which included getting in my way, knocking over the milk, and screaming while being carried out.

What does Epifanio do anyway, I wondered, *besides babysit Elton?* He didn't seem to have a job yet strutted around like the boss, even though it was clear Zunilda was the pants—not to mention the brains—of the operation. Little Elton wouldn't taste any of my experiments, of course, so I left some for

Zunilda and took the rest home, figuring the chili would keep. In this weather, who needed a fridge?

Over *mate* that evening, I told Margarita about the in-service and how much I loved studying Guaraní.

"I'm glad you like it. Our language is very sweet—*Jhe-ë ñane ñe-ë,*" she said with great affection, pouring the steaming water out of the Thermos up to the rim of the *matero* and handing it to me. I gladly took the warmth into my own hands and sucked on the bombilla, awaiting the rush of earthy flavor.

Ah! A hint of lemon…probably *cedrón*. The temperature was perfect, as it always was with Margarita. I had a habit of burning my tongue when I drank *mate* at home because I could never wait long enough for the water to cool.

"By the way," she said, "it's *cedrón*." She was teaching me about the *yuyos*.

"I knew it!" Actually, it wasn't that hard to tell.

"I also put something else in it," she said, baiting me. "What do you suppose *that* is?" Uh-oh, this would be tough. There were so many.

I'd been looking up different remedies in my medicinal plant book and was blown away by what I'd found. Now, I believed in the curative power of plants, but some of them had properties that sounded almost too good to be true. For example, *cedrón* was lemon verbena, which came in two varieties: *Lippia citriodora (cedrón Paraguay)* and *Lippia chilensis (cedrón Capi-í)*. Both plants were at once sedatives and *at the same time* either nerve fortifiers (*citriodora*) or circulatory stimulants (*chilensis*)! It appeared these *remedios* were good for just about whatever ailed ya—except of course they did nothing for intestinal parasites, contrary to what most campesinos believed.

But what had Margarita added? After a few seconds, I shook my head and handed her back the *matero*. "*Ndaikuaai, che,*" I said with great affect, trying to sound like a real *paraguaya*…and trying to hide my annoyance at not knowing. She smiled—she had me!

"It's *capi-í katy*, considered a *refrescante* and usually only consumed with tereré, but I like it. Besides, it's good for the kidneys."

I was always impressed when people said things like that (and they always did)—I wouldn't have had the slightest idea if my kidneys needed fortifying or not. How could you possibly know your kidneys from, say, your bladder? Of course doctors did, but how many of them were there around these parts? Easy answer: too few.

And it wasn't that Margarita *couldn't* know where her kidneys were, because she very well could. So I decided to give her the benefit of the doubt even as I wondered what this *remedio* might do to me—as far as I could tell, my plumbing was in decent shape.

"You were saying?" I prompted.

"Yes, Guaraní can be so beautiful." She looked out at the sky. "*Araí* is 'cloud.'" In the setting sun, the clouds looked like pink cotton candy.

"*Ara-tirí* is 'lightning.'"

"I can see it," I said, gesturing with my arm, "streaking across the sky." That was what I wanted to say, anyway; what I actually said was "flying across the sky" because I didn't have a clue how to say "streak" in Spanish.

Margarita smiled and said, "*Sununú* is 'rolling thunder.' It sounds like it, don't you think?" She repeated the word a few times. I nodded. No question, the names sounded like what they stood for, in an oddly visual way.

"Here's another—guess what it means." She closed her eyes and threw her head back, loudly inhaling through her tonsils, then leaned her head forward and exhaled with a guttural "*kororö.*"

It was obvious: "Snoring!"

"Yes! *Don Pedro o-kororö etéreí-na,*" she said, laughing as if this was the funniest thing she'd ever heard. I only hoped I would never have the pleasure of experiencing it for myself.

I shivered and said, "*Che ro-ú,*" and Margarita laughed so hard she nearly fell off the chair.

"You want to eat me? Have sex with me?" she howled. "I think you mean you're cold, *'Che ro-y.'*"

My face caught fire. Oooops! So much for not discussing my body temperature with anyone. At least it was only Margarita. Guaraní was full of traps, wasn't it? I didn't remember Carmen mentioning that one.

Just then we heard Sarita calling for Margarita, who popped up immediately. Her devotion to her *comadre* knew no bounds.

"See you tomorrow morning." She smiled as she went inside, and I sat in the foyer contentedly serving myself *mate* with herbal tonics and enjoying my solitude in the nippy yet stunning sunset.

Then I started thinking about home, and as always it took mere seconds for the tears to build up, overrun their dams, and start inching down my face one track at a time. Their heat against my cold cheek shocked me and made me laugh, which made me cry even more—crying and laughing, it was definitely "the same release." [57]

Joni understood.

It was so cold there was only one thing for the weather to do, and that was naturally to get even colder. Over the next few days frosts like no one had ever seen killed sugarcane, tobacco, corn, bananas, and vegetables, and caused many farmers to lose their investments for the year.

In the office one farmer reported losing two to three hundred thousand guaranies' worth of crops. "Oh well, it's God's will," he'd said with a little smile. I was floored: How could the people be so *tranquilo* all the time? They just accepted whatever happened to them without railing against it...though I had to admit, railing against Mother Nature *was* a bit foolish. Needless to say, Epifanio's and my garden—all that produce I was eagerly awaiting—was destroyed. I railed like hell.

The following week I was sitting in the sun in the doorway of the office making member certificates when a young woman about my age approached. She said her name was Agripina Romeros and she was from Jaula-cué, a compañía off the *ruta* a few kilometers from San José. Velázquez knew Agripina's family, of course. They had built a fogón six months ago, and Velázquez wanted to check it out. We made a date to go there on Tuesday morning and stay for lunch.

Hopefully Vargas would let us use the car, as I'd planned to take the bus to Villarrica Wednesday morning for supplies and wanted time to prepare the night before. I had three clubs going now, and everything was running smoothly. It felt good to be working hard. Things were looking up, the worst of winter surely over.

Anna-í sent word that we would have to postpone the site visit, which was fine with me—I wanted to have more to show for myself before she came to observe me.

---

57 Joni Mitchell, "People's Parties," 1973.

The weekend was surprisingly warm, more or less. It was now the end of July and, I hoped, winter's "pique." I spent time cleaning dead plants out of the garden and writing letters. Mom had been upset because the mail wasn't going through, so I had to explain why she hadn't heard from me. I'd thought it was because the lady at the post office in Caazapá thought the postage was twenty guaranies when it was in fact twenty-five, but it turned out to be something agencywide.

We'd been informed during the in-service that PCVs would now be using the diplomatic pouch to send mail. No one knew why—we were discovering the PC was disinclined to share much information—but other parents must've gotten alarmed and sent telegrams like Mom did when their children's letters stopped. I realized I should stay in closer contact with my family. I remembered Ellyn saying she'd met a man with a ham radio who loved having PCVs over to use it; he worked for USAID. I was determined to call home the next time I went to Asunción as it had been seven months since I actually talked to anyone in my family.

In the office Monday morning, a socia brought word that the president of the club in Cabajú Retä was sick and wanted to cancel the meeting, so I typed out my monthly report. The next morning Velázquez and I set out for Jaula-cué to visit the Romeros family. The visit did not go quite as planned. Days later I described it in a letter to Mom:

> Now, my fantastic, terrifying, divine three days in the campo. I went out to visit a family I knew, who live 2 kilometers outside a compañía of Caazapá, "Jaula-cué," which in Guaraní means "what was once a cage for birds." I went with one of the daughters who now lives in Caazapá (there are 10 children). These people are campesinos. Subsistence farmers, but well-fed and so serene and happy. We left on a Tuesday. Up till then I'd been a little constipated (I have to add this so you can note the extremes I went through). That Tues. out there I finally got that problem solved. But—eating meat gave me a toothache that I had <u>all</u> <u>day</u> <u>long</u>. We planned to leave that afternoon, but the family wanted me to stay, and I felt

brave ("Oh, probably not <u>too</u> many bugs in the bed") and decided, What the heck.

That night some people came over (guys, too) and, since this family has some money and a battery-operated record player, we danced. Now, I was angry because there was one fellow who was practically set up for me, and he made me want to vomit. So, ANGER. I didn't enjoy the evening much. I have to add that during the day I had an absolutely wonderful time with the family— LOVE, CONTENTMENT. That afternoon I had <u>mate</u> with the mother who is big and strong but not too well now because of menopause. In the <u>mate</u> she put a "remedio"..."for the intestines," she told me.

Well, the next day [full moon] I woke up with my period. And it was raining. When it rains in Paraguay the roads close. So here I was, walking around with rags ("on the rag"), rinsing them out every few hours, SUFFERING because all I wanted to do was go home. We tried to leave, walked to the main ruta, but there were no more vehicles passing, road too wet. I cried and cried, was <u>so</u> miserable. Walked back to the house, sat around the fire in the kitchen all day, felt better, laughed, loved, glowed with the family (the girls are my age and looking for husbands). That night we sat around the fire and cooked dinner, a combination of special more-or-less dishes. One is a corn flour-grease baked-on-a-stick thing *[caburé]* that I loved and ate a lot of. Too much.

The next day I woke up sick to my stomach. Was sick all day, even threw up. The mother fixed me two kinds of tea and that's all I had all day (except for three soft-boiled eggs that I threw up). This and my period. By this time I was resigned to staying (Thurs.). The day wasn't all bad, I slept mostly. That night everyone came in to entertain me and we laughed. Can you imagine what it's like to sleep in a mud house out in the campo? Well, that night the bugs <u>did</u> find me and bit me to pieces. Still I itch.

The next day the road opened and I finally went home, dirty, tired, astounded. I loved it, and yet I hated it, and my emotions were so intense, so strong. I suffered more than I have ever suffered in my life (physically) yet I had such a tremendous good feeling inside, too. It was incredible. I love those people. Somehow I changed after that, but it's so recent I can't really tell how yet. It was all so different from anything I'd ever known or even imagined in my life!

I knew something inside me had changed because when I'd said good-bye to Mamá before leaving the house, she'd held me for a long time and said, "*Ro jhai jhú*, Emi." Without thinking I'd answered honestly, "*Ha che ro jhai jhú aveí, Mamá*," after which I got tears in my eyes because I wasn't sure I had ever actually said "And I love you, too, Mom" to my own mother.

In my journal I wrote "The overwhelming feelings of love and happiness I felt while there were only comparable to the extreme feelings of misery and despair that I also felt. I couldn't have felt one without the other." Reading over it later, I thought, *Misery, yes, but despair?* Where had that come from? It finally hit me that being stuck out in Jaula-cué at the mercy of the Romeros family had deprived me of something I'd treasured all my life yet always taken for granted—my freedom.

Velázquez and I had gone out there to check on the family's fogón, which they'd clearly never used. But when I sat around the fire with everyone that night, I realized how difficult it would be to change tradition. The Romeros family didn't use their brand-new stove because sitting around the fire in the kitchen all together like that on cold winter nights—with the camaraderie, the food, the shared experience, the bonding—was an integral part of their lives. Losing the fire would mean giving up more than mere ash and smoke. It was the foundation of their family, the hearth...the heart.

Who was I to come along and try to change all that?

One highlight of the experience was eating my first *yvapurü*, the fruit in the song "Mis Noches Sin Ti." It was like a purple grape only larger, with bitter skin and white, gelatinous flesh that was difficult to eat because of the huge seeds. But I was blown away when I saw the tree itself: the fruit was growing right on the bark and branches, even the roots! The girls said the tree was called a *jabuticabeira*. I'd never seen anything so weirdly cool, real yet something right out of Dr. Seuss.

Another highlight was that I finally discovered the true purpose of mandioca: mandioca made it possible to swallow the gristle! Hallelujah, brothers and sisters! In the campo even the chicken was tough, so I'd mixed some with mandioca in my mouth, chewed it up, and voilà—it slid right down my throat. *Meat and mandioca go together like coffee and donuts...Scotch and soda...Astaire and Rogers...all the great couplings.* I couldn't wait to tell Diego.

The girls showed me how mandioca was planted—by using five-inch cuttings from the stalks, no less—which increased by orders of magnitude my regard for the humble tuber that basically cloned itself and could thrive in any kind of soil. I gave up the fight.

Chalk one up for mandioca![58]

I had to laugh every time I flashed on yet another highlight of my stay on the "farm": watching the rooster hump a duck, a sight ignored by the others and, I could tell, titillating only to me.

The day after I got home from Jaula-cué, Saturday, July 26, was Dad's birthday, and I was back at work in the office. It felt strange. Last year at this time I was with my family in Battle Lake at the first memorial birthday gathering for Dad, when we buried his ashes on the shore. It was sobering to remember he'd given his life so we could still go there. I wondered what my family was up to this year but didn't get as sad as usual.

Things went well after I got back. I was busy with the usual flurry of forming clubs—Tayy-í said yes, which made me happy—working on the school garden, and planning meetings. The ultimate goal was to have the members plan the meetings themselves so they could learn the rules of procedure, but for now I'd have to do it.

I'd been back a week when we had a 4-C meeting in San José, where I presented the notebook project I had in mind. The socias seemed to go for the idea. I also gave my talk on the three food groups. I didn't get the impression much of the information penetrated, though, and realized it might be more difficult than I'd thought. Back at the office I wrote in my work log: "Next time we're

---

58 It turns out that mandioca was and still is preferable to bread—especially now that obesity and diabetes rates have skyrocketed because Paraguayans eat less mandioca and more wheat products.

going to begin our notebooks, I'll give my basic soybean talk, the subject will be 'Proteins' ('Formadores'), and by cracky they're going to at least know the three groups when I'm done."

The next Thursday, August 7, Montoya and Velázquez took me with them to talk to some farmers about a work plan with the bank. I wrote: "Farmers do plan, then borrow money. Interest 1 percent monthly, 12 percent yearly (if they wait a whole year to pay)...A guy borrowing money now to plant cotton pays in May, only 10 percent (gee whiz, what a real ganga)." Even I could see it wasn't a deal at all—it was just being proposed as one. (Of course I wasn't exactly being objective in my reporting.)

August seemed to fly by. I was reading a lot to stay inspired and copied this poem into my journal one night:

Journal entry 20 Aug—When the sun rises, I go to work,
When the sun goes down, I take my rest,
I dig the well from which I drink,
I farm the soil that yields my food,
I share creation. Kings can do no more.
—Ancient Chinese, 2500 BC
A moth has just expired in my candle's flame.

In September I started reading *Lord of the Rings* and was spellbound by my first foray into fantasy, such an escape I felt guilty. But it gave me something to look forward to in my house alone at night...and to keep me from thinking too much.

I hadn't been much of a reader growing up. In fifth grade I got stuck on a book called *Kildee House* and pretty much stopped reading after that—I was too busy with horses and school. But I couldn't believe how good it felt now to kick back and surrender to the exciting adventures taking place in a magical—though clearly allegorical—land.

It was early spring, and the 4-C clubs were humming along. Velázquez and I made home visits in other compañías to try and generate interest.

One morning I drove to Yegros with Morton Kramer, a PC "operative" passing through Caazapá compiling data for a study on the effectiveness of generalists in the Peace Corps versus PCVs with degrees in their service area. I wondered what he might find, as I didn't think anyone had a degree in agriculture except maybe Tomás in Yuty. Along the way we ran into a traffic jam...of cows! Honking did nothing to move 'em along. When we finally got to Yegros it was fun surprising Gino, who naturally had no idea I'd be showing up. He played his guitar and and sang a catchy tune called "London Homesick Blues,"[59] about being lonesome in a foreign land. I would definitely have to learn that one.

Morton had brought my mail, including a letter from Mom—she was planning to visit over Christmas! The news filled me with equal parts excitement and dread.

One weekend Epifanio, whom I now called "Fancho," and I planted zucchini, green beans, cauliflower, and broccoli, with the chickens' help—*yeah, right*. All the little bitches wanted to do was eat the seeds. And who knew hens had personalities? One of them was downright mean. Even so, how could I ever kill and eat them? The "gals" were endearing themselves to me, all right, with their *kara, kara, kara* (what hens said in Spanish), but I had to admit they were pretty dense.

I liked being busy, but oh how I *loved* going home and reading Tolkien. The humidity draped the earth in a Middle-earth kind of fog, the perfect environment to read about the hairy-footed hobbits and their quest to save Middle-earth. I loved going out into the misty night wearing my poncho and imagining myself in Rivendell, enchanted.

Then I got stuck in the campo again, in San José, with a family that didn't have it together. For two days I was cold and hungry and covered with bug bites—not even blowing "jujuy, jujuy" into my hands could cheer (or warm) me up. When they killed a chicken to feed me, I was chagrined to be such a burden. I couldn't wait for the *ruta* to open, so I walked the fifteen kilometers home...in my rubber boots. I decided to put my foot down—no more getting myself in this situation.

The wet weather kept us in town for the most part, and one day I didn't come to the office at all because the rain just wouldn't quit. Vargas got pissed and about a week later handed Velázquez and me a memo with the new schedule:

---

59   Gary P. Nunn, 1973.

"M–F: 7:00 a.m.–noon, 2:00–5:00 p.m.; Sat: 8:00–noon." *Oh yeah? We'll see how well mister big boss himself adheres to it.*

I walked into mayhem one Saturday at the pensión. Don Pedro was sitting on a chair, bare from the waist up with a towel over his shoulders, while Sarita fumed about, the wet remains of a stogie clamped between her teeth. She seemed angry with her husband. At least a dozen others milled around, talking in low voices. Margarita held her finger to her lips and motioned me to sit down, which I did.

Finally Sarita stopped and stood behind don Pedro, holding a pair of tweezers and admonishing him in a rash of unintelligible Guaraní. She lifted the towel from his shoulders to reveal a large bandage taped to his upper right back. I wasn't sure whether to flee or lean in for a closer look, but the truth was I couldn't budge.

Sarita tore off the tape (causing don Pedro, decorated veteran of the Chaco War, to wince) and lifted the bandage, causing a murmur to pass through the spectators like a wave. Underneath were three red lumps about the size of quarters, each with a small, oozing hole in the middle…and sticking out of each hole was the whitish tip of what looked like—blecchh—a larva or something!

Seeing the look on my face, Margarita whispered, "Don Pedro was out in the campo a few weeks ago. He left his shirt to dry on a bush and a fly laid eggs on it. He never checked for them, which is why Sarita is so angry."

I didn't understand. How, exactly, did they get into his back?

Holding the towel under one of the holes, Sarita began tugging at the larva, gently, so as not to pull it apart, I guessed. She coaxed and pulled, each time getting a better, closer grip with the tweezers, tugging and coaxing until all of a sudden its body, which was twice as long as the tip sticking out and wider at its base, popped out, along with some pus and blood. An involuntary "OHH!" passed everyone's lips as if a fútbol goalie had just taken one in the *cojones.*

Sarita set the thing on a napkin. It was a maggot, clearly, and quite possibly the grossest thing I'd ever seen in my life. Its length was the width of a dime, its creamy opaqueness ringed with crinkly brown lines. It looked like a tiny, rubbery seashell. Pedro sat stoically as Sarita extracted the other two, each getting a response like the first, especially the third, which was the largest and had already started growing little wings.

Feeling queasy, I looked at Margarita, who answered my unasked question: "When the eggs first hatch, the tiny larvae (called *ura*) burrow into the skin. The only way to get them out is to wait till until they get bigger and then cover the hole with plastic so they can't breathe—they come out looking for air and *POP!* You pull them out." I groaned. That part I knew all too well, as it was etched on my retinae forever.

She said as if to a small child (she knew I was cavalier about such things), "But of course we want to avoid the *ura* in the first place, which is why we iron our clothes after they have been drying outside."

¡Holy Mary Mother of God! Now I knew why the Paraguayans ironed everything, even their underwear. I resolved to *never* hang my unmentionables on the fence again. Could you imagine anything worse than having those horrid things...*down there?*

Later I looked up *ura* in my Guaraní dictionary, but it said only "a worm that grows under the skin and in wounds." I couldn't help but wonder what kind of fly had laid the eggs, but I had an idea.

A week later I went to Asunción for a joint training with PC and SEAG. At the PC office I was amazed to learn that Patty Hearst had finally been arrested in San Francisco, where she'd been hiding right under the cops' noses! Good detective work. I would never forget her kidnapping: I'd just returned to Stockton after Dad's death and was shocked when it happened practically in my own backyard. The list of crimes Patty had committed—with a machine gun, no less—was staggering. That girl who called herself an "urban guerilla" was in some hot water, all right...although surely Daddy would get her off.

I also found out that two more girls from our group had left, including Jessica. She'd reportedly had some major dental work done and then split, saying that was what she'd come here for in the first place. Why was I not surprised? The other girl had let herself be seduced by a terminating PCV—a real Southern jackass, if you asked me—and gone home with him. Wouldn't you know, she and I had gotten along fine. What a waste, I thought, to sub-jugate her own life and dreams to his, to just throw away her life like that.

But then again, what did I know about love?

It had been raining, and I was walking to Villa Morra when some boys in a car swerved close to the side of the road and splashed through a puddle, completely covering me in street muck, after which they sped off laughing and honking. Furious, I picked up a rock and threw it as far in their direction as I could, but it fell just short. *Bastards!*

That was when I heard whining in the bushes. I lifted some leaves to see what it was. A little dog! He was white—or had been once—with long hair, sort of terrier-like and God knew what else. As he lay there panting, I noticed a blood-encrusted gash on his side. I had to help him—I'd rescued a couple of dogs in Stockton and even gotten a reward for one.

So I picked this one up and headed to Ian's, who, even though he was an ant guy, would surely know what to do. At least he lived close by. Fortunately he was home, but it was awful wondering what he thought when he saw me—for one thing I was filthy, and of course "the" party had been here. But he seemed oblivious as we bathed the *perrito* and dressed his wound, which Ian figured was probably from a bullet that had only just grazed the lucky fellow.

I told Ian about the *ura* incident. He said the culprit was the botfly, which was what I'd suspected—we'd had to guard against them at the Thayer stables as well, picking the yellow, capsule-shaped eggs off the insides of the horses' legs so they wouldn't ingest them. How lovely that here in the tropics, so-called "human" botflies went after people as well. From now on, before donning any item of clothing, I would give it the third degree.

Ian said he couldn't keep the little mutt, so I had no choice but to bring him home with me—I couldn't just abandon him, could I? He was fluffy like a cloud and sort of came into my life like one, so I named him Araí.

That was one long-ass bus ride back to Caazapá! It wasn't until after I got Araí fed and settled in a bed I made for him in a crate outside my kitchen that I realized he was more than a little cuckoo, perhaps as a result—or the cause—of his recent trauma. His pointy ears curved out and up like horns, and when he wasn't running around in circles or doing flips, he stared at me with his head cocked like the RCA dog. He was so sweetly nuts I couldn't help but fall in love with him. I decided to start eating my midday meals at the pensión again—I'd been cooking for myself—so I'd have leftovers to feed my little *jaguá-í*.

Emily's rescued dog Araí outside her kitchen in Caazapá with his trademark expression, imagining something in the shadows.

The Fellowship of the Ring was awaiting me like an old friend. You had to love Frodo Baggins! I admired his courage—I didn't think I could have resisted the temptation to use the ring and become invisible. Reading the book put me in a place I was sure I had dreamed of at some time, somewhere in my subconscious. The dark forces in the trilogy scared me, though. I knew they were based on historical figures and couldn't stop thinking about Stroessner and the other megalomaniacs here in South America, who had also cast an ominous pall over the land.

One day—a miracle!—a plastic sword appeared on a table at the pensión. I raced over to it, brandished it, and did some *kendo* moves with it that I'd learned in aikido (circle over your head and then down and around as if you're cutting off someone's head), yelling "In the name of Elendril, Elven-King!" I wasn't sure those were the right words, but it didn't matter…I was possessed, unable to resist the spell of the sword.

Ah, full engagement—there was nothing better. I only wished I could have that feeling more often.

Caazapá's spring festival was postponed for a week because of rain and ended up being held September 28, the day before the fiesta of the Battle of Boquerón, a national holiday. There was a parade with marching bands, floats, even a beauty queen. I wondered what such an honor might entail. If it was anything like the States, the queens would have an opportunity to experience things they could never have imagined.

At the dance I got asked by two guys to be their girlfriend. One of them was a high school boy I played basketball with who knew perfectly well I was too old for him. Jesus! I was learning to say no to these cheeky boys…and be firm: "No, I don't *want* a boyfriend, thank you." Would it never stop? I had to admit, though, Tito sang well and was looking good.

The next day it rained but the soccer game went on, and Caazapá—which had moved into the semifinals and was undefeated with two ties—beat San Juan, 3–0. The whole town was beside itself with glee. I wrote Mom: "It's getting warm, has been very rainy. Springtime, wildflowers, fruit blossoms, WEEDS! Paraguay is a paradise."

"It's because of *Caraí Octubre*," Margarita said at lunch on the first day of October as she set down a bowl of steaming beans and corn with fresh cheese and substantial shreds of beef—at last, the infamous *jopará*! It looked delicious.

"What is 'because of Mr. October'?" I asked, blowing the steam away and stirring the soup with my spoon to cool it down as my salivary glands went into overdrive.

"Well, October is the month when people used to run out of food, and sometimes still do," she said. "By the time October rolls around, the money from the farmers' cash crops is spent, and the food from the *chacras* is eaten. What they planted in August or September, like grapes or watermelon, won't be ripe until mid-November at the earliest. So if the families haven't put aside enough food, they could face hunger and possible starvation."

"*¡No me digas!*" was all I could think of to say even though I of course didn't want her to stop telling me. Before I knew it I was spooning the soup into my mouth uncontrollably, slurping it to avoid burning myself (a trick I'd learned in Japan, where slurping was considered good manners). I preferred beans to meat any day.

"Yes, so what Caraí Octubre does is he comes into our houses and steals our food in the middle of the night and puts it in a long sack on his back. To keep him away, we have to eat well on this day, preferably bean soup, and share our food with guests. That's why," she opened her palm toward the food, "because of Caraí Octubre, Sarita has very generously given you your meal today for free."

"Oh my gosh, please thank her, that's so nice," I managed to say as I put down my spoon for the first time. Only in Paraguay would people feel obliged to stuff themselves—and even more, share it with others—when they were in danger of starving.

She sat on the edge of a chair and said, "You were asking about examples of *jopará* in Guaraní. There are many, but these are some of my favorites." She chuckled. "Gossip is *radio so'o*, 'meat radio.'" I smiled—the perfect image!

"*Sombrero ka'a* refers to a man who 'gains the favors' of a lady at the expense of her boyfriend...or husband," she added coquettishly.

I laughed out loud. Now, why would she pick that one? And how did a straw hat represent a guy cuckolding another guy—usually called "putting horns" on him?

Before I could ask, she said, "But my favorite example of *jopará* at the moment is..." She looked around and then at me. Her voice was practically a whisper: "*Ña mandá ha ña mondá*, which refers to the party bosses: 'They rule us and they rob us.'"

Margarita wasn't laughing anymore. I was shocked to hear her criticize the Colorado Party—it was dangerous for us both. I just nodded.

She fished around in her apron pocket and pulled out a bone wrapped in paper for Araí, which she slammed on the table, then winked. I thanked her as she jumped up to get back to work. I'd have to ask her what that was all about… at my house, where the walls didn't have ears.

That morning I had attended a presentation by the nutritionist and the midwife at the health center. They were a little nervous but knew their stuff, as well as their audience: they understood what the campesinos had and what they needed. The nutritionist, Odila, said she'd like to be the next *educadora del hogar*—welcome news!—and wanted to come to our meeting in San José on Friday, which was fine with me. Anna-í and Diego would be there as well to observe me in action, so I figured we might as well make a spectacle of it.

I still didn't feel comfortable being in front of a lot of people but was faking it the best I could. In my teens I'd had acne and regularly saw a dermatologist. My self-confidence had suffered, and I'd learned to avoid the limelight. That of course was impossible here, where you carried around your own spot that was always trained on you.

The rain refused to let up, so of course Velázquez and I couldn't get any work done even though we were adding clubs in Boquerón and Rojas Silva. All the clubs had decided every two weeks wasn't enough, so we were prepared to go to the campo in the mornings as well, which of course bothered Vargas because he needed Velázquez in the office for some unspecified reason. (I figured it was really because he didn't want us to hog the vehicle.) Vargas pretty much kept to his own schedule and was gone a lot—which didn't bother me—usually without informing us (or at least me)—which *did* bother me. A lot. I never knew where he was if he wasn't sitting at his desk or talking to people—mostly farmers, granted—on the stoop.

Then one afternoon he reamed Velázquez and me, Velázquez mostly, for not getting enough work done. Velázquez had spent a lot of time helping me get started and consequently neglecting his own work. We got an oral whippin' that scared me and ticked me off, frankly, because the rain had been a big factor in our lack of accomplishment.

After all was said and done, though, I liked Vargas. I knew he walked a tightrope between supporting the campesinos in their efforts to rid themselves of the middleman, and supporting the middleman himself—the local honchos (which as a merchant he must have been as well). I wanted to support Vargas because I knew he was under a lot of pressure to get results. We all were. I was glad Anna-í was coming soon because I needed some advice.

The day before the observation it rained but cleared in time for Velázquez to go to Villarrica the next morning to collect his paycheck or some damn thing and forsake our planned trip to Rojas Silva. *And so it goes.* (I'd been using that line from Vonnegut a lot lately.) In the afternoon I had to ride my bike to San José, where I met everyone coming from Asunción, which turned out to be Anna-í and another PCV, Alonzo, not Diego. Odila didn't make it (no surprise). I had to admit I was relieved Diego wasn't here to evaluate me in my first formal observation.

As the girls began trickling in, Antonia called me over and said she didn't want to be president anymore but wouldn't give me a reason. Wonderful, and with my supervisor present! I asked her to not mention it and said we'd just elect a new one next week. Off to a great start.

The plan for the day had been to make *croquetas* and *crema* (custard) from soy, but it soon became apparent that the socias assigned to bring the ingredients weren't going to show up. This was turning into a disaster! But we got through it somehow: I gave my presentation, Anna talked a little, and I managed to smile as Alonzo took pictures. Afterward Anna gave me suggestions but seemed a little condescending, which made me feel bad. I concluded in my SEAG log it was "pretty much of a *nada* reunion. Depressed—want to get going."

How long had I been saying *that?*

Adding to the difficulty was the uniqueness of each club. In Rojas Silva few of them spoke Spanish (nice), and in Boquerón people apparently had money and didn't want fogones (fine), but they also wanted manual arts instead of nutrition, which added to my workload but was all right. I worked even harder to learn the traditional *aho-po'í* and other types of needlework so I could teach them. It made sense to start with a sewing box of some sort, and a Nido milk can seemed the perfect container, as everyone had them. I worked on a proto-type, with a cotton lining and piqué fabric on the outside.

Vargas grudgingly gave me permission to work at home a couple of times when it rained. I felt the need to be there for Araí, who was seeming more and more deranged. He never left my side when I was home, and I was pretty sure he was deaf. I often took him for rides on my bike, which I could tell he loved; people we passed would stop us so they could pet him, saying *"Mi-i-ira un poco."*

In a letter from Mom that Anna had brought I learned that my grandmoth-er—whom I adored and had more in common with than my mother—was coming to visit as well, so I started planning a fantastic voyage for the three of us. I figured we could spend a couple of days in Asunción, a few days here in Caazapá, then shoot over to Yguazú Falls and on to Río de Janeiro, which was where I really wanted to be. I worried a little about Nanny, who was seventy-three, but she was in good shape and shouldn't have any problems.

I sent that itinerary to Mom in a letter on October 9 with a list of things to bring me, including vegetable seeds and a tape of Marty Robbins's *Gunfighter Ballads*, my favorite album when I was ten (I'd played it over and over until my brother hid it from me). I wanted to learn "El Paso." Mom had asked about my chickens; I told her we would eat them when she arrived. I said I'd try to call her in November when I went to Asunción for the in-service.

At the next reunion in Tayy-í—I biked the four miles there—we got three new members, the socias demonstrated their understanding of the food groups, and we made cookies out of toasted soy flour. A few guys showed up as well, guitars in hand. It turned out practically everyone, in-cluding the irrepressible Olimpia, played guitar and sang. I was goaded into doing the only songs I could remember, "Your Cheatin' Heart," "Mercedes Benz"—I was delighted when they told me Janis Joplin had hooked up with a sexy Brazilian rock star for a while—and of course the requisite "Bésame Mucho," which was the only song in Spanish besides "Guantanamera" that I could play and sing convincingly (though it was in the wrong key for my voice). I requested "Mis Noches sin Ti," which the cute guy with super curly hair crooned beautifully.

I couldn't help but notice how well people sang here—they all had nice voices, full of vibrato. And the Paraguayan songs were different from ours back home, reminiscing about places as much as people.

This club was by far the most on the ball. I enjoyed everything about the afternoon, including the ride back, where I passed people walking and oxcarts creaking home after a long day. Small *motos* flushed birds out of the brush as they putted by, often carrying someone on the back sidesaddle.

Araí was over the moon to see me, especially when I gave him the bone Olimpia had insisted I take. Feeding him wasn't easy—I couldn't just go to the store and buy dog food. Sometimes I got liver for him from one of the vendors in the municipal market. I mostly gave him leftovers from what I ate and hoped for the best. He was starting to calm down and put on weight. I let him sleep next to my bed but not on it, and the back door stayed open at night (it was warm enough now) so he could go in and out.

Despite Margarita's protestations, my proximity to Zunilda's house allowed me to feel safe with the door open. I had assured Margarita that my ferocious guard dog would warn me about any creatures, real or imagined, that might try to breach the castle keep and make off with the princess. But she had met Araí and was not convinced.

By mid-October, after more wet days—one rainy afternoon of which I snuck out to watch the fútbol team practice for the big game against Iturbe next Sunday—I had another new club, in Arroyo Guazú. The plan was to go to Boquerón in the mornings and Arroyo Guazú in the afternoons. It was a lot, but I'd asked for it—anything beat sitting around all day.

There was clearly a need for these clubs.

San José provided some drama when the girls said they didn't want the officers who had just been elected the week before. No one brought ingredients for the cooking demonstration. They said they didn't want to study cooking with soy anymore. Jesus! But the good news was they were determined to keep going. I had to hand it to them for knowing what they wanted—or didn't want—and speaking out.

Later Vargas told me the farmers in that area weren't keen on growing *soy*. I guessed that would've explained why the socias never brought soybeans when they were supposed to. Why hadn't he told me sooner? I realized I had no idea what really went on around here.

I spent one wet afternoon finishing my last diaper for Elena, who was due to have her baby any day now. I also wrote to Mom:

> As far away as I may be from my <u>real</u> home, I am learning that the family system is one of the most important things I've encountered…
>
> My friend Elena hasn't had her kid yet. We're waiting, waiting. She's really spaced out, and as I see her every day, I am, too! I've been embroidering diapers, etc. I love Elena and am even going to be there when she delivers. I have this fear, though, that she's going to start labor one night and I won't be there. Soon I'll start to sleep with her. Her husband works in another town, and old Aunt Vicenta can barely walk.

A couple of days later, Elena and Vicenta had vanished! Vargas assured me they'd gone to Boquerón, not to worry. I was disappointed but also a little relieved, as I wasn't sure I could handle watching a baby being born. I wondered where she would have it now, as there was no clinic in Boquerón. I appreciated Elena's courage—my own mother had birthed her babies under total anesthesia. (I, of course, planned to avoid getting into that position in the first place.)

More rain came, and then it was time for Sunday's face-off against Iturbe, which Caazapá lost, 2–1. Rumor had it our team captain was bought off, but I didn't want to believe it because I knew the guy, more or less. I wondered if there weren't often rumors like that when a team lost a close game, especially one against the neighboring town, where the rivalry would be most intense.

The next day as I arrived at work, Velázquez said, "I swept this morning and now it just needs to be mopped." *Excuse me? I'm the one who sweeps every damn day, and now you've decided it's* your *job to sweep while* I *mop? Do you think you're doing me some kind of favor?* God, Velázquez could be annoying. But of course mop I did, all eight incisors pressed firmly into my tongue, which I knew must be covered with calluses by now.

San José and Tayy-í were gangbusters over the fiestas they were planning before summer break, which was fast approaching. Both clubs wanted to raise money for *planchas*. I had to get permission from the officials for both clubs and buy drinks, snacks, and cigarettes for San José (the socias would pay me back); Tayy-í would buy its own cantina from a *despensa* near the edge of town.

I also worked with Odila and the midwife planning a Mother's Day event in which we would give presentations on issues around pregnancy. As I wrote home, "I will speak on hygiene and health. 'Wear shoes,' I'll say, 'so you won't get hookworm!' and everyone will do as before. Well, perhaps one or two out of 50 will be affected. It's a frustrating occupation."

One day I rode my bike to Tayy-í in the morning, getting back just in time to hop the one o'clock bus to San José for our reunion and "this time for sure" preparation of *crema*. In my work log I wrote: "Gotta slow down! Crema turned out ok but next reunion will be in [another socia's] house." It seemed the girls couldn't agree on *anything*.

Yet despite the frenzied nature of my existence, I would find myself smiling every now and then because I couldn't stop thinking about the in-service next month and our trip to Concepción. I was more than ready for a little "PCV and me" time. Who knew what adventures lay ahead as we chugged up the mighty Río Paraguay? And after that, three generations of Oswalt women tearing up the streets and beaches of Rio de Janeiro. It was a lot to look forward to...what I seemed to thrive on.

On October 28 I wrote to my grandmother, apologized for not writing, and told her I was excited she was coming for Christmas and how I loved sitting in travel agencies looking through brochures. "May make a good tourist yet!" I wrote, then undoubtedly terrified her (sometimes I didn't know why I did the things I did) by continuing:

You'll like Paraguay, it's nice and sizzling. In Río we'll find you some golf courses. Are you going to bring your bikini? Get ready to drink and dance all night long. In Paraguay get ready to swat mosquitoes all night long. And use the New York Times for toilet paper (the toilet paper we use to sand wood).

I've been working hard lately. For what? Sorta discouraged right now. At least there's a Japanese restaurant in Asunción where I go to console myself. I want to return to Japan.

Tonight I'm going to see a Canadian lady friend who's married to a New Mexican gentleman friend, works with USAID. She'll think I'm hungry, when in fact I've gained about 10 lbs. Maybe we'll go to the show at the Marine House (US Embassy)…

Aren't you glad I wasn't kidnapped by leftist Argentine terrorists? (Sometimes I wish I was.)

I didn't really mean that last bit, of course—I was just prone to making inflammatory statements, like the time I told Dad I wanted to go to Cuba. He'd stormed around for a week after that. I would never forget his favorite quote: "If you're not a communist at the age of twenty, you haven't got a heart; if you're still a communist at the age of thirty, you haven't got a brain." I understood what he was saying but couldn't possibly agree with him…and now I'd never have a chance to prove him wrong (or vice versa).

I'd been so busy I'd written only once in my journal, so I devoted my second and last October entry to wrestling with whether or not Eastern philosophy denied free will (free will was important to me even though I seemed to make a lot of bad decisions exercising it). If the Buddha said, "All life is suffering, and the way out of suffering is to have no desire," then where did initiative, creativity, come from? Wasn't accomplishing something the result of a desire to improve our life in some way? Or were we just supposed to sit back and accept whatever befell us, be it fame or famine?

I of course couldn't accept that idea, writing in my journal "JUST HOW FATALISTIC ARE THE EASTERN RELIGIONS?…My theme for the present: Achieving a balance between my search for self and my 'quest' to engage myself in and 'better' society."

A book I'd picked up in Berkeley called *Phases of the Moon*[60] gave me insight into this rather ongoing internal dilemma. The concept, based on W. B. Yeats's poem by the same name, aligned lunar phases with traditional sun signs. This

---

60   Marilyn Busteed, Richard Tiffany, and Dorothy Wergin (Boston: Shambhala Publications, 1974).

"guide to evolving human nature" helped me see how, because of my lunar phase (22, half moon waning), I was trying to shed personality—the clarity and self-differentiation of the full moon (Virgo's "all the world's a stage")—and replace it with character—the use of senses other than sight, the feeling of oneness with one's surroundings of the new moon (the deeply intuitive, empathic core of Pisces). I was smack in the middle, tending toward both sides and swinging freely back and forth.

No wonder the Furies visited me on a regular basis!

One quote about Phase 22 that I felt an affinity with but wasn't sure I understood was "for my strength is made perfect in weakness." It sounded like something from the Bible. People did seem to think I was weak because I deferred to others—though I believed it took strength, not weakness, to put others first. Maybe that's what it meant.

From another book I copied Robert Frost's "Santa Fe Sketch," the final line echoing the first: "The valley was swept with a blue broom to the west." It was true, mountains always looked blue in the distance. God, I missed the desert! I could almost hear the mourning doves: "Throo coo coo. Throo coo coo." My heart ached as I thought about how growing up in such a vast space had taught me to focus on far horizons…and how it wasn't until I went to Japan, where life was in miniature—and everything was art—that I'd learned to look at things close up.

I closed the journal, said good night to Araí, put him in his basket on the floor, read a few paragraphs of my new book, *The Source*, which was fascinating but dense, blew out the lamp, climbed between my sheets, and fell asleep.

It was still dark when I awoke with a start, disoriented but furious once I realized some goddam *thing* had just bitten me on the back of my goddam *knee*!

I found my flashlight, threw back the sheet, and confronted the little bugger…but saw nothing. I sat rubbing my bite, which smarted, when I saw a black speck appear on the sheet. I reached for it, but it jumped up and landed a short distance away.

A flea! In my goddam bed! I'd never actually seen one before. Our family dogs had disgusting bulbous gray ticks but never fleas. I glanced over at the culprit. He just sat there looking innocent with his ears pricked—little devil!—and his head at forty-five degrees. "You're lucky you're cute," I muttered.

I turned back to the *pulga* and grabbed for it, but it jumped again. The chase was on. This was war! I was determined to get that little varmint. I'd always heard about flea circuses and knew they couldn't be real…but if this was not a fucking circus, I didn't know what was. I lunged forward and slapped my entire hand over the speck, shouting "Gotcha!" But when I lifted my hand… nothing! It had gotten away again. I'd have to wait.

And wait. Rage and despair began to build up like steam in a boiler. Finally I saw the flea, grabbed it, and got it where I wanted it. Thanks to Yeats's crazy old men, I knew what to do: crack it between my thumbnails. I started to do that when I realized just how tricky it was going to be to trap a miniature kangaroo between two slick surfaces.

Sure enough, the first time I tried, the thing escaped. By now I was out of my mind. It appeared again; I grabbed it with the fury of a madwoman, slapped it between my thumbnails, and—CRACK!—heard its exoskeleton snap. Victory! I cackled like a witch for a while as I wiped my nails with newspaper and watched to see if any more showed up. None did, thankfully, so I lay back down, fearing the worst.

Sleep eluded me as I waited for another prick in the dark. Thoughts swirled around my head: my upcoming in-service and trip to Concepción…my summer vacation starting in December…my family coming to visit…my fleas.

I hated to admit it, but Araí would have to go.

I fell asleep fantasizing about returning to Japan and teaching English. I loved that place with a passion and, as I hadn't been able to finish my journey there, felt a nagging need to return. Besides, I couldn't imagine anyone in Japan having fleas.

A few days later I found a good home for Araí with Antonia's family in San José. They had agreed to take him, and I knew he'd love running around outdoors and having one adventure after another. It was hard to leave him, but I'd be able to see him whenever I went out there, so everything would be all right.

The *pulgas* were finally vanquished after a few more nights—I was loath to spray insecticide on my bed—though not without leaving me exhausted and miserable from losing so many nighttime hours to those little "shites," as Steve would say. Flashing on Steve made me happy because I could already hear Jorge Cafrune and his beloved voice on the record player singing about *Catamarca*, the place I just knew I had to visit.

It was warming up, so I started doing yoga again before *mate* in the mornings with Margarita and was proud of myself for being so disciplined. I liked the warrior poses, and mountain pose was exactly how we were taught to stand in aikido, relaxed yet ready, shoulders back and down, knees unlocked, weight evenly distributed throughout the feet. My favorite, of course, was child's pose, where you curled up into a little ball to stretch your lower back—probably no accident it resembled the fetal position.

Of course the best pose of all in yoga was the final resting pose, *shavasana*: dead man's pose.

"What's this?" Margarita asked one humid morning. She took a drag off the bombilla and started making a sound like something going down the gullet: *"mocôcô, mocôcô."*

"Easy! Swallowing!" I shouted, and she smiled. I loved being the star pupil, even if I was the only pupil.

"So, how's your work going, Emi?"

I sighed. "Pretty well. We're forming new clubs, trying to get people to come to the reunions. But it's so frustrating. They're on their own schedule. And when they say they'll come next week *'si dios quiere,'* I want to scream! I always say, 'Of *course* God wills it—*Are you kidding me?*—so I know you'll be there.' Then they don't show up."

She was smiling as she handed me the *mate*. I sucked it down and passed it back. "What does God have to do with them showing up to a meeting, anyway?" I went on. "Can't they just decide to go and then go? They don't have to sit around waiting for God to tell them, do they? They can use their free will, can't they?"

I was on a roll. "And why do they always say *ikatú*? I learned in class that *ikatú* means 'maybe,' which to me means someone will at least *try*...but then they don't come. What's up with that?"

Margarita waited patiently for me to wind down, but my exasperation surged instead: "And when they do come they're always late, *always!*"

She smiled. "Are you finished? Good. First of all, Emilia, when people say *ikatú*, they don't really mean 'maybe.' You know we have a roundabout way of addressing things here. People don't want to tell you directly that they won't be there...so they say they *might* be."

I looked at her deadpan. "So if I mean 'no,' then I should say 'maybe'?" She smiled and nodded. I had to admit it wasn't that different from saying "I'm not cold" to mean "I'm hot" or "good-bye" for "hello."

"As to people always being late," she said, "when you have nothing, time is the only thing you *do* have. Your campesinos are exercising control over their lives in the only way they can: how they allocate their time." I nodded. It made sense: Who wanted to be tied to a stupid clock, anyway? I realized now how events had their own time frame, and Paraguayans tended to finish one thing before starting another without worrying about the hour...unlike us time-obsessed neurotics in the "first world."

Margarita swooped in for the kill: "And of course the expression '*si dios quiere*' is what people say because they don't want to be too presumptuous about what God does or doesn't want...and it has the added benefit of absolving the speaker from any responsibility whatsoever. It's very useful—you should try it sometime." I rolled my eyes and she mimicked me, and then we laughed.

"How many clubs do you have now?" she asked, pouring herself a *trago*.

"Ay, Margarita, I'm going crazy with so many. I have five and can barely keep track of them all. And Boquerón wants a club as well. I'm starting to tear my hair out. But it'll look really good on paper. I'll have a lot to write about in this month's report. I'll include the names of the clubs and socias."

Margarita shot me a look, and then I realized why: I was about to supply the Paraguayan government with names of people in the campo who were involved in organizing and educating themselves, pursuing democratic principles, reclaiming sovereignty over their lives, demanding their rights as citizens. People like me.

The kind of people the "benevolent" dictator seemed hellbent on eliminating.

The *mate* had lost its flavor, so I headed home to get ready for work. "Ours is not to wonder why, ours is but to do or die" looped through my mind as I walked. Where had that come from? I didn't know, but it was true enough: I was expected to turn in those names. I could only trust that we were doing the right thing here in the long run and not inadvertently putting people at risk.

But how could I rationalize it by saying I was "only doing my job"?

When Araí wasn't at the gate to welcome me home, I started to cry and couldn't stop. Without him, I really didn't have a reason to smile in the mornings. Being home in Tucson with my family was all I could think about, which was of course ridiculous because they were coming here to me. So I called off my little pity party and went to the office to write my report—without names. I would beg forgiveness later if necessary.

I wasn't a spy...was I?

Tayy-í's fiesta was the next Friday, October 31, good ol' Halloween back home, a holiday I hated—naturally—even though I loved it as a kid. But it annoyed me how Americans were such conspicuous consumers and so gullible that they followed the subliminal commands of the advertisers and bought tons of candy (i.e., poison—let's face it) to give to bratty kids who'd been conditioned to believe they deserved something for nothing. One of my biggest pet peeves about America was the sense of entitlement people seemed to have.

Nevertheless, when Friday rolled around, I forgot about all that. The evening was mild under a clear, moonless sky. Half of Caazapá showed up in Tayy-í, it seemed. Lights were strung up around a grassy *cancha* and powered by generator, Tito's band provided the music, the cantina did a splendid business, and a good time was had by all.

Olimpia's friend with the curly hair asked me to dance a few times, and everyone was gushing as if we'd just returned from our honeymoon or something. Olimpia told me he wanted to know if he could be my boyfriend, which floored me. But there was absolutely no way I could go out with the young man, who, although quite handsome and congenial, probably hadn't attended much school in his life, for starters. What would we talk about once the passion had fizzled?

I just smiled. "But I *have* a boyfriend," I lied apologetically, feeling like a chump.

After the fiesta I was talking with a couple of town girls and asked as nonchalantly as I could if they thought Tito had a girlfriend—he didn't seem to be with anyone at dances (we'd only said hello tonight) or when I saw him around town. The girls assured me they didn't know.

The next morning Velázquez and I drove back out there to help clean up and encountered a fuming Olimpia. "We're short," she muttered, grabbing my elbow and leading me out of earshot. She was speaking Guaraní at a very rapid rate that could have been Swahili for all I knew.

"*Castellano, por favor, cuñataï i porä,*" I said with a smile but got none in return. I'd never seen her so mad but could now understand where she got her reputation for being a firebrand—which was what I loved about her. It was muggy and she was sweating.

"I think Felipa took some of the money from the cantina," she said. "I know we made more than the amount she turned in."

It struck me that this was the second missing-money issue here in Tayy-í. I assured her I would look into it but wouldn't be able to give her an answer until I talked with Vargas and Velázquez. She agreed and calmed down.

It took a few hours to clean everything up. Except for the cantina, everyone was happy with the funds raised—the new queen had even danced while people stuck bills in her gown—and the socias were eager to begin ordering their *planchas*.

Driving home, Velázquez and I discussed the cantina problem. He suggested that I talk to the owner of the store where the socias had bought the supplies. I told him he was a genius. We drove there but the *despensa* was closed till Monday, which was fine with me: the weekend was already half over, and I just wanted to mellow out at home.

On Sunday I worked on peanut recipes and my needlework sampler, without which I would have nothing to show—nor any credibility whatsoever—when Tayy-í started embroidery. The socias had proposed holding a soybean-cooking exposition where they would also sell items they'd stitched, which sounded excellent. The best part was that the idea had come from them.

It had been warm and my house was stuffy, so that night I left the back door open, thinking how I missed my "guard dog" but not his little circus. Clouds had rolled in, and the night was pitch black. I blew out the lamp.

My head was no sooner on the pillow than I heard a light tap on the shutter. A tremor shot through my body and I sat straight up, scalp tingling.

"Emilia, it's Tito. Open the window."

Tito? Oh my god, what a relief it was someone I knew! But how was this possible? The girls must have told him I'd asked about him—that hadn't taken long! And now here he was, bringing me a *serenata* with his friends. My stomach turned a few cartwheels. Tito liked me?

"One moment," I said as I fell out of bed and slammed on some shorts and a T-shirt. Shaking, I fumbled for the flashlight and switched it on. He tapped again and whispered, "Emilia!"

"Un momento!" My heart was beating so hard I thought I might faint as I walked over to the window and unlatched the shutter. A hand caught the wood and swung it out. It was Tito all right, smiling, as was I.

"Turn off your flashlight," he said, and I did. But something wasn't quite right.

"You didn't bring your guitar?" I asked. "And..." I peered into the darkness, hearing nothing. "Where are your friends?" All of a sudden I thought about the open back door—was this some kind of ambush?—and turned around in a panic, flicking on the flashlight as if drawing my six-gun.

But no one was there. I switched off the light and turned back toward the window, where I could just make out Tito's silhouette.

"Don't worry, Emilia," he said softly. "I came here alone because I thought you might, you know...want to keep it a secret."

"Keep *what* a secret?" I asked, figuring his friends were probably out there trying not to bust up. I was disappointed he wasn't going to serenade me—I would've even been happy with "Feelings."

"Well, I was hoping I could come in and...visit you." A few scenarios went through my head, when he said: "Here, give me your hand. I have something for you. Close your eyes."

I hardly needed to do that as I couldn't see six inches in front of my face, but I did what he said and held my hand out through the glassless pane. He took it and put something in it that was warm and felt hard and soft at the same time.

Holy shit! He had wrapped my fingers around his erect penis! I let go immediately, repulsed but suppressing a laugh: *That was original.* How had the cheeky devil managed to pull it off?

"Emilia, I want you, I need you. Please let me come in."

I was stunned. His pleas sounded pathetic, but I had to admit my hormones didn't care. After all, I was a red-blooded American twenty-something, wasn't I? I wouldn't exactly say I was liberated, but I was trying to be. If guys could do it, why couldn't girls? I'd been feeling pretty lonesome…wouldn't it be nice to be held and loved by someone I was attracted to? By all accounts I was very much a single woman, a free bird.

In the space of a few seconds my life passed before my eyes: my failed attempts at love, the lonely nights, the tears. Maybe this was what I needed to get over some of my hangups. Of course I knew there were lots of reasons *not* to do it, but if we kept everything confidential it might be okay. After all, we were consenting adults. Perhaps later we could "go public."

"Are you sure you're alone?" I said, peering into the black and trying to elicit a sound from a hidden collaborator. But I heard nothing.

"Yes, yes, I'm alone, I promise you. Please, Emilia." I looked into what I could see of his eyes. There was a good chance he was lying, but some unknown force made me suddenly cast my fate to the wind.

"Okay, go through the gate there and come around back."

I couldn't believe I'd actually said it! As I closed the shutter, I was too embarrassed to look at him. I crossed to the open back door, thinking *At least he asked permission*. But by the time I saw him there I was pretty sure I'd made a mistake.

Nevertheless, weak as water, I let him in. I thought we should talk a little first, but he kissed me right away, a nice kiss—at least he hadn't been drinking. He gently guided me onto the bed and sat next to me, murmuring sweet everythings. He definitely had the lingo down. We fell back onto the mattress, and I couldn't help but think how glad I was the fleas were gone.

It was exciting and passionate, urgent…though ultimately unsatisfying. A short while later, he said he was sorry but he had to get up early to study and could he come back sometime? I said he could if he swore to tell no one. He solemnly promised and then, with a kiss, disappeared into the night.

Was it destiny, or all my own doing? I didn't know, but I had to admit I was happy to have found my Paraguayan *amante*. I'd thought that was the last thing I wanted, but it just felt good to be with someone. I'd have to keep quiet about my tawdry behavior, but it was a secret I knew I could keep because, even though the experience wasn't exactly mind blowing, I was more than willing to practice until it was.

After my pulse finally returned to normal, I hit the sack with Linda in my head singing about meeting at the dark end of the street—just the thing I thought I would never do, and now here I was. Yet secretiveness was second nature to me, being part Scorpio and all. And, yes, there were advantages to keeping the liaison clandestine, the most important of course being that I could bail when necessary with no repercussions. But I did feel a little coerced—what would've happened if I'd said no?—and wasn't sure how the balance of power would work out in the end.

Oh well, "When in Paraguay..."

I overslept in the morning and couldn't get out of bed—the sheets were redolent of Tito, and I luxuriated in it. When I dragged myself to the office half an hour late, two socias from Tayy-í were waiting for me on the stoop. I was relieved my workmates weren't there to see me arrive so late and in such a state, what with that scarlet letter emblazoned on my forehead and all. I unlocked the door and we went in.

The girls started talking and the spell burst.

Apparently Olimpia had been sharing her opinions freely around the community. Felipa claimed that the money she gave Olimpia was all she'd collected. The socias were worried that irreparable harm could be done if we didn't get it resolved right away.

"Let's go to the *despensa*," I said. I locked the office door and we started up the street. The girls were obviously upset, whereas I was just hoping to score some *mate* from the shopkeeper. I was in luck—he had both yerba and a suggestion.

"Did the candy and cigarettes sell out?" he asked as he passed me the *mate*, which I practically inhaled. The girls looked at each other, shrugging their shoulders.

"Perhaps some didn't sell and needs to be returned. I had to close early Saturday for a wedding, so I wasn't here if anyone came to do it."

It was clear we'd have to go to Felipa's house and find out, so we flagged down a truck heading in that direction and sat in the back on sacks of rice.

When we were dropped off fifteen minutes later, we still had to hoof it another kilometer or so. We got to Felipa's house but found no one there. The issue would just have to wait, as there were no trucks to catch going back. It took a couple of hours to walk, the last few kilometers by myself after the girls reached their own homes.

I told myself I was being punished for my sins of the flesh and had to laugh. Seriously, though, it was time to find a horse. Not even the bicycle could have made my life easier today.

When I got back to the office, sweating and dehydrated, Vargas had just arrived and was quite put out with me: I'd apparently left the keys in the door, and they'd been dangling there for hours. Anyone could have come in, etc. I felt bad and apologized like crazy even though I wondered why anyone would want to get into the SEAG office. Vargas gave no explanation as to why he'd arrived so late, but then again he didn't have to, did he? I didn't even ask where Velázquez was.

At that moment two more socias from Tayy-í came in, looking sheepish, each trying to get the other to step forward first and talk. By this time I was about at my wits' end...I needed some tereré! Fortunately, Vargas thought of it too and left to ask his wife to prepare some for us. As they lived next door, he returned in a flash.

Finally one of the girls spoke. "Felipa is my aunt. She had to leave suddenly because my grandmother got sick. She didn't know I had taken the rest of the cantina home to return it to the *despensa* on Saturday afternoon. But the *despensa* was closed and we couldn't do it then. We came to town right now and returned everything. We just wanted to show you we have the money. We'll take it back to Tayy-í."

They had the money, all right. That settled it...something a simple phone call could have resolved back home. Olimpia was right to be concerned about the money, but I just hoped her words hadn't compromised our attempts to unite the community. It was becoming more and more obvious how little people trusted one another here—like Mexico, I figured, it was family first and the rest need not apply.

San José was planning their fiesta for this coming Saturday, but I would be in Asunción at the in-service, blissfully unaware of whatever problems they might cook up.

The *chivato* in front was topping out with flaming red flowers whose yellow stamens fairly throbbed as they exploded in all their male glory...whoa! The days were hotter than hades, though, with absolutely no ventilation in my house, and sleeping at night was next to impossible. I might have turned into a mummy were it not for the spray bottle of water I used for evaporative cooling. At least in the winter you could bury yourself in blankets, but now there was no escape—you just had to make friends with your sweat glands.

The week passed quickly. I saw Tito once in town, but he practically ignored me. Oh well, that was our agreement.

While packing on Friday I reached into my *ropero* for my leather sandals, brought them out, and saw that they were coated with bright green mold. The fungus covered almost everything else as well, its earthy stench perfuming my clothes with "Mildew No. 5." *Tranquilopá.* I just hoped the organism wouldn't take root in my skin, too, constantly irrigated as it was.

In Asunción I was shocked to find Polly gone and the original twelve— why did the phrase "dirty dozen" keep coming to mind?—reduced to five. We heard that Polly, who'd apparently built a school as a VISTA volunteer, couldn't get anything done in Villeta because she was discriminated against. Another theory was that because Villeta was on the river—which I'd thought sounded ideal—it was marshy and mosquito infested. Despite Polly's reasons I was sad she terminated early, even though I knew she didn't like me (she'd allied herself with Jessica long ago).

Ellyn and I spent the week at Steve's house because, as I wrote Mom, "we decided he needed some company." I listened to Jorge, Mercedes, Los Chalchaleros, and a 1964 album by Eydie Gormé and Trio Los Panchos, *Amor*, that had a touching song called "Sabor a Mí,"[61] which Steve said was Mexican and about—what else?—love lost and a taste that lingers.

One night after Ellyn went to bed, Steve and I were looking through his bookshelf, where I noticed a copy of Pablo Neruda's *The Captain's Verses*, a book I'd fallen in love with in college. I pulled it out and said, "This is one of my favorite books! Talk about passion...you can really see why romance

---

61 Álvaro Carrillo, 1959.

languages are called that." Steve started to say something but checked himself.

I read aloud, with my best dramatic interpretation (I felt relaxed enough around Steve), about how I, the condor, soar above you walking and suddenly, in a flurry of wind, feather, and claws I assault you and lift you up in a shrieking cyclone of furious cold…Whew, it left you breathless! I hated to admit it, but the violence was erotic.

"Good job," Steve said. He paused. "Actually, the 'Romance' languages are called that because of their Latin roots, as in 'Rome,' not because they're romantic."

Duh! I usually hated being corrected, but for some reason I didn't mind so much when Steve did it.

"You know Neruda was murdered by Pinochet, don't you?" he continued. I shook my head. I knew all too well what Pinochet was capable of but had no idea how Neruda had died.

"There's controversy about it, of course. He was in the hospital for stomach cancer, which was the official version of how he died, but it was later revealed that he'd called his wife and asked her to come pick him up. He told her he'd been sleeping when a doctor came in and gave him an injection in his stomach. He figured it was poison and, sure enough, he was dead within twelve hours or so."

I shuddered. First Victor Jara and now Pablo Neruda. What kind of swine were these dictators, to kill their national treasures with such impunity? It was inconceivable.

In Guaraní class we learned some subtleties about the language, such as how to make a command sound more like a polite request. It was said in the most supplicating manner and sounded like it should be followed by "I'll be your best friend." I figured it would be useful—*"Ejumí-na reunión jhape"* would get people to show up at the reunion "happening" for sure. *Yeah, right.*

Carmen also told us about *e-á* [ay-AH], something I'd heard Margarita say when she was impressed or flustered. Carmen said it was equivalent to "wow," which she pronounced in the most adorable way: "wuau." I'd used *e-á* myself and smiled to realize I was starting to think in Guaraní.

After class one day, some of us went to the Hotel Guaraní for a beer. We were asking each other how things were going when Miriam shocked us. "Because I live alone, the men all think I'm a prostitute. For the first couple of months a different guy showed up every night wanting sex." She blushed and looked down at her glass.

My eyes about popped out of my head! Had that been Tito's intention? And here I thought he *liked* me. Thank God he hadn't tried to give me any money. Up until his arrival I'd felt safe in Caazapá, under the protection of my neighbors and the pensión. But now I could see how maybe I'd just been lucky. Margarita was right: I should have taken the "snakes" more seriously.

"Fortunately, after I explain who I am and what I'm doing here, they leave me alone." Miriam looked at each of us in turn, her hazel eyes glistening. "I decided to befriend some of the merchants' wives in town, so they could, you know, *defend mah honah!*" I appreciated the comic relief of her Southern damsel in distress and chuckled with her.

Someone asked if she still had visitors. "Not as many, thankfully," she said. "Do you realize...if a woman simply looks a man in the eye here, he thinks she wants to have sex with him? That's what the mayor's wife told me. You know, I just don't remember being told that in training."

I squirmed. I obviously didn't remember either: I had a bad habit of making eye contact with men. I couldn't help it—being direct was my nature. It wasn't that I was naive...not after Callison professor Mickey Gibson made it clear in the Yucatán that if he and an old man from Mérida whom I had befriended and trusted had been sitting at a café and seen me walking down the street toward them, they would've made a bet on which one could get me into bed first. Scumbags! And Mickey was my professor, no less. (I later realized he might have been protecting me, in his own twisted way. I got the point, regardless.)

I didn't really trust men but rather felt compelled to challenge their ignorant behavior—and let them know I didn't fear them—by looking them straight in the eye. Now I saw how such bravado could get me into trouble here.

Miriam continued. "Actually, I'm really happy because a few weeks ago I bought a small *carreta* and a horse, and I drive to all my meetings now. I usually pick up a few socias along the way. It's fun, and the people love it." I couldn't imagine driving a cart, but it made me even more determined to find myself a horse. What was I waiting for? I'd noticed a pretty little bay with a crooked blaze in Caazapá…maybe I could find out who owned him.

The bill arrived and Ellyn scrutinized every item. When she got her change, she counted it carefully. Did she trust no one? Of course I knew she was right and I should do the same, but it just wasn't in my nature.

Thursday morning we awoke to loud cheering and honking of horns: Spain's Franco was dead. I wrote a letter to Mom telling her Río hotels were expensive at twenty-four dollars. That night (and the next), Ellyn and I went out with a couple of guys she'd met—*How did she do it?*—Peter and Carey. Carey, red haired and carrying a cane, claimed he was the "Carey" of Joni's song. I didn't believe him, of course, until it turned out he knew the lyrics better than I did (I had no idea the words were "Matalan Moon"). Anything was possible, I guessed. He wanted me to sleep with him, but I just couldn't.

Around ten of us left the port of Asunción early Saturday to spend the next twenty-four hours on the ferry to Concepción. We drank gallons of tereré and beer, slept on deck, talked, read…anything to fill that gaping maw of time. Gino and Tomás were there, as were a health volunteer named Raúl, Alonzo, and another English friend of Ellyn's named Alfred. We discussed plans to buy a turkey and some chickens, feed them for a few days, and then—whack!—off with their heads.

Except for the constant rattling of the motor, the ride upriver was peaceful and, more important, smooth. There didn't seem to be many towns along the way, only a million kinds of flora. Because it was so flat, you couldn't see much beyond the shore. Every now and then a little "island" of shrubbery floated by on its merry way to Asunción and beyond. We saw a few capybara, or nutria, the hundred-pound rodents we'd heard so much about. They resembled giant rats, only less menacing—more like pigs.

When the ferry finally docked, we could barely keep our eyes open as we rode in horse-drawn taxis through the charming colonial town to Ellyn's, a sweet house with real bathroom and kitchen lit up with real light bulbs. We met

Ellyn's roommate and a few other PCVs who lived here, hung out, drank *mate*, ate dinner, and then crashed. The next day we bought the birds, which we put in the backyard. For some reason I grew fond of the turkey and hated to think it would be in my stomach in a few days.

Tuesday was my birthday, the big two-three.[62] We had a party, and Ellyn even baked me a cake. How different from a year ago, when the Peace Corps was still a cosmic question mark in my life. I enjoyed spending time with the other PCVs and wondered how hard it would be to return to being alone in Caazapá.

The day before Thanksgiving I fasted, figuring an empty stomach would help me better appreciate the Pilgrims' hardships. Soon it was time to dispatch our fowl. I couldn't do it, but the guys had no problem. First they poured caña down the turkey's throat to get it drunk so the meat wouldn't be full of adrenalin, caused by fear, they said, which made it tougher. (I could see why.) Then they commenced to separating the birds from their heads. The yard was a mess as chicken zombies ran around, blood spurting everywhere; I could see why the Paraguayans just twisted their necks.

The turkey turned out to be smaller than we thought, so Ellyn—who'd invited a lot of people—had to buy a couple more chickens from the neighbor. Thankfully, these arrived already deceased. We cleaned the birds by first dunking them in boiling water to loosen the feathers and then plucking them. At one point I stuck my hand up the rear of one to pull out its innards and inadvertently forced some air through its voice box, resulting in a loud "AAWCK!" All of us jumped and then laughed, relieved to discover the thing was neither alive nor possessed. It was a sober reminder that we had taken its life to sustain our own, and I gave thanks like never before.

Because Concepción was so far north, it was even hotter than Asunción, so using the gas oven indoors to cook the birds was out of the question (it was also too small, of course). Instead, on Thursday morning the guys lit a fire outdoors in the beehive-shaped oven, the *tatacuá*—which resembled the huge termite mounds I'd seen around Iturbe, so abundant in some places that farming was

---

62 That same day, November 25, 1975, at a meeting of Southern Cone countries in Santiago, Chilean President Augusto Pinochet formalized Operation Condor, with the United States later providing communications, intelligence, and other support.

impossible—and sat around tending it as they sipped caña and swapped tales of indeterminate height.

The women were inside preparing the poultry when Ellyn's neighbor came around sticking her nose into things. This turned out to be fortuitous as she tsked-tsked us into believing we didn't know what we were doing (that much was obvious), that the fire in the *tatacuá* wasn't hot enough, that she'd better cook the birds at her house. For a fee. *Ndaipori problema*—by now we were sick of the things.

We made mashed potatoes, stuffing, and as many of the other trimmings—including pies, of course—that we could fashion out of local ingredients. Guests started arriving. As we prepared to sit down to a lavish feast (relatively speaking…forget cranberries here), we heard someone clapping outside the front door. Ellyn went to open it and found a young soldier standing there.

"Hello. I'm here to monitor your event," he said shyly.

Ellyn looked him up and down, then turned to us and said, "I had to notify the 'authorities' that I would be having guests at my house. Now they send this pipsqueak. I say if we have to have a representative from the police station, let's have the comandante himself!" She turned the unwitting boy around and herded him down the street, returning in a few minutes to say the chief would be along shortly. I didn't like the sound of that but held my tongue.

It was obvious you didn't mess with Ellyn. My love and respect for this extraordinary woman were in that moment given a lifetime guarantee.

The chief showed up, all charm of course, and despite my reservations we enjoyed a wonderful meal full of laughter and fellowship that naturally made me think of my family back home and how I longed to be with them. I couldn't believe I hadn't gotten around to calling Mom last week! I missed everyone, but mostly I thought about Dad. What would he think of my present situation? Better than Japan, certainly. It bothered me that I wasn't dreaming about him anymore. I wasn't forgetting about him, was I? Was that how you moved on?

Maybe he was just settled into a little corner of my heart now, as Margarita said.

The adventure was over all too soon, and with promises of doing it again next year, we were back on the boat, back to Asunción, and back in our sites. As I fell into bed in Caazapá, I couldn't help but laugh thinking about the raft that the guys were now set on building and floating à la Huckleberry Finn down the Río Paraguay for two weeks. *Two weeks!* I didn't see how they could possibly make it happen.

That week I bought a kid, as in goat, for the *visita*. I was getting good at this! Actually, I couldn't go anywhere near the thing—my neighbors would keep it in the meantime—because I knew I would change my mind and not be able to kill it. Or have it killed, as I obviously had no intention of doing it myself. I mean, chickens were one thing, but a *mammal*? I winced every time I heard its guilt-tripping little bleats.

Zunilda said she could provide a daily *comida* for me, for a reasonable price, and I gladly accepted—cooking for myself (which I was back to now that Araí was gone) was too much of a chore. I usually ate with them but would sometimes just pick up a plate of food from her and take it home to eat in peace.

> *Journal entry 14 Dec—Eating Zunilda's comida with wooden chopsticks, in walks Epifanio, says: Emilia, if you'd like to use a fork we have forks. What depths of poverty he must imagine my life falling into!*
>
> *Last evening, recording on the tape recorder for Sam & Steph…Elton reciting, singing, us talking in Guaraní. Later, supper (same thing as lunch, only the meat cut up, and all drier—name changed, too, to "estofado").*

It was actually kind of nice being back in Caazapá, where the woodsmoke never left your nostrils and the chickens never stopped scratching. I finally got up the nerve to ask Fancho how the chickens could lay eggs without roosters around—we had no *gallos*—and he looked at me with a mixture of astonishment and pity. Using exaggerated gestures to make sure I understood, he practically fell down laughing as he explained the fowl facts of life.

"Ay, Emilia, Emilia…the chickens lay eggs regardless of whether there are any roosters around to 'make love' with them. It's just that the eggs are not fertilized, as in…no *concepción*."

Boy, was I ignorant. I realized the last thing I wanted was to be discussing sex of any kind, even feathered bipeds, with the likes of Epifanio, who was a bit of a simpleton…everything with him was a crude double entendre. I honestly didn't understand what Zunilda saw in him other than his good looks and "fun guy" persona. Then, again, I had to wonder what Zunilda thought of me—several times she'd complained about the teaching profession in Paraguay and tried to get me to talk politics, but I'd resisted. She undoubtedly considered me as much of a dunce as her husband.

Of course the heat and humidity started to make me grouchy, as the clubs were on break for the summer and there was nothing to do all day but sweat. I couldn't wait for my family to arrive so I could get the hell out of this intolerable place.

Look out, Copacabana, here we come!

Part VI

My Awakening

—⁊⁊—

Martín

What defines patriotism, for me, is the idea that one rises to act on behalf of one's country. As I said before, that's distinct from acting to benefit the government——a distinction that's increasingly lost today.

Edward Snowden
The Nation, October 28, 2014

The road to my conscious awareness (the *"conscientização"* of Paulo Freire) was long and difficult. Each circumstance of my life determined my final social commitment.

My childhood as a street vendor set me on the search for answers to innumerable questions. In those years I was being cared for by an aunt, who had me work as a helper in her kitchen from four to seven each morning and sell empanadas from seven to noon daily in the corridors of the School of Agriculture in San Lorenzo, a military-style boarding school of two hundred fifty secondary students. I attended primary school in the afternoon.

One very cold day I fell asleep curled up in a corner of one of those halls with my two baskets of empanadas. When I awoke, I found I was covered with a blanket and my baskets were empty. My first reaction was to panic, but I calmed down after I found an envelope containing full payment for the goods. It was the nicest surprise of my life.

My aunt—who would force me to go to bed early every night by peppering me with her rosary as she recited the "Third Joyful Mystery"—lined the bottoms of my baskets with pages from the newspaper *La Tribuna*. While my customers were in class, I busied myself reading those stray pages, discovering what was happening in the world, near and far. What attracted my attention most was news of the General Assembly of the United Nations, which seemed to me something from another planet. I was especially fond of the character of then Secretary General Dag Hammarskjöld (working out his name and its spelling made for difficult reading), whom I considered to be the "leader of the extraterrestrials."

I also enjoyed listening to classes being held at the school and was intrigued by the history of the French Revolution. Sometimes the teachers would forbid me to look in the window, so I would take my usual position on the floor but with my ears tuned in to learn what was happening with Danton, Marat, and Robespierre. The figure of Robespierre in particular captivated me.

Another part of my time was spent doing homework on my spacious desk—the tiled floor of the corridor. During breaks, students would crowd around to buy empanadas from me, surely less for the quality of the goods than out of compassion for the disproportion between my height and the size of the baskets.

But my desire to learn was stronger than the hardships of my young life. The students would look over my homework and take turns helping and encouraging me. I remember two nurses and a professor and his wife who were concerned enough to give me vitamins and mineral-rich tonics. On weekends I visited my schoolmates' homes and helped them with their homework. As a reward, their parents invited me to stay for meals, which helped sustain me through the week.

During this time I was fascinated by the dictionary, which contained beautiful, full-color illustrations and seemed to know everything—nothing escaped its attention. This led me to think the dictionary was also something from another planet. I dreamed of having my own dictionary someday. It was an obsession and almost a nightmare. I decided to turn to the only extraterrestrial I knew of, and asked a student at the School of Agriculture where Mr. Dag Hammarskjöld, secretary general of the UN, lived. He said he didn't know this man or his organization. We talked some more.

"But why do you want his address?" he asked me.

"Well, because I want to write him a letter and ask him to send me a dictionary." The student stared at me and ran off. Shortly thereafter a group of his friends arrived, and one of them said, "You want to write to the secretary general of the UN to ask him for a dictionary?"

"Yes," I replied timidly. The group burst out laughing and made fun of my naive plan. I was deeply upset as I belatedly understood it must be impossible to correspond with the extraterrestrial Hammarskjöld.

However, I did have a friend with whom I could openly discuss extraterrestrials. We spent many nights gazing at the sky, and I told him my friend Hammarskjöld's office was on one of those stars. My friend replied that the headquarters of the UN was on the moon, and he was quite sure of this because his grandmother had told him so.

My passion for the dictionary was so great that I gave up the fun of recess to pore over the one copy my school had. Reading it transported me to a magical world, where I felt immeasurably happy. I would look at the picture of Robespierre and strike up serious conversations with him.

After primary school, I entered the School of Agriculture—not as a vendor but as a student. It was there that I was initiated into political life, participating in the activities of the Colorado Party Youth. Encouraged by my family, I became a member of the National Republican Association (Colorado Party) at age fourteen. The campaigns for the renewal of the central committee leaders excited me. The first candidate I supported was a student named Waldino Ramón Lovera. His eloquence impressed me, and I tried to be like him.

When Stroessner carried out the military coup on May 4, 1954, his artillery troops occupied the School of Agriculture and for a short time shared our facilities, which covered some four hundred hectares. In those days people talked about Stroessner as the most honest military man in the country, a friend and defender of the poor. This is what was said by my schoolmates and at my aunt's house.

I, too, was a fan of Stroessner because I sincerely believed he would solve the problems of our family and our nation. The sacristan from the church had told me that Paraguay once experienced a golden age, when there were no rich or poor and we were all equal and happy. He was talking about the Jesuit settlements during the Spanish colonization, and the practice of the philosophy of Saint Augustine as expressed in *The City of God*. I naively thought Stroessner would bring back that experience, so I didn't miss a single event in his honor.

My town named its main street after Stroessner, and I remember that in his speech—the first I had heard—he harshly criticized liberal governments, calling them "legionnaires" and "traitors" and "communists" because they were responsible for the grave economic situation the country was going through.

The speakers who described Stroessner's personality never stopped repeating a word I loved hearing but had trouble pronouncing: they said he was a *pundonoroso*—honorable—military man. I looked it up in the dictionary, and knowing what it meant increased my admiration for the man. My uncle Virgilio, however, had a different opinion.

Virgilio was leader of the bakers' union, and when he drank too much he would do unpredictable things. Once he was moved to urinate calmly on the commemorative plaque in honor of Stroessner's visit to San Lorenzo. He told me Stroessner was "not an honorable, but rather a dishonorable military man" because in 1952, when Stroessner was colonel of the Paraguarí Regiment, he supported efforts to raise the price of electricity in Encarnación (a city in southern Paraguay) to an outrageous extent, even though he himself was from Encarnación. The angry reaction of the people met with Stroessner's harsh repression, so the Colorado Youth of Encarnación declared him persona non grata and an enemy of the Paraguayan people. After Stroessner became leader of the nation, he took revenge on the president of the Colorado Youth of Encarnación and sent him into exile.

Uncle Virgilio also held Stroessner responsible for the assassination of the agrarian leader of the Colorado Youth, Dr. Roberto L. Petit, which happened on May 4, 1954—the day of the military coup that put Stroessner in power.

The things my uncle said surprised me, but as he said them when he was drunk, I didn't take them seriously. My main concern was getting him home; if he couldn't stand up and walk, I didn't have the strength to move him. I had a hard time convincing Uncle Virgilio it was time to leave.

Little by little, however, those who only the day before had been protagonists of the events celebrating Stroessner began to disappear from the nation's political stage. I'd been a Stroessner supporter because of them. Later, it wasn't even possible to talk about them, and finally they were openly attacked. This was when I first began to have doubts about the regime.

The restrictive measures began after the failed general workers' strike of August 27, 1958, demanding higher wages. Repressions intensified in May 1959, with the dissolution of the Chamber of Representatives, which had tried to impeach the chief of police of Asunción (who ten years later was appointed ambassador to Bolivia) for his brutal repression against students gathered in Plaza Italia to protest an increase in the price of tickets for the urban transport system.

Sanctions and anticommunist hysteria on the airwaves continued—even Pope John XXIII was accused of being the "wayward mentor" of the Second Vatican Council (1962–65). I began to realize that the threats coming from the popular radio program "The Voice of Coloradism" negated my convictions, and I decided that whatever the program defended must be false and whatever it attacked must be true.

After graduating from the School of Agriculture, I was secretary general of the Department of Agronomy and Veterinary Science of the National

University from 1962 until my arrest in 1974. During the entrance exams, we received "orders from above" to admit only those candidates who had recommendations from the military, from the private secretary of the president of the republic, from some of the nouveau riche (smugglers and drug traffickers), or from the official party administration. This made me feel like an accomplice to injustice that I was powerless to counter. My tormented conscience was soothed when, very discreetly and through professors and friends, I was able to favor one or two applicants who had received the highest scores but not been "recommended."

The system for assigning jobs at official primary and secondary schools had one peculiar aspect: the candidate had to appear before the minister of education armed with a letter of recommendation from the president of his or her local Stroessner Colorado Party faction. Who were these people? Local party factions that constituted the political and social support of the dictatorship—the foundation of the Stroessner system. The president of each base, as a reward for his loyalty, enjoyed certain privileges.

Faction leaders in rural areas benefited from municipal taxes; gambling on cockfights, horse races, and games of chance in general; patron saints' days; and contracts for public works. Furthermore, they were merchants who paid no taxes and monopolists of the country's produce, bitter enemies of agricultural cooperatives and any kind of farmers' organizations. They cooperated closely with the powers of repression, the army and police, denouncing their neighbors, torturing them, and burning their ranches.

In urban areas, faction leaders were associated with the police and army, exploiting prostitution, smuggling, drug trafficking, and other activities. The majority held university degrees in law, public relations, or economics, or were alumni of the US Army School of the Americas in Panama. They were prominent members of the anticommunist organization led by the president of the Institute of Rural Welfare, a landowner and member of the oligarchy.

At party meetings local faction presidents shouted the highest praises of General Stroessner, declaring their fervent love for the fatherland and saying they were "at the service of the people." These were the shock troops the regime counted on unconditionally to suppress any kind of demonstration, the real "eyes and ears of the tyrant." Their fanaticism was morbid because it was no more than a tool for defending their privileges, and it resulted from the political-training courses they received regularly from the Stroessner party administration.

The abuses carried out by faction presidents affected the teaching profession, a subject that merits special consideration. These men humiliated my colleagues who wanted to work, and the price my female colleagues almost always had to pay for a recommendation was to submit to the sexual appetites of those "local leaders," followers of General Stroessner, who in this way assigned the most important positions in public administration.

Soon after I joined the board of the Federation of Paraguayan Educators, I discovered there was institutionalized terror in the field of teaching. Every day we received complaints about the abuses our urban and rural colleagues were suffering. Witnessing what the teaching profession and the entire educational system were going through turned me against the military-political regime in power. Conversely, my confidence in the struggle of the teachers' union grew when I observed the fortitude of some of the leaders, in spite of the prevailing political situation.

The plague that devastated the teachers did not end with the local party minions; there were also the usurers. As payment of wages was nearly always delayed by the supervisors, teachers had no choice but to "sell their salaries" in advance to lenders, who would charge 10 to 20 percent interest. These lenders were mostly the supervisors' husbands, who divided their spoils with then-administrative director of the Ministry of Education, Pastor Coronel. He assured the usurers that they would get an automatic reduction in their withholding tax through the payroll under his control. All this led us to assume that Pastor Coronel, in complicity with the minister of education, purposely caused the delays.

Another blight no less important was the "purchase order," the trading of which for half its cash value was common when teachers had to pay for emergency expenses not covered by the Institute of Social Welfare, such as hospitalization in a private clinic.

It should also be mentioned that teachers who had contributed 20 percent of their salaries toward social security (retirement, Institute of Social Welfare, the National Workers' Bank) were for the most part not entitled to paid sick or maternity leave because the budget wasn't enough to cover even a quarter of the annual demand. Nor did the Institute of Social Welfare make a provision for such benefits. Hundreds of files were arbitrarily "frozen" by the Treasury Department, forcing those who had been teaching for over thirty years and no longer had the strength or desire to do so to continue working.

In sum, a low salary made up largely of social security benefits, usury, the abuse of purchase orders, legal actions, and the unethical activities of local party presidents transformed *twenty-five thousand* Paraguayan teachers into an army of persecuted debtors. I openly shared my concerns with others in my community.

We all knew that the minister of education had built a palatial mansion with fees collected for the legalization of titles, certificates of study, and other services. We were aware that these fees were a brazen assault on the finances of heads of families and a betrayal of the national constitution, which mandates free education. We were certain that when the dictatorship fell and democracy was instituted, the minister's mansion—a shameless replica of the White House—would be converted into a modern local school. Just the thought of this calmed our anguish.[63]

As a student in the Department of Philosophy in 1962, I was deeply affected by Professor Luis Alfonso Resck's fiery speeches against the regime. I admired his courage most of all. In the same department my fellow party member Leandro Velásquez was also critical, but we did not trust him as we knew he was working for the all-powerful minister of the interior in administration in Puerto Presidente Stroessner.[64]

I recall how the McCarthy-like actions of the US State Department affected the National University in Asunción. An American "expert" by the name of Ralph Burns was sent to the university, where students witnessed his picturesque yet deplorable efforts to assist in educational reform. What he actually

---

63 This vision is on its way to becoming a reality—if the mansion is not torn down first.

64 As mentioned earlier, Leandro Velásquez went on to become leader of PORA, the Armed Revolutionary Workers' Party. He died under mysterious circumstances in Argentina in 1976 (no doubt a victim of Operation Condor).

did, however, was add fuel to the anticommunist fire started by Stroessner on May 4, 1954.

Burns sent an official document to the authorities in which he claimed not to understand why students were politicizing the university. He said he found it odd that Paraguayan students were inclined to discuss politics, a sphere of which they had no special knowledge. Burns advised the Paraguayan authorities against building residential areas or dormitories for students and professors—so common in American and European universities—because they "could facilitate meetings or visits with the communists." According to Burns, any proposal for change had to be communist inspired, and there was only one way to fight this temptation: athletic competitions.

Burns deliberately proposed developing sports and recreation because, rather than being educational, the experience would wear out the university students, act as a sedative, and prevent them from posing problems of substance. I realized that in the opinion of the American expert, the National University should continue in its role as factory, producing unscrupulous professionals and obedient employees who would be indifferent to issues of justice and exploitation.

One event that led me to think about the danger Stroessner's government posed to Latin American democracies was what I saw at Aeropuerto Presidente Stroessner in late 1965. By order of the minister of education, every teacher in the central zone was called to attend a reception at the airport for the "victorious" Paraguayan troops returning from the Dominican Republic, under the command of Colonel Cubas Barboza. It was then I discovered that Paraguay had been the first country to send reinforcement troops backing the North American invasion of the Dominican Republic in April—and that Stroessner had also offered Paraguayan soldiers to support the shaky pro-US regime in Vietnam. (It was later said that Colonel Cubas Barboza had been arrested and jailed in Villarrica. Out of regret for having joined the occupation force, he'd tried to lead a military coup to overthrow the "constitutional" government of General Alfredo Stroessner.)

By that time I had graduated from law school at the National University. Several of my classmates became government officials, and I would often run into them in court or at parties. From them I found out that Hugo Bánzer's fascist coup d'état in Bolivia was prepared in Paraguay, and that Bánzer himself had held several meetings with Stroessner and the army's intelligence service days before the overthrow of General Juan José Torres.

(Much later, in 1973, I would read in the Buenos Aires magazine *Gente* (People) that the Paraguayan government had also been implicated in the Chilean coup. By using diplomatic pouches to smuggle in millions of dollars to the Paraguayan Embassy in Santiago, Stroessner had subsidized the truckers' strike and thereby helped incite civil unrest.)

That same year (1965) I became director of the Juan Bautista Alberdi Institute, named after an Argentine national hero and defender of the Paraguayan cause during the Triple Alliance War; this had made for smooth relations with the Argentine Embassy in Asunción. There I discovered that the Paraguayan government, through the mediation of the Argentine ambassador, was supplying automatic weapons to the Anticommunist Alliance of Argentina, a death squad organized by the extreme right, in complicity with the military governments of the Southern Cone, to crush the supposed "subversive outbreak."

In 1968 the first municipal election of the "Stroessner Era" was announced. I honestly thought it would be the first step toward the democratization and moralization of the country, as established in article 3 of the party program: "The government will be organized on the basis of freely expressed popular sovereignty, and the establishment of balance and harmony among the administrative powers to guarantee a stable democracy." Under this illusion I joined the electoral campaign and was appointed a member of the San Lorenzo delegation of the Governing Board of the Colorado Party.

We were called together by the board to receive a briefing, along with the other presidents and members of the central zone. The education minister's brother was the main speaker. He focused on the need for a police force to prevent General Stroessner's enemies from criticizing him (that is, exercising their civil rights) and portrayed the party as being on the verge of failure. The belligerent primitivism of the talk was clearly a result of the speaker's nervous tension.

I myself had criticized the regime, and at that moment I had the feeling I was the target of his attack. I couldn't get rid of a searing anxiety that increased the longer I watched him. His trimmed, rectangular mustache called to mind the face of Hitler, and the hollow timbre of his voice reminded me of the clown-like Mussolini I had seen in the Chaplin film *The Great Dictator*. As the speech progressed, the room filled with an atmosphere of repression and censure, which the speaker encouraged with his violent rhetoric. It became unbearable. Confused and distressed, I left the room where hate was being preached in the purest Nazi style.

A few days later I was visited by a fellow member of the San Lorenzo delegation of the governing board. We had a very important conversation in which he amicably expressed his disagreement over my behavior at the Colorado headquarters. Suddenly he asked if I would vote for Stroessner in a sovereign election. In view of my silence, he continued, saying he would never vote for someone who did not respect article 4 of the Declaration of Principles of the Colorado Party—which unequivocally opposes rule by dictatorship or of the few—or who did not believe that democracy guaranteed the move toward an egalitarian society without special privileges or exploited classes...an ideal my visitor believed Stroessner was steadily moving away from.

He continued his explanations, expressing doubt as to whether authentic Colorados could vote for Stroessner in a free and democratic election. Therefore, he anticipated that in the future fraudulent elections would continue, violence would be unleashed, and the state of siege would be institutionalized. He likewise stressed the need to act with great prudence, saying change could be achieved only from the inside, only if a solid alliance could be forged of all parties interested in democracy and economic progress.

In speaking of the tactics to use in that uncertain future, my colleague emphasized that, above all, we had to overcome the lack of communication among the Colorados themselves, we had to overcome this isolated world into which repression and censorship were driving us more and more. He felt we should call to the Colorado Party's attention the fact that certain acts promoted by Stroessner were demagogic, such as wearing a red scarf around the neck or the obligatory "invitations" the president received every day to graduation ceremonies, whether in medicine or law, dressmaking or hairdressing—the only important thing was that the head of state be present, as it was all about public display.

My fellow Colorado then said he had observed that the Alberdi Institute had not yet invited the president to hand out diplomas. He told me my attitude of systematic opposition to appearing next to the chief of executive power was completely misguided—he considered it political nearsightedness and said it would cost me dearly in the long run.

In time his opinion proved correct.

He added, "All that glitters is not gold, and not all those who cheer for Stroessner truly support him." He said the regime was corroded by corruption and would inexorably end in failure. For now, however, it was necessary to remain in the country and inside the regime's apparatus, if possible, like the Trojan horse. Further, he said I should not forget that for the democratic cause, increasing the number of exiles was always a point for the opposition. Argentina and Brazil were true escape valves for the regime. With the systematic bleeding going on, Stroessner controlled the explosive Paraguayan boiler, fueled by years of injustice. Exile should be the last resort, as in the end only internal pressure would decide the fate of this regime that was not of the people.

My friend advised me to think over the content of the Colorado Party's Declaration of Principles, adding that the *democratic and progressive* branch of the party was the one with the best prospects in the long run, and it would fill the political vacuum when Stroessner was defeated. Economic policies like those in effect today, he added, left no room for the great majority of the people. Foreign monopolies appropriated everything, and there was no surplus that could serve as the basis for a policy of national commercial and industrial development.

The conclusions of my fellow Colorado could be summarized thus: (1) the Colorado Party was an organization of the people with two main sides, one answering to the great majority (the democratic and progressive Colorados), and the other to the minority whose interests conflicted with those of the people (the Stroessner Colorados); and (2) the democratic Colorados were aware that the present regime was incapable of solving the country's economic and social problems. They also knew a united "people" was much stronger than the reactionaries.

He said the progressive current of the party would gather around the figure of Roberto L. Petit. For that reason, he thought it urgent to spread the ideas of this leader of the Colorado Youth, after first uncovering the facts behind his assassination.

This conversation was crucial in that it helped change the course of my political journey. I understood that the principles of the real Colorado Party responded to the aspirations of the people of the Guaraní nation. It was a powerful notion that motivated me to fight for those ideals. From that moment on, the nature of the regime and its contradictions became clear to me.

At the time, there was controversy among researchers of the Guaraní language over the correct way to write "Caacupé," the town on the highway from Asunción to Presidente Stroessner. Some favored the use of the letter *C*, while others favored *K*. Because of this, I was inspired to identify the two types of Colorados in the same way. The Colorados were the authentic, progressive ones, and the Kolorados were Stroessner's upstarts, social climbers, opportunists, the nouveau riche. In my conception, the Colorado leaders were the ones who did not sell themselves and could not be bought. The reactionary camp of the Kolorados, on the other hand, housed the figures of Alfredo Stroessner and his henchmen, all of whom had a price.

The visit of Nelson Rockefeller to Asunción in 1969 caused repercussions in Paraguay. Students of the departments of Engineering and Medicine at the National University, along with those from the National High School and the Catholic University, organized demonstrations protesting the unwelcome presence of this representative of the United States. As was customary, the demonstrations were suppressed with the utmost violence.

But our spirits were lifted when we heard stories about the reactions of some of the relatives of those who had carried out the repressive acts: they had argued with the perpetrators and sometimes even gotten into physical fights with them. These stories convinced us that in the very heart of the pro-Stroessner "family," contradictions had emerged that would inevitably be resolved in favor of the new Paraguayan society.

Those of us who were not part of the Stroessner power elite suffered from the grave economic situation in Paraguay. Generalized corruption in business and institutionalized smuggling stood in the way of industrial development and made us more and more dependent as a country. To silence possible protests and promote fear, the government used massive arrests, mostly of innocent people.

In this social and political climate, the only reliable source of information about what was going on in the country was the Catholic newspaper *Comunidad* (Community). This voice of the Paraguayan Episcopal Conference (CEP)[65] opened my eyes, which may be why I began to doubt what I read in the official newspaper, *Patria*. The two differed significantly in how they portrayed the nation's problems.

According to the government publication, the main challenge was to rid Paraguay of communism. The regime was not the least bit interested in eradicating tuberculosis, misery, or ignorance, which were frequent concerns of *Comunidad*. The CEP's publication stimulated my interest in liberation theology (with its emphasis on serving the poor) and the doctrine of Christian democracy, and I became even more attracted after talking with its leaders.

When I was a member of the auxiliary committee for the health center in San Lorenzo, I asked the director why he didn't demand at least minimal medical supplies from the Ministry of Health, as the center distributed only aspirin and purgatives to a population of more than fifty thousand. In private, the doctor, who was not a Colorado, explained that he ran the risk of being dismissed if he dared even to repeat his request for sterile gauze or gasoline for the ambulance.

"I have been head of this center for ten years," he said, "and it has been ten years of moral suffering because of the government's indifference to the humble people who work on the land, in the municipal market, or with the small manufacturers in the area." The doctor lived in a world of permanent conflict

---

65 An agency of the Catholic Church that provides a forum for the bishops of Paraguay. It published *Comunidad* until forced to stop in 1969; it then published *Sendero* (Path) from 1973 to 1992.

between the threat of dismissal for not belonging to the Stroessner party and the need to work and serve the community. So far, the government had not tried to get rid of him because he had the total support of the people, but he was a special case.

Captain Cecilio Giménez, whose house was across the street from the municipal market, also lived in conflict. One day he confided the following to me: "We have to face the fact that in the past, people came to the market to buy meat, milk, fruit, and vegetables. They were happy. Now the vendors complain because their goods are rotting; sales have decreased despite the fact that the population has doubled. The people are hungry, the children malnourished. Can you tell me what is happening?"

I took advantage of the opportunity and compared Paraguayan society to a colony of bees in which 5 percent of the population consumes 90 percent of what is produced by the majority—farmers and workers—who do not get a fair price for their work. Logically, the difference ended up in the pockets of the few, the idle. I reminded him that in Paraguay there were four uniformed officials (police or military) for each worker, so there was no way the budget could support that 5 percent, adding together the entire repressive apparatus.

With a thoughtful air he answered that, in his experience, only communists knew the cause and effect of social phenomena, and my explanation reminded him a little of what the parish priest had told him about me. The priest was suspicious of my loyalty to Stroessner's politics because I frequently spoke with my students at the Alberdi Institute about social issues like the one Captain Giménez and I were discussing. After this unequivocal statement, there was an awkward silence. The captain changed his manner, took on his usual posture of Stroessner-like authority, and dismissed me with a coldness that left me puzzled.

That night I could not sleep for fear—fear that Giménez would inform the police about everything I had said about the corrupt and repressive nature of the regime. From that moment I was often overcome by an anxiety that reached all the way to my bones. At the same time I completely rejected everything that smacked of Stroessnerism and its fanatic "Kolorados."

After attending political events, I would feel depressed. My conscience demanded that I put a stop to that sham, that I publicly withdraw from pro-Stroessner politics and enlist in the ranks of those running the Colorados in Buenos Aires. I dreamed that they would not use the red scarf anymore, but rather a broom that would represent the actions of the authentic Colorado ideology in power, sweeping away once and for all the injustices that prevailed in Paraguay.

On the other hand, I never forgot what had happened to a colleague who, for having questioned the legitimacy of Stroessner's "constitutional" government in his history and geography class, was taken to police headquarters and threatened with torture and imprisonment if he continued his "subversive teaching method." With this precedent I was afraid my conscience would betray me and I would start telling my students—many of whom were children of "Stroessner bosses"—what I really felt as we discussed subjects like democracy, dictatorship, and habeas corpus in moral and civic education classes.

Fear of repression consumed me, and the daily tension at work gave me an ulcer. The stress was intensified by reprimands I received from the Ministry of Education. They said that thanks to me, the Alberdi Institute had become a hub of resistance, and they told me to immediately get rid of all opponents of the government. As a defense strategy I gave ingenuous explanations—for example, that I didn't know whether a given professor was in the opposition. To buy time, I promised I would take advantage of the end of the school year to proceed with the purge, a promise I obviously had no intention of keeping.

Things got out of hand when I approved the list of colleagues to be the first occupants of the Teachers' Village of San Lorenzo housing project, where I acted as president of the Association of Educators. The Teachers' Village was the result of my colleagues' collective effort, and the first occupants were—according to the authorities at the Ministry of Education—"for the most part professors in opposition." From that time on, my presence in the "official world" no longer inspired confidence, and they made me aware of this at every turn. Friends who knew what was going on advised me to proceed with more prudence and, above all, to keep my distance from the teachers' cooperative because, according to the government, it "reeked of communism."

Around that time we also had an offer from the Mexican actor Cantinflas to hold a fundraiser in Asunción for Paraguayan teachers. However, a very angry minister of Education summoned me urgently to his office and shouted that Cantinflas would *never* be able to set foot in Paraguay because he was a communist and, furthermore, I had better stop practicing democracy in the classroom because it was communist inspired. From that moment, he added, we were prohibited from reading Paulo Freire's subversive book, *Pedagogy of the Oppressed*.

Through teaching and labor-union activity, I was discovering little by little the world of lies that the oppressive system was weaving to hide its injustices. This was the subject of a continuous dialogue I held with Celestina. Probably to cheer me up, she said she found my state of conflict positive because she considered my growing class consciousness a sign of pedagogical labor in progress.

Celestina was more mature than I politically because she came from a family that read and discussed national and international issues. Among her relatives were people of all political persuasions—Febreristas (one of the allowed opposition parties) for the most part, like her, but also honest Colorados, Liberals, communists, and members of the military. She was my refuge, my consolation, and she enabled me to tolerate an atmosphere filled not with oxygen but with burning fear.

My ulcer got worse, and it became clear that no remedy was going to be effective if I remained in this tense situation, under constant threat. For that reason I applied for and won a scholarship from the Organization of American States (OAS) that had been advertised in the papers. Sure enough, a course at the Catholic University of the North (in the Atacama Desert in northern Chile)—in an environment where justice still prevailed—did much to heal the wound.

My stay in Chile inspired me to dream of an Alberdi Institute that would produce the future forgers of democracy in Paraguay. From then on, I felt the need to go beyond individual action. The task seemed very burdensome to me, so I decided to share my pedagogical worries with colleagues who had progressive concerns, for the most part former seminarians.

In my search for the causes that had led to the consolidation of the dictatorship, I discovered that Paraguay's landlocked geography and the Guaraní language had helped strengthen our national identity very early on, but those same factors had contributed to making the country an island within the context of South America. The surrounding countries almost always lived with their backs to Paraguay, and vice versa.

After I returned home, I attended the opening of a chalet in the town of Caaguy-rory that belonged to a navy lieutenant. I knew the young sailor's job was fighting small-time smuggling operations in which poor people brought in food from Clorinda, Argentina, for their own consumption…while at the same time protecting the pro-Stroessner "big fish," whose smuggling amounted to millions of dollars.

The guests' conversations centered on the furniture, pottery, ceiling, and other items, all imported from Brazil. Nothing there was made in Paraguay except for the mandioca they served with the steaks—even the meat was from Argentina. After the drinks (whiskey and "high-quality" beer), the conversation intensified, but the topic did not change: furniture, statuary, chandeliers, the roof, crystal imported from Europe for the mansions of ministers and government entities like the phone exchange, health service, and others.

Everything I saw and heard made me think again about the great difference between the *C* and *K* Colorados. I thought about the people of my town who did honor to the public offices they held by living modestly. For the Stroessner administration, though, honesty was a crime of lèse majesté, or offense against majesty, and those who led a life of austerity were persecuted relentlessly.

In 1972 I went to Argentina to pursue my doctorate in the science of education at the celebrated National University of La Plata, with a scholarship from the government of Argentina. I was deeply moved by the thousands of my compatriots exiled there with no possibility of returning to our country, thanks to Stroessner's whim. When I spoke with them, I found that they were extremely homesick. They lived with the hope of returning to their native land as soon as the political conditions were right. To deny a citizen the right to return to his country of origin seemed to me an act of unpardonable cruelty.

According to the rules of doctoral study at the University of La Plata, I had to present a plan for my dissertation within six months. I had two options.

On the one hand, I could write a dissertation extolling the virtues of the educational system imposed by the dictatorship. To achieve this I would do as the recipients of the regime's scholarships did: request an audience and offer the "leader" the fruit of my efforts. This would result in a good job for me in the bureaucratic machine and an easy path in my country.

On the other hand, I could uphold the truth and denounce the Stroessner educational system for benefiting the dominant class exclusively and serving the interests of underdevelopment and dependency. I met with Celestina in Posadas, Argentina (across the border from Encarnación), and together, aware of the consequences, we chose the latter.

The research and writing of my work took many months.[66] I analyzed different problems that figured into the complex panorama of my country, and the impact of politics and economics on Paraguay's educational system. In particular, I mentioned the cultural penetration of Brazil and North America. I also discovered that implementation of the Itaipú Dam would have grave consequences for Paraguay if measures were not taken to change the economic structure of the country.

I defended my dissertation, *Paraguay: Education and Dependence*, in August of 1974 and afterward went straight to the main office of the National Commission of Argentina for UNESCO and the OAS office in Buenos Aires to inquire about job vacancies in the area. I presented my application in hopes of securing a position that would make it possible for me to leave Paraguay immediately and "honorably."

On more than one occasion I wrote Celestina that my fear of returning to Paraguay was tearing me apart body and soul. Aware of the danger surrounding

---

66   Although I did not know it at the time, some of the materials given to me for reference involved a counterinsurgency study, Project Camelot, begun by the Special Operations Research Office (SORO) of the US Army in 1964. SORO's director, Theodore Vallance, described Project Camelot as "a study whose objective is to determine the feasibility of developing a general social systems model which would make it possible to predict and influence politically significant aspects of social change in the developing nations in the world" (cited in *Wikipedia*). After word about the study got out in Santiago and Washington in 1965, the project was canceled, only to be continued in a more discreet manner. But the fact that I referred to the "top-secret" plan in my dissertation was a pretext for Stroessner to treat me harshly later. Although President Kennedy was not directly linked to Project Camelot, he had encouraged the US military to undertake counterinsurgency studies—precursors to Camelot—after the Bay of Pigs debacle in April 1961.

us, and foreseeing the possibility of exile, we'd sent our older children, Ricardo and Lincoln, to study in Argentina.[67] My morale was very low, but our commitment to the teachers at the Alberdi Institute who had accompanied us in the task of reflection and consciousness-raising eventually caused us to rethink our plan to settle in Argentina.

In the end Celestina and I decided to return to San Lorenzo because we were truly convinced we needed to remain in the place where we could best contribute to the revolutionary cause. We had two objectives in mind: transformation of the Juan Bautista Alberdi Institute into a teachers' cooperative, along with the operation of trade workshops for electricians, carpenters, pavers, etc., and completion of the construction of housing in the Teachers' Village.

All these experiences gave rise to profound contradictions within me that led me more and more to want to know the cause of what was wrong, a definitive explanation for my dissatisfaction. Through my awareness of what was happening in my conflictive society, I saw that in the eyes of the dictatorship, I was becoming a highly dangerous person who needed to be "neutralized" or "liquidated." It behooves me to provide some background information along these lines to explain why I was supposedly so dangerous.

A few years earlier I had reconciled with Captain Cecilio Giménez, who had fortunately reconsidered his arrogant, pro-Stroessner stance while serving as local Colorado Party leader in San Lorenzo. He made this decision after promising not to badger opposing teachers and professors—those who in Stroessner-speak were referred to as "contrary." The local party presidents' authority had far exceeded legal limits during that time, and they had become police-like agents answering directly to Stroessner's political police, led by Pastor Coronel.

Captain Giménez had been replaced by Felipe Salomón and wanted to regain the presidency of the local Colorado Party. So I began supporting

---

67 After I was imprisoned, my sons were not able to return to Paraguay immediately, as they too ran the risk of being detained or kidnapped. They later accompanied my mother in all of the negotiations. Ricardo had the magnificent idea to send a note to the general director of UNESCO in Paris, telling him about the violations of human rights in Paraguay and my case in particular. Then Ricardo and his siblings organized a campaign of support and reported their mother's untimely death to the *Círculo Paraguayo de Médicos* (a doctors' union).

Giménez, which attracted the interest of many party members, and we saw that we could be successful in the elections. The opposing ticket was Salomón and a veterinarian whose merits were based on the embezzlement of funds from the municipal coffers and from the National Service to Fight Against Hoof and Mouth Disease, and on the creation and promotion of brothels that trapped young rural women migrating to town.

As our campaign grew, so did our popular support. We arranged for me to qualify as a candidate for an important post at the national level. Our opponents got all their money—much more than we had—for advertising, finances, and logistics from Stroessner's private secretary, Mario Abdo Benítez. In spite of everything, they beat us by a slim margin in an election that was clearly fraudulent, as usual.

This happened in June of 1972. Our adversaries understood the real possibilities we had with Captain Giménez in the next election. Thus began a two-year period in which they spun the *ñandutí* of intrigue designed to neutralize and liquidate the Giménez-Almada ticket, which stood for freedom in the time of Stroessner's greatest political, military, and police power.

Because Celestina and I had a thirst for justice, we chose to unite with the poor and dream of a society in which we could communicate without fear and grow without poverty and in solidarity. We had resolved to "preach by example," to teach human rights, to be the means by which the people could have their say, their good news—*the distribution of wealth and not of poverty*—through an economy of communion, on a more humane level.

We were very aware that in the regime's context of injustice, corruption, and repression, temporal values were above those of the spirit, so much so that ill-gotten resources and material gains were exalted and became ends in themselves. For example, we could barely tolerate that teaching jobs were assigned by local pro-Stroessner party presidents and usually given to incompetent people; that the electoral farces were all flagrantly manipulated; that the regime's profiteering had no limits (perpetrators would even sell children under the pretext of legalizing adoptions); that the calculated theft of state property was tolerated; that the dignity of women was sacrificed in an anti-Christian society; that the environment was being destroyed through the concession of thousands of hectares of land—to the police, military, and local party presidents via the Institute of Rural Welfare—and the merciless felling of our forests; and that peasants and indigenous people were then persecuted and the land made into giant cattle ranches and farms for producing export crops to obtain cash.

Under Stroessner, Paraguay had changed from a republic into a "banana republic," in which disunion and inequality held sway. Consequently, the flame of justice lit very quickly in our hearts, but our decision to unite with the poor became our "mortal sin."

As a result, Stroessner declared us guilty.

Part VII

All I Want
December 1975–May 1976

—∿—

Emily

*Where you find the greatest Good, there you will also find the greatest Evil, for Evil
likes Paradise every bit as much as Good does.*

Wallace Stegner
All the Little Live Things

Río de Janeiro! The most enchanting city I had ever imagined, and I was actually *here*! The geography was spectacular, from the delightfully phallic Pão de Açúcar (Sugarloaf) to Corcovado with its impressive art deco statue of Christ the Redeemer standing watch over the city. With all the other rainforest-covered hills jutting out of the sea, the big bay dotted with islands, the sapphire Atlantic, the white lace of the waves on the sand…it was paradise for sure. I'd nearly wept as we beheld its splendor for the first time. Rapture. Now I understood.

The surf was perfect, the beaches clean and adorned with human bodies that made your gonads tingle, male and female, string bikinis and banana hammocks, all shades of glistening espresso and caramel and vanilla blending smoothly in the bosom of the warm and seductive sand. I got horny just thinking about it. Where was your *amante* at times like this?

I didn't plan to tell my sister about Tito—it'd been just the once, after all. I still wasn't sure how I felt about it but had to admit I was hoping he'd come back.

Yes, my *sister*…Virginia, named after my paternal aunt. I went to pick up my mother and grandmother and came back with Ginny, whom they'd sent in their stead, as Nanny couldn't make it (she was okay, just had to have a little "procedure" on her cervix) and Mom couldn't leave her alone. So my sister and I were now in stunning Río after almost getting stuck in rainy, hot, insufferable Paraguay.

Ginny said she'd barely gotten off the plane from Chicago—where she'd started acting school but was returning home to Tucson—when Mom asked her to come to Paraguay to check up on me. That kind of ticked me off…I didn't need no stinkin' checkup! But when Gin said Mom was worried about everyone, Nanny and us, I felt bad. It wasn't as if Mom didn't have her own problems. I was sure my letters didn't help—I tended to spill my guts out in those.

Just being around my sister had made me more relaxed than I'd been in, well, about a year. Her hair was short and she'd filled out some, though she was still "skinny Ginny," and damn if she didn't still have that inner tranquility I could only long for. She reminded me that in our family she'd been known as the whiner and I the pouter, which made me laugh because it was so true. I'd always had trouble controlling my emotions. Well, we all come into this world with a disposition.

I had to laugh remembering how my father would never let me stomp off during an argument (usually political), so I'd stopped initiating them. I could never win, anyway—Republicans had a way of stating their case that was irrefutable. "Don't contradict me," I could still hear him say, and I felt like I'd been yelled at. (I'd always been hypersensitive.)

Gin and I had gotten along even though she was my kid sister—not close, but not distant, either. As the middle child I must have felt displaced by her, as I was barely two when she was born and—WHAM!—Dad wasn't "mine" anymore. (Mom always seemed tied up with our big brother.) But after leaving home and being so far away from Ginny and everyone, I realized how much I valued our friendship—especially now that Dad was gone.

We'd cried when we discovered we both blamed ourselves for Dad's death. It was only natural—it was also only natural that we would try to change the other's mind. We both missed Dad body and soul and agreed we would've gladly suffered the consequences of his choosing to live rather than sacrifice his life for us…which we could only hope hadn't been in vain.

I took Ginny to Caazapá, where she got a kick out of meeting everyone and drinking tereré. I swear, ice never tasted so good—I would never again take that precious resource for granted. I couldn't bring myself to kill the kid, so I traded it for a sheep that Zunilda would cook later.

Then the worst happened: it rained like hell and we almost got stuck in Caazapá for Christmas, even spent a wretched night in Maciel waiting for the train, true desperados by that point, so desperate we were even willing to go south, to Argentina, when all I really wanted was to go north, to Brazil. The southbound train had derailed at San Salvador, just before Iturbe…but when it finally came through Maciel at 1:00 a.m., *no one woke us up, even though we'd asked them to!* I was beside myself with rage. But my sister fared far worse; as I wrote in my journal, "Poor Gin's having some nasty bouts with the bugs. Damn near afraid to sleep in any beds anymore. I'd wanted her to experience the 'campo' but not like this!"

I couldn't believe I'd actually planned to bring my grandmother to this inferno! My sister and I barely—and I mean *barely*—made it out on the bus (it came close to not leaving). But after only twenty minutes we were forced to stop in Ñumí, a village north of Caazapá with *absolutamente nada*, for four agonizing hours, to wait for the road to dry…which by this point my sister thought was a perfectly reasonable thing to do.

When we finally hit pavement, I wasn't sure I would ever stop.

But stop we did, at Yguazú Falls and the lovely pink colonial Hotel das Cataratas, on the Brazilian side of the falls, complete with coatis and toucans. (I'd seen it on that fateful field trip from the Argentine side and fallen in love with it.) No rooms were available, so I used every wile I could muster. A generous young English-learning waiter winkingly offered us his room, which we winkingly refused. Then a vacancy turned up. It was sheer heaven. I fell in love with the falls, even got up at sunrise and jogged down to the base of Devil's Throat—getting soaked from the mist—in hopes the relentless, raw power could somehow purify me (and thinking those rocks would make for a pretty hard landing).

Two days later we arrived here in Río. Our first three nights had been at the Regina Hotel near Flamengo Beach, between Copacabana and downtown at the mouth of Guanabara Bay, 170 cruzeiros (about eighteen dollars) a night, with a refrigerator, our own bathroom with occasional hot water, and a superb breakfast on the top floor.

From there, Sugarloaf looked like a gigantic shark thrusting its head out of the water and about to rip you to shreds, just like the one we saw on posters everywhere of the ridiculous-looking film by some upstart named Spielberg. Gin said she'd seen it in Chicago and screamed out loud, which made me laugh—still the same ol' scaredy-cat.

We went to see Chaplin's *The Great Dictator*, a seemingly odd choice for a Latin American country, and thought the whole film hysterical, from the upside-down airplane scene to Chaplin's brilliant lampoon of the long-winded "Tomainian" language with its overly concise English translations, and our favorite, the dancing-with-the-globe scene. Why did dictators have to look so alike, anyway—Stroessner, Pinochet, "Adenoid Hynkel"? Mussolini, aka "Benzino Napaloni, Dictator of Bacteria," was a total buffoon, as were "Herring" and "Garbitsch." (Gin was distressed when I told her Goebbels—or was it Mengele[68]—was rumored to be living in Paraguay.)

---

68   Josef Mengele did live in Paraguay, in 1960 and from 1963–64, in a German community called Hohenau. Though reported to have drowned off the coast of Brazil in 1979, he is rumored to have returned to Paraguay under an alias not long afterward and lived as a madman in Nueva Alemania (New Germany). He is said to have thrown himself in front of a bus in Asunción five years later ("Mengele

What a genius Chaplin was, and so talented. I hadn't laughed that hard in a long time. But during the final speech, when the "fake" Hynkel gave his call to action, asking people to fight for freedom and democracy, to resist the "machine men with machine minds and machine hearts," saying we were coming out of the darkness and into the light, and greed and brutality were being defeated—I got choked up. If only it were true.

The movie had been made in 1940 and—like *The Hobbit,* written in 1937, which also spoke of defeating the "darkness" and the machinery of war—was clearly a vindication of underground efforts to break free of tyranny. Over coffee later, Gin and I agreed that the current government of Brazil, a military dictatorship as well, must be pretty tolerant to let the film be shown here despite its subversive undertones.

Either that or they just didn't get it.

Journal entry 29 Dec—Gin is having a good time but has a cold of sorts and is not in the best of spirits. She gets fed up with me because of my "take life as it comes" ways—even more pronounced after a year in Paraguay—she, being the Capricorn she is, likes to know exactly WHERE she is going and HOW she will arrive...

Journal entry 30 Dec—Morning. Went to the beach today at 6:15 and jogged/ walked to the end of Copacabana. Only three hours of sleep last night—went to the "Cestinha," a "discotheque"...Had a terrible (tragic-comic) time with Ginny getting rid of two nice-but-only-too-typical Italians. I thought I would lose my mind. How weary I am of this eternal chase/woo/conquer game. Just give me purity!

"You taught me to read," Ginny said one day, "when we used to play school out in the carport." I remembered dragging her out there and being the teacher—I'd always loved school—but had no idea I'd actually taught her something. It was a good feeling.

She also told me about a dream she'd had in which she was riding in a rocket toward outer space. She was sitting in front of a *Jeopardy!* -like panel, and

---

in Paraguay," Graeme Wood, Drexel University: The Smart Set, 5 February 2008, http://thesmartset. com/article02050801/).

a smooth-talking game-show host had offered her the answers to "all the questions of the universe," with just one caveat—once she knew the answers, she would never want to go back to Earth. She'd woken up immediately.

"I think humans were meant to ask questions and find their own answers," she said. I'd never heard my little sister sound so wise. Even back in Maciel, after using the skankiest latrine I'd ever seen, she'd said, "You know, Em, this is reality, not Chicago." She was losing her innocence, all right.

Ellyn arrived, and we moved into a former PC–Paraguay volunteer's apartment two blocks from Copacabana Beach, where we spent most of the week when we weren't sightseeing or sampling restaurants or dancing samba all night. Ellyn's parents had flown in from Minnesota (they were staying at the Sheraton, shameless extortion at thirty-eight dollars a night), and I took to them right away. We all went to see the Cristo—with its unbelievable views— and the luxuriant Tijuca Forest, where we saw shrines with offerings of food that the guidebook said were left by followers of Macumba, an African-Brazilian religion with various sects that were apparently growing in popularity.

I lived for the *vitaminas* made with fresh pineapple or papaya every morning before hitting the beach and getting burnt to a crisp. Portuguese was fun to try to speak, sounding like a cross between Spanish and French. We pretended to shop for expensive gems in carpeted stores along the wavy black-and-white mosaic boardwalk; I bought an inexpensive stone pendant that had a cross in it, called the *cruz del sur* (southern cross). I found it hilarious that I would end up wearing a cross after all, and that people would think I was Catholic.

On New Year's Eve we celebrated the bicentennial of our nation with liberal doses of the local sugarcane rum called *cachaça* [cah-SHAH-sah]…and paid dearly for it the next day, barely even remembering the thousands of people on the beach who were celebrating Yemanjá, the Queen of the Sea, by dancing and singing and sending little paper boats out into the surf with offerings to appease the "giver and taker" of all life.

Sadly, all too soon it was over. When we said goodbye at the airport, Gin said she felt a lot better and wondered if Mom hadn't sent her here for her own good as well as mine. I was doing better, too—I felt I could handle anything life had to throw at me now. The last thing I said as we hugged was "Tell Mom she doesn't have to worry about me." *Yeah, right.* I would miss my sister.

At least Ellyn and I still had the cruise to look forward to.

On January 5 I wrote a letter on Hotel das Cataratas onionskin stationery with the imprint "Tropical" to Mom et al.:

And now it's over, this wonderful break, this taste of city and salt water and international atmosphere. I feel ready to return to the tranquility of Paraguay but not so ready to resume my work. I've achieved a certain peace of mind in the past few weeks, that shouldn't be interrupted by worries of responsibility to many others. But I suppose that old thought pattern will return, too. Planning and organizing and being diplomatic, ick!

This city is such a magical place, with its climate and unique combination of Latin "mañana" attitudes mixed with African "samba," FIRE. There are hills throughout, much like San Francisco, that add to the diversity of the place. Such a vacation atmosphere. But the gold and glitter wear off after a bit, one realizes the blacks and whites don't mix all that well, that 85% of the people in Brazil (Rio) are not upper class, nor even middle class. Yesterday when we came home from our weekend cruise we passed kilometer after kilometer of cheap block apartments that are government built and crowded...People flood to the city to find jobs when times are rough, and what do they find there? A lifestyle they will never be able to adopt, not even emulate, yet a growing desire within, every day, every TV commercial, every newspaper ad, to have it. These apartments looked like prisons...The rich are rich and the poor poor, there is no middle class as we know it.[69]

Ellyn and I just returned from a three-day yacht cruise...a great trip! There were 21 altogether: 4 Swiss, 1 Italian, 1 French, 1 Irish, 1 Australian, 1 Brazilian, 3 English, 4 English-Brazilians, 5 Americans... The air was so international, 3 or 4 languages going on at once (everyone spoke English, or could). Now I want to learn as many languages as possible. We had to drive 80 kilometers south, to a coastal village called "Itacuruçá"—a Guaraní name!—where we boarded our ship, an old combination sail/motor that was all wood and so strikingly beautiful... the "MAKAIYA." We stayed in the bay, never hit the open sea; but the bay was huge, hundreds of islands and we would go for 3–4 hours without

---

69 The income gap in the United States has been widening since the 1920s.

stopping, from one island to another. The first day we went to an island, anchored there, swam, snorkeled, ate, drank, talked, read, etc. and had a barbecue on the beach that night. (Needless to say we all drank a lot and got absolutely plowed.) We were all sunburned, too.

Saturday wasn't as nice—no sun. We left the island and went to a small tourist town, Paraty, where it began to rain, so we spent the night on the boat in the harbor. Went out for a fish dinner and dancing afterwards. Sunday was sunny again, we headed toward another island and swam, snorkeled some more...what a delightful occupation! Swimming in and amongst rocks, watching fish who think you're just one of them—I saw yellow and black striped, blue and black striped, speckled ones, anemones, star fish—plants swaying with the waves. I loved it. Everything about this easygoing beachcomber life I like. My next journey may take me to an island somewhere, among fishermen.

Well, it was so nice having Gin here, she is a real joy to have around. Just wish Mom and Nanny could have come...

On January 26 I returned home to Caazapá, and it felt different. I felt different, too, separate yet wanting more than ever to be a part of life here and get back into a routine. Rumor had it the office would get a Paraguayan *educadora* (Odila?) soon. I could only hope it was true.

In honor of the rainy and cool weather—a welcome, if brief, respite from the heat—I copied a poem by Li Po (701–762 AD) into my journal:

If you were to ask why I dwell
among green mountains;
I should laugh silently, my soul is serene.
The peach blossom follows the flowing waters.
There is a heaven and earth beyond
the realm of man.

February 1, 1976, Dear All,

Hello from Asunción. I returned here after four miserable days in Caazapá...

Did I tell you about our American folklore night? We had a show, a benefit for the asylum, and had everything from magic acts to square dancing to a song jamboree. I sang "Cheatin' Heart" and a couple of duets. It was great fun, and we made nearly 40,000 guaranies (around $320)...There was a wild party afterwards, put on by an army colonel and his wife, netted 17,000 guaranies. Even the US ambassador came to the show! (His son performed some "magic.") His wife liked it and he <u>pretended</u> to, but I think he was politely bored...

Well, it's a new year, I've made some resolutions. Hope I can fulfill them...

Love you all—In the struggle, E

Journal entry 3 Feb—Paraguayan holiday, Día de San Blas. Well it is most interesting to imagine what I'm doing, that is eating mutton off my very own sheep. Eating a bone, a meaty bone, awrghh! Chew, tear, chew. Licking greasy fingers. Listening to Phoebe Snow. Rocking out on "Down by the San Francisco Bay." Someone could come here and cut himself off entirely, forever from the rest of the world. The US hardly exists for me now...

Journal entry 4 Feb—I CAN'T BELIEVE IT..."MALACARA"[lit."BAD FACE"] FOR MY HORSE! ALWAYS MY FAVORITE HORSE AROUND CAAZAPÁ! AND I'M ONLY RENTING HIM! YIPPEE!!

Journal entry 6 Feb—What a day! Finished flipchart...read some SOURCE... washed hair, dishes...visited Elena on Malacara...ate polenta and soy... almost went to sleep...got to the office...went to San José, had cramps, couldn't play volleyball...saw Araí and want him again. (Sure he's crazy but I don't think he belongs in the campo!)...yoga...dinner w/ Elena...

What pisses me off is when Vargas reprimands me for sloppy office hours, then turns around and for one whole day doesn't show up in the office! And I go to his store to buy coffee & candles, and he's sitting there drinking tereré. Fooey!

I really have enjoyed this week, but probably only got through it because it was only 3 days long. Well I'm at the point where I finally understand what I'm doing, and finally understand what a good situation I've got (even after Tito came over last night...)

WORK LOG 12 FEB
    a.m. Oficina—Club 4-C Prep.
    p.m. Tayy-í—Nice reunion, Velázquez talked a lot, motivation to work plus some cotton bichos [bugs]...I'd talked to the socias before re: fiesta, gardening project, then manualidades [handicrafts]...Then played some music. Everyone's stringing tobacco, also harvesting peanuts. Rolling cigars, big fat ones. I do love the girls there, all the folks...

Journal entry 12 Feb—Lincoln's birthday...Today I rode Malacara to Tayy-í. The road was funky, just stops in the middle of a swamp...Well I did eat peanuts, and had a glass of milk at Olimpia's, and smoked a li'l stogie back at [another socia's] again—had a great time on ol' Mariposa [Butterfly] (oops, I mean Malacara) even though he tried to throw me one time, or so we thought.
    The moment of truth is fast approaching (er, my candle's burning out).

WORK LOG 13 FEB
    a.m. Lluvia [Rain]—Oficina.
    p.m. San José-mí—Girls didn't show up, only two who live in house where we went (Blanca and her sister). Angry 'cuz I don't come no more. Velázquez had reunion in San José, not too big but he said farmers asked him to help form comité [commission]. HOORAY! He's very enthused.

Journal entry 13 Feb—Wow, Zunilda's telling me last night that I need to put on more lotion, that my hands are rough, that to hold my hand is like holding the hand of a man. And then talking about my sister, how fine her skin is, how delicate her hands and feet (well, it's so true) but así es luego, tengo la piel de mi papá [that's just how it is, I have my father's skin].

Work was revving up, with all the clubs planning fiestas, it seemed. I'd almost forgotten it was Valentine's Day. It was a Saturday, and I worked that morning getting permission from the police chief for the dance in San José-mí.

I hated going to the police station. The officers treated you with a thinly veiled contempt they disguised as respect. Their little game of cat and mouse amused them but infuriated me. They could do anything they wanted with you—all in your best interest, of course—and made sure you knew it. I shuddered to think what *really* went on in that place. Risking rudeness I made excuses, as always, to avoid the chief's invitation to tereré.

But oh, how I loved my horse! He looked like my first true love, Schoolboy, who'd won me lots of ribbons and trophies when I was ten. Malacara was petite but truly the prettiest *cabajú* in town. What a coincidence he belonged to Zunilda and Epifanio. It was handy to be renting my house *and* horse *and* getting a daily meal, all from the same people...and all for peanuts, only thirty-two dollars a month.

Emily trying to get her horse, Malacara, to pose for the camera.

I was definitely looking forward to dinner at their house tomorrow for Día de los Enamorados. Zunilda was barbecuing the tyrannical hen—we'd had to sacrifice her to keep peace in the roost. (Maybe we needed a *gallo* after all.)

One thing for sure: I was counting the days to my upcoming trip to Asunción, where I'd be helping train some new PCVs in ag extension. How could it possibly have been twelve months since I was in their very shoes?

Journal entry 14 Feb—Valentine's Day. Be Mine. Didn't send a single valentine. Somehow you lose it when you're not surrounded by it…I live in two worlds, Caazapá and Peace Corps, I'm getting so involved in Caazapá and don't particularly want to change that…

Whew something noteworthy today. The school PTA meeting in San Miguel. I didn't want to go, had had a bad time [earlier] and was angry. Came to the office, wanted to leave but stayed to have a smoke. Velázquez came in the vehicle with a Rojas Silva profesora (directora) [principal] and said "Ja ha pues" ["Let's go then"]. Well I didn't want to go, to leave Malacara at the office, to leave so late and miss the asado of my chicken, etc. but was forced into it. I closed the office and sat in the back of the car smoking, saying little. "Un ratito, nomás" ["A little while, is all"] Velázquez says, and I know I'm going to have a miserable time.

We get there (after a nice ride which I did enjoy—"A new road for horseback" I told myself) and I'm argel [ahr-HEL] as hell. Don't want to speak (I thought they're inviting me to ask for plata [money]. We go into the school and what should result after one of Velázquez' inspirational but taxing (after the 3rd or 4th time) speeches but an open-fire between some parents (about 30 in all, one-room schoolhouse w/ desks, blackboard) and the maestra [teacher], who just happened to live across the road, wealthy, almacén [store] and cocina a gas [gas stove], heladera [freezer] and everything. They accused her of giving free time to students ("recreos") and selling them things from the store. Or making them clean the school, yard, etc. Their arguments were not strong, not unified. To be sure, there are problems, and the people are not to be ignored. But no one was looking for solutions, only recounting grievances, and I thought I was going to go crazy…

Afterward we ate w/ the maestra, chicken, sopa, salad w/ tomato, onion, potato—exactly what Zunilda etc. had, más soup. I mellowed out...and they commented on how "adaptable" I am. I just threw it all away, that's all. Decided it's too late to worry about Zunilda. But came to the conclusion I couldn't really worry my little head that can only hold so much over a [minor] thing like a parent/teacher dispute in San Miguel, Caazapá, Paraguay. I mean there are some really important things going on in this life!

For example: A man full of revelation, but without desire, has equal (to the joy of Spirit) joy. (TAITTIREEYA UPANISHAD Book II, Joy) May He protect us both. May He take pleasure in us both. May we show courage together. May spiritual knowledge shine before us. May we never hate one another. May peace and peace and peace be everywhere.

Yo he dicho [I have spoken].

Wed 18 Feb, Dearest Nanny,

I'm in Asunción now, helping to train the new group of volunteers...we're teaching manual arts, visual aids and home improvement. It's so hot!! Seems strange to receive letters about snowstorms and Santa Claus.

When I think about all you've gone through—hopefully it's over by now—I feel so bad. Somehow you just keep on truckin' and that's what I love about you...

I've been on a vegetarian diet since I came to Asunción...now that I eat with my neighbors I eat too much meat. But I do love them, especially their 3-yr-old boy. Our favorite pastime is sitting around being gross ("dirty") with each other. That's how Paraguay is, gut level...

My friend Ellyn is here also, for tech training. I've learned a lot from her about methods of education (she's 25, has been teaching for several years). Think I may just go into teaching, someday, the government no longer appeals to me as a place to work. I do want to be politically active, but from the bottom not the top...

Your loving granddaughter, E

—Napkin Haiku—
The Cerro Corá chopp bar,
no fruit juice?
Well, bring me a cafecito,
*   then,*
black karma, bad
*   mud...*
(but it's cheaper)
Amidst the impurity
—the luscious impiety—
look!
White innocence
in wide straw hats:
*   suspender'd*
*   Mennonites.*
Comes the coffee
top foam in yin/yang symbol
a good omen...
*   like the Mennonites!*

Journal entry 27 Feb—Just read THE WISDOM OF INSECURITY by
Alan Watts.[70] *He states my thoughts exactly as I've learned from Eastern*
philosophy..."I" am part of everything, "you" are part of everything,
therefore I am part of you; or the experience of you is as important as the
experience of anything else. In any situation, the "I" is only a side product
of the true experience. If you're reading something and think "I'm reading
this," then in effect you're no longer reading it, simply thinking you're

---

70   Alan Watts (1915–73) was born in England and became fascinated with Eastern philosophy at a young age, publishing articles on Buddhism and Zen when he was only fourteen. He moved to New York in 1938 and then to Chicago, where he became an Episcopal priest for six years. In 1951 he moved to San Francisco to teach at the American Academy of Asian Studies and soon became a counterculture celebrity. He died in his sleep at age fifty-eight, leaving behind at least twenty-five books and an extensive audio library of over four hundred talks. He considered Buddhism more a form of psychotherapy than a religion.

reading it. *Stepping outside the situation (what I'm famous for, in my own eyes).Watts says: Learn to live right and everything will fall into line of its own right. I agree...*

Journal entry 28 Feb—Fiesta tonight [in Caazapá], carnaval. I'm wearing a mask that I made, a "Lone Ranger" type covered w/ red & white polka dots...

The president's coming! Por fin.Yesterday eve a reunion (women): plans for visit. My job: serving "cocktails."At last, my debut as cocktail waitress! And my first president! Even having a dress made (well, it's something to write home about...) Noticed how the women present at meeting were anybody's anybody...

Tía Sarita told me Zunilda talks a lot. Zunilda doesn't like the way Tía Sarita has her little chicks on leashes.Yesterday evening, walking w/ Perla— Perla says, "Tía Sarita thinks I'm walking with a guy, that's why she's gotten up and is coming over to meet us."Then when Tía Sarita reaches us she sees me and says "Whew I thought it was a guy" and we all laugh amiably...

I use roughly four gallons of H2O a day...

Journal entry 1 March—Día de los Heroes. Mariscal López died today in 1870...

Last night at the fiesta...I begin to see clearly what "festejaring" is, "going together"... You meet someone (at a dance, or just around) then if you like each other, the guy comes over to visit for awhile...from there it either makes it or it doesn't. Fiesta:The girl, not knowing what the guy is thinking (she likes him still, but he's messing around) sits contentedly until some fellow (not boyfriend) asks her to dance. She must comply, or sit still the entire night. Soon many boys ask her to dance...but not her boyfriend. Later: She:Why didn't you ask me to dance? He:Well you looked busy enough.That is, he blames it on her! The males have all the prerogative.

2 March 76, Dear Everybody,

I'm in Villarrica now so thought I'd drop a line. I came to buy paper for teaching (out of my own pocket—the Ministry of Agriculture is hard put to provide for these things)...This Friday Pres. STROESSNER is coming to Caazapá, finally, to inaugurate: Antelco bldg. (telephone); Colorado Party building; School of Agriculture; a few campo schools; plus various and sundry others (my house, for example). Well, you'll never guess what I'm going to be doing when he comes: serving "cocktails" before lunch to the officials of the town (and big Al)! This is my big chance! I'm on the road to fame and fortune in Paraguay! Pray for me, you may read about this, you know, Time Magazine, N.Y. Times, whatever.

I wrote a letter to the Middlebury Summer Language program, read about it in the want ad section of the Times (which I use for t.p.)...

We've been celebrating Carnaval in Caazapá. What this consists of is 4 nights of fiesta that end with everybody quite soaked either from sweat (mucha samba) or more likely water. It's the custom to throw water on everybody for Carnaval. What sophisticated fun, ne?...E

Journal entry 5 March—"Presidente Alfredo Stroessner" visits Caazapá. Here I was yesterday, an "exemplary Colorada" painting in giant red letters: Alfredo Stroessner, yeah yeah yeah. The town is super Colorado now.

Journal entry 6 March—He came, and he went (Stroessner). I got in with some ministers, got to stand right in front...("Who is that rubia?")

At the inauguration I took a picture of Vargas and a couple of SEAG agents beneath the sign I'd painted with Margarita—under duress—that proclaimed Caazapá's support of Stroessner *por siempre and para siempre* (forever and always). Later, standing in front of Stroessner in the foyer, I had to admit being that close to such a powerful person was exhilarating...though I wasn't about to buy one of the ubiquitous portraits of him being hawked by everyone, it seemed.

The fanaticism made me uncomfortable, though, so I was only too happy to go back to work the next week. And work I did. Velázquez had to go to Asunción, so I caught a ride to Rojas Silva to talk about the upcoming fogón demonstration we wanted to have there. In the afternoon I went to San José-mí to give the socias the permission slips for their fiesta April 24. They had quite a bit in their *fondo*, 7,683 guaranies (sixty-one dollars). We decided to make a squash-based dessert at the next meeting; I would bring the vanilla.

I returned to Rojas Silva the next morning and talked more specifically about the fogón course, but the people said they were embarrassed about their kitchens and didn't want the SEAG women to see them. I wondered if there wasn't something more to it, but decided Velázquez would have to talk to them.

Things were feeling tenuous all of a sudden, out of whack, Yeats's "widening gyre" on the verge of spinning out of control. It was clear I was trying to do too much.

On Tuesday a boy showed up from the telephone service, ANTELCO, to tell me I had a call. As no one here had phones, if you wanted to make a call you went to the ANTELCO office in your town, told the operator you wanted to call me in my town, then sat down and waited while the operator put the call through to the ANTELCO office in my town. After the call went through (*if* it did), a messenger from the ANTELCO office in my town would come to my house and, if he found me there, tell me I had a call. I would then walk to the ANTELCO office in my town and receive your call…presuming you were still in the ANTELCO office in your town and hadn't gone home out of irritation over the long wait.

Fairly straightforward.

It was Anna-í, asking how things were going.

"I've decided to have just a few clubs and concentrate on them," I told her. "Having more with meetings every two weeks isn't enough to keep the momentum going." Fortunately, she agreed.

About an hour later Ellyn called, and the whole ANTELCO process was repeated. I loved that we were speaking English and the operator had no clue what we were saying—this obviously rare denial made her so apoplectic she looked like one of those withered crones made from dried apples.

The next night I rode Malacara to Tayy-í and spent the night at Olimpia's. I liked doing it but realized I didn't want to make a habit of it—I still got nailed by bugs.

I wasn't looking forward to the next Saturday; there were too many things going on and I was dreading them, feeling out of sorts…afraid the tide of good-will was ebbing once again.

Journal entry 13 March—No emotion…A very nice day, though COLD, overcast, freezing, poncho weather! And today the asado (Colorado Party, I was invited because I helped at the Stroessner asado) and I helped make "morcilla," blood sausage at don Roque's house, and I enjoyed myself in the kitchen with the women (though I didn't talk much, didn't understand the Guaraní)…

Then came home, went to the asado, ate some of the blood sausage—after I'd told myself and know I didn't really want any—only ate it because it was there, it was there, like Paraguay is here, I'm only forcing myself to adapt because I'm here, it's good practice…

Then the meat…and teasing about boyfriends, like always, it's always the same thing…Of course I value the laughter, but my mind is being slowly drained of anything worthwhile…To be or not to be, I only am, I only participate because. Because it's here. Because I'm here. Not because I really want to. Why do I need the cross-cultural experience? At this point I'm integrated. Integral. I would go to the dance tonight only because it's a dance, I love to dance…not because I see any real reason to go. I am expected to go. Would rather stay home and read EXODUS.

In fact that's precisely what I intend to do. Don't know what's come over me. Naturally I vacillate, back & forth, haven't attempted to deny that…

This is most unexpected, because I have been adapting. I love adapting. And it is something I've never felt before. Aren't I ready to return to something where I fit in a bit more, something to which I am a functioning part? I feel so separate here, I cannot communicate my religious beliefs with anyone, I cannot communicate my visions, my interpretations of history, my impressions of present and past experiences…Minds here are concerned only with the here and now of Caazapá. And that is a very real thing, eternal almost…

And here I am, only minutes later, all choochy [dressed up] and ready to go to the fiesta: Ángela and Perla could go only if I went (this, the first time we haven't been accompanied by a "señora"). Meanwhile I'm freezing and wondering how the night will end.

Lipstick!

Next door Fancho and Zunilda are having it out. He got angry at Zunilda 'cuz she went to the asado, now isn't that a bit ridiculous? He's been impossible lately, grabbing touching telling me he wants to fuck me, eat me, etc. I'm getting very upset about it, "threw" an avocado at him this evening, but in fun almost, it's all in fun, oh yes ho ho ho...

Talk of "love" lately, with Lambote, the town drunk (ex-famous musician, traveled the world until he lost the use of his hands). A true poet, bohemian—says South Americans love, North Americans mere materialists.

Journal entry 15 March—Went to Villarrica today... Stopped in San José on the way home, work purposes (fogón)... Ended up bringing Araí home again. I couldn't leave him there, all covered w/ dirt and fleas and matted, bloody hair. Gave him a bath...but I can't keep him here. He'll give me fleas again! Oh woe is me.

Accompanied home by Miguel, Catrasto...mere kid. Wanted to sleep w/ me. Routine. Shit I've never turned down so many men before in my life! They expect it.

Journal entry 16 March—Fortune today [Tarot]:

Past—The world (Success in all undertakings)

Present—Strength (Triumph of love over hate)

Future—Wheel of fortune (Ups & downs; good luck)

Later...night—A somewhat frustrating day. Reunion in San José-mí that turned out well...I left there went to Rojas Silva to inquire about fogones (all without vehicle of course, catching rides wherever possible). As it turns out none of the families in Rojas Silva wants to build, for one reason or another...I went to one house, the socia there hid in the kitchen (and I know she was there!) until I left, didn't want to tell me she wasn't going to build her fogón. Whew these campo attitudes and manners are too much...

Tired this afternoon, frustrated, no one would pick me up to go home. But the sunset very colorful and cheering, somewhat...

WORK LOG 17 MARZO

a.m. Limpieza de oficina [office cleaning]—About Rojas Silva—It appears there's only one family that wants to build...Called PC Asunción... STILL NO VELÁZQUEZ. NO RAIN! Good-bye, cotton.

p.m. Manualidades—Stayed home, actually, weather a bit rainy. Began apron for ña Juana.

Ña Juana was an elderly widow I'd befriended in the neighborhood, who lived alone and agreed to watch Araí whenever I had to leave (now that I'd brought him back from the campo). I liked being around her because she made me laugh and was kind to animals. She was tickled with her apron, modeled after the one I'd made for myself in seventh-grade sewing class and still had at home—if Mom hadn't gotten rid of it, too.

The next few days were nothing but a rainy, muddy mess. I went to the office anyway and worked on handicrafts, including making another apron, this one for Aurelia, Sarita's cook. The roads would be closed for a long time after this deluge, and work would come to a halt…but these were perfect conditions for making a cup of tea in the evenings and reading some inspiring texts.

[Written on a sheet of paper]
FOUR NOBLE TRUTHS: (1) Life is "dukkha" (suffering); (2) Cause of suffering is "tanha" (desire); (3) Cure of tanha is overcoming desire; (4) Overcoming tanha accomplished through Eightfold Path.

EIGHTFOLD PATH—Right knowledge, Right aspiration, Right speech, Right behavior, Right livelihood, Right effort, Right mindfulness, Right absorption

"Budh" in Sanskrit means both to wake up and to know.

"My daily activities are not different,
Only I am naturally in harmony with them.
Taking nothing, renouncing nothing
In every circumstance no hindrance, no conflict…
Drawing water, carrying firewood,
This is supernatural power, this marvelous activity."
    —Sayings of the Lay Disciple Ho

Journal entry 20 March—Time flying, much activity. Nights spent at hotel, taking advantage of the waning summer nights, I suppose. In general all's

well. Lot of time spent with Zunilda and family. Today (RAIN!) began making invitations for Olimpia's niece Olga, March 30...

Reading THE ONLY DANCE THERE IS,[71] has some helpful insights for the "consciousness" searcher..."Risking your position,""Making love with the unknown,""You've got to risk it all (give it all up) to have it all." I sense that's what I'm doing, but only out of loneliness, really. I've gone through many periods, stages here—now it's a kind of boredom's set in, very little novelty, I've run out of things to say...need to re-energize. Difficult for me to live out in the open always.

Ram Dass also talks about love, as a state of being or a place within each person that allows him to love, that is love, love and consciousness the same thing. (p. 60) "Being in love" is loving something "out there"—"I am in love with that connection to the place in me that is love"...

Mantra: OM MANI PADME HUM

OM = (like Brahma)—One behind it all, the unmanifest

MANI = Jewel or crystal

PADME = Lotus

HUM = Heart

"The entire universe is like a pure jewel or crystal right in the heart or center of the lotus flower, which is me, and it is manifest, it comes forth in light, in manifest light, in my own heart." (p. 9)...

I suppose my "goal" in life, if anyone were to ask me, would be to become enlightened, or at least continue to enter into higher states of consciousness...I am immersing myself more in "life" here, but at the same time am increasingly separate...because it's not the community of seekers I'm looking for. Just regular folks, is all. And not even that, really. I'm here, in a small town in rural Paraguay, S. America...What for??!!!

I can't sit at my desk and become "enlightened" if I go not out into the world and demonstrate or merely live my enlightenedness, spread it around.

Been reading the New Testament, too...The story of Jesus is marvelous... I'm drawn to the Bible now, it sits opened upon my desk (with the Spanish version of GOOD NEWS FOR MODERN MAN)...

---

71 Ram Dass, *The Only Dance There Is* (Anchor Press, 1974). Ram Dass (formerly Dr. Richard Alpert, renowned Harvard psychologist and psychedelic pioneer with Dr. Timothy Leary) is a spiritual leader in the US. He coined the phrase "be here now" with his 1971 book by the same name.

Life here is so linear, people have no time for "philosophy." Well, of course, there are a few...

p. 79 "Despair is the necessary prerequisite for the next degree of consciousness. That's absolutely a prerequisite."

Journal entry 21 March—Spring equinox (autumn here)...Finished Ram Dass, really turned on by his syntheses! I feel it's important to read the original, ancient texts... As I've said, the Paraguayans are...simply Zen, in a way...Yet I see now how they're stuck in the 2nd and 3rd chakras.[72]

1st—Muladhara—red—bottom of spine—survival separateness

2nd—Svadhisthana—orange—below navel—sensual gratification, sexual desires, reprod.

3rd—Manipura—yellow—navel—power mastery, ego control

4th—Anahata—green—heart region—compassion (of Buddha)

5th—Vishuddha—blue—throat—communication, creativity

6th—Anja—indigo—brow—intuition, perception

7th—Sahasrara—violet—crown of head—wisdom, understanding...

How naive I am! This morning some campo guys "woke up" in the policia, were arrested for taking part in a serenade last night without official permission. "I don't understand," sez I, "why permission is necessary." Zunilda and Epifanio were quick to assure me that serenades often result in looting, molesting, rape even murder. I didn't know what to say...So unfortunate something like that must be exploited...

WORK LOG 23 MARZO

a.m. Tayy-i—Weighed tobacco...With and w/out fertilizer (w/out naturally came out ahead). But it's all farcical, there's no CONTROL

p.m. Ciudad Club 4-C—Finally broke down—sick of not working. Going to have a club here, more or less...the same manualidades class I had before. Won't be Club 4-C so much as a cooking and manualidades class.

Journal entry 23 March—A dream...night before last: My lot was drawn to be the one to "escape." (What had I done? If anything? I don't know)...All's

---

72 A chakra (Sanskrit for "wheel" or "disk") is an energy center in the body.

that was important was the escape. Didn't have to escape to anywhere, merely get out from under the press.

After that: Zunilda, Epifanio, Chinooka [their housegirl] are killing weeds w/ pesticides...I tell Chinooka not to go near my land w/ poisons—but it comes out all garbled, I have to repeat it.Whether in English/Spanish I know not.

Fascinated by Jung!...

Stopped by DoctorVera's to deliver message...Now as a result I'm filled with an urge to live with a family, that family. And I think one of the reasons is: I'm looking for a father figure. Not that I'm "looking" so much, as somehow I feel as if I've found something. In Dr.Vera's presence I feel comforted, sort of, calm; he's so graceful and wise, soft-spoken, authoritative yet gracious, fair, just. Noble.And I could learn many things. I'm tired of Epifanio's irresponsible antics. How to approach the matter...

Journal entry 24 March—Today got the courage up to ask Sra.Vera if I could live with them. I think she'd like me to, but the problem is her father is returning, and a room must be prepared for him.We'll see, that's all there is...

Things had slowed down at work again; for some reason the vehicle wasn't available, which threw everything off. None of the socias showed up for the meeting in San José. I talked with Antonia, who said the girls were probably working in the *chacra*. (I had tried working in the *chacra* once but could barely even lift the hoe! They were probably out there barefoot as well, picking up some damn parasite.) Antonia gave me money for a volley-ball net the club wanted me to buy in Asunción; they didn't have much left over for *planchas*.

I felt frustrated but was trying to go with the flow. It was actually kind of liberating. Why bother making plans? I began to see how the Paraguayans embodied the Buddhist concept of "impermanence." Of course that's not what they would have called it, but that's how I understood it: Things never stay the same, and we're doomed to suffer if we try to hold on.

Then one day I got the surprise visit of my life.

Journal entry 31 March—It all happened so fast...Sitting one evening knitting, not wanting to venture out for lack of initiative, I hear a voice at the door, somewhat "English"—"You've got company"—and thinking it Steve, rushed to the door, a big kiss already in the making...A bit into the light, and..."Wait a minute, who are you?"

Jamie Brownhill's the name, from Australia, got parientes in Colonia Cosme. We sat and had wine, then went to [Catastro's] despedida [going-away party] at the hotel...Went out on a serenade next day. I went to Sarah's anniversary asado, then Sunday Jamie and I went to the colonia. 4 old Aussies there, speak English, all married to Paraguayans...We stayed with Wallace Wood, a marvelously well-informed fellow (listens to BBC). His wife, no teeth, always making cakes for tea, and breads. We ate so well!

Jamie turned out to be quite a fellow and we had a wonderful time, stayed an extra day because the truck that was to pick us up broke down. Fine!...Jamie left wanting me to go with him. And the thought had crossed my mind. But at this point I can't! I've worked too hard to try and like this place. If he would have come earlier chances are I would have—Bolivia, Colombia, USA, Australia. Ah, pipe dreams...

Last night Olga's b-day party in Tayy-í, came back on horseback at night, so dark! Beautiful...All the excitement was just what I needed. I'm heading toward tomorrow full speed ahead (or heading toward today...)

[On a postcard that says *Haga frío, haga calor, como un buen mate...no hay nada mejor!* (Whether the weather's cold or hot, there's nothing better than a good *mate!*)]

Hello All—I've finished a year of service!...The other day an Australian fellow blew in, was on his way to visit "relatives" in Colonia Cosme, an old Aust. colony founded in 1894, about 21 km. south of here. So we went! There are four old guys there, 75–80, sons of the original inhabitants, speak English. It was great!...All my love, E

WORK LOG 3–5 ABRIL
Villa Florida Conferencia [SEAG]

[On a hand-painted watercolor of bird flying upward at a forty-five-degree angle]
The conditions of a solitary bird are five:
The first, that it flies to the highest point;
The second, that it does not suffer for company, not even of its own kind;
The third, that it aims its beak to the skies;
The fourth, that it does not have a definite color;
The fifth, that it sings very softly.

—San Juan de la Cruz, "Dichos de Luz y Amor," IV-8

10-IV-76, Dearest Nanny, Received your letter of 28 March. I value your thoughts on what I'm undergoing. Actually sitting and drinking coffee in a restaurant alone doesn't make me sad, because I'm so familiar with it. True, I'm not the loner I once was…but a hot cup of coffee, a clean table top, a good pen and some inspiring paper (not like this!) are all great comforts to me—but you're right, there is no one to complain to about the coffee ☺…E

[Two weeks later]
AH—WHAT AN INTERLUDE!!
Journal entry 14 April—Period, this morning…FULL MOON: Rode Malacara at sunset, watched the moon rise. Why has the moon always symbolized the feminine, the deceitful? Surely just because it comes and goes doesn't mean it's deceitful, on the contrary, you know it will come again…Semana Santa [Holy Week] in Paraguay: chipa, sopa & asado. I've eaten 3 chipa so far today! One of doña Sara's, one of Perla's, one of Margarita's. Visited ña Juana. Everyone asks you about chipa, if you're making it…

Journal entry 16 April—GOOD FRIDAY. Celebration of Christ's death.[73]

Journal entry 17 April—"The flight of the alone to the Alone." Plotinus

Journal entry 19 April—Semana Santa in Paraguay...Chipa by the Dozen!

Journal entry 20 April—Early a.m., before office. We have a list to sign now, to assure that we arrive on time. Why doesn't Vargas sign it? Should last about a week... Drizzle. Do I leave tomorrow on the train? <u>Nothing</u> will keep me from Steve's wedding...

[Later]...A strange thing happened this morning...I was preparing to have breakfast (at the office—was going next door), telling Velázquez that I felt hunger...stretched...and a hunger pain seized me—and didn't go away! A cramp-like feeling, doubled me over for a good 10 minutes...

Coordinating gardening projects with some elementary schools. Amazing... They'll soak you for everything they can (maps, flags, seeds)...

Journal entry 26 April—I'm reluctant to go to bed because I know I shall be bitten by bedbugs. This is making me into a rather depressed state...

Tomorrow: Get dog.

Spray bed.

Office—mop?

Laundry.

Interview at school.

Arrange: pay house, horse?

Make decisions.

---

73 On this same day, the torturer Sapriza arrived in the town of San Juan Bautista with orders to elimi-nate suspected communists, in what would become known as the *Pascua Dolorosa* (Painful Easter). Scores of campesinos who lived in surrounding areas—all of them members of the Agrarian Leagues—were imprisoned in the jail at Abraham-cué. Eight were executed, some in front of their families, and many more taken to Asunción. Most were sent to the Emboscada concentration camp in September. Some were never seen again. A similar raid had been carried out in Jejuí, near San Pedro, in February 1975—only weeks before my PC group arrived there for training. There, too, people had been killed and lives destroyed. No weapons or "subversive" materials were found in either case, but in both instances the leagues' coffers were emptied.

Be firm.

Breathe.

Li Po:"Lazily weaving a white-feathered fan I lie naked / a green dell in the mountains. I hang my hat on a jutting rock / I cool my head with piney air."(Contentment)

WORK LOG 27 ABRIL

a.m. Escuela #256 Huertas Escolares [School Gardens]—Talked w/ directora—invited me to teachers' reunion Thursday. Can't proceed w/ gardens until next week.

p.m. Oficina—Stuck in office, lack of a lack of a vehicle (no more 2:30 micro). Guess I'm a mentirosa [liar].

Journal entry 27 April—88. How toWrite a Chinese Poem (ZEN FLESH, ZEN BONES[74])

"A well-known Japanese poet was asked how to compose a Chinese poem.

'The usual Chinese poem is four lines,' he explained. 'The first line contains the initial phrase; the second line, the continuation of that phrase; the third line turns from this subject and begins a new one; and the fourth line brings the first three lines together. A popular Japanese song illustrates this:

Two daughters of a silk merchant live in Kyoto,

The elder is twenty, the younger, eighteen.

A soldier may kill with his sword,

But these girls slay men with their eyes.'"

Arranged today to move [back] into Díaz! I think I'll like it very much. Don't know for how long I'll stay, though...I just lost my lack of transportation (a lack of a lack of transportation: no more 2:30 micro. And I <u>refuse</u> to sit and wait; and I <u>refuse</u> to go at 10:30; and I <u>think</u> I refuse to go at 12:00) (Though of course that's what I must do)...

WORK LOG 28 ABRIL

---

74 Paul Reps and Nyogen Senzaki, *Zen Flesh, Zen Bones: A Collection of Zen and Pre-Zen Writings* (Boston: Charles E. Tuttle Co., Inc., 1957).

a.m. San José-mí.

p.m. San José——We missed the reunion! Went w/ Vargas [late] to S.J.-mí first, to weigh cotton…then to S.J.——everyone had left! Haha, this is almost the last straw, as far as no vehicle is concerned.

Journal entry 28 April——Been uncompromisingly warm lately, hot at midday…and I am covered with bug bites. How ludicrous, if, after all my attempts at decision, the one thing that drives me from Paraguay is the BUGS!!

I'm not making anything happen anymore, trying not to fret…Yesterday for example, I wanted to go to a reunion in San José-mí, on the 2:30 bus. No bus. Today, planning to leave on 12:00 bus, first San José-mí to apologize, then San José for reunion. "No, Vargas said he'd take us" sez Velázquez, so I gladly wait til 2:00. We fool around, stall more in San José-mí (meanwhile I'm forced to consume nearly ten tangerines) and by the time we reach San José: no more socias. What can I say? I don't really care any more. All I want is to get them their fogones, start a few gardens, and split.

Told Zunilda this evening that I'm moving. Took it kinda hard. Affair complicated by the fact that there's a feud between Zunilda and Tía Sarita at the moment. How absurd! It's because of Zunilda's big mouth (she always speaks her mind, I respect her lack of diplomacy). Just to see the inanity: Has to do with credit vs. paying. It seems that when Sarita needs something and doesn't have the money on hand, she buys on credit from Zunilda; when she has the money she goes elsewhere. That's what Zunilda says; Sarita's story is different, naturally. Are there any attempts by one or the other to understand the opposing view? Surely you jest! But this is what makes life jump here, like the fleas in my bed make me jump (shit)…

> *Tangerines sit plump and naked on a plate,*
> *their garments strewn carelessly upon the dirt floor.*
> *In me senses are excited at the analogy,*
> *but everyone else just eats them…*
> *[Tarot] Reading: Question: Is change in the future, radical?…*
> *Future——The hermit, reversed.*

Despite the warning of the upside-down hermit ("terrible loneliness, a feeling of being left out in the cold, an outcast on the fringe of society"), my mental health was improving—I'd always loved being a scholar and found Eastern philosophy especially illuminating—even as I feared yet another plot twist in the continuing *telenovela* of my life, *Diary of a Mad PCV*.

PART VIII

TOMB OF THE LIVING
MAY–JULY 1976

—⟶⟵—

MARTÍN AND EMILY

It is easy to stand in the crowd, but it takes courage to stand alone.

Mahatma Gandhi

9

MARTÍN

On May 3, 1976, eighteen months after my arrest, some of us prisoners were ordered to prepare our things and move out of the cell at the First Precinct. Guards led us to the rear of the building, where several red *perreras* sat idling. Twenty-five of us were crammed into one of them and taken away, destination unknown. It was approximately 11:00 p.m. Very soon we arrived at another police station. As I was the last in, I was the first out.

A corpulent superintendent, hysterical about the arrival of the "communists," came toward me threateningly. I later found out he was a well-known torturer and son of a great advocate of teaching in Paraguay. From every direction men pointed machine guns at us, ready to fire. The tension was thick, and the slightest reaction on our part could have cost us our lives. Everything seemed to indicate that the superintendent had received instructions to provoke us—but we prisoners understood perfectly the need to remain calm.

The next morning we found ourselves in a soldier's latrine, although we had no idea where. We were concerned about the health of some of our companions, especially the older ones, most of whom had participated in the Chaco War and had more recently been tortured by Pastor Coronel's thugs.

The latrine was cold and the odor intolerable. A young university student from Carapeguá sat on the floor near the toilet, his face swollen and his eyes practically bulging out of his head. I too had severe intestinal pain and was constantly losing blood. After a few days we were transferred to two cells, each about five meters by five meters, which already held a few detainees.

The guards told us we were in the Third Precinct, in one of the cells of the Interior Ministry's Office of Technical Affairs, also called "La Técnica."[75] The place

---

75 Stroessner had carried out his coup on May 4, 1954, and in early 1955 sent the lawyer Antonio Campos Alum to Panama to train at the School of the Americas, where some of the US Army-taught

was known to the outside world as the "Sepulcro de los Vivos" (Tomb of the Living) because it held the oldest political prisoners of Latin America—and because of the crimes committed here.

The atmosphere was dismal, the conditions subhuman. Thirty people were packed into each of two cells. Inside the cells was a toilet—though no water to flush it with—and across from them was a wall that closed off the air, impeding ventilation. The cells had colonial-style grated steel doors; I felt like I'd been transported to a Roman prison. As a child I'd seen one in the movie *Quo Vadis* during Holy Week, and it was just like a cage. From outside, officials and sergeants observed us like strange beings from another planet.

We eventually found out that we were in cell number two and, in addition to those just arrived with me from the First Precinct, in cell number one were Antonio and Ananías Maidana, Alfredo Alcorta, Julio Rojas, and a few others I recognized. Most of these men—except perhaps the first three—had spent approximately twenty years in prison without ever being tried. A judge had ordered them freed but Stroessner had not allowed it, so the Maidanas and Alcorta remained in prison.

I was later transferred to cell number one and discovered morale was high there—as it had been in my previous cell—despite the physical and psychological challenges the prisoners faced. My new cell had improved security: the door had a double grate and a long iron chain with three padlocks. The time it took to let us out of the cell was longer than the time we were allowed to hug our loved ones during the weekly visit, which was five minutes. The visitors' room was next to the guards' office, and the intense police scrutiny intimidated our visitors.

I had my first-ever encounter with real communists at the Tomb of the Living. It is ironic that Pastor Coronel was the one who put me in direct contact with frontline militants. At the time I was picked up, I believed—like many of my fellow Paraguayans—that communists were terrorists who had no regard for the country or the law. I truly thought they had no respect for God, family, or any existing institutions. However, my contact with them changed my opinion.

---

courses included torture. Alum returned in 1956 accompanied by Robert K. Thierry, an intelligence colonel and Korean War veteran. They formed the Office of Technical Affairs that same year, thereby establishing the first "school of assassins" in Paraguay.

As a result of my harsh prison experience, I had slowly developed an attitude of extremism and revenge, and had come to believe that the only way to fight the dictatorship was through armed revolt. I thought the only alternative for my country was to eliminate all the officials who served the regime.

It was with great surprise that I discovered the communist patriots did not share my ideas. I call them "patriots" because I saw for myself that their commitment to the cause of the nation, the pureness of their convictions, and their clear intransigence made them worthy of this title. Most of those who were there had sacrificed their freedom, their health, and their family lives to establish a more humane society within our country.

The official voices of the dictatorship tended to repeat phrases such as "In Russia, children are separated from their parents," "The Cubans are trying to set the continent on fire," and "The communists are corrupt and heartless people." However, my own experience living beside them made me understand that those statements were unfounded. Most of the comrades displayed a strong sense of family and a moral rectitude that I had seldom found in people who said they respected the values of Christianity and humanism.

Those awful "barbarians" who, according to some, scorn religion and preach violence, were respectful and attentive every Sunday when we listened to mass on Radio Cáritas. And when I would take extremist positions, they would respond calmly, "Changes, comrade, do not happen overnight. Be careful not to make the same mistakes as the dictatorship. It's not true that all military personnel are crooks; many of them are respectable people who will stand with us when things change. Within the bourgeoisie are many honest people we must join with to create a strong front against the dictatorship, in an open platform of democratization that will take into account the interests of all."

I never saw in these fellow prisoners evidence of a grudge or the desire for retribution. For them, ours was not a fight among people but rather among classes. Paradoxically, this was how they were able to view objectively certain attitudes that were representative of the dominant classes. "What would be surprising would be for them to act differently," they said. "By acting as they do, they are simply defending the interests of their class."

I slowly opened up to my companions, who at times reminded me of the early martyrs of Christianity. We talked not only of our families, our beliefs, labor and political struggles, and the future of the country, but also of poetry, art, and the trees that would be flowering out of sight beyond the prison walls. And as people's vital energies seem endless, there were always anecdotes and jokes.

On weekends we would play chess, but our main topic of conversation was soccer. We followed the national championships passionately, especially the games between Olimpia and Cerro Porteño, traditional rivals in our world of fútbol, especially for the Liberators of America Cup. Like most of our fellow prisoners, Antonio Maidana was a Cerro fan, while Alcorta and I rooted for Olimpia. These differences provoked heated discussions that were followed with interest—even friendliness—by our guards.

During one of our conversations, Antonio Maidana told me a story. One day Alfredo Stroessner Jr. showed up inebriated at the Third Precinct and, in an arrogant voice, asked one of the officials, "Where are the communist leaders? Who is Antonio Maidana? Who are Rojas, Alcorta, and Ananías Maidana? Bring me the key to their cell so I can liquidate one by one those traitors who have sold themselves to Soviet imperialism."

Maidana stood up and looked him in the eye. "I am Antonio Maidana. The traitor, the enemy of the nation is not I but your father, along with everyone in his group. I am not serving any foreign powers, just the poor of my country. You are the ones who have sold yourselves: to US imperialism. Leave me in peace and get out of here."

The argument went on, becoming more and more heated. The officers were terrified and couldn't bring themselves to obey young Stroessner's order. In the end, the communist leader's firm and calm attitude disarmed the young tyrant.

"We'll see who wins," the president's son said as he walked away.[76]

The lack of sunlight had a serious effect on our health—the slightest change in temperature would result in a cold or the flu. Representatives of the International Red Cross had persuaded the authorities to promise they would let us out in the sun three times a week, but the doctor in the Third Precinct took no action toward making that happen. It was even said that he profited by

---

76 In January 1993, at age forty-six, Alfredo "Freddy" Stroessner Jr. lost himself to his addiction and died of a barbiturate overdose (thought to be intentional), predeceasing his father by thirteen years.

the prisoners' suffering, as only a minuscule amount of the medicine and milk sent to us by humanitarian groups actually reached us.

I looked at my cellmates and admired the human body's strength to endure such deprivation. Sometimes I felt much too tired, physically and emotionally, to keep on living that nightmare. The lack of sunlight affected me most. The darkness, the dampness of our cell, the insufferable smell of the toilet in that small space—it all threw me into a deep depression.

At times my restless mind carried me to the brink of insanity, but my cellmates' serenity brought me back and made me consider my situation more calmly. As an escape and a way to avoid giving in to the temptation of aggression, I would think of the past. I remembered my childhood in Puerto Sastre, my teenage years at the San Lorenzo School of Agriculture, and my experiences teaching at the Juan Bautista Alberdi Institute.

Puerto Sastre, located in the Chaco on the Río Paraguay north of Concepción, was a microcosm of the general reality in the country. I remembered the mansions belonging to the English administrators of the tannin factory, the comfortable homes of the Paraguayan employees, the workers' barrio where I used to live, and the shacks of the indigenous people who did the hardest labor. I rekindled the image of my mother washing clothes belonging to the factory owners, the mischievous figures of my little dark-faced friends playing with whatever was at hand, and me trying to catch them as we played *tukaé* (tag).

From agricultural school I particularly remembered my illustrious professor Rodolfo Valek, whose exemplary conduct made a lasting impression on me. Valek was fired during summer break of 1954. I never found out exactly why, but it was evident that don Rodolfo was out of place in that environment of conformity and lack of imagination. We admired him for several reasons. Unlike many of his colleagues, he was pleasant and friendly to us—he despised violence and was always willing to explain his actions and the coursework he assigned. We were especially enthusiastic about how he worked side by side with us, taking the shovel to dig, using the machete to cut trees.

Before the school was moved to San Lorenzo, it operated in Viñas-cué. The Ministry of Agriculture established the courses and programs of study, but the way in which they were carried out was left up to the teachers and students. Courses were organized in small production cooperatives based on a particular crop. So if a class decided to concentrate on corn, for example, all of the activities—planting, crop care, harvesting, and sales—were focused on corn. Profits were shared by the institution and the students and were used to purchase clothing or organize field trips to rural areas.

The students liked having a say in their schooling and began to request other reforms and demand even more participation—but these were denied. Strikes followed, and the government opted to close the school in Viñas-cué and reopen it in San Lorenzo. Teachers and students who had led the movement were expelled.

There were more strikes in San Lorenzo. In 1955, we organized a protest against the poor quality and meager portions of the food. The director was fired, and the government appointed a member of the military as head of discipline. He immediately closed the school library, saying it was "the cause of all the problems on the planet." The director went on to enrich himself in the Ministry of Agriculture and Livestock.

9

EMILY

Work got busy again in May (I still couldn't think of May as autumn). The school gardening project in Caazapá was going well, the 4-C club in San Jose-mí began their garden, and I gave a talk on home gardens, one I'd worked hard on to get just right. However, the lack of professionalism in the office began to annoy me, and even though I liked Velázquez, I was starting to lose it with him.

I'd decided to move back to the pensión mostly because of Tito—his visits had become unpleasant, and I didn't know how else to break free of him. He didn't really talk much and had no apparent interest in me as a person. He'd come over only a few times but was starting to be controlling. And it turned out he wasn't that good in bed. I'd tried to feel good about the affair but just couldn't after a while—guess I wasn't much of a women's libber after all. In truth, he was making my life miserable.

Why had I ever let him "visit" me in the first place? What a mistake that had been. I would have to start making better decisions.

I also moved to get rid of my bug problem—thanks again to Araí—once and for all. I was being sorely tested but tried to stay strong and just keep putting one foot in front of the other. My journal became my refuge and, though it smacked of narcissism, a place I escaped to regularly as my state of mind swung from low to high and back again.

Journal entry 4 May—Whew! So much going on (work-wise) that I'm having a difficult time convincing myself I'm no longer happy. A sort of grim acceptance / determination has superseded the self-indulgence of misery...

Pulgas in bed last night, at the pensión...I sprayed my house w/ Baygon and—(shudder)—DDT (the stuff!) so's couldn't sleep there...

To call Anna or not to call Anna.

Have you ever slept in a bed with fleas? They crawl on your knee, it tickles, you want to throw up (you know they're fleas). End up crying yourself to sleep— After killing 3, one gets away, you've seen it, the biggest monster enlightenment satori yes! pulga you've ever seen, and the red-neck mother jumps just as you're closing in with fingernails clacking, the kangaroo jumps—and disappears. You know he's around somewhere. The lights go off. You weep for home.

I'm insensate. Nothing matters. All very ludicrous, absurd. Doing the work. But no love. I'm only staying for the work. That is not right. That is a sin.

Well, to the campo.

WORK LOG 5 MAYO

a.m. Ciudad [city]—Planted perejil [parsley], repollo [cabbage], rabanito [radishes], remolacha [beets], lechuga [lettuce]

p.m. San José—San José will order 11 planchas.

8—Tayy-í

8—San José-mí

11—San José

27

5—Arroyo Guazú

Velázquez wants "us" to clean the office, to prepare for the visit of [a Paraguayan colleague]...yet he doesn't lift a finger to the fucking thing while I'm in the campo, he wants me to do it is all, he can't even clean his own desk for crying out loud or sweep the floor Jesus Christ!

Journal entry 5 May—Justice in Paraguay: The rule in Caazapá, no loose animals in the street...So a soldier goes around and fucking SHOOTS animals in the street! (Happened today when I was working in the school garden.)...

Anna is coming after 14–15 May in Villarrica. Perfect! Maybe what I have to do is lower expectations of myself. These would be my reasonable goals:

Collective garden in San José-mí.

Fogones for everyone.

Expositions for everyone.

But there will be an educadora here soon enough! I can't live for others! I'll go crazy if I stay here!

Journal entry 6 May—People tell me I'm not as pretty, because I've lost weight...They like their meat with lots of fat...

Last night I had a fantastic dream about Dad, I woke up crying before dawn, and continued crying until there was light in the sky...

Journal entry 9 May—Sitting in my house, all packed up, no posters on the wall, just blank faces echoing Eric Clapton ("E.C. was here")...

Moving is always sad, of course...Chaos, disarray, a feeling of abandonment. The home a house, skeleton, four walls and tear-stained Paraguayan paint. Bookcase barren, table-top bare, shivering with the cold. The order now disorder. The personality no longer...My last night using batteries!...

Zunilda's little kitchen helper came over today with a nasty-looking foot, infected in two places, nickel-size. My first reaction: "Sure, I'll help you out, but I'm so glad I'm not a doctor." Then as I was washing it and applying the ointment & band-aids, I really got into it, felt like a healer. Compassion overwhelmed me!

9 May 1976, Dear Mom,

HAPPY MOTHER'S DAY!...

It's starting to get nippy here, beginning to rain more again. Forecast is for a frost early this year, perhaps June...a very crippling thing in Paraguay, where before last year's frost that killed 70% of the sugarcane, bananas, other crops there was hardly ever anything of the kind...

This morning I'm riding my bicycle to a compañía 4 kilometers away, to begin a gardening project there in the school...

There was a huge Colorado party reunion here this weekend, for young Colorados. Two main themes: "re-election" of the president (Stroessner's going on 23 years as "president"—the constitution must be changed to allow it); and a lot of anti-commie talks, with the waves of extremism filtering in from Argentina, Bolivia and other places. Naturally I attended not one reunion; but the locale was a block from my house, and I listened to a lot of fanatic shouting. The people here <u>love</u> Stroessner, are very nationalistic. I tend to ridicule (as most Americans) but the USA could certainly use a little patriotism.

Who's it gonna be for US president?...When California's Jerry Brown runs for president I'm going to work on his campaign...

Loving you, E

WORK LOG 10 MAYO

a.m. Galeano-cué (school garden)—Went well. One teacher (of 3), Angelina, knows about gardens, so she'll take care of the rest. We made one tablón, I'll return Thurs. a.m. to plant. They'll prepare more in the meantime (hopefully). I took seeds.

p.m. Tayy-í—Ate at Olimpia's, helped w/ her huerta...Her sister-in-law has one, too—Wow, made me feel so good!

WORK LOG 11 MAYO

a.m. Oficina—Got pissed at Vel. for not sweeping office. Didn't speak all morning. Phone calls...Did cartulinas on different veggies, what seasons, distances, etc. translating leveler directions.

p.m. Escuela #256—No reunion in San José-mí—Vel. finds it convenient to tell me as I'm boarding the bus (why not sooner?). Spent the p.m. moving to hotel, mostly.

WORK LOG 17 MAYO
ASUNCIÓN (DOCTOR—WITH PERMISSION)

17 May 1976, Dear Everyone,

You'll never believe what happened: Day before yesterday I shat a roundworm! Well it didn't bother me nearly as much as my recent flea and bedbug attack did. Needless to say, two days ago I'd about had it & was ready to come home. Luckily I turned to a veteran PC member [Ben] for advice...he gave me the kick in the rear that I needed...I feel fine, except that I've been pretty low lately, spiritually...

Will write soon—Love always, E

Journal entry 18 May—A talk with Ben, Sunday. "You have no integrity," he tells me, "You're undependable and fickle." Never started anything he didn't finish, sez Ben. I was brought to anger—at myself, of course, for indulging in my own pains and sorrows. I've decided to develop ME. I'll stay, I need to show myself I can do something. I'd hoped this change would come about in me, and it was Ben gave the kick I needed.

Went to Asunción for ascaris treatment. The new doctora's professionalism is questionable...gave me pills for hookworm, which will not cure roundworm, and can even cause the roundworms to become activated, push themselves out through my intestinal lining. I must buy the correct remedy.

It feels good now to be here, in my room at the Hotel Díaz. Today is a beautiful day: sun permeating everything, shining into my window and illuminating the vacancy within my soul.

I'll always be grateful to Ben for caring about me so.

Journal entry 22 May—[In Caazapá] Listening to BBC! Doesn't come in too well, but I can understand it. A nice feeling. Maybe I'll keep up a little with what's going on. Ever since visiting in Colonia Cosme I've wanted to connect my radio to a high copper wire. Saturday p.m. is evidently rock and roll time…

I'm all chusky [pretty] now! Make-up and all! How good I feel! Everything moving fast, pounding, but I'm in control. Not like riding wild stallions with one finger, as Kathy L. put it before.

God, I hoped Tito wouldn't be at the dance tonight. I'd checked and his band wasn't playing. He'd gotten angry when I moved to the pensión, and I'd been doing my best to avoid him. Why had Perla begged me to go in the first place…and why had I agreed?

As I got dressed, I thought about work and how it was becoming a huge comedy of errors—only without the comedy. In addition to everything else that was happening, earlier that day I'd prepared our monthly report and gone to a meeting by myself in San José. The club had gotten some new members, so they elected a new secretary and treasurer. Then the old treasurer showed up! Oops, foiled again. Nothing seemed to be going right.

Journal entry 26 May—Almost pay-day! Whew, what a motley past few days…First the dance was a drag…I had to dance w/ Tito. I did it "for him"—he wanted to dance slow bolero, to show how intimate we are. Oh why did I give in? Got sick, had diarrhea. Next day, "Día del Agricultor," not too many aggies, only a few old folks just wanting to go to mass. We had to lower the flag to raise [it]. Beautiful fog. Then I came home & took my bicho medicine. UGH!

[Final entry]
  WORK LOG 27 MAYO
  a.m. Oficina.
  p.m. Tayy-í—God if my hemorrhoids don't kill me first.

—*INTERIM*—

Journal entry 6 June—*Unbelievable, the things that befall me whilst I neglect writing in my l'il journal. My last entry = taking bicho medicine…Shit! The medicine did me in, I shat all day (as I was supposed to), followed the capsules with epsom salts ("purgante") and had a very disagreeable taste in my mouth all day. Washed my hair—didn't <u>feel</u> bad—and ña Sara nearly walloped me. "Your face will swell up." Needless to say it didn't. The next day, though, ugh, in bed all day, too worn out to move. Then on Tuesday…my old hemorrhoid appeared, worse than ever, hurt like crazy. It's raining by now, no escape. Ooh, so sore, can't sit down. Ride my bike? Ha! But went to San José-mí and San José.*

Thursday luckily a busload of municipalidad dudes went to Villarrica (special permission) so I got to go along. This is the day I got so pissed at Velázquez, ranted and raved, told him what a dummy he is ("You don't even know what day of the week it is!"). It was good to get this out, the emotional part, now perhaps I can "help" him with his work instead of anticipating his not doing it & getting angry when he doesn't. He asked me to type the calendar, his job, and I noticed that for this month he's got "Elaboración de Informe" ["Fill Out Report"] for the 18th! (due the 21st). So…

To Asunción! And to the doctora…who promptly tells me: "That <u>will</u> have to be removed!" Wonderful, so I go to the Hospital Bautista where Dr. Talavera lances the bugger, hurts like a son-of-a-bitch on the way home (BUS!?). Local anesthesia in your ass isn't the most pleasant sensation in the world. Another appointment for next week, Tuesday. (This is Friday.) Meanwhile by Saturday (Ben's party) I'm ready to go, and do dance a bit…Spent a pleasant weekend, till Tuesday. "Well, looks fine, but it'll have to come off sometime; now or later?" Hastily I replied "now." Mistake! Why not wait? That night I decided not to do it. But fate had decreed (bullshit by the way about fate decreeing). So:

IN THE HOSPITAL—*I'd doubted all along, having considered more "natural" alternatives; perhaps a "home remedy" of doña Sara's. But I was soon convinced (how!?) that I oughta go ahead with it. I went by myself, after a dentist app't. Jeez my poor body. What a feeling, to be undressing alone, in a hospital room, knowing that in a few hours I'll be lying in this very bed in some sort of agony (I'd had a preview of how painful it is to mess with your asshole). Dr. Sosa had called me into his office to tell me it wasn't necessary to perform the operation <u>now</u>—We discussed the matter, decided to go ahead (what if it gets sore again in the campo?).*

299

First…the enema. Never had an enema before, that one liter of warm H2O sure cleans you out all right. Then I hang out in my bed for about an hour reading. "Aw, c'mon sure I don't really want this to happen but let's get on with it." Then: two big shots in the ass → OUCH!, "pre-anesthesia." And blood out of my finger. When I'm starting to feel pretty good they roll me out, down the hall, to the operating room. I'm digging it, looking around me, taking it all in…

It's over in a flash. Don't really remember being taken back. But when I wake up there's Ben…I explain my experiences but am very delirious. Injection, sleep. That's how it is for 3 more days (daze), injection sleep injection sleep. My butt was so sore! Began to dread having to ask for "calmantes" (Demerol?)… From there it was pain and sleep, consoling visits from [PCVs]…Averaged 3 injections per day, UGH! Plus Valium. Food not too good.

Found out later I coulda been sent home!

Journal entry 12 June—Sitting before my heater in Caazapá…Arrived this afternoon after a two-week absence—and I'm off again tomorrow! To the week-long SEAG cursillo in Caaguazú. Can't imagine what that will be like.

Close scrape with Death today on the bus…not my own, but the feeling of being nearby when someone gives up the ghost is uncanny. The lady (young) was brought to the bus in a bed, then put on, groaning. I looked into her face and at first saw a red ball. She didn't move much during the trip, upon her (brother and sister?) carriers' laps. "Wow, to think you'd have to wait for the 4:00 micro to take someone sick to the hospital," I thought.

When we arrived the chofer and guarda told them they'd have to go to Dr. Vera's house (private) because now there's no one at the medical center. We dropped them off to closed doors. "What a day to get sick," I thought. "As if you can choose." They carried her off and I gasped when I saw her face: a sickening yellow-white with black circles around her eyes. "God I think she's dead" I thought, turned out later she was! She "died" on the bus (actually a little while later). I was shook, and so was Chelo, who'd run into the whole affair a few minutes later. How tragic!

Journal entry 13 June—Saw EASY RIDER ("Busco Mi Destino" ["I Search for My Destiny"]) tonight, imagine that flick reaching all the way to Caazapá!

Of course it was shot to pieces, left out some of the best parts, Jack Nicholson's first imitation of rooster (after drink)...Of course Tito's being there, by my side, trying to put his arms around me and hands on me made me sick to my stomach.

This afternoon I went to Juana's [to drop off Araí]. Her patron saint day, San Antonio. When I arrived the women (and a couple of small boys) were praying. A single candle lit, a picture of San Antonio, an altar with plastic lace cover, one or two other saints, a burnt-out candle...the women praying using a rosario. What repetition! But an atmosphere worthy of mystical musing. I did my own praying, admitting I didn't "understand" what the women were garbling...but it was a true enough medium, <u>something</u> was happening! Later, sitting in Juana's "kitchen" (now a "kitchen" due to 3-foot wooden "wall") having mate...animals running around afoot, farting—her little goat, 3 little pigs, a tiny kitty. I can never think of anything to say. End up telling stories of my "past."

We're leaving tonight at 3:30 AM for the cursillo in Caaguazú...

[Another girl from our group] is gone! Left Friday. Too bad...

[Ten days later]

Journal entry 23 June—Almost a year since I began this diary.

Puerto Presidente Stroessner. Believe it? I'm on my way to Saltos de Guaira. AWOL. Beautiful!

10

MARTÍN

While still at the Third Precinct, I recalled an article I'd read in 1963 on pedagogy stating that in the Middle Ages, universities functioned as real "corporations"[77] made up of students and professors, where work in community was a priority. Remembering my old Professor Valek, his concern for others and his pedagogy of participation, I'd promised myself I would follow

---

77 A group of people authorized to act as a single entity; perhaps "collaboration" would be a better translation.

his example. The conditions already existed, as I was then director of the Juan Bautista Alberdi Institute.

In 1972 there were forty-four professors, twenty-five of whom, like me, shared the philosophy expressed in the message sent out by the Catholic Church in Medellín, Colombia (Conference of Latin American Bishops, 1968) that education should prepare the people of Latin America for the new kind of society in which they wanted to live. Among our spiritual mentors were Aníbal Ponce and Paulo Freire, from Argentina and Brazil, respectively. We were also inspired by the recent educational reform in Peru, implemented during the presidency of Juan Velasco Alvarado.

It was not the best time politically for us to be carrying out an experiment in pedagogical self-management. Suffice it to say, during that same year the Paraguayan Ministry of Education distributed to all elementary schools the infamous *Decalogue Against Communism*, in which teachers were warned about the supposed dangers of Marxist ideology. Aware of the risks inherent in following a progressive pedagogy that would have no support, we contacted local, national, and international pedagogical organizations such as the Association of Educators of San Lorenzo, the Federation of Paraguayan Educators, the Catholic University, the World Confederation of Teaching Professionals, and others to let them know what we were doing.

To define the principal directions for the development of our plan, we formed a group of mostly Christian professors, of similar ideologies, and met for several days. We were influenced by the message from Medellín and by the events of May 1968 in France, and we naively believed that we could change academic institutions within a repressive and reactionary political system. We decided to make our teaching more democratic, with the community participating in the decision making. The people of San Lorenzo would no longer be marginalized within the school I was in charge of—they would now be the protagonists.

With the objective of getting rid of old top-down, authoritarian practices, we decided to periodically evaluate the director and professors. Students and professors evaluated the director in general assemblies, and professors were evaluated by their colleagues and students. We tried to get the students accustomed to practicing rigorous self-critiques, as well as individual and community self-management. Students rated their professors based on several criteria, such as competency, capacity for dialogue, imagination and creativity, and the ability to connect with the community.

At this point there were many who wanted to get to know the real face of Paraguay. Many students and teachers critiqued themselves and others, knowing that this long and difficult path was the only way. They put a lot of energy into confronting their reality, with the result that our school in San Lorenzo was transformed as an institution. A new atmosphere surrounded our efforts.

We continued, convinced that we had to get to the bottom of the problems in education. We had to critique and analyze the culture transmitted by the school in order to re-create it in light of new values. In education, asking questions is fundamental if there is to be genesis and change, and in this way we developed an evaluation tool that we called the "school thermometer." Before we applied it, we meticulously studied social history and the structure of domination and dependence at each stage. The description of the individual and his bio-psycho-social development followed.

We determined three types of educators derived from different concepts of the individual and education: the traditional school, the merely progressive school, and the new, "open" school, based on dialogue and the facilitation of learning for individual and social self-direction.

We tested the instrument all the way to the upper levels of the primary school. It proved to be simple and allowed us to measure the "temperature" of each classroom, according to whether the teacher was authoritarian, permissive, or democratic. Use of the thermometer became widespread.

The most important benefit was, without a doubt, the awakening of the educators' and students' consciousness of their concrete reality, and the rich implications that emerged regarding the circumstances of the country. *Where are we? How do we live?* We discussed these questions and agreed: Paraguayan society was—and still is [in 1978]—feudal. The power relationship is from lord to serf. Official education favors individualism and allows development only up to the point of reflective thought. Above all, it prevents entry into social awareness and participation, and impedes the learning of problem-solving and creativity. Young people graduate from school into a society for which they are not prepared but to which they must adjust, even if they do not adapt. Finally, they live without resolving their own identity, much less that of their homeland.

All our notes, figures, and information regarding the thermometer were destroyed during the period of persecution. But even though the scientific interpretation of the data is missing, what remains is Paulo Freire's assertion, which we made our own: "Education is an act of love; as such, it is an act of courage. It cannot fear debate, the analysis of reality; it cannot flee from creative discussion, or it would be a farce."

Several professors subsequently took it upon themselves to initiate a project to turn the Alberdi Institute into a teachers' cooperative. In that climate, and with the new pedagogical atmosphere, we happily observed the desire to learn that motivated our students and, above all, their willingness to share in the struggles of the people. On the chalkboards we had written: "The new individual and the new society will be the fruit of brotherly solidarity with the people, which emerges through living together and through shared efforts."

Many barriers were broken down, and new horizons could be glimpsed. Of course, not all the professors at the institute shared our point of view. The "reactionary group," as it was called, protested strongly when I requested that exams be returned to students after being graded. They claimed this could damage the teachers' authority and put them in the position of being controlled by students and parents, who, in their opinion, were incapable of exercising competent judgment.

We knew perfectly well the risks we were taking, but we were convinced that our experiment was an exercise in justice. The awareness we were working toward for our young people, as well as our country, motivated us to continue.

One day, in front of the morning session of the fifth-year high school students, a young professor demanded that I stop immediately the process of reform because, in his opinion, it would inevitably result in chaos. His warning did not frighten me—the confidence of most of the parents and students was the best proof that our pedagogical activities responded to the aspirations of the educational community. The reactionary group went to the Ministry of Education and denounced the "communist" experiment we were developing, thereby starting up the machinery of repression.

One of the first measures adopted by the authorities was to provide financial support for another institute that had just appeared across the street from us, headed by a former teacher at the Alberdi Institute who'd had a close relationship with my wife, as the two colleagues were from the same town. The school was named in memory of the mother of a pro-Stroessner senator. The senator and the director of the school went to the Government Palace and presented to Stroessner the "critical problem of San Lorenzo." The president ordered the Treasury to set aside resources for subsidizing the school, even though its students would still be paying tuition.

During summer break, these two women unleashed an intensive campaign of defamation against the Alberdi Institute, urging the families of San Lorenzo not to send their children to such a "subversive" institution. To attract students, they offered tuition costs much lower than ours. Their campaign had no effect, so they changed tactics. I later discovered the next steps they had taken toward dealing us our final blow.

The president and vice president of the pro-Stroessner faction of the Colorado Party in San Lorenzo, along with others, brought in a clerk from the National University of La Plata and introduced him to the president of the republic, on his birthday, as "the University Professor Doctor Espinosa." Espinosa had arrived from Argentina with a copy of my doctoral dissertation, which was used to get Pastor Coronel involved.

Pastor Coronel—formerly a functionary of the Ministry of Education and Culture and a future key element in Operation Condor—now had three pieces of "irrefutable evidence" against me, provided by those named above: a list of subversive individuals, with my name at the top; a partial history of the development of the Alberdi Institute under my direction; and my dissertation criticizing the educational system in my country.

Several members of the community had an active role in portraying my wife and me as communist militants. I knew precisely who they were.

Earlier that year, in May, the teachers' union had carried out numerous activities, including the Congress of the Federation of Paraguayan Educators, where I had acted as president, vigorously demanding a substantial wage increase and stability for teaching jobs. This was the last straw. The authorities badly needed to put a stop to such demands and teach us a lesson. I turned out to be the ideal scapegoat.

On November 26, 1974, they ordered my detention. In the eyes of Stroessner's dictatorship, I had committed several grave offenses in the areas of politics, labor, and education. The strongest proof against me was the experiment in educational self-management at the Alberdi Institute and the dissertation I'd written to earn my doctorate, in which I argued: "In Paraguay, education fulfills the role of legitimizing the system in force, and it is organized in such a way as to produce underdevelopment and dependence."

Later, when I was in prison, I made my situation worse by trying to teach my fellow inmates at the Emboscada concentration camp how to read. I had definitely committed the most terrible crime against tyranny—education for freedom.

10

EMILY

I was AWOL, all right, and I wasn't exactly sure how it happened. One minute I was at the wheel of a SEAG vehicle, a VW bug, smokin' down a curvy road—¡Qué curvas, y yo sin freno! (my high school friends hadn't called me "Emmy Granatelli" for nothing)—toward Caazapá after the conference in Caaguazú, singing along with a Brazilian radio station playing all Beatles tunes, happily belting out every single word of every single song, in harmony at times, much to my male colleagues' terrified delight (I was surprised they'd let me drive)...and the next minute I was on a bus to Porto Guaíra, Brazil, having finally made up my mind to terminate and go live in San Francisco with my college friend Kathy, study Chinese, and practice aikido. She had invited me in a letter brought to me in Caaguazú by a PCV, and I'd taken it as the long-awaited *sign*.

I would no longer have to adapt myself to my surroundings in a place I no longer wanted to be—I would instead provide myself with an avenue toward self-understanding and realization. I felt free and unassailable.

I had to admit it came up suddenly. At the conference I'd talked with a PCV who was about to terminate early. I'd been angry at the guy for quitting, and now here I was doing the same thing, feeling I'd be going against my *self* if I didn't pursue the opportunity with Kathy in San Francisco, convinced another year would be too late. I was grateful to Ben, who was also there, for helping me straighten out my values and teaching me integrity, how to live fully and from within myself rather than "accepting outside norms and trying to make them my own," as I wrote in my journal. I really meant it this time.

I'd confronted my reality at last and been forced to admit that everything I'd built so far was going up in flames around me.

Something Gino had said at the *cursillo* was really weighing on me. He and I were having a late beer; I could tell he was agitated and asked him what was wrong.

He chuckled bitterly. "I guess it's being around all these government... functionaries, who pretend to be so righteous when in fact they're nothing but hypocrites."

I remained silent, hoping he'd continue. He did.

"You see, I have a girlfriend in Yegros named Lorena, beautiful Lorena, who is a student at the university in Asunción. She lives with her aunt there, but I met her in Yegros, at a fiesta. One day a couple of months ago I was walking with her across campus when I, idiot that I am, started singing the anti-Stroessner song I'd learned from some guys in my site—hey, I'm a musician, I learn songs. Besides, I am very verbose about bad-mouthing that son of a bitch every chance I get."

Gino's English was attracting attention in the bar...never mind that he was practically shouting.

Thankfully, he lowered his voice. "Sorry, it's just that at UT I studied government and international politics with an emphasis on Latin America, and definitely learned to hate all the *dick*-taters down here who I know are kidnapping, torturing, and murdering innocent people." He stopped and took a deep breath.

"Anyway, the tune is 'Military Madness.'[78] It's a Graham Nash song that's been translated and goes something like *'Militarismo mata mi patria, qué tristeza me cobra.'* Well, here I am just a-singin' away about how sad I am that militarism is killing my homeland when all of a sudden I notice something wrong—*no Lorena*. She wasn't walking with me anymore. I looked all over but couldn't find her *anywhere*. She. Had. Disappeared! I couldn't imagine where she'd gone and didn't know where her aunt lived. Tell you the truth, I was scared shitless. I waited a long time, trying not to look conspicuous, and finally decided she couldn't still be there. I ended up taking the late bus home. God, did I feel terrible."

His jaw muscles twitched. "About a month later I saw her in Yegros. She really chewed my ass out and told me to *never* do that to her again. Then she said…because of her family's connection with the Liberal Party (her grandfather had been active in the forties and fifties), a few months before I got there she'd been a victim of one of Stroessner's 'commie sweeps.' His goons came to her house late at night and forced her to go with them. They held her prisoner for about a week, during which time…" He cleared his throat and was silent a while.

"During which time they beat her and raped her, repeatedly, and when they released her they told her to tell her family and community not to fuck with Stroessner and his 'people.'" Gino practically spat out the last words: "But they're not people—they're *animals*. I can't imagine how she must have felt when I started singing that song, absolutely terrified she could be picked up again."

I was too stunned to react. When he spoke again, his voice barely audible, I thought he might cry.

"She is happy to have survived and didn't need some stupid-ass, loudmouth gringo drawing attention to her. There isn't an apology sufficient to

---

78 From the 1971 album *Songs for Beginners*.

cover that one. I made a pathetic attempt, though," he said with a rueful smile, "which she graciously accepted."

This Texan was suffering!

I said, "I'm so sorry, Gino. But it's not your fault. You couldn't have known. We all have things to learn here."

"True," he said, "but the stakes are way too high to be fucking up like that. I have to remember I might be endangering the people I'm with…including you, I suppose."

I glanced around the bar again but saw nothing out of the ordinary. I did feel sick to my stomach, though. How could people do that to each other… and get away with it? Several minutes passed as Gino fiddled with the label on his Pilsen Paraguaya.

Finally I said, "I asked Miriam if her situation had improved, and she said things were going well, she hadn't had a 'visitah' in a while." A smile flickered on Gino's face as he continued to stare down at his bottle.

I hadn't had a "visitah" in a while, either, since I moved back to the pensión to get away from Tito. It had been obvious for a while that he didn't want to make our relationship "official." When I'd asked if we could go out publicly, he'd given me reasons why our arrangement was so much better, and the scary thing was I followed his logic.

Things had become much clearer after PCV Theresa explained that here in Paraguay a guy visited his number-one girlfriend on Monday, Wednesday, and Friday evenings and "made nice" to her father on Sunday afternoons… whereas the lesser girlfriend got visits on Tuesday, Thursday, and Saturday. I had to laugh, realizing Tito had always shown up on nights reserved for number two.

I'd honestly thought I might die that night at the dance, when he practically humped me! As far as anyone knew, there'd never been anything between us. (Or had he spread a few juicy tidbits around town?) And then, at *Easy Rider*, after I rebuffed his advances—gestures that further reflected his lack of respect for me (though why should he have any in the first place?)—he'd asked, rather threateningly I thought, why I'd been talking to Lambote, and whether or not I'd "slept with the Australian."

My blood pressure shot up. Had the SOB been spying on me? The thought put me on edge: What right did Tito have to snoop into my life, anyway? His days of harassing me were over though, thank God. Of course there was no way I could tell the Peace Corps about him. It would cause an uproar in my site, and who knew how it might end? Besides, I couldn't deny the affair had been consensual.

The truth was, I hadn't "slept with the Australian"—oh, rest assured Jamie wanted me to and I was filled with desire for him, but I was trying to be chaste. (Tito just couldn't imagine two people of the opposite sex sleeping in the same room and not being overcome by lust.) And as for Lambote…damn it, I could talk to Lambote whenever and wherever I wanted.

The hemorrhoidectomy was what ultimately did me in. My recovery had been excruciating and interminable and ended up derailing my whole life. When I'd finally returned to Caazapá, work became impossible because for some reason our SEAG office—with a Paraguayan *educadora*, Mami, now at least—was back to having no vehicle, which demoralized us and made us want to throttle each other.

Sick of being at the mercy of people and events I had no control over, I decided I'd had enough, and the next thing I knew—I was here in Brazil. I was taking this trip as a symbol of my imminent future of living in the moment, on my own terms, taking each day as it came, stopping whenever I was ready, turning off a side road if I felt like it…a real rolling stone, answering to no one but myself. I needed it badly.

It was also my last chance to visit the area, and for that matter nearly the last chance for *anyone* to visit Sete Quedas [SEH-chay KAY-dahss] (Seven Falls), which would be entirely submerged once Itaipú Dam was constructed and the reservoir filled…all in the name of "progress." Both Paraguay and Brazil would ostensibly benefit from the accord, which had been signed by dictators Stroessner and Médici in 1973. A couple I met in Puerto Stroessner said construction had begun last year. Ten thousand people would be forced to move, and Sete Quedas—the largest waterfall in volume in the world—would simply cease to exist.

This was almost more than I could bear. I'd wanted to go for tourist reasons, but now I knew I had to see these *cataratas* before they were obliterated in such a brazen manner. Did man's hubris know no bounds?

A black gentleman I sat next to on the bus helped me find the Hotel 7 Quedas, exorbitant at thirty-five cruzeiros (about three dollars) but nice: hot shower, double bed, blue-flowered wallpaper. I could hear the roar of the distant falls.

In the morning I waited for the *circular* at 7:00 but it didn't arrive until 7:30, too late for sunrise shots, but it didn't matter because the fog was too thick for pictures anyway. In fact the footbridges, suspended from cables across the deep gorges, disappeared into the mist. The first bridge was hair-raisingly bouncy and slick—looking down at the whitewater below terrified me, threatening to make me lose my balance—but I eventually got the knack.

I was soon trucking over the bridges pretty fast, figuring, with my luck, if one were to collapse it would surely be the one I was on. But thinking that didn't stress me out—*au contraire*, it made me laugh and filled me with a sense of abandon. If this was my day to die, then so be it...I might as well live it to the fullest.

Fatalism could be useful after all![79]

Between bridges I explored every path, even following one to the edge of a cliff overlooking the river far below. I bushwhacked down and found myself in a quiet spot with ponds, huge basalt boulders, water plants, grasses...and beyond, the spray and roar of the immense cataracts, divided into seven groups along a huge cliff where water tumbled off whole and smashed into vapor on the rocks below. Birds trilled and early-morning sun dried the ground, warming it.

I climbed back up to the path and continued toward the ceaseless crash. It sounded like a huge machine and I kept ducking, thinking there were planes overhead. I ventured out to the farthest point on the slippery rocks and sat down. My seat got wet but it didn't matter—I was out in the elements, alone. I sat there and absorbed everything: the constant roar that flushed out my thoughts, the mist and the oxygen given off by the incredible flora, the rainbows everywhere, the birds cruising on thermals overhead.

---

79 On January 17, 1982, nine months before Sete Quedas was destroyed, a hundred-yard-long suspension bridge collapsed, and eighty tourists lost their lives. Eight survived.

All of a sudden I understood the Buddhist teaching about the world's being an extension of our body. We were all the same! The answer to the problem of existence wasn't "out there"—it was inside us the whole time! I felt supremely happy…even if I couldn't join the birds in their little joy ride in the sky.

I took it all in and felt part of Nature, Nature that just *was*, Nature that was taking its own course, that didn't "make progress" like that abomination a few miles away, which would destroy these falls and so much more. *Human beings belong to the Earth,* I thought. *What makes us think the Earth belongs to us?*

Then I couldn't help myself, I started to cry, loudly, for the destruction of this place, for the sad state of the world in general, for my father, my family, all my misdeeds, my very being. I sat there, cheeks plastered with tears and mist and snot, sobbing and begging forgiveness from the universe, from Mother Earth, from God.

I no longer recognized the person I had become. Nor did I want to. I felt worthless. What had happened to me? But it wasn't time for self-recrimination. All I needed now was to empty my mind. *Just breathe.*

Some time later I arose from my perch, stiff and spent, an empty vessel, sustained by a rare inner peace (it was all I ever wanted) as I headed back, floating over the bridges and down the trail to town.

At breakfast the hotel owner was lamenting the loss of Sete Quedas after Itaipú—which he said meant "singing stone" in Guaraní and was the name of an island in the Río Paraná—but tried to be positive by pointing out, "We'll have the biggest lake around, thirteen hundred square kilometers." He didn't convince me, though—it was obvious he was anxious. He would have to move his whole family—where? He didn't know, but he had a brother in Minas Gerais. He said Itaipú was owned by the government and all the revenue would go to the politicians, who would only end up squandering it. I felt sad and helpless, which made me mad.

My granddaddy, Harry Oswalt, had lost his cabin on the Gunnison River in 1961 for the same reason: it was flooded after a dam was built to provide electricity for the booming West. For thirty years he'd driven from Kansas, where he designed and built farm machinery, to Colorado to fish for rainbow trout, his passion. When he'd had to close the cabin, it was as if he left his heart there… he died that winter.

The globe was becoming overcrowded! Some time ago I'd written in the back of my journal—which was fast approaching—that world population in 1972 was already at *three and a half billion*, a truly frightening number, surely close to the tipping point.[80] Soon all the humans would consume the earth like so many larvae on a wool coat. I'd been a senior in high school when the first Earth Day was observed and knew our old Mother's goose was pretty much cooked—especially if everyone on the planet enjoyed the standard of living we did in the US.

Across from that page I'd written: "Fleas: live 1-1½ yrs—lay 3–5 eggs daily (400–500 in a lifetime), takes 10 days to hatch. ABC Diario *(ABC Color)*. Groan!"

The next day I took a bus to Foz to see Yguazú Falls for the last time. A blue-eyed, Spanish-speaking German campesino sitting next to me said that 50 percent of the folks in this part of the country were German, usually the storeowners and wealthy farmers. There were definitely a lot of blonds here—that was the first thing I'd noticed about him.

"Germans are hard workers. The Brazilians don't like to work...like the Paraguayans," he divulged. That last statement offended me. I knew plenty of hardworking Paraguayans. But I also had to admit I'd come close to feeling the same thing.

So far my solo jaunt had gone well, acceptable rooms and food and not too much macho harassment. The room I got in Foz, though, at the Hotel Brazil, was a real pit—tiny space, couch bed, single sheet, bathroom down the hall—and at forty cruzeiros wasn't even cheap. The place reeked of cigarettes and perfume. I had just checked into my room and was heading back out when I heard Guaraní spoken in the hall. A couple of cleaning girls, obviously Paraguayan, were speaking it to a Brazilian man who was flirty and acted like he didn't understand. It sounded like they were saying "you smell bad."

I left the hotel and walked down by the river, where a shantytown had sprung up. Most of the homes had been constructed from thin sheets of plywood and were truly houses of cards. So many children...I wondered what they ate, as they had no *chacra*.

---

80 World population doubled in 2011, to over seven billion.

These had to be some of the people we'd learned about at the *cursillo* in Caaguazú. Record numbers of Brazilian farmers had been driven off their land and were now settling along Brazil's western border and immigrating to eastern Paraguay, joining the scores of displaced Paraguayans headed for the same area. Most of these new "residents" were in fact squatters, but land was plentiful so no one seemed to mind—although some SEAG agents claimed that much of the land had been stolen from the indigenous Aché.[81]

During the *cursillo* we'd visited a family whose house was similar to other campesinos' homes in Paraguay except that it sat in a shady forest. Of course everyone was slashing and burning the trees to create farmland. Some agents alleged that wealthy Brazilians were snapping up land in eastern Paraguay because Stroessner was selling it cheap. I thought how disheartening it must be to know your government had absolutely no intention of acting in your best interest and there was nothing you could do about it...if you wanted to stay alive, anyway.[82]

What I'd learned from others at the *cursillo*, especially Gino, had affected me as well. Maybe Paraguay *was* becoming too dangerous and it was time to get out.

Later that night at the hotel I got up for a drink of water and saw a man enter a room, then heard him unzip his pants and take them off, followed by girls' voices from the same room. This was a bordello, all right! I made the mistake of asking the teenaged desk clerk for a cigarette; he followed me to my room saying he wanted to "help" me sleep. I closed the door and locked it in his face, but he came back later and knocked for fifteen minutes. He must have had a key! I heard boot heels scraping the floor all...night...long, and I jumped every time the man snoring in the next room turned over. At least *someone* was sleeping.

---

81 The Celestina Pérez de Almada Foundation has taken up the cause of the Aché, who suffered genocide under the Stroessner dictatorship after multinational corporations like Industria Paraguaya obtained the rights to land reserved for the Aché and sold it to foreign investors.

82 Land issues continue to plague Paraguay (recently in Curuguaty, for example), as large GMO (genetically modified organism) soybean producers move in, destroy the environment, and evict—often killing—small farmers who have worked the land for generations.

As I sat there on the bed, fully dressed with my shoes on, too scared to sleep, my sheet around me like a Superwoman cape (that was a laugh), I started beating myself up pretty bad. Where was the intrepid traveler now? How had I become so despicable? I'd read over some of my journal entries from past weeks and been appalled at how I'd described myself as an "exemplary Colorada," referred to protesters as "commies" and "extremists." I'd even gotten swept up in all the hype and been excited about meeting Stroessner.

At first. Thankfully I'd come to my senses, and as I stood in the crowd that day in front of him, watching him pick up a baby and kiss it, what I was actually thinking was how easy it would be to assassinate the bastard. After my short stint as bartender afterward, I made an excuse and went home so I wouldn't have to shake the hand of the dictator—thanking Ray for the inspiration.

Still, I realized how callous I'd become to the Paraguayans and their situation. In my writing I'd called them just regular folks, said they had no time for philosophy, they would soak you, they were stuck in the second or third chakra, even worse. Jesus! Where did I get off being so judgmental? It wasn't their fault their government had failed to prepare them for the modern world.

And the situation with the parents versus the "authority," in San Miguel? I couldn't have been less concerned at the time (hadn't felt it my place to intervene)—we even shared a meal with the *maestra* afterward! And yet now I could see what an important issue it had been. I hadn't stood up for those good parents who were trying to do what was right by confronting a person in power who was taking advantage of their children.

Had I stopped caring about the Paraguayan people?

I thought of everyone I'd come to know—the folks at the pensión, my neighbors, my socias, my workmates...and I knew the answer was a resounding "NO!" I hadn't stopped caring. I still cared, a lot—hell, I *loved* those people, like family. Paraguay, too. And I still cared about being a good PCV. I realized if I quit now, I wouldn't be any better than the girls in my group who'd already gone home. In fact, I'd be *worse* because at least they hadn't spent any more of the Peace Corps's money, whereas the agency had paid all my expenses, including my trip to Brazil, had invested in me for the last year and a half. For what? An incomplete job?

I shuddered to think what JFK would think of me. I realized his inaugural address was much more than just the iconic line about asking not—our president was talking about struggle and sacrifice, telling us we had to stand together to help people defend their human rights.

I looked at my ring, our family crest engraved in carnelian. (My grandfather had commissioned the crest in the 1930s.) *Volenti nil dificile*, it said, "for the willing, nothing is difficult." I shivered. This value was the very cornerstone of my family, what had inspired my Irish-American ancestors to be upstanding members of their Pennsylvania communities, to be doctors and ministers and cofounders of colleges, to serve their country in the American Revolution and the Civil War and First and Second World Wars, to hand down the values of integrity, self-reliance, and perseverance. My grandfather, Thomas Alfred Creigh—who had studied under Woodrow Wilson and corresponded with him regularly—even put together a booklet called "On 'Making One's Mark,'" which he'd given to his five children on Christmas of 1935, when my father was eighteen and a freshman in college, the country still in the throes of the Great Depression.

I was making *my* mark, all right—a boldface demerit. This was my family legacy, for God's sake, and I was clearly nothing but a fraud. Here I was, alone and miserable again.

Things were certainly going splendidly.

Light was leaking through the broken shade when I finally dozed off; though it was quiet at last in that den of iniquity, by then nothing could have stood between me and oblivion. A few hours later I boarded the bus to Asunción and berated myself the whole way back. How had I managed to lose control over my life…yet again? I felt I had no choice now but to throw in the towel and go home.

I stopped by the PC office to tell them I was terminating. As if in a daze I picked up a letter from Ginny, bid farewell to a few folks, and wandered around the city, hiding from people I knew, haunted by something Dad had told me before I left for Japan, the last time we would ever talk face-to-face. "What I fear most," he'd said, "is having to duck into doorways to avoid meeting someone in the street." And here I was, doing just that.

Later, alone in my room at the Stella, I found out I hadn't loaded my film correctly and didn't have a single photo of Sete Quedas. I kicked the wall so hard my big toe swelled up and turned purple.

Back in Caazapá I sat in front of my "two-bit p.c. 'heater'" in my room at the pensión, dreading having to say good-bye to everyone. And wouldn't you know, the letter from Ginny said, "I miss you terribly, but my pride in your staying outweighs all that."

I spent the rainy Fourth of July hunkered in my bed freezing. What a laugh—I was independent, all right. And alone. All I could think about was how freedom was a two-edged sword: it required responsibility, and too much of it could land you on a slippery slope if you weren't careful.

I had to figure out what to do with Araí; Sarita said she couldn't take him. Thinking about the day I'd brought him home from the campo choked me up. After the reunion that day in San José I'd gotten on the bus to Caazapá, but when we pulled out Araí started running after us, his legs pumping as fast as they could, tongue flapping sideways in the wind. *Please stop,* I begged from the rear window of the bus, *stop running, just stop, turn around and go back!* But he kept going for an agonizingly long time, and my heart broke.

It was obvious the little guy didn't want to stay in the campo—who could blame him? Dogs weren't exactly "pets" out there. So I'd yelled at the driver to stop the bus, jumped off, and run to meet Araí in a scene right out of some silly *novela.* I scooped him up, carried his filthy, bug-infested derrière at arm's length onto the bus, and took off without looking back. What else could I do? The courageous cuss had taken his fate into his own paws, and you had to love that.

Fortunately, ña Juana said she'd be happy to keep him. I said good-bye to Araí for the last time, surface tension the only thing holding back my tears. This time he didn't try to follow me home.

Journal entry 12 July—New journal, new Beginning. Awakening. Emergence from the cocoon, weak, wings still wet and folded, can't fly. But the metamorphosis has taken place...I hereby christen this journal..."CHRYSALIS...a song of Hope."

Journal entry 15 July——More quotes from Kerouac (Dharma Bums)…
"When a baby is born he falls asleep and dreams the dream of life. When he dies
and is buried in his grave, he wakes up again to the Eternal Ecstasy." p. 51

"And when all is said and done it doesn't matter…Sad understanding is
what compassion means…I think therefore I die." p. 68

[About Gary Snyder] "Never said nothin that wasn't plain ordinary talk of
Tao[83]…(Like me)…He's got a little bit of the Fool in him and little bit of the
Moon Goddess too." p. 113

"Praise Lord, if you can't have fun turn to religion." p. 129

"Music blends with the heartbeat universe and we forget about the
brainbeat." p. 136

Today: Bike-ride to Tayy-í. Beautiful clear day, blue sky and white cotton-
ball clouds. Sailin' down the road, downhill, the last time! Appreciation. First
stop: Fernández. Naranja lima [lemon orange]. Visit to huerta…problems…I
don't know shit! Yes, we'll tell Velázquez, he'll know what to do…You always
get the feeling of being taken care of in the campo, a chair is always provided,
something to eat. Velázquez and Mami were to go to a reunion here last Thursday,
didn't show. Great way to start…How much older Olimpia's grandmother
looks! (How many more winters? I ask myself, undoubtedly echoing her own
preoccupations.)

[Socias] preparing sugarcane, for molasses. I have a glass…sweet, but not
overly, a freshness, greenness. Taking Instammatic pictures, snapshots. Ah, give me
a good camera and set me loose for a week! Visited the school garden in Galeano-
cué, all planted but plagued by plagas, insects and virus, too much, no recourse.
No money…At Olimpia's went to bring mandarins, as always, the end of the crop
this time, chiquititas [teeny ones]! It's cold and Olimpia wears her only sweater
inside-out, so's not to dirty. All trips out there over the past year all dream-like,
I decide it will always be this way, no sense in holding on. "Non-attachment.""I
think therefore I die."Tired, so much easier to frown, but I sing instead. Why worry?

Journal entry 16 July——"All alone, without friends and loved ones,

---

83 Chinese concept [pronounced "dow"] meaning "way," "path," or "principle"; equivalent to Japanese
"do" [doh], as in "aikido."

Alone but for my own innermost thoughts,
May the Buddhas pour out their infinite compassion,
That I may have no fear or terror."
            Prayer #20...TIBETAN BOOK OF THE DEAD

Journal entry 17 July—Today on the street, the town drunk-poet [Lambote]
stopped me, or rather I stopped him (no fear this time, feelin' high and good
even, devil-may-care...). He prophesizes, saying:"You're on some kind of misión
here, you didn't come just to work, what ideology [are] you? Be careful, they'll
get you" and I trying to explain my "ideology"—LIFE IS DEATH—but not
political, today the poet-artist-anarchist isn't interested in my artistic-poetic-
anarchic endeavors. A warning! From a sage...

The office held a *despedida* for me, of course—someone going away was
always a big deal. Everything seemed in good shape here, and I left feeling
confident that Vargas, Velázquez, and Mami would make steady progress toward improving the lives and livelihoods of the campesinos.

Or not.

One thing was certain: I had worked my butt off in agricultural extension!
To what end would remain to be seen.

Bidding adiós to my family here was of course the most difficult, especially
Margarita. I hadn't seen much of her lately. Of course I'd been away a lot, but for
some reason we rarely had *mate* together anymore. On my last night, after dinner
and sad farewells to the others, I finally corralled her into my room to say good-bye.

"Emilia, *¿Qué se hizo de vos?* (What became of you?)" she asked in that
pained tone guaranteed to make you feel guilty. (I knew she couldn't help it.)

"I was going to ask you the same thing!"

"You first," she insisted as she sat next to me on the bed.

I told her about Sete Quedas, and she gave me the Guaraní word for the
sound made by a waterfall, *chororó* [shoh-roh-ROH], which sounded more like
a babbling brook than the pounding madness I'd just come from.

She could barely contain herself so I nodded to her.

"Chelo and Fernando are engaged!" she said with a huge smile. "I'm so
thankful."

"That's wonderful, Margarita! Please tell her how happy I am for her." I was leaving on the 3:30 a.m. bus and wouldn't get to see Chelo—or Margarita—again.

Suddenly Margarita turned to me and said, "Oh, Emi, why do you have to go?" I threw my arms around her as we both started to cry. I had many excuses but could never tell her the real reason. All I could say was how sorry I was. We wiped our tears with the tissues she'd brought and were quiet for what seemed like a long time.

"Margarita," I finally said, when it was obvious we'd have to go to bed soon, "Who exactly is Lambote? He said I should be careful, that I'm on some kind of mission here—which I'm *not—not that kind, anyway*—and that 'they' would get me. Who do you think he was talking about?"

Composed now, Margarita stood up, grabbing my hands and looking me in the eye as I got up, too. "Lambote used to be a fine guitarist who unfortunately drank too much and ten or so years ago had an accident of some kind—he won't talk about it so no one really knows what happened. Now...Emilia," she practically whispered, "even though things have gotten more tense here for some reason, I don't think you, with that diplomatic immunity you told me about, need to worry. But it's probably a good thing you're leaving, seeing as how...well..." She looked toward the door and then back at me. "Tito works in the Colorado office and all."

What? How...? When...? Who...? I had many questions, but none passed my lips. People just *knew*. They knew and they still loved you.

I hugged Margarita and then said good-bye, my cheeks wet again as I closed the door and slipped between the sheets at the Hotel Díaz for the last time. My dream of March 23 was proving to be prophetic—I needed to "get out from under the press," all right.

Have you ever broken down bawling in your room and tried not to make a sound? I pressed my pillow to my face so hard I thought I might suffocate.

PART IX

EL CÓNDOR PASA
AUGUST 1976–JULY 1977

—⚮—

EMILY AND MARTÍN

We must let go of the life we have planned, so as to accept the one that is waiting for us.

Joseph Campbell

11

EMILY

M y Peace Corps career might have ended there but for the generosity of Gary and Todd and their belief in me as a volunteer.

In August I found myself miraculously still a PCV and resurrected, as it were, in Piribebuy [pee-ree-bay-BOO-ee], a town in the *cerro* (hills) two hours east of Asunción and south of Caacupé, on paved roads, where I began working on a latrine project with a sanitation engineer named Trini. I'd found the job myself and was now a health volunteer with the National Public Health Service, SENASA.

I couldn't forsake JFK, so I'd realized termination was out of the question—my work here wasn't finished. I had to get a grip, start all over, reinvent myself. Again.

I was counting my blessings because I thought for sure Todd and Gary were going to kick me the hell out this time. I was also thankful to be out of ag extension. In SEAG we were teaching democratic principles in a very undemocratic place, despite Stroessner's claims to the contrary. Where would it all lead? We empowered women to organize through democratic means, yes…but they were still "organizing," which could raise suspicion. Were we setting our socias up to be harassed—or even worse?

The new *educadora* would have to answer those questions for herself. The good news was I had never been reprimanded for leaving the socias' names off my monthly reports. The bad was I realized as long as the current government was in power, we were fighting a losing battle.

Leaving Caazapá hadn't been easy, but I was relieved I'd taken action and escaped when I did. I couldn't help likening myself to Max the cat—and even though I probably didn't have many lives left, my luck hadn't run out entirely because Piribebuy, population five thousand, was "simply divine," as Mom would say.

"The arroyo that runs through provides me an insurmountable daily joy," I wrote home. "Just the walk down there, looking up at green grassy hills, trees, houses here and there...and the stream itself, especially at sunset...picture-book!" The "stream" was the Piribebuy River, where women gathered in the mornings despite the cold—not that they had any choice—to beat their laundry on the flat rocks and spread it out to dry under the bluest of skies. There was even a waterfall close by, a small and inviting one, called—you guessed it—Chololó. (The water looked clear despite being just a few miles downstream from the "laundromat.") The sounds and colors soothed my bruised being.

What a relief I was still here in Paraguay! Every time I heard a *polca*, or sat down to have *mate* with someone, or looked out over acres of verdant date palms and sugarcane, I was thankful I hadn't uprooted myself too soon. The country did have its charms, after all.

This was my last chance to make good. I had less than a year to honor my oath to the corps, and I understood all too well how fast the time would pass. I had to admit, the last year and a half, at times unbearable, had flown by.

Tell you one thing, though—I was done with crying. Fed up. And I was done with people manipulating me. From now on I would be in complete control and wouldn't need nothin' from nobody. I would get my bearings and make something of myself, so I could finish here and go home a success.

Besides, I was doing the best I could, so everybody could just kiss my ass. I'd found my bottom—it was all up from here. But I didn't want to wallow in this negativity; I wanted to return to the serenity I'd felt at Sete Quedas, the peaceful feeling of belonging, of gratitude, thanks, gracias...grace. I knew it was up to me.

I looked at my family ring. I'd always worn it facing away, as if to seal wax on a letter, but now I took it off, turned it around to face me, and slid it back on my finger. I was willing, and anything was possible.

Wed. a.m., 4 August 1976, Dearest Mom and Everyone,

It's early and I'm sitting by the window of my new kitchen in my new house listening to Radio Caacupé and giving thanks that it's finally raining. Actually I have much to be thankful for, primarily an inner peace that I can only attribute to my current situation and Buddha...

My work has only begun: I've met the chief of police and the president of the Colorado Party headquarters here in Piribebuy. I must meet the "mayor" and the priest. One thing about working in Peace Corps, you deal with important people. I knew the minister of agriculture…Tomorrow I go to Asunción for a conference for the health volunteers. I'm so glad I changed into this program! The fellow I work with here is a gem and a hard worker (Paraguayan).

Just a note to say I'm quite alive and well in South America…

Missing you all—Amor y besos…E

Journal entry 4 Aug—Rain, finally, graceful. Thankfulness everywhere. I welcome the cold and grey and wet. Such fine smells! Blossoms of peach, pear, lapacho…

I was renting half a house from a woman named Elsa. She and her three-year-old son, Jesus María, lived in another house in town, which was a relief because even though I felt sorry the kid had to have a girl's name, he'd already shown his capacity for being a right little shite. Besides, I didn't really want to share the kitchen.

It was nice having two rooms. In a letter home I wrote, "I'm renting the house for ₲5000 ($40) a month, a bit steep…but I have a stove with oven (that just ran out of gas!), a bed, a clothes closet, a cupboard, dishes, tables and chairs. Therefore I don't mind. Maybe later I can pay less (rent shouldn't be more than ₲3,500…I make only ₲18,900)." The queen mattress felt luxurious. The backyard had a gate that was rarely used, and I felt safe being so close to the houses on either side.

Piribebuy had electricity but no running water, and once again I had the pleasure of using a latrine out back—though it was much closer than in Caazapá. The cistern was still dry despite the rain, so I grabbed the bucket and started down the cobbled street from my new house to look for a well. My head was abuzz with thoughts about a PCV I'd met who was pregnant with a Paraguayan's baby and planned to have it here and get married. She was so *tranquila!* How could she possibly know this was *it*, he was *the one*? I admired her courage but didn't envy her future, babies not being my thing and all.

I saw a pretty girl around my age walking briskly uphill toward me and had to laugh because her fast pace reminded me of me. I stopped and said to her, *"¿Moó-pico oiko la y, cuñataï i porä?"*

She smiled and replied in Guaraní, "My name is Cristina. We have water at my house. Come with me and I'll give you some." She turned around, put her arm through mine, and started leading me down the street in the direction she'd just come from. It became clear there would be no resisting Cristina—she was fiery and feisty and every bit the Sagittarius I wasn't (we quickly established that we both had birthdays in late November, hers two days after mine, me a year older). Her home, which she shared with her parents and sixteen siblings, had multiple rooms and a dirt floor. I was welcomed with open arms by her mother, María, who thought I was the cat's pajamas. Cristina filled my bucket and then walked me the six blocks back up the hill to my house. She of course knew Elsa—everyone knew everyone here

I fell immediately in love with my neighbors, ña Fernanda and her daughter, Petronita, and Petronita's (I assumed) daughter, Angela, who was twelve. Ña Fernanda was old, probably in her sixties, and went around with a chewed-up stogie always on the verge of dropping from her lips as she pulled them back into a broad smile. Come to think of it, everything about ña Fernanda was broad. She always wore a black bandana, and it was obvious there'd been no man around the place for a while.

They ran a *despensa* where I could get supplies and three Kents *sueltos* for ten guaranies. My parents were both heavy smokers. I'd always hated it when people around me smoked, but doing it yourself wasn't so bad. I wasn't a real smoker; I only did it because they were there. Surely three a day couldn't hurt.

Ña Fernanda, Emily's beloved neighbor in Piribebuy.

Cristina and I became best friends, though I had to keep my distance a little because Cristi, God bless her, was itching to take over my whole existence. She was a natural-born leader, but—while it was true I was a natural-born follower—I had to draw the line somewhere.

It turned out she was fervently Catholic. One day she asked me if I believed in God. "It depends on what you mean by 'God,'" I answered cheerfully, ready to spar. But she just frowned for a second and then grinned, and that was the end of it. She said Piribebuy was more religious than most towns because of its proximity to Caacupé, the "spiritual capital" of Paraguay, where the statue of the Virgin of the Miracles had been discovered. I'd seen the statue. The virgin had light-brown hair and blue eyes—a miracle indeed!

I knew quite a bit about Caacupé because I'd stayed there a couple of weeks looking for work. At the Hotel Uruguay I'd met an American agronomist with USAID, Don, who claimed the United States was making a mistake sending big farm machinery to Paraguay. "Once it breaks down there's no way to fix it," he said, "and the campesinos can't afford the gasoline to run it in the first place." Don, who was married, said he might have some projects for me, but when it turned out one of them was to have sex with him, I quickly cut off his innuendo and moved to Piribebuy.

In Asunción Ellyn finally introduced me to her expat friends the Blevinses and Lauers. Mr. Lauer worked for USAID as well. Both families were happy to put us up, which was great now that Steve was married. They were nice people but asked a lot of questions, I thought.

I finally called Mom on the Blevins's amateur radio by patching through some ham in Oklahoma. It was pretty cool how it worked, just like in the movies.

"Hi, Mom. It's Emmy. I'm here in Asunción. Hope you're doing well. It's a ham radio, so you have to talk and then say 'over.' Over."

"Hi, Em. Yes, I'm well. Over." Her voice shocked me as I hadn't heard it in over a year and a half.

"Mom, you have to talk for a while before you say 'over'. . .it's not really like having a conversation. Over." Neither of us was used to talking much and it took a while, especially with an audience, but we finally got going. We exchanged news, and I tried to talk her into coming to visit.

"We'll go to Yguazú Falls, then Buenos Aires, and then over to Bariloche, where we'll cross the Andes into southern Chile and take the train north to Santiago. Over." She said she'd consider it. I knew she wouldn't.

"Over and out," Mom said when she was finished.

"Over and out, Mom. Eighty-eights!" I replied, which Mr. Blevins had said meant "hugs and kisses." I liked spending time in their home and with their kids, who were high school students at the American school here, where Mrs. Blevins taught. It was a lively household—no different from any with teenagers in the United States.

The Lauers, on the other hand, lived alone in a rambling house on a large lot with trees. Their children attended college in the States. Mrs. Lauer hid her drinking but managed to get soused every day by noon. One morning Mr. Lauer drove me to the PC office. At a red light, he turned to me and said, "Sometimes a man likes it when you just grab his penis and squeeze it tight, like this." He demonstrated—with his hand only, thank God. *Whoa, guess he's not getting any action!* That was the last time I stayed with the Lauers.

Ellyn told me later that Mr. Lauer had tried to grope her while she was sleeping. What was up with all these Yanquis acting like barbarians, anyway? Weren't we supposed to be the "civilized" ones?

The Lauers had talked me into taking a kitten they couldn't keep; she was two months old and had been spayed. I named her Ara-tirí Overá, "lightning strikes," because even though she was completely black, to me she was like a ray of light, in a yin-yang sort of way. She needed to be held a lot, but she knew to pee in the dirt—*and* cover it up. Little genius! She slept with me in bed, nestled between my neck and shoulder. Angela was smitten right away and started calling her "Tili." After Tili discovered she liked to stretch out on the grain sacks in the *despensa* and taunt the mice, she became our collective kitty. They wanted to keep her, and I was happy knowing she'd have a good home when I left...which was only nine months away now and bearing down on me like a bullet train.

11 August 76, Dearest Mom and Everyone,

It's a beautiful "spring" day, warm afternoon, sun offering what heat it can through grey cirrus clouds (it finally rained), songbirds filling the air with cheerful music. In the distance a drum is keeping time undoubtedly to some group rehearsing for tomorrow's parade... The 12th of August was the date of a decisive battle in the Triple

Alliance War, and it took place here in Piribebuy. (Aren't you glad I always choose towns with easy-to-pronounce names?) I'm sitting in my kitchen, flowers in the window, sun shining in, drinking a cup of coffee...My life has become so tranquil and enjoyable. I can't believe this is the same me!

My house is so nice, especially my stove and oven. I'm doing a lot of cooking: breads, granola, soup, casseroles. I want to begin a garden, but the problem is my neighbors' chickens get in my yard. In fact, every two days one of these chickens lays an egg in my garbage crate; and, being "sin verguenza" (shameless) as I am, I haven't told my neighbors. My rationale: if they can't keep their chickens in their own yard (their pig, too, for that matter!) or even regulate where eggs are laid, then I can't be held responsible. Don't you agree? The chickens drive me crazy, always want to come into the house...

We've got a latrine project in one community...We do interviews at the houses, assess the problem, have a reunion where we teach parasitosis and importance of latrines, then form a commission and get them to build latrines, or well, or help to protect a natural spring, whatever is necessary. In the campo towns here there is a remarkable lack of "community." We have to identify the community's leaders and go to them...

Last weekend the health volunteers had a conference in a place called "El Tirol," a swanky hostel in some "mountains" (I always say quote mountains because they're actually quite small) near Encarnación...a day of meetings re: the health program, problems, solutions, recommendations, etc. Of course nights are free, and we took due advantage. The place had heated floors!...

I'm in great health once again, both physically & mentally. Plus spiritually, always higher...E

Journal entry 17 Aug—Write in here so little now—

Today gave a charla [talk] at 4-C club, went so well!! I was relaxed, and the "motivational" theme was very appropriate. I attempted to give the girls

something to think about...or rather, give them an idea of what it is to think. Stressed the idea of <u>preventive</u> as opposed to <u>curative</u> approach to good health. I asked questions about what we covered (What is good health? Preventive health? Mortality rate? etc.) and they answered them, remembered! Then had mate with the carnicera [lady butcher], a decent woman, told her I had "frialdad"—for some reason I was experiencing sharp abdominal pains, ever since this morning—she put in a remedio for "barriga" and I'll be damned if the pains didn't go away...

Journal entry 19 Aug—Thought-pattern for an afternoon (not-so-typical)—or—"I know you think I meant to do it to you but I didn't."

Part I—Sweeping leaves. Wonderful pastime, mind-less activity, the kind as "leaves" mind open for random thoughts to enter, a kind of Zen initiate first-job in the temple: sweep! (Remember the delight when Gayle had me sweep & mop the floor my first day at Fat City...)

Part II—Still sweeping leaves, fade from one reverie to another, now thinking about [a fellow PCV] and what he sez about having a "goal" when he speaks, or an end in mind, perhaps doesn't quite realize what he says at the time but isn't satisfied unless some doubt or question has been clarified...And I ponder this...

Part III—And musings fuse into more musings. I'm sweeping away. Feeling the muscles relax, feeling my body transform itself into energy and work and the sheer bliss of it all..."Qué guapa!" and here's my neighbor, the lady I've been wanting to talk to about using part of her chacra out back for my garden. So I ask her (in Guaraní) (natch) if she's going to use it, yes, she says, going to plant mandioca tomorrow. Oh, I sez, I was wondering if mebbe I couldn't use a little patch for a garden, and we discuss fencing (in Guaraní) (all) to keep out the chickens and pigs, and I tell her I was thinking 'bout using the spot next to my house but the land is bad, yes "iva'i la yvy" she says, needs fertilizer. We chat some more, yes isn't Guaraní fun then I continue sweeping and realize: Well I'll be damned if I know whether or not I can use a corner of her chacra for my garden!...

Part IV—And I think: "Now that I've got the leaves swept into my garbage pit I really should burn them, but here's this guy here fixing the neighbor lady's fence so's she can keep the pig out of the mandioca she's planting tomorrow, and the smoke is gonna blow right his way, so's I'd better not..."Then decide to write a letter, have a cup of café, come in to heat the water and think (forgetting completely about the hombre on the fence):"Well I'd better burn the leaves so's I can say my job's complete"and I go out and set the blaze, only then remembering why I'd decided to wait awhile, and so I mumble an apology and that's the end of the story. (He doesn't mind anyway, he's used to folks exercisin' their will without consultin' him.)

And oh, it's a glorious spring day, the sun is beginning to win the battle for supremacy against the cold air. But oh the cold when the sun goes down...

Journal entry 20 Aug—Ah how I love mate in the morning...Remember all last winter: get up, do yoga, wash, dress, then head over to the pensión at 7:00 for mate with Margarita—EVERY DAY!—the first time, really, I'd acquired a routine like that...And we'd sit and chat, I usually listening (to stories of pomberos or more interesting things like who's getting married,"ryé guazú"[big belly], etc.)...Ah, those frosty winter mornings with Margarita, huddled over the brazier, watching the auburn morning sun slant through lapacho and chivato leaves. And Margarita's bountiful jardín, claveles [carnations], dalias like the ones she gave me, white and yellow, and green, purple variegated plants proliferating in all parts, well-kept, a very fertile place in all...

And whenever I'd arrive early, before 7:00, before Dávila and Montoya and [a colleague] had left for the bank, they would tease me about being so early, would ask me in Guaraní if I fell out of bed ("Nde re-á nde rupá gui?") (Of course I never knew what time it was because my clock was always at least ½ hour fast)...

And then I'd go to the office at 7:30, have breakfast with Elena around 8:30–9:00, café de soja or cocido con leche—with galletas, UGH! But I was stuck, and I really loved being with her, now quite pregnant, even if I did have to give up some personal values...I knew she depended on me, since [her husband] was working in Stroessner—arriero [a resourceful person (lit. "muleteer")]!—and came once in a fortnight, if even that often. I would have merienda [snack] sometimes, too, and Elena thought I _needed_ it after a while, like any young Paraguayan between the ages of merienda and mate...So it was *more of the same, sugar and crackers (the golf-ball ones, the only "bread" you could get in Caazapá then, the wonderful soulless staple that campo families would sell milk and eggs for...). But I loved Elena and so it didn't matter all that much...*

I described my work in a letter home dated August 25:

I just finished (or am finishing) a film strip for tomorrow's reunion in the campo. The film strip is called "Pepe Pynandy y la Sevo-i" which means "Barefoot Pepe and the Hookworm." This is the first time I've tried to use my "artistic talent" on a project of this sort... it's great fun! You take a strip of plastic (sheeting, like) and shade in the background spaces with magic marker. Then you draw—or TRACE—your pictures with black Indian ink. Then you take another strip the same length and iron them together (iron <u>not</u> <u>too</u> <u>hot</u>, I almost learned the hard way). The pictures are all very simple, stick figures mostly, but I want to work some more in this to see what I can do.

I'm so happy working now! Like never before. I feel like I'm doing what I envisioned myself doing when I considered joining PC...I think nothing of spending nights or Sundays working...Tomorrow after the reunion we'll eat at one of the houses in the community. The people will probably kill a chicken...The reunion is to teach about parasites, and convince the folks they really oughta build sanitary latrines. ("Come on, you guys!")...I've started running, too, which makes me feel <u>so</u> <u>great</u>...One afternoon a week I help out at the 4-C club in town, teaching nutrition...

Strange sights in Piribebuy. Twice in three days, funeral processions have passed in front of my house, with the people wailing and screaming and tearing hair and generally making a scene. I've <u>never</u> seen that before (processions à la oxcart)...

Well, about the reunion this morning...went off without a hitch, and was fun to do. Only 25 people came though (30 later) and that was discouraging at first. I was almost demoralized...but when it came my turn to teach I just stepped right into the role. I like teaching now. I told about the parasite cycle and its relationship to latrines as best I could in mixed Spanish/Guaraní; Trini helped me out. I also tried to instill the idea of "preventive" as opposed to "curative" health. Then I mentioned ways to "break the parasite cycle." Next came the film strip, which everyone liked (Trini read the script in Guaraní). And finally, Trini and I sang the "Sevo-í" song in Guaraní.

You should've seen us going to the campo on his motorcycle...guitar in my right hand, film strip in my left, a huge (2' x 3') portfolio in his lap. We could have used a pickup! Then there was this old guy verging on senility who insisted on adding his own comments to our lectures (Trini talked about location and construction of latrines). A bit exasperating, though harmless enough...At one point I told him in Guaraní, "Listen: I'm teaching now... you can teach when I finish." He shut up for about 30 seconds. After the reunion about 7 men got together and seemed quite interested in building latrines. So they'll be the commission. I suppose we'll have another reunion later, and more will come...

Gin, the name & address of the holistic doctor:

DR. ANDREW WEIL, RT. —, Box —, TUCSON. 85715

Maybe he'd be interesting to talk to. If you look him up, tell him I found his name in New Age Journal...

It was almost spring but the nights were chilly still, so when I wasn't using my oven to bake, I sat in front of it with the door open to stay warm. I knew people said not to use the oven for heat, but I wasn't daft—I kept the kitchen door open, too. It must've been enough because I was still alive and kicking, the proverbial phoenix risen from the ashes.

In a letter to my grandmother I wrote, "Who are you voting for, Nanny? I've applied for an absentee ballot; afraid I'm a Democrat all the way. I've always thought government is more a common 'good' than an evil that should be done away with. Or at least it could be a good thing..."

I was excited and proud to be able to vote for president of the United States all the way from here, and was definitely leaning toward Jimmy Carter. He wasn't part of the corrupt system and would surely never compromise his integrity. I loved that he was a farmer. Plus I was certain he would stand up for human rights—someone had to.

11

MARTÍN

At noon on September 7, we received an order to prepare our things and move out of the Third Precinct. After inspecting our belongings, checking our pockets, and patting us down to make sure we weren't carrying weapons (which was completely ridiculous, of course—how in the world would we have acquired them?), the officers pushed us into a *perrera* and we left, not knowing where we were going. There were about thirty of us packed in like sardines, and we bumped uncomfortably along the dusty road. Fortunately, the maneuver took place on an autumn-like day. We remained serious and silent, but every face expressed curiosity about where this move would take us.

I wanted to believe our state of being was changing, that we were being transformed from the death of that infernal tomb into the living, even if it was of the lowest biological category—half men, half beasts. In my delirium, thoughts of my companions as cartoonishly grotesque monsters made me feel like laughing.

The trip took about two hours. Then the van stopped, the metal door opened, and we were ordered out. We found ourselves in the patio of a feudal-style fortress as a caravan of military vehicles entered as well. Revving motors, loudspeakers, orders, and shouts filled the air, as each group moved according to its own rhythm—the military personnel with nervous agitation and the prisoners confused, slow, trying to guess where we were and what was happening.

Inside the fortress were at least a hundred prisoners who had apparently also just arrived. Soon more showed up. In the end there were about four hundred of us—men, women, babies only a few months old, nursing from the breasts of their tattered mothers. With curiosity I watched every detail of this scene, which seemed to be out of a World War II Nazi concentration camp. A child in his pregnant mother's arms cried. I thought he was probably hungry or thirsty, but it turned out he was suffering from a serious intestinal illness.

The mother was Gladys Ríos de Mancuello, from Argentina. Her Paraguayan husband, Carlos Mancuello, a graduate of the University of La Plata, had also been arrested (on November 25, 1974, the day before me) and almost a year later declared "disappeared" by the police. (I had learned this from the young man's father and uncle, a former commissioner and first officer, respectively, who had shown exemplary conduct as we shared a cell in the Third Precinct.)[84] I went to a sublieutenant and explained that the mother needed to make some herbal tea for her sick child. The officer appeared to be moved, immediately ordering some soldiers to build a small fire. But I don't think Gladys ever had time to make the tea because we were ordered to move into the dark cells.

We spread out on the floor of a small area, twenty-five of us lying next to one another, some covered and some not. One of the prisoners told us we were in the Emboscada concentration camp, in the zone called Minas-cué. Originally a fort built in the early nineteenth century by dictator Rodríguez de Francia to fend off attacks from indigenous peoples, it had been turned into a prison camp in the 1930s for Bolivian soldiers captured in the Chaco War. I looked around and discovered new faces as well as people I had already met at Investigations and the First and Third Precincts.

The afternoon passed slowly, and the generator-powered light bulb in the hallway went out at 9:00 p.m. After locking the deadbolts and padlocks, the guard ordered silence. Thus began our new lives in yet another hell. As if it weren't bad enough, this one included a shortage of potable water.

Prisoners at Emboscada suffered from extreme thirst. Water was brought from the Piribebuy River to the prison in military trucks or by burro. The containers

---

84   Carlos Mancuello spent twenty-two horrific months at Investigations and was then officially "disappeared" (i.e., extrajudicially executed) on September 22, 1976. Gladys had her second child in prison in August 1975; they were released on November 2, 1977.

used were dirty gasoline or oil cans. Eventually, after many disputes with the authorities, we were allowed to use an old well about twenty meters from the latrine, which provided between thirty and forty liters per day, mostly for drinking—personal hygiene was a privilege reserved only for police and military personnel.

The abysmal food and lack of air in the cells made our incarceration even more difficult. Many of the new prisoners protested the poor conditions, but any protest was taken to be a manifestation of rebellion and would result in new threats of torture. The authorities blamed the protests exclusively on the communists, saying "they" wanted to cause "uneasiness and chaos." This was why some of the comrades I had befriended in the Third Precinct were occasionally returned there.

The Paraguayan Committee of Churches sent us food, but the authorities often appropriated it. One day we requested information on the list of supplies sent to the prison. The authorities did not hide their displeasure; they responded that from now on, questions regarding food rations would be considered subversive and, therefore, liable for punishment.

There were twenty-five cells, and by initiative of the authorities themselves, a council of delegates from the cells was formed, solely to organize the cleaning of the prison and communicate orders from above to bring about "better behavior." In the beginning, delegates were elected directly by the inmates of each cell. Even though the council met in the presence of a prison representative, we would address issues that went beyond what was established, visibly irritating the guard on duty.

Readings and discussions that we held inside the cells also flouted the guards' vigilance. The issues we discussed in secret meetings were later taken to the council of delegates. Because of this mobilization, we were able to achieve something that was prohibited everywhere else in the country: the ability to think and express our ideas.

Later, fearing the "communist" threat, the authorities changed strategies and appointed the delegates themselves. But this didn't stop our line of action; rather, it fortified our struggle, increased morale, and emboldened demands for more humane treatment.

The first cell I lived in at Emboscada was number seven. There were twenty-three people in a space measuring three by four meters and nearly two meters high, with a ceiling of reinforced concrete, a thick wooden door, and a window measuring twenty centimeters a side—our only source of air. The polluted waters of the Piribebuy River caused dysentery in the prison population. The state of hygiene was intolerable. If we needed to relieve ourselves at night, we had to use empty Nido milk cans—often the same ones we used the next morning for our breakfast.

When summer arrived the cells became veritable ovens, with temperatures rising to 45 or 50 degrees Celsius (113 or 122 degrees Fahrenheit) and practically roasting us alive. Hunger, diarrhea, heat exhaustion, mosquitoes, and other maladies caused upheavals among the prisoners, which were immediately treated as subversive uprisings. We also reacted strongly to the prohibitive prices in the prison cafeteria, a business run by prison commander Colonel José Félix Grau.

I relayed our cell's demands to the comandante, who was from San Lorenzo. As punishment I was taken to the feared cell number twelve, which housed those who had remained in prison the longest, most of them communists.

While I was still in cell number seven, I had represented my fellow inmates before the council of delegates. In that capacity I made it known to Colonel Grau that we were profoundly displeased that the prisoners from cell number twelve had a different schedule from the rest of the prison population, and we thought it unfair that citizens who had suffered more than fifteen to twenty years of captivity were still being detained for no more than an offense of conscience. I also requested that on Saturdays we be allowed to hold sports competitions and cultural events.

Colonel Grau categorically denied my requests.

The weekly arrival of the *perrera* created anxiety among the prisoners. Guards emerged and began selecting those who were to be taken to the Office of Investigations for torture. So-called lawyers from Investigations required the victims' presence so they could prepare the paperwork to be sent to the Department of Justice, specifying the systematic offense of disturbing the "public peace"…that is, violating the infamous "Law No. 209." The lawyers and torturers—as well as judges of the dictatorship—were in charge of getting signatures for such "confessions" by whatever means they could. After one or two weeks of torture and terrible mistreatment by specialists using "the precise pain, in the precise place, in the precise amount" (phrase used by US torture instructor Dan Mitrione), the prisoners would be sent back to Emboscada.

Normally, the superintendent directed the selection process. Sometimes he would call my name and tell me to "behave," saying he was being very patient with me but his patience could run out, and at any moment the authorities could call me in to "settle accounts." He would usually speak to me in a paternalistic tone of voice, as if his only intention was to help me.

The atmosphere at Emboscada was one of perpetual fear. The psychological abuse culminated in the shooting exercises the police and military forces held right outside the prison, their intent being to remind us that they were well armed and there was no possibility of escape. At the request of my cellmates, I presented objections to Colonel Grau during a council meeting regarding the humiliations we'd been subjected to at the Office of Investigations.

He did not respond.

Our prison was located at the lowest point in the arid, rocky zone of Emboscada. Inmates held there during the Chaco War were forced to cut stones, which were then used as building materials or to pave streets in Asunción. This particular spot was called Minas-cué, "where the mines were," a name that evoked the period of forced labor by Bolivian prisoners.

The concentration camp consisted of an area about one hundred meters on each side surrounded by a stone wall more than seven meters high that could not be climbed; there was a walkway on top where guards were always on patrol. On the outside edge was a guardrail to keep people from falling off, but there was no such rail on the inside. The entire building was against the stone walls, with few windows, all of them barred.

We prisoners lived in that hole called Minas-cué. There were children, seniors, sick people, pregnant women, and people of all nationalities, religions, and ideologies. A girl who was only four years old had been forced to stay there while her parents were sent to Investigations. She became obsessed with escaping and invited my daughter, Celeste, who was staying with me there at the time, to break out with her. That was the day Colonel Grau accused me of indoctrinating Celeste with Marxist-Leninist theory and ordered me to send her home (although she had no "home" to go to at the time; my mother was in Argentina with the boys and, under the circumstances, could find no one to care for Celeste).

Emboscada was organized so that the teenagers were in charge of two specific tasks: carrying water from the Piribebuy River and collecting firewood from the surrounding area—both under strict military supervision. The mistreatment these adolescents suffered, as well as their contact with politicized adults, stimulated in them the development of a political awareness they did not have when they arrived.

The women were especially remarkable. They worked elbow to elbow with the men and showed admirable strength and courage, despite having lost husbands and sons and undergone torture themselves. During the delegates' meetings, they were the ones who spoke up most for human rights. A lucky few shared prison space with their loved ones.

Living together with everyone made me realize that, although there were around four hundred of us in that military fortress, in practice all three million of the country's inhabitants were oppressed by the military, a situation that fed the flames of rebellion within us every day. An entire country held prisoner. An entire nation without freedom. A whole people living as if in prison, without rights—a prison ignored by the world.

Every time I got the chance, I reminded my companions of the long struggles people had initiated throughout history for their freedom. I talked to the farmers about Christianity, its vicissitudes and its final triumph.

At times we thought we could feel the slow but inexorable approach of the moment when all the accumulated suffering of a quarter century would simply burst. I recall that many would think of this and want to hear the poem "Parto" ("Birth"), by Julio Correa, which I had memorized. It spoke of the oppressive forces in the world today and how the people's pain was the pain of childbirth, and that freedom was about to be born.

One thing was clear to us: the only way to combat and defeat the current fascist dictatorship was the united, coordinated fight of farmers, laborers, students, and all the popular sectors. We were also convinced that at this point in our struggle it was necessary to avoid discrepancies, theoretical or otherwise, that could interfere with the united force behind the one great objective. It was while we were in this state of mind that a few noteworthy events occurred.

Before or after the night patrol, during the cleaning chores, or at any time, I would chat with young officers and tell them that ours was a just cause and Stroessner's politics, condemned throughout the world, were steering the country towards a precipice. They asked me what I would propose politically, and I said "the Colorado Left"—in other words, a Colorado ideology that would advance toward a social democracy, taking up again the ideas of the authentic Colorados. I stressed to them that uniting the honest Colorados inside the country with those who were living in exile, along with all of the opposition, with no exceptions, was the only way to undermine the dictatorship.

At first the officers listened to me with interest, but as I got deeper into the subject, a few became uneasy. And of course someone told Colonel Grau that I was now heading a full indoctrination campaign, but instead of being for farm workers it was for the prison officials.

One day I ran into Colonel Grau. He acted very cordial and even invited me to discuss some issues regarding the prison. He told me he was worried about the health of some of the older prisoners and was negotiating with his superiors to allow the "poor souls" to be moved to cell number twenty-five.

Suddenly, he very politely asked why I had forsaken Colorado ideology for subversion. I responded that it wasn't true, I was convinced more than ever of the justice of the Colorado doctrine. In fact it was my identity as a Colorado that made me oppose all the abuses Stroessner had committed against the doctrine, among them office holding for perpetuity, character worship, political stagnation, the takeover of our sovereignty and economy, and cultural and educational colonialism. I pointed out that I was against "peace" and "order" imposed from above, against the state of siege, the corruption of public administration, contraband, white slavery, drug trafficking, and all the rest. I concluded by saying it was not a mystery to anyone why, under that regime, Paraguay had become an international refuge for common crooks and fugitive war criminals from Europe.

"You, Almada, have been very influenced by the communists," he responded.

"No, Colonel, I have been influenced by the popular vein of the Colorado Party, and I will dispute anyone who tries to strip my party of its historical content, its liberating power, and its social justice. I think the name with which our party was born into civil life, the National Republican Association, fairly expresses the desire for the unification of the Paraguayan people against oppressors from within and without. My words are in regard to those ideas."

"The fact is, Almada, you have read a lot of communist texts at the university in Argentina, and now you want to bring into our midst a foreign ideology and a foreign revolution," he said.

"No, Colonel. The Colorado Party advocates a nationalist revolution, rooted in Paraguay's own traditions, despite the experience of world history. The Colorado Party therefore does not acknowledge ideological, political, or cultural metropolises, or foreign dictates, and it answers only in the interest of the people, seeking the welfare of the republic."

He said, "It's been proved that there have always been rich and poor, but you people here at Emboscada want to fix the world in a day. That is impossible, Almada. You're just dreaming."

"No, Colonel. History teaches us that the gap between rich and poor is not a question of fate. The new society we want to bring about requires that we overcome the injustices that reign in our country—5 percent of the population is very rich, 10 percent middle class, and 85 percent poor. This situation can be remedied with an anti-imperialistic, democratic, popular Colorado government based on the unification of farm and industrial workers and the rest of the exploited population. The government we envision will make changes to free Paraguay from dependence and respond to the essential needs of the people. One of these needs, Colonel, is what motivated my concern as an educator—the democratization of teaching. As you know, education in Paraguay under Stroessner's dictatorship benefits only those in power and perpetuates our underdevelopment and dependency. We want the Colorado government to guarantee authentic democracy and open the way to a socialism in which wealth, not poverty, is distributed."

"That is communist language, Almada!" he exclaimed.

"No, Colonel, that is genuine Colorado language. You have apparently never read the Declaration of Principles in the Charter. I know it by heart: 'Power actually exercised by the people and, specifically, access by the working masses to own land and other means of production, as well as their participation in the political process and in representative bodies, and in the administration of social security services, constitute the only guarantee of genuine freedom and an indispensable instrument in the creation of an equal society without privileges or exploited classes.'"

"Everything you are saying sounds good on paper," he said, "but in practice it is impossible. Our country is poor and cannot guarantee everyone an education. Put your feet on the ground, Almada, you are too much of an idealist."

"Then how can you explain that in a supposedly poor country, the government in power sets aside more than 50 percent of the national budget to maintain its military and police? Or that in a country whose economy is based on agriculture and livestock, the Ministry of Agriculture is at the bottom of the national budget? Military service is obligatory, and the rule is followed to the letter, whereas free elementary education is also obligatory but not enforced. Why? According to official reports, each year one hundred thousand children have no school to go to. Does that seem right to you?"

He sighed. "What would you propose?"

"Among other things," I said, "a substantial increase in the education budget, and the transformation of private institutions into cooperatives, from elementary through university, assisted and controlled by the State."

"That is communism because it eliminates private property."

"No," I said, "the property is still private, it just acquires a social function, in line with the spirit of the National Republican Association, the Colorado Party."

"You have a distorted view of the Colorado Party, Almada."

"My Colorado ideology," I said, smiling, "is written in the future, because it advances toward a society without privileges or exploited classes, as expressed in the Declaration of Principles, article 4. It's true the party was formed in 1877, but it reformulated its entire theory and practice according to the demands of our times, on February 23, 1947, at a historical convention in Asunción."

"You are hopeless, Almada," he said. "You are too much of a fanatic. Maybe those ideas can take root in the future. Until then, calm down and behave yourself."

Notorious for his cruelty and ferocity against political detainees, Colonel Grau was known at home and abroad as the "Butcher of Death." The preceding dialogue took place during a unique period of his life—his wife had just died—which I believe explained his willingness to listen to me.

12

EMILY

I was in Asunción at the PC office on September 21 when a pale Todd bolted out of his office, shouting that a Chilean diplomat named Orlando Letelier had just been assassinated in Washington, D.C., only nine blocks from the White House. How could that even happen? Who had done it…and why? On the bus back to Piribebuy, I realized there was still a lot I would never understand.[85]

—*Napkin Haiku*—
  Hop a 31, find a seat, watch the street—
  Mariscal López.
  Let's meet for a beer…
  Where? Beneath the chivato tree,
  we'll toast you and me.
  Them wheels of fortune:

---

85 The October 11, 1976, issue of *Newsweek* reported that, according to the CIA, "the Chilean secret police were not involved," a story later found to be a cover-up by then CIA head George H. W. Bush, who naturally wanted to maintain ties with his communist-fighting allies in Chile's army and protect Manuel Contreras, the head of Chilean secret police (DINA), who along with Pinochet was behind the assassination. Bush was never questioned about the false cover story, and the FBI was soon onto the real culprits. The tragedy marked the beginning of the end of US support for Operation Condor.

In 1998, after Pinochet was nearly extradited from England to Spain, Secretary of State Henry Kissinger—who has always denied US involvement in the assassination—was reported to have begun making careful inquiries before traveling abroad, seeking to avoid, in his words, getting "Peenoshayed."

The Plaza Uruguaya,
blind man's violin.
Singing songs in Guaraní——
he turns his head, sees me.

Some PCVs I knew were terminating and I found it unsettling, as I wrote in my journal: "Such small ripples in the everyday ocean of everyone else's lives, and for them tidal waves…It's such an anticlimax to finally leave, it's like death, one is so very much alone, no one can possibly feel what the leaver feels. And life does go on, after all…"

Across the street lived some members of a band, Los Ídolos de Piribebuy, who had actually recorded some albums. I bought one, *La Corona de Éxito* (The Crown—Peak—of Success). I got to know the brothers Alcaráz and Filemón Roa and played guitar with them some evenings. Playing music with people was fun, like speaking a common language. It struck me how fortunate these guys were to need so little "terrain"—the instruments themselves—to make a living, whereas farmers in the campo required hectares of land…and of course backbreaking work. (It was true, though, musicians covered a lot of terrain on the road.)

Mornings were warm enough to start doing yoga again. I loved how the out-breath was as exhilarating as riding a wave…and how if we were constantly aware of this, we could live fully half our lives in ecstasy! I reveled not only in the poses but also the meditation…just a few minutes of freeing my mind of thoughts left me feeling relaxed and energetic at the same time, "transcendent" as it were.

October snuck in before I knew it. One morning the neighbors' sow died in my patio, certainly not by my hand though I confess I may have entertained the odd craving for bacon. But what a fiasco! I was sorry for their loss; the thing was useless to them now—they couldn't very well eat it, could they? I felt the family's pain as several men dragged the corpse away, but I wondered if they didn't blame me somehow.

Journal entry 3 Oct—Poem from the day I left Caazapá:
Lookin' around the room at the stained green walls——

There's nail holes where maps once hung, without a lamp, the light bulb falls.

'Lone in this emptiness, where light hangs on empty spaces,
where echoes hang on bare corners and walls hide Time's erases.
It's a familiar scene, this still-life of movin' on.
Lookin' back to where you've been, lookin' up and wonderin'
why wanderin's your only destination.

Journal entry 4 Oct—*Terrific storm today...The rain came slowly...but the wind! It was another scene, holding doors and windows shut, cursing when the door flew open and blew my desk's contents all over the living room, taking up the rug after it was already wet, etc. No da gusto [It's not fun]. Che añó [I alone]. But no worry: I've got a pretty little banana bread in the oven...Can't believe how home-based I've become. Short excursions out, nomás, but several times a day. Like now: Mate with ña Fernanda and ña Petrona...*

Journal entry 7 Oct—*Brief escapade to Asunción, prime motive: president "debates." Not a debate, really, I didn't care for the format*—*but have no suggestions. Would like to see more of a dialogue between the two men. This was a farce. But I at least heard J.C.'s voice...Hopefully we'll be hearing it for some years to come...I feel Carter can make things happen...He's a farmer with charisma. Let's form a sort of agrarian party (agrarian-based social democrat)...*

Journal entry 10 Oct—*Sunday. Trini's grandfather's funeral...Beautiful days. Thick, almost, with sunshine and warmth, yet a cool fragrance and damp. You can feel the sun is working full force to reach through to you. And that energy you pick up...*

Dream I had last night: Wowie!: Riding in a huge camión toward Caazapá, but we turned off just before...The truck was air-conditioned, the day very hot. We rode to the middle of a plain and stopped, driver getting out, going to visit something, right back. But there's water, running, on the ground...and the ground is sandy, desert. "This is the beginning of a flash flood" I protest. I know deserts. He denies what I say. I get down from the cab, and the water's to my knees. Before I have time to turn around, the water's upon me, a wall of muddy water, white with rage, is upon me, and it's black.

I experience no struggle, no sensation of suffocating, of drowning, dying. Where are my thoughts? My thoughts are on the Tibetan Book of the Dead. My mind is with the Mind of the Universe. My body is floating in fog.

The flood's over. I'm wet but still alive (at least the state I recall as once being my existence). The story resumes. Ellyn has survived also. Where are the others?

The sun comes up.

Journal entry 11 Oct—Evening mate. Ara-tirí Overá has just finished her filets. I'm rejoicing over being alive. I feel more alive than ever. This afternoon I went swimming in the arroyo...Ah, was truly glorious! I've been looking forward to a swim for a long time now. The feel of the body as it moves through the water, the cool enveloping mass. To feel every muscle, every joint, every part of one's self move; moistened, smooth. And what could be more joyful than swimming in a river...Always clean...

There are many people swimming and bathing, mostly young men; noise reverberates outward, upward, toward the town. I'm embarrassed a bit to strip, so sit on a bench awhile. Finally I decide SCREW IT, I WANT TO SWIM AND THE SUN'S GOING DOWN! So off comes my T-shirt and my jeans, lucky I have a tank suit even if it is a bit small. Fooling around, I ask if the water's cold (got to break the icy stares). I can always get a few laughs. I swim, I sing the sevo-í song, I swim some more. Afterwards I feel so damn good.

Journal entry 29 Oct—The PC meeting was successful, the cursillo was successful...even our 3rd volleyball game was successful! (Though I played miserably.)

Some of my happiest moments were playing volleyball for my barrio, María Auxiliadora. The games were at night under the lights and well attended. One time after I scored a point, someone yelled, *"¡Adelante, Yanqui!"* and I had to laugh. But I wasn't really that good, and when Cristina's sister Hilda returned to Piribebuy I got bumped off first string, which stung even though I knew it was the right decision.

On November 2, I listened to the election on my scratchy radio, my heart in my throat—Carter *had* to win!

12

MARTÍN

As happens with sound in an echo, what was happening in the United States had repercussions in Paraguay that found their way to our feudal dungeon in Emboscada. For example, during the presidential elections of the giant up north, we political prisoners favored the Democratic candidate, Jimmy Carter, while our jailors preferred the Republican, Gerald Ford.

We were aware that regardless of whether Carter or Ford was the next occupant of the White House, the Paraguayan military dictatorship would continue receiving the same unconditional line of credit to keep the police and military apparatus going. We nevertheless liked Carter because during his campaign he preached the defense of human rights, clearly with the intention of improving the discredited image of unpopular governments created and maintained by the United States itself.

Just as for voters in the US, for the political prisoners and authorities at Emboscada, Election Day was charged with emotion. The official radio station transmitting the elections announced with great hype the initial results showing Ford ahead. Government officials celebrated the triumph of the Republican, which was also a triumph for the Paraguayan government, while we prisoners remained anxiously silent. Later, the results showed Carter ahead and we reacted with resounding applause, to which the authorities responded with threats and insults.

Some of us cried when Carter was finally announced the next president of the United States.

13

EMILY

I felt elated and proud that I had actually voted for the next president of the United States (my first vote had been for Nixon's opponent, George McGovern, in 1972). But I also felt trepidation—now "we" were behind the wheel of this juggernaut *sin freno*. It would remain to be seen whether Carter could fulfill his campaign promises.

Mom wrote to say she was coming to visit. I was sorry but relieved that Nanny would be staying home. At the travel agency in Asunción, I tried to get reservations at Hotel das Cataratas but was disappointed to discover it was booked for the month of December.

"We'll see about that," I said to the agent with a wink.

Things were starting to heat up, including the weather. I'd invited some PCVs to my house for Thanksgiving, after which Cristina would host her and my birthday parties at her house on Saturday. Cristina did everything by the book, literally; she showed me the bound volume she used to keep track of what was happening and who was attending. (She even had her own purple stamp—not to mention one of those elaborate signatures everyone seemed to have that was a "stamp" in and of itself.) These events naturally required approval by the local Colorado officials and the police chief. I still hated how they had to know everything.

Journal entry 24 Nov—My two-day Thanksgiving fast became a 24-hour Thanksgiving fast. Tomorrow, my birthday: 24 years…

Li'l kitty is hunting cockroaches and other big-size bugs these days.

How beautiful, the chivatos in bloom! I am thankful at least that I can appreciate Beauty. And I do, I do.

[Later] The dreams I've had lately, of gasping for breath while swimming, hair suffocating me…Where is Buddha? What a sanctuary, to be living in God always. Is man meant for that? Is that serving God?

The articles on fascism in East West Journal (September) are startling. How timely! Saying: Don't be carried away by emotionalism, "spiritualism," because it's potentially fascist. (Pre-WWII German youth were also involved in a "back-to-earth" folk movement. The almost "religious" states of mind were easily diverted into a group-relatedness and pride—NATIONALISM— that was used in some one person's scheme for world hegemony and unified status.) Group identification is the prime factor. And a zealousness, deep conviction... [86]

Journal entry 28 Nov—After the Thanksgiving fest... We were 8... We all worked hard to get the food on the table and in our mouths, and it was Good. I don't know on what my fears were based the night before, I suppose an ego thing, that no one would come. It turned out to be the best birthday ever!... The Paraguayans showed they care... Ña Fernanda and Petronita sent budín [pudding], the parrillada lady made chipa guazú [chipa with meat]. I was buzzing with felicity.

I was nearly raped last night by "Pupi." He came in my window as I was sleeping (after we all got shit-faced at Cristina's party). I honestly think he thought I wanted it... but my attempts at first to talk him out of it were in vain, he's a huge monster and I couldn't budge. I told him he had no self-respect, that I would tell everyone if he did anything to me, etc. Nothing worked. Soon he was quieting his mouth and concentrating on other power spots. I let out a yell that scared him, before I knew it he was gone! What a narrow escape... Of course I'll tell no one here. How can I?

---

86 In 1958, Cité Catholique, a traditionalist Catholic organization created in France in 1946 (and supportive of the Nazis), was introduced in Argentina along with a doctrine of counterrevolutionary warfare and brutal repression of terrorism. As it did in the Algerian War, the group provided the ideological support necessary to justify the torture carried out during Argentina's ensuing "dirty war" in the 1970s. Among other things, soldiers were told they were "doing God's work" by eliminating the "subversives" (aka "communists"). In fact, the group's founder, Jean Ousset, developed the concept of "subversion" as a force trying to undermine Christian order.
Interestingly, the United States saw a similar development in the 1930s, as business leaders chafed against the New Deal and began to fund conservative religious leaders to preach "faith, freedom and free enterprise." During the Eisenhower administration, this "conflation of Christianity and capitalism" was fully realized when "under God" was added to the Pledge of Allegiance and "in God We Trust" to paper money (the phrase had appeared on coins since the Civil War). What president or candidate today does not close a speech with "God bless America"? Yet Richard Nixon was the first to do so, in 1973, and Ronald Reagan made it gospel. See history professor Kevin M. Kruse's revealing book, *One Nation Under God: How Corporate America Invented Christian America* (New York: Basic Books, 2015).

Crap! Why hadn't I put a screen on that window? And how was it even remotely possible I hadn't woken up as "Pupi"—the perfect nickname—must have fallen through it? He'd tried his best to get my attention at Cristina's party, but I'd ignored him because he was such a dolt, which apparently pissed him off—or in his delusion convinced him I was dying to have sex with him. Was it really *my* fault, though, just because there was no screen?

Oh, I get it. It's my *fault for leaving the way open because, after all, in such a situation, what's a man to do? Of course a* man *can't be expected to control himself, now, can he?* Why did it take me so long to figure things out? And what compelled me to keep tempting fate like that?

I might have been trusting, but I wasn't timid. When I felt that SOB on top of me (fully clothed, thank God) in my bed, separated only by the sheet, I made up my mind I was *not* going to let him rape me. He had me pinned, but after trying to talk sense into him and then screaming, I bit him as hard as I could on the neck—I wasn't about to give up. He yelped and rose up, angry; I was afraid he might hit me. But he got off me and somehow fell back through the window, landing with a thump and stumbling away.

I felt pumped to have fought the brute off, even though I knew he was probably just too drunk to force the issue. I never asked ña Fernanda if she heard anything, and she never mentioned it, but I did wonder about the lies the bastard would undoubtedly be spreading. Good thing he lived in Asunción and I wouldn't have to see him around town.

Still, his insolence—and the fact that he was getting away with it—filled me with such rage that I forgot to thank Miriam for her thoughtful telegram wishing me a happy birthday *"con cariño"* (with affection). I was touched that she would think of me, especially as Ellyn had said another girl from our group just left for the States with her Paraguayan fiancé (say what?)...and now we were the last three left! Here I'd worried about Miriam more than anyone, but she was doing just fine, was doing a great job, in fact. Ellyn was an über volunteer, too, though I never doubted *she* would finish—now I just hoped she wasn't serious about that good-for-nothing *novio* of hers.

Journal entry 8 Dec—*Pilgrimage last night to Caacupé, in the rain. A mess but welcome relief from sizzling humidity...with Cristina and cousin Felicia. We began by bus, then disembarked somewhere between Caacupé and Ramal— So many people walking! From Asunción and Stroessner and all points in between...Why do they walk? It's the custom, perhaps no one really knows, but there's a vague, primitive sense of sacrifice, sublimation of desires for a higher spiritual being, that this effort will return to one in worldly ways (people do the sacrificial walking, then pray to the virgin and ask for something in return... the supplicants).*

Arriving in Caacupé, to find streets filled with people, stands selling food, plastic recuerdos, plastic junk, shirts, straw mats...people sleeping everywhere, preferably under an awning of some sort...children selling candles a diez [at 10 each]...chipa, empanadas, caña...gente! Gente! Gente! A renaissance fair (and only 3 SENASA inspectors sent?!).

The drizzle continued but created no problems. There's misa [mass] in the plaza, people paying respects to the virgin in the church. Candles lit and offered. In the marketplace the Hermanos Villalba Palacio de Juegos, bingo and merry-go-rounds and ring toss. Asado. Plastic junk. Caacupé ceramics. Religious festival? You'd never know it. Temporary stalls fairly well built, bamboo, no rain inside. Young girls, women in white dress, light blue capes, so weary, how far have they come?

We follow Cristina. Cristina is very autocratic. She's always the one to say: Vamos [Let's go]. Cristina decides where to go and Cristina says when. Felicia and I follow her like groupie fans, but how can you not love Cristina? Her ultimate concern is Mankind. I'm certain she would sacrifice anything...

I've heard too many misas this week. I have my period (I think) [full moon], unprepared. We go to Cristina's aunt's to sleep: no room! I decide I'm bored, want to go. We listen to another misa, then return home to Piribebuy. The Catholic services move me in no way whatsoever, neither the walk, nada. NADA! I am incensed to hear the priest reading from the Bible and knowing the people take that for gospel truth. Don't all people have the right to think?...

I did my good deed for the day: Last night in Caacupé, the church officials were looking for the parents of "Ramón Amarilla"...The people at the policía

were looking for Ramón. They couldn't hear one another. We informed the police.
A happy reunion, presumably. Each was waiting for Godot.

Some PCVs held another *peña*, which I wrote in a letter home was a "'folk festival, American style' to help raise money in one of the towns. We're trying to figure ways of getting people to continue raising money, working together to recognize community needs and solve them." This *peña* was in Guarambaré, and I had to admit it was fun singing and playing my guitar on stage—nerve-racking, yes, but fun.

We stayed overnight with a PCV who lived in Guarambaré. In the morning some volunteers were smoking grass (strictly forbidden, of course) and invited me to join them. Then they decided to go to mass. What a trip! I saw the ritual in a whole new light, literally—the acrid incense, the smoke, the mesmerizing drone of the priest's voice, the consumption of Christ's flesh and blood. (I didn't take communion myself, of course; I knew from having to attend five o'clock mass with the Spencers before horse shows that if I did, I'd go to hell. I didn't believe in hell, of course, but wasn't going to take any chances…unlike my sister, whom God must have pardoned because even though she'd broken the sacrament, she was still aboveground, as far as I knew.)

The rite had always seemed barbaric, cannibalistic even, but at that moment— *I got it!* I experienced an exaltation I'd never felt before, a oneness with something "beyond"…a direct perception of God, if you will. Either that or the rhythmic swishing back and forth of the censer had me hypnotized. I had to laugh thinking how my Presbyterian forebears would have disapproved of such "spiritualism."

The thing was, who needed a priest to enter that space? Not me—I could get there (and often did) through yoga. It *was* the same place, wasn't it—"at-one-ment"? I hated how the Church made people think they couldn't get close to God without an intermediary, preferably someone wearing gold-accented scarlet robes who was privy to the church's secret incantations and "licensed" to give benedictions.

But then I remembered Margarita's telling me once about the Farmers' Agrarian Leagues—a concept President Carter would support for sure—and how priests were risking their lives to help campesinos achieve land reform by helping them overcome their dependency on the system (that is, their fear of reprisal) and take their lives and education into their own hands...a concept that obviously threatened Stroessner's need for an ignorant citizenry.

Chalk one up for the priests! It took courage to do what they were doing out there.[87]

13

MARTÍN

After lunch we would have an hour of obligatory rest in our cells, usually with the doors open. I often took this opportunity to talk with the farmers. These fruitful—though clandestine—conversations turned into a study group. Our first task was to analyze the *Guaraní Primer*, the official text for teaching literacy in Paraguay. We gradually understood the alienating aspects of its contents, including its biased vocabulary and systematic disregard for the social realities of the country, along with its emphasis on individualism.

In the same cell another discussion and reflection group developed, and we came to see that despite our misfortune, we were using this siesta to cultivate and enrich ourselves spiritually. Our restlessness grew each time, and eventually we could no longer keep our meetings a secret.

We became aware that many of the campesinos, influenced by Christian movements, had amassed a wealth of experience. Our cellmates couldn't help but praise the work these farmers had begun in their respective communities. I was surprised to observe the ideological sophistication many of them had. With deep humility and absolute confidence they said to me, "There is no such thing as an ideologically neutral adult-education or literacy course. Education always implies a political choice and a commitment either to those at the top or those

---

87   For more information read the excellent book by Penny Lernoux, *Cry of the People: The Struggle for Human Rights in Latin America—The Catholic Church in Conflict with U.S. Policy* (New York: Penguin Books, 1980).

at the bottom." They told me of the interesting unofficial literacy experiment in which they had taken part in Tuna (Misiones) and Colonia Jejuí in 1975, using the teachings of Paulo Freire. The experience had ended in their punishment through brutal repression.

I had several opportunities to talk to parents who had participated in the literacy courses in Tuna. They recalled with great fondness the methodologies and prevailing enthusiasm within and without the classroom. They told me that for their children, going to the *escuelita* in Tuna had been a source of happiness. There, they said, the usual problems of absenteeism and discipline were nonexistent.

One Sunday, during the sporting events—which Colonel Grau was now letting us have—we met to discuss the topic of Tuna more carefully.

A member of the group said, "One day I was summoned by the town's chief of police for having a meeting at my house, where we discussed the issue of the weekly *minga* (see footnote 7). Everyone who had been at the meeting came to the summons. The chief—who was extremely annoyed by the presence of my twelve companions in his station of only seven officers—remarked, 'I have summoned only González, this dangerous character. The rest of you, who asked you to come?' One of them answered, 'Chief, sir, we all attended the meeting. We came here together, and we will leave together. In terms of responsibility, all of us here are González.' From that moment I have been considered a communist and systematically persecuted until my arrival here at Emboscada."

Other farmers weighed in. "I'm here because I let a Spanish priest stay at my house while he taught in our little school." "I was a member of the parent committee." "I committed the offense of donating a portion of my land for the site of the school." "I am a Colorado, and I was the leader of the *compañía*. I am here because I neglected to inform the authorities of the 'subversive education conspiracy.'"

I asked if they could give me a concrete example of the teaching methods used. One answered, "Among the many exercises, there was one in which we were supposed to calculate the difference in the profit made by a farmer who sold ten kilos of corn to a store owner, a cooperative, and directly to the consumer. When the Ministry of Education found out, they said the exercise was in conflict with the official education program and classified it as 'suspicious.'"

Another man said the police had seen the following in his notebook: "Because men will be full of self-love and love of money, and will be conceited, haughty, blasphemous, disobedient to their parents, disloyal, unable to govern themselves, ferocious, loveless, traitors, stubborn, swollen with pride, adoring of pleasures..." During a torture session the police tried everything they could to get the man to reveal the names of the people who had given him that supposedly extremist text. The bishop's intervention was required to prove that it was not political propaganda but a passage from the New Testament.

On another occasion, we focused on the case from Colonia Jejuí. Those who had taken part in that educational experiment explained, "We took it upon ourselves to teach our own children. After finishing our work in the field, we held classes in a shed, following a program we had created. We also had the support of Father Braulio Maciel, whose parents were farmers. 'The Gospel,' he would say, 'is the Good News for the poor. It is God's response to the oppressed and the exploited in our land. This is why my place is here, among the campesinos.'"

The man continued. "Our children don't know Spanish, only Guaraní, which was also taught in our school. The state schools are too far away, in addition to the fact that farm children are at a cultural disadvantage. The obligatory language in those schools is Spanish, and the curriculum is made to reflect bourgeois values from the city."

I asked how the adult literacy classes were taught.

"We would discuss certain words depicted in drawings and simple charts. These words had two characteristics: they were made up of syllables that could be combined with each other to make new words, and they referred to our material and social reality, the concrete reality of the farmer—words like 'work,' 'school,' 'hunger,' 'plow.' As we discussed these key words (in an exercise called 'problem posing'), we learned to analyze our own situation and the causes of our oppression. And in the practical math course," he continued, "I remember we learned things that directly mattered to us, like how much the middleman earned for a kilo of corn we sold him, or how much the taxes would be on our equipment."

He paused for a moment. "Father Maciel told us that during the last century, Paraguay was the only free and independent state in South America. Back then our country had a model system of social security, as well as advanced industries and technology. As everyone here knows, the first train in South America was in Paraguay, and it had no foreign financial assistance. The *pa-í* (priest) also explained the reasons why our country is now among the poorest in South America. He said the Triple Alliance War, provoked by our neighbors Argentina, Brazil, and Uruguay—who were following orders from England— had destroyed the emerging Paraguayan state."

I was impressed by his grasp of history. "Regarding Father Maciel," I said, "you were accused of spending time talking to him about Marxist issues instead of religion."

Taken aback, the farmer asked, "Where did you hear that?"

"[Another prisoner] and I were recently taken to Colonel Grau's office," I said, "and Grau showed us some documents signed by a Chinese clergyman, in which those accusations were made."

The farmer shook his head. "That is part of a defamatory campaign created by that man so he can take our lands. It's true that Father Maciel and I did not spend time discussing immortality of the soul or things like that. But we were convinced that standing up for the poor was also part of the church's message."

I realized that I had been living with my back to reality—I had overestimated official knowledge and underestimated the abilities of our campesinos. Now that I was in direct contact with them, I was discovering their intelligence and enormous potential.

I also realized that Paraguayan farmers are clearly aware that our educational system ignores most of their real-life problems. It fails to address issues that directly affect them, such as property ownership (rural estates, small holdings, tenancy), commerce as a form of social exploitation (cornering of markets, production costs, usury), education as a social process, and others. After listening carefully to these farmers, I agreed that the pedagogical approach used in Jejuí and Tuna could be the starting point for a national literacy campaign when Paraguay became free and we began to build a new society.

Our movement in the concentration camp was beginning to take shape, and I became the object of strict supervision. To avoid problems, we decided to formalize the literacy program in a meeting of delegates attended by Colonel Grau. During this meeting we requested permission to leave our cells during the rest hour and hold our classes beneath the *guapo'y* (ficus) tree. Grau grudgingly authorized the request and named a captain as supervisor.

Unfortunately, the captain requested assistance from the Ministry of Education, and once again the official literacy course, with its alienating characteristics, was imposed. The authorities had ended the movement just like that, by taking it over. Grau ignored those of us who had been teaching literacy and adopted the initiative as his own, presenting himself to public opinion within the prison as someone who was "very interested in the quality education of campesinos."

We didn't give up our efforts, and they finally paid off. We acquired a degree of comfort and improved working conditions, now that we were able to organize into work teams with weekly shifts. Of course these activities were rigidly controlled. We were given chairs and wooden tables (no longer having to sit on the ground to eat), better food, water, air, better treatment, a few visits...all thanks to everyone's coming together, as well as to domestic and international pressure. The efforts of opposition parties from within the country and from outside, along with the intervention of churches, the International Red Cross, Amnesty International, and the Human Rights League (from France), among others, played a fundamental role in improving our situation.

14

EMILY

Mom arrived at Aeropuerto Presidente Stroessner, and as she walked through the gate it hit me: *Two whole weeks alone with my mother? Tranquila, nomás.*

After a couple nights at the Stella—which thankfully met with her approval—I took her to Piribebuy for a few days. Naturally, she charmed everyone. She did well using the latrine and taking *baños triangulares* in the shed. I was telling her how to dip her hands in cold water and rub them together to make warm water to put on her face, when she stopped me.

"Don't forget, honey, I grew up in Oklahoma during the Dust Bowl." She knew about roughing it, all right...which was probably why our family never once went camping. (In all fairness, though, she had spent much of her child-hood at Granddaddy's cabin—as did her kids when we came along—which had an outhouse and only a woodstove for cooking.)

I pointed out the new screen I'd put on the window, but she was hardly impressed. Well, it *was* just some chicken wire I'd scavenged. To hell with the mosquitoes, I just wanted to keep out the "snakes." I wouldn't tell her about Pupi—why frighten her like that?

Mom had just turned fifty-one. Her birthday was six days before mine, but she was a Scorpio, a sign I mistrusted, especially as I had a lot of it in me. She'd had a facelift the year before and it looked pretty good, even though I of course found the idea appalling.

Journal entry 14 Dec—Mom's visit: At home in Piribebuy. Mom is taking it all like a real sport. She really has a good attitude. It's so funny to see her walk down the Asunción streets, a gringa you can be sure! One thing frustrating for me, though...her lack of assertiveness...All her life Mom has either been faced with familiar circumstances, or else had someone to hold her hand when she hasn't. She admits this: Also, that her generation was taught "What to think, not how"...Of course one of my values is compromise. But lately I've come to assert myself. "This is what I feel. I exist, too!" And feel I have a right to. It concerns recognizing basic needs, and not feeling as if I have no needs. Because if I suppress them, I am a conglomerate of suppressed needs...It isn't as if they don't exist...

A *perrita* in heat being harassed by a gang of barrio dogs found sanctuary in our latrine. With all those *perros locos* waiting there for her to come out, we couldn't go near the thing for a couple of days and had to use ña Fernanda's. But Mom didn't let it faze her—as long as she had cigarettes and vodka, she was fine. Of course she was quite pleased with me, now that I had my own little nicotine habit.

Emily's mother, Bonnie Lou, sitting in the doorway of Emily's house in Piribebuy
with Ara-tirí and waving "good-bye" to people passing on the street.

One afternoon we sat on my front stoop chatting and saying "adiós" to everyone who walked by. I cringed as she told the same old stories.

"I never understood why you didn't marry that Davies boy, what's his name, Henry? He is so darling." She took a drag off her Aqua Filter. "And I'll never understand your comment about not wanting to live in a house with a white picket fence." It was true, I could have taken up with Henry Davies, the cutest guy in my class (a basketball player, no less) and lived "happily ever after," but I just couldn't do it—it would've been way too easy.

Before I could answer, she said, "You quit talking at fifteen." I rolled my eyes. How could I tell Mom that as a teen I'd thought her shallow? She didn't work, in other words, contribute to society. All she did was play golf—a game I hated because of the water it wasted—with the ladies and write and perform ditties for their awards luncheons. I had to admit she was good at what she did, but to her dismay I'd wanted no part of that "gilded cage of iniquity," my clever term for the country club. (Dad had incurred wrath there by breaking with tradition and voting to include Jewish members. He'd been overruled…and later ostracized.)

Mom went on. "When you were a baby, you always pushed me away." I gave her a sad look. I couldn't explain that one—I'd just latched on to Dad, I guess. He and I were quite a pair, "akin" in so many ways: him letting ten-year-old me be his chauffeur and careen the golf cart around the course, pedal to the metal, calling me "Eagle Eye" for my ability to spot balls in the rough; me advising him on my brother and sister at his request; us eating a sunrise breakfast with the farmers in Battle Lake or sipping Scotch and watching the Super Bowl to critique the commercials.

"As a toddler you would see something across the room and head straight for it…but then inevitably trip and fall before you got there."

Tell me about it! Was this family story to be my fate? Would I be forever doomed to learn the hard way, to crash and burn before reaching the object of my desire?

There *was* a possibility I was brain damaged.

"Mom, don't forget I also had a concussion when I was fifteen, after that psycho Altar Bound bucked me off for no reason. You remember how messed up I was—I didn't even know what day of the week it was. Ginny and Kathy Spencer told me I kept asking them what happened, over and over." I chuckled at the memory.

It was Mom's turn to roll her eyes, and I knew that look: *I told you so*.

"I still don't remember anything about it," I continued, "though I do dream every now and then about sliding along the ground on my stomach headfirst and taking in a mouthful of dried horse manure."

"You could've broken your neck, you know," she snapped, and she was right. My mother had always worried about us riding, which was why, she claimed, she'd rarely gone to the horse shows. I always wished she had, like Dad. Mom and I barely even saw each other when I was growing up; from age nine to fifteen I walked to the stables and back—a mile each way—six days a week, after school and on weekends (we had Mondays off), learning discipline and hard work…and being raised by my surrogate parents, Mr. and Mrs. Thayer. It was all my own choice, of course. At only thirty bucks a month, the price was definitely right.

I went on. "The first thing I remember, vaguely, in the hospital was a nurse putting something next to me saying, 'Now if you have to throw up, here's a bowl'…and the first thing I remember clearly was barfing all over the floor. They really loved me after that."

I smiled, thinking of the Romeros family and history repeating itself.

Mom wasn't smiling. The injury had been pretty serious. I'd had to lie flat on my back without lifting my head for twenty-four hours, staring at the ceiling, starving—the only thing they would let me eat was Jell-O, which made me gag.

"Maybe that's why I quit talking. You know, I haven't been quite right since." She laughed, obviously thinking I was kidding.[88]

I'd lost interest in riding after that, preferring to brave the new world of teenagers, basketball games (boys' only, as there was no girls' b-ball in Arizona until Title IX was passed—two years after I graduated, naturally), and about fifty times the horsepower: my used silver Opel Kadett with a four-on-the-floor

---

[88] "Damage to the prefrontal cortex from severe trauma or from even milder events, such as a prior concussion, can also result in unusual behavior and/or the inability to make rational decisions." Dr. David Williams, *Alternatives for the Health Conscious Individual* (May 2015, 18:5, p. 2).

that Dad bought me for my sixteenth birthday. Man, I loved that car, and my dad for surprising me with it. I hadn't even asked for one.

"¡Adiós!" Mom waved. She was getting the hang of it.

She reminded me why they had transplanted the family to Tucson in 1960, when I was seven: she'd thought she was going to die of Hodgkins because of a spot on an x-ray—no second opinions then, apparently—and didn't want it to happen in her hometown with everyone, as she said, "breathing down my neck." She and Dad had decided to raise us kids to be "independent" in the event of her death (which she'd obviously cheated). But what exactly had that meant? That we would never form close bonds? Bonds could be shackles, too, couldn't they?

Then out of the blue Mom looked at me, took my hand, and said, "And I'm so sorry I got rid of your toy horses. It was an accident, you know. I put them in the wrong box because I was an absolute wreck. When you asked me about it, I got defensive, I don't know why…"

I stared at her. And all these years I thought she'd done it out of spite. I realized I'd never once thought how difficult it must have been for her to move out of her prized home—and stature—in the country club.

I smiled. "It's okay, Mom, I know you didn't mean to." I just couldn't feel angry about it anymore. She was still a member of the club and worked in the pro shop, had a suitor or two but nothing serious. She said she knew we all blamed ourselves for Dad's death, but begged me not to.

"Your father was a very smart man. But when he started having financial problems in 1970, he made some risky investments. Then everything backfired. He predicted things would get worse before they got better, and he was right— the economy didn't start to rebound until about the time you left, January of 1975."

That figured.

"He was humiliated that he'd been unable to, as he said, 'manage his affairs'…which he took full responsibility for—he wanted no one's pity—even though those unscrupulous land developers in Río Rico had taken advantage of him."

Those lying sacks of shit! I'll get you, Irv Jennings, I was thinking (Dad had named Jennings in a letter), but I kept my cool.

She recited what she'd written for Dad's funeral, which amazingly enough she still knew by heart (well, she *had* been an English major at the University of Kansas):

BONNIE'S THOUGHTS—January 16, 1974

Why? Because he was strong, not weak.

Because he loved his family far more than himself.

Because he was funloving and ever happy, and could not like himself when he could not be that.

He asked for little, gave much, all his life—so why not give of himself one last time? (For the good of all.)

He acquired a role as a perfect person (honest, helpful, kind, and loving) and could not face being a lesser person in his own opinion.

He loved the life he had, and would not settle for less.

His life belonged to him—and he handled it in his own way.

He always seemed to know what was best—and we have no right to criticize.

He was master of his life—master of his death.

He would not leave his wonderful life a sad, broken man. He loved all of us too much for that. He loved all of us too much, period!

She got it. We held hands and cried discreetly—after all, we were still on the stoop. I realized how courageous she'd been. *"La pollera colorada"* blasted out of a slowly approaching *parlante*, a small pickup with giant speakers that went around the neighborhood from time to time, either announcing fiestas and sporting events or proclaiming the merits of some goon running for office.

Mom said, "When I saw the letters on his desk, I just couldn't break the trust and read them, destroy what little dignity he had left. And you can believe I've regretted that decision every single day since. As soon as the sheriffs pulled into the driveway, I knew what had happened."

She told me about the stock market crash in September 1973 that caused Dad to lose half his investments practically overnight. Jesus! That was when I'd first arrived in Japan, so depressed I'd lost the will to live—and worse, lacking the courage to do anything about it—totally unaware that my father, too, had for years been hostage to the same relentless inner monologue that insisted *"You're nothing but a failure"* over and over until you were beaten to a pulp.

You didn't need bars to be a prisoner.

September 1973. I would certainly never forget that month and year as they pertained to South America but didn't know the US stock market had crashed at the same time. So that was what Dad had meant in his last letter to me when he explained the situation: "And then September came."

Mom gave me all the reasons why Dad's financial meltdown hadn't been my fault, and I had to admit some of it was true—my college expenses would have been manageable had the economy not been in the toilet.

"Your father flew to Kansas in early November to go hunting with friends, and I think he had a small stroke," she said.

I disagreed but said nothing. I alone knew what had pushed my father over the edge—the telegram he'd sent me on December 29, 1973, responding to my request to stay in Japan the whole year instead of just one semester (the original plan): ARRANGEMENT FOR YOU TO STAY LOVE YOU LETTER FOLLOWS DAD. He didn't write the promised letter until two weeks later, on January 15...*the day before he died*. And once he'd written it, he had to follow through with his plan, didn't he? There was no honor in the alternative.

"Sometimes you have to do what you have to do," he'd said in our last phone conversation, before the telegram, when I'd asked to stay. At the time I'd thought my father was telling me I would probably have to come home— I'd had no idea he was talking about himself, and what he felt *he* had to do. The weight, some days, was still almost more than I could bear.

But I knew if I didn't let it go, it was going to kill me.

"What do you think of Patty Hearst?" my mother asked when we were finally kicking back on the air-conditioned bus to Yguazú Falls. "Her getting thirty-five years and all. The poor thing was brainwashed, you know."

"She wasn't brainwashed," I retorted. "That was the defense Bailey used to try to get her off, but it failed. No, I think she just saw for the first time what life was like on the other side of the fence, so to speak, and realized how privileged she was. Didn't she send out a greeting to all her 'brothers and sisters' after she was arrested? I think she just came to her senses."

"White middle-class guilt," Mom said, looking at me. "What you have."

I decided not to react, but she was probably right. I just didn't understand why I should have so much more of everything simply because I'd had the "foresight" to be born north of the border, so to speak, and to relatively wealthy parents—though we saw how *that* turned out.

But I couldn't give in. "Perhaps, but she's far from middle class."

"You know what I mean."

"I'll bet she's shitting a few bricks right now, pardon my French."

I knew how to stop a conversation with Mom cold.

Could I have been Patty Hearst? Sometimes I wondered, though I drew the line at violence. She'd adopted the name "Tania" from Che Guevara's comrade, and was obviously caught up in the whole movement. Her grandfather had been quite the populist in his day, even helping FDR—whom Mom hated, naturally—get elected president. I loved it that Patty said her father "could have done better" when he distributed the two million dollars' worth of food the SLA had demanded for the Bay Area's poor. But was it worth thirty-five years in the slammer? Not to me. But then again, no one would kidnap me in the first place.[89]

In the Foz terminal we locked up our luggage and hopped a local bus to Hotel das Cataratas, hoping I could repeat the coup last year with Gin and get a room despite no vacancy. After a bit of cajoling they finally procured one, so I grabbed enough money for the round trip and left Mom in the bar, telling her I would get our stuff and be right back. The *ônibus* hadn't arrived at the hotel yet, and I wanted to experience the jungle, so I walked a few hundred yards down the road and around some bends to where, for a few surreal moments, it was just me and the steamy, ear-splitting rainforest.

---

89 Hearst's sentence was commuted to twenty-two months (which she had already served) by President Carter in 1979, and she was pardoned by President Clinton in 2001.

The bus I was waiting for passed going the other direction, and I gestured to the driver to let him know I'd be getting on when he came back. He nodded and kept going, but then stopped. When he pulled away, left standing there was a Brazilian army officer.

Crap! Just the two of us for a long, empty stretch of road. The officer, visibly agitated, started toward me.

"I'm a tourist, traveling with my mother, who's here at the hotel, and I was just out here enjoying the jungle and waiting for the bus," I said innocently.

But he was approaching fast, and I got a bad vibe from him.

"I am a member of the Peace Corps of the UNITED STATES OF AMERICA. I work for the GOVERNMENT of the UNITED STATES." I was firm. I was shouting.

I was terrified.

The unsmiling officer reached out to grab me and said, "Let's wait over there in the shade." *In the shade? Are you kidding me? A person could disappear forever in those trees!* I yanked my arm free and ran toward the road, wondering what I was going to do next when—a miracle!—two cars approached going toward town. I waved my arm but the first one went by. Suddenly I realized: no one was going to challenge an army officer! My heart was pounding so hard I thought it would shoot out of my chest, and I couldn't breathe for the fear.

For the love of God, please let the second one stop! It was a taxi and started to pass...but then it pulled over. I ran and got in as fast as I could, telling the driver to take off *"AGORA!"* He peeled out as I slammed the door shut and fell over on the seat. He leaned forward and looked at me wide-eyed in the rearview.

"Oh, *muitu obrigada*, thank you very much," I said between pants, my voice shaking along with the rest of my body. *Heart, still thyself! Just breathe.* I peeked out the back—the officer stood in the middle of the road, shrinking as we drove away. What if he was memorizing the license plate number? He didn't appear to have a gun, but I ducked back down just in case.

"I don't have enough money to pay you because I was going to take the bus," I explained to the *taxista* in breathless Spanish/Portuguese/sign language. He gestured with his hand and said something I didn't understand, but it was clear he didn't mind crossing the authorities. I was certain he'd risked his life to pick me up. After dropping me off at the bus station, he didn't want to return to the hotel—hardly surprising—so I paid him what I had minus the amount I needed for the bus back, which wasn't much, and he honestly didn't mind. I thanked him for saving my life and he just laughed.

I wasn't laughing, though, as the *ônibus* approached the hotel on my return—what if the whole damn Brazilian army was there waiting for me? Needless to say, it wasn't. But two close calls in a row...I would *have* to be more careful from now on. I didn't mention it to Mom, although every time I thought about it I nearly had a panic attack: I'd never been so scared for my life.

That night, as I took my first bath in months, I thought about the waterfalls pounding down outside and the force they created, airwaves so strong they made the windows rattle nonstop. I thought of Yeats's lines about a waterfall in Scotland, which always came to mind here: "Nothing we love over-much / Is ponderable to our touch."[90] I was thrilled to be back in my favorite place again, safe—and to be sharing it with my mother, my friend.

[On an aerogram titled "Views of Foz do Iguaçu City"]
19 December 76, Dear Gin and Sam and Nanny—Guess where we are, Hotel das Cataratas. I used my Peace Corps special personality pass and finagled us a room. Certainly lovely...The weather is warm but Mom is doing well, wonder how she keeps up with my wild ways. Think we're going on a helicopter ride. Gin: Remember our friendly waiter? Well he recognized me, he speaks English well now. We went to a "despedida de soltero" one night in Piribebuy, Mom got the royal treatment, listened to folk music in Guaraní (with harp et al.) and even danced the polka... She was a real hit...We're havin' a real good time, wish you were here...I'll let Mom fill in the other side. Miss you all! Love, E

Hello, Loves—I keep forgetting it is nearly Christmas until I come upon a decorated tree (not many) and each day ask myself Is this the day? Strange. But we certainly are having fun & working hard

---

90   William Butler Yeats, "Towards Break of Day," from *Michael Robartes and the Dancer* (Churchtown, Ireland: Cuala Press, 1921).

at it. What I mean is—all the crowded buses, the heat, the dust. Yet it is all so beautiful—and my worn feet and tired gams soon heal when I see the breathtaking sights. Yguazú is a highlight—but I shall never forget the pre-nuptial party in Piribebuy & the royal treatment Emmy & I got. You'd have thought <u>we</u> were getting married!—Anyway, we check out of this fabulous hotel in about an hour—then the helicopter ride over the falls—then the bumpity bus to the Paraguayan side to catch the high-class one to Asunción. We will shop tomorrow (Mon.) & get me ready for the boat trip to Concepción (hairdo & manicure)…
XOXO Mom

We'd dared each other to take the helicopter ride over Devil's Throat, which the pilot said marked the border between Paraguay and Argentina. But the chopper dipped around so much that even with the new Olympus Mom had brought me in hand, I was too terrified—not to mention nauseated—to take a single shot.

I'd promised Ellyn we would visit, so we took the ferry to Concepción. Mom enjoyed the trip though it was a bit rustic for her tastes. It had been raining and the town was a swamp. Of course Mom wanted to take one of the buggies, so we arrived at Ellyn's covered in mud. She was living with a family now, the Laviccios, and after we got cleaned up, she told us about them. They were prominent in town, Liberals, the father a doctor.

"One of their sons, Rodolfo, is a teacher in Asunción," she told us. We were sitting in the living room and no one was home. Ellyn looked around anyway and continued in a low voice. "He got picked up a few months ago and put in prison. His parents are such good people, and they were beside themselves with worry. I wrote a letter to Minnesota Senator—Vice President-elect now, yay!—Mondale…and Rodolfo has just been released! I don't know if Mondale had anything to do with it, but we're all so relieved. Rodolfo's not a communist…he's just not a Colorado."

Ellyn's act was definitely courageous. But she blindsided me when she said she was thinking about marrying her Paraguayan boyfriend and staying here forever. Marriage? Good lord—what was the world coming to?

"I'm staying at the Sheraton," a man said to Mom on the flight to Buenos Aires. After we landed, she took one look at the dive I'd chosen for us and said *we* were staying at the Sheraton, too. As we didn't have a reservation—and it was only two days before Christmas—they had to see if they could squeeze us in, so wouldn't we like to have dinner in the restaurant on top of the hotel while they found us a room?

We took the elevator up, emerging into the foyer past a couple of soldiers. Through a window on the far side of the room, I saw an amazing sunset over a harbor dotted with boats, and naturally started over to take a picture. Suddenly I heard metal clicks and felt hands on my arms as two soldiers pulled me back. Of course I wasn't about to resist. Mom and I just stood there, eyes locked.

"You are prohibited from taking photographs here," said one of the officers.

We explained that we were tourists, *nomás*, I just liked to take pictures, I was only interested in the view, I'd be more than happy to put my camera away. They called the front desk to check us out and then graciously allowed us to be seated. Later, in our room, we had the exact same view of the harbor. It was dark by then, but I could take as many pictures as I wanted in the morning... which I did.

It turned out the boats that weren't yachts were ships, and they looked to be naval vessels! No wonder the military police didn't want me snapping pictures...under their watch. But what exactly did they think I was doing from my room right now? It made no sense. *Rent a room at the Sheraton and be within range of the Argentine navy—now that's security.*[91]

"Buenos Aires has more fountains than Paris," our taxi driver, Juan, fairly crowed the next day as he drove us around the city speaking Spanish in that authoritative-sounding way they had, with an accent that sounded Italian, like they were telling you off or pointing out everything wrong with you: "And then THAT and then THAT and then THAT."

---

91 The Sheraton Buenos Aires itself had been the target of an attack by the Montoneros and ERP when a bomb exploded there in October 1972, killing a Canadian woman and gravely wounding her husband. Several attacks on naval vessels were successful as well.

There definitely were a lot of fountains—I especially liked the controversial one that Juan said the authorities kept moving around called "The Nereids" (sea nymphs), with its voluptuous naked bodies, sculpted in 1904 by Argentine Lola Mora (you had to love the sound of "Lola Mora")—and statues, too, most of them touting some idiotic military victory or another.

"It looks very European," Mom said as we gawked at the ornate architecture. I could only imagine, as I'd never wanted to visit Europe, as Joni sang, so cold and old and "settled in its ways."[92] Latin America was where the action was, man, where you never knew what would happen next…at least I used to think that was a good thing.

Juan took us to the Palace of the National Congress, the halls of "injustice," as he wryly put it. "Many of the bronzes and marble statues here, both inside and out, were also sculpted by Lola Mora."

How cool it must have been to be Lola Mora!

"The Casa Rosada's distinct color comes from limestone and bulls' blood," he said as we cruised to the other end of the Plaza de Mayo. Pink hardly seemed appropriate for a presidential palace…but "bulls' blood"? Sounded like a macho boast to me. The Argentines did love their cows, though, especially in the form of sweetbreads—which, I had discovered the hard way, were never meant for human consumption.

We paid Juan and got out to walk around the plaza. It was quiet, only a few passersby. Rodin's *Thinker* sat there to inspire me. I snapped a picture of the Pink House—surely that was allowed here. No one tried to stop me.

Downtown, political posters covered every available surface, revealing a running dialogue. On the window of a liquor store, a poster that said "Enough! Of subversion / You can and should combat it" covered older ones from the People's Revolutionary Army (ERP) that said "Violence? Who generates it?" The ERP posters featured a red hammer and sickle, which was a little disconcerting. Someone had tried unsuccessfully to scrape these off.

---

92 "California," 1970.

Posters in Buenos Aires warning against subversion and violence (Christmas 1976).

On one vacant storefront, a young man with red plastic bucket and brush was gluing a large poster over some smaller ones, themselves on top of others. I thought how brave the young man was until I got closer and saw that his posters said "Summer Courses: Philosophy, Psychology, Sociology, Archaeology." *Not too "subversive," surely…or were they?* There seemed to be an air of normalcy about the place.

The next day the streets were empty. It felt eerie until we remembered it was Christmas. We exchanged some macramé jewelry we'd bought from a street artist and went up the elevator to eat.[93]

---

93   I wasn't aware until 1981, when I read Jacobo Timerman's *Prisoner Without a Name, Cell Without a Number* (New York: Alfred A. Knopf, 1981), of the horrific "death flights" that took place in Argentina, in which hundreds of innocent people, a third of them women (including two French nuns), lost their lives in the Río Plata and Atlantic Ocean after being drugged, stripped, and thrown out of airplanes…even as my mother and I sipped cocktails at the Buenos Aires Sheraton. Three of the victims were cofounders of the Madres de Plaza de Mayo, whose remains were washed ashore in December 1977 (a year after my mother and I were there), buried in a secret mass grave, and positively identified in 2005. The Mothers and Grandmothers of the Plaza de Mayo are still active today.

"So…my very first extension agent, in Iturbe—remember, the one who was too much of a smartass for his own good, the so-called tree 'specialist' who said I couldn't *possibly* like the *chivato* because it was nonnative and a weed…" We were en route to Bariloche and I was explaining how I'd chosen to visit the Bosque de Arrayanes.

Mom interrupted: "Excuse me. Didn't you once liken your beloved *chivato* to the mesquite tree? Also 'beloved,' I believe?" I nodded, suddenly on guard.

"Well, I hate to tell you, but your mesquite is 'nonnative and a weed' as well." She looked at me and smugly sipped her vodka through the little airline straw.

Grrr. Why did grownups always have to ruin things by being so logical? I struggled to stay positive—traveling with your mother could be a bitch!

I took a breath. "Anyway…he was the one who told me about it. The *arrayán* is a tree with cinnamon-colored bark. It's rumored that Walt Disney went to the forest and got the idea for *Bambi* there." Mom and I looked at each other—making sad faces and crying "Bambi!"—and then started to laugh. Everything was copacetic.

In our room I read that Bariloche, evergreen and snowy in winter, sat at 2,930 feet…only a few hundred feet higher than Tucson. Yet it felt so mountainous. It also supposedly had a "cool, Mediterranean" climate—wasn't that a contradiction in terms? The photogenic town was obviously geared toward tourism—one man sold photos of *turistas* posing with his llama.

To get to the *bosque* we had to take a ferry across Nahuel Huapi, the ancient lake that reflected the peaks surrounding it, snowcapped even in summer. Seagulls flew behind the boat catching bread that passengers flung in the air for them—how could the birds keep up?—and hot coffee was available on board. It was perfect…until I overheard a man saying that Hitler and Eva Braun were rumored to have hidden out in this area until the early 1960s.

"After all, their remains have never been found," the man reminded his companions. The news was unsettling though not surprising, after all I'd learned.

When we walked through the forest, the *arrayanes* did cast a dappled, fawn-colored light that looked familiar—Walt had been here for sure. We agreed the stately, twisted old trees created an atmosphere of tranquility.

The *tranquilidad* evaporated the next day, however, as we crossed the border into Chile. "Everybody off the bus and into that room," said a young soldier, pointing with his submachine gun. We did as we were told.

The officers seemed unnecessarily rough—or at least disrespectful—with some of the passengers, mostly young men, who must have had problematic passports or something in their luggage. But did they have to be such automatons?

"Attention, everyone…you must now go in that room over there." They herded us into the new room. I was starting to get nervous. I mean, I'd never questioned the power of my US passport, but what if something went wrong? What if they didn't return it? If anything happened to us here in the middle of the freakin' Andes, no one would ever know—we'd simply never be heard from again.

But we finally made it through and got back on the bus to Puerto Montt, at the southern tip of mainland Chile. Now we could relax and enjoy the ride.

In the hotel dining room I immediately identified two Americans, just by the way they sat and gestured as they talked—Mom was impressed—so we chatted with them after dinner. It turned out they were astronomers in the Atacama Desert, a seemingly God-awful place—except for stargazers—that took up the whole northern third of Chile. The next day the four of us went to the town of Ancud on Chiloé Island to eat some "serious seafood." We ordered huge bowls of steamed *mariscos*, and that was when I discovered I hated seafood, especially sea urchins. Blecch! Seriously, they were vile.

On the train heading north toward the equator, Mom and I talked about US politics and the recent election. She'd always been a Republican even though I suspected she was just parroting others' opinions. She of course voted for Ford, and I didn't want to rub it in too much how unusual it was for an incumbent to lose (even though Ford hadn't been elected in the first place). We agreed on one thing, though: even the most cynical among us had to admit the United States was one of the safest places in the world to be, as far as our judicial system was concerned.

"Though our country isn't perfect," she said, "where else would you want to end up in jail? At least our rights are protected and we have the presumption of innocence."

"Yeah, if you're white," I had to throw in.

Undaunted, she continued. "We enjoy smooth transfers of power after elections with no coups, we have freedom of the press, and we don't kill each other over differences of religion or politics...well, not much, anyway." She smiled wistfully and looked out at the glittering Pacific Ocean.

"Yes, that's all well and good, and aren't we Yanks just wonderful?" I said a bit too sarcastically. "But it's important for Americans to understand how the rest of the world views us, and that's something we don't seem to want to do. You know, Mom, Americans take so much for granted. Our lives are so good, and why? Because we've exploited the hell out of, quote, developing countries in Latin America and the rest of the world, for one. We say we're only helping them, but we're the ones doing the developing—to serve our own needs, naturally—and the profiting, of course, as if the world were our factory and everyone worked for us. We want *them* to increase production to meet *our* demand, so we sell them machinery and stuff they can't afford or use, which creates huge debt they'll never be able to repay. Sanctions will then be imposed, of course, which will only hurt people more. It almost seems like a giant plot by the 'haves' to squeeze every last drop out of the 'have-nots,' to turn them into indentured servants, as it were."

"You've always had an overactive imagination," Mom said, pointedly stubbing out her cigarette in the train ashtray.

I didn't let it stop me. "And now we're helping Stroessner incite civil unrest and eradicate its most intelligent and creative citizens...we're working *with* fascists, whereas not long ago we were killing them in Germany. How can that be?"

She looked pained. I knew she understood, but I also knew she wasn't about to give up her lifestyle. (She'd bought a house in a different country club and was doing well, all things considered...Dad's life insurance had kicked in and saved her.) It wasn't *her* fault there was inequality in the world.

"Maybe your Jimmy Carter will change things," she offered warmly, patting my hand, and that was that.[94]

We arrived in Santiago the next morning. The city was like Buenos Aires with its imposing architecture, but there were a lot more soldiers—not to mention beggars—on the streets. We tried the local drink, pisco sours, and agreed they were pretty good. Pisco was a brandy, of all things.

The next day I accompanied her to the airport. I hugged her and said, "I love you, Mom." It was the first time I'd ever said it, and I was surprised how good it felt. I finally understood what "unconditional" meant when it came to loving your family.

"I love you, too, sweetheart," she said, blowing me a kiss as she walked through the gate onto the tarmac.

Whew, mission accomplished! I still had a couple more days here. I went to see *The Sound of Music*, for the first time ever, and was struck that the von Trapp family was running from—who else?—the Nazis. What was it with all the Nazis lately, anyway?

I caught a taxi. "That's the Presidential Palace," the driver said, "La Moneda, where Allende was last seen alive." *La moneda...*"the coin"?

"It used to be a mint," he added. That explained it, although I wondered how people felt about their government's blatant association with money, the love of which was of course "the root of all evil."

Was Pinochet at this very moment signing decrees at the desk where his soldiers had murdered Allende?[95]

I didn't ask about the stadium where Victor Jara and so many others (including two Americans, I'd heard) had been executed—only three and a half years ago, when I was a world away in Japan—hard to believe. I remembered a conversation

---

94 Carter's human rights platform made an immediate difference: two weeks after Carter was elected, Pinochet released hundreds of political prisoners. Also, on September 6, 1977, President Carter hosted Stroessner himself at the White House, bringing up the dictator's human rights "problem" in a visit that likely prompted Dr. Almada's release eighteen days later (see http://www.presidency.ucsb.edu/ws/?pid=6580). Carter distanced himself from the right-wing regimes and cut military aid, but long-lasting change came slowly: military dictatorships in the Southern Cone lasted through the 1980s—BOL '82, ARG '83, BRA '85, URU '85, CHI '88, PAR '89. As for Operation Condor, Dr. Almada maintains that "the condor still flies."

95 In 2011 a Chilean court exhumed President Allende's remains and ruled his death a suicide—a theory long held but never confirmed. Ironically, Allende took his life in the palace's Salon of Independence.

I'd had with Steve a few months earlier about the stadium. We were listening to "Ode to Joy" from Beethoven's Ninth, and I'd said I found it unsettling because I associated it with the horrendous scenes it played behind in *A Clockwork Orange*.

"Yes, that film was definitely disturbing," he'd said. "And Hitler, you know, had the song played on his birthday. But Miguel Ríos wrote new lyrics in 1970, and his 'Himno de la Alegría' has become an anthem of freedom everywhere. In fact, did you know that after the coup in Santiago in 1973, groups of women stood outside the stadiums—at great risk, mind you—and sang the song over and over to give the prisoners hope?"

I hadn't known but was glad I did now. Steve found a copy and we'd sung it together: "Come, sing, dream singing, live dreaming of the new age… when all men will once again become brothers." We were both crying by the last chorus, and I knew we'd been thinking the same thing: *There but for the grace of God.*

By the time I left Santiago and flew home, I was more than ready to get back to my life as a PCV—which was scheduled to end May 6. First on the agenda was Tom's highly anticipated wedding in Yuty. I described it in a letter dated January 27:

I'm in Piribebuy now, just back yesterday from yet another sojourn—soul-journ—and this time it was truly that. A group of 18 vols took the midnight train (that famous one that burns wood and derails and sometimes arrives on time—Gin knows!) south to Yuty for Tomás's (PCV) wedding to Miranda (Paraguayan). What a trip! Left at 6 PM and arrived at 8 AM. We were like little kids, or better yet outlaws or even hobos, climbing all over the slow-moving train under Paraguay's incredible star-blanket. There was a group of young Paraguayans also on the train, getting off at Caazapá (that's right!) for the patron saint festival.

The wedding was super…we danced till 4 AM. The next day some of us got on the train north again…and I got off at Caazapá. This was Sunday. I was pretty apprehensive at returning to Caazapá, what with all that's happened to me there…but it turned out to be the most rewarding experience I've had. My old family was so glad to see me, and I've never felt so content in my life, being with them. It felt so "right." Well that night we danced till 2 AM. Monday I went out visiting—whew! Faces so familiar and dear, I'd never realized. I was SO GLAD to see them all again! And I talked to people about important things, something I'd always felt was lacking before.

I realized how much more involved I was in Caazapá than here in Piribebuy—not only due to time (1 year 3 months as opposed to 6 months) but the entire emotional spectrum that I experienced in Caazapá is at opposite poles from the detachment I've maintained from P. It's been all work here, and minimum social involvement... So: Caazapá. I'm glad I left, it was necessary. But I never knew I was capable of such feelings for a place. For once I didn't resist. I didn't resist the food, I didn't resist little or no privacy, nada. And the energy I received from being open at all times... WOW!...

I got to be godmother...wonder if it means I'm marriageable, hope not. Tom's town is Yuty, 96 mi. past Caazapá, no lights...The ceremony was illuminated by a couple of kerosene lamps, several candles—and the bride's brother's car lights!...18 americanos in an outback town of 3500–4000—I think it was a somewhat outstanding impact...

What I saw in myself during the trip was how "Paraguayan" I've become. I'm getting to the point where I <u>love</u> speaking Guaraní, want to learn more; where I <u>love</u> the folk music, want to learn more. Mom, in all sincerity, I just don't know how I can leave when May rolls around...

Journal entry 2 Feb—So much energy in the air...Visitas from everywhere, all houses teeming with life, tatacuas smoking and producing sopa, chipa, asado; all in preparation for SAN BLAS, Paraguay's patron saint. Elsa and her little ones have moved in to the room next door, and I actually thrive on the activity...

Journal entry 8 Feb—These things I see here, every day; it seems only right that I record them. Else why am I privileged to see these dramas unfolding before my very eyes, I the distant observer involved yet only a step away from escape.

The old lady last night, that vieja [old woman] in rags who lives by herself, who can imagine how she feeds herself...Curly blonde-gray hair, tied back with dirty triangle scarf, her dress a series of rags, really, but presentable, not too dirty... and her charity shoes, loafers with heels no less! (As Petronita teases her, just right for the fiesta.) She carries an old beer can (16 oz.) with 5 G [guaraní] bills stuffed in the top—oh rich meade—this for kerosene. Another set of cans, rectangular and attached somehow—these for oil and alcohol. Plus her two new baskets, which she carries on her arm so proudly, brand new and yellow straw:"I'll sell the big one for 350 Gs" she admits but it's worth less. Who knows where she got it?

How kind is ña Fernanda to her, her twin in age but ah so unfortunate, this is hell on earth to be old and alone. Ña Fernanda listens respectfully to her story, forehead creased, puffing on her ever-present cigar, as she measures out 5 Gs worth of sugar and kerosene. Ña Fernanda lets her have her say, because she feels such profound pity (I imagine). But this passes; it's the teasing everyone wants, even the old beggar, what else is so familiar to her? And no one would tease if he didn't care, isn't that right? She leans on her bamboo cane, back straight but hunched at the waist...I play a few notes on the guitar I'm carrying (from the "mbaracá-jhape" [guitar happening] at Meza's) and she winces, doesn't like the music...Could it be because she has no time nor room in her meager existence for pure joy?

Journal entry 10 Feb—Been in Paraguay 2 yrs 1 mo...

Journal entry 11 Feb—Elsa says I sleep outside because I have FAITH (this in response to my assertion: I'd rather die by a snake-bite due to sleeping with my window open, than keep myself locked up and paranoid)...I've slept twice now at ña Fernanda's, outside—DIVINO!

Saturday afternoon, 12 Feb 77, Dearest Nanny,

Thought it was high time to get a letter off to Nanny-O...

Things are going very well for me now...The chief obstetrician [Norma] (the <u>only</u> one) at the health center and I will begin a Mothers' Club this coming Tuesday, which will last 6 weeks. We'll include sex education, nutrition, hygiene, child nutrition, etc....plus some manual arts (diapers) and an attempt to push the services of the health center (most babies are born in the campo)...Most of the women (14) are campesinas.

I'm programming it, so to speak, and although I have a guide to use, many particular decisions still rest with me: such as, what material will actually be covered (I'm making the visual aids for the "obstetra"); the formation of a commission, president, V.P., etc. so that they can perhaps work as a true "club" and have a treasury. I'm also conducting a small survey, to see how many have had children before, if any have died, of what, is this their first birth in the health center, what are some of their feelings about the health center vs. the traditional "curanderos" (witch doctors) in the campo, etc. I have high hopes for the group.

What is so right about it, is that I'm "designing" the program, and the actual teaching will be left to the staff. This could be frustrating though, too, as only indirectly can I oversee what is actually taught. I have ideas on what should be included in the class on menstruation and child-conception...and nutrition, etc. I'll have to wait and see this first time what the obstetrician includes in her talks.

There are so many deaths among children here, due to diarrhea and subsequent dehydration (the belief is that, if a kid has diarrhea and vomiting, giving him water will make it worse...it's so tragic, that it's water the child needs more than anything else). I'm also unofficially in charge of visual aids at the health center. And another project I'm working on is with a grade school here in town. Essentially, it's a teacher-education program, including hygiene, parasites, some nutrition, etc. The teachers then present the subjects to the students, and it all comes to a grand finale in a program of some sort, with theater and songs by the kids, displays, anything.

To that program we'll invite parents and offer the cement floors we sell for latrines, in hopes some construction will result. One thing I've learned is not to begin a program that will have no practical follow-through. All this planning and programming is most beneficial to me in many ways...I do like teaching and will undoubtedly explore this field further...

The lady who owns my house has moved in with her little boy and Ana, their 12-year-old helper. I asked them to, and really do love the chaos…having them around eases many tensions. It's very un-Paraguayan to live by yourself if you're a woman, and I've become Paraguayan enough to actually FEEL how strange it is. Now I can have friends over (guys, especially) and no one thinks anything of it. I have my official guardians. Also, I have my own "apartment," as the doors between the two big rooms remain closed (Mom can explain). So I still have privacy, when I want it. I really love the folks here…

It's been terribly hot lately, had some rain yesterday which cooled things off nicely…but we're back to sweatsville today. March should bring some cool southerlies…I'll stop at 4 pages…I could go on and on, but my fingers are beginning to ache.

HAPPY VALENTINE'S DAY!!

Love love love…E

P.S. My volleyball team won the championship!

Journal entry 14 Feb—Monday a.m.—DÍA DE LOS ENAMORADOS—Waiting for 8:00, going to teachers' meeting. Will present ideas for project. I think they'll be responsive, as the directora at least seems to be. This work—so far—is extremely enjoyable.

Fairly eventful weekend—Friday night Verna's b-day (didn't eat my cake!) but I was pooped, tired of singing the same ol' songs and being the same ol' simpática Emilia…Saturday a.m. at health center, Sat. eve cena [supper] here with Elsa's relatives—good. Then Sunday—(bought guitar with Elsa's ANDE [electric company] money, gent joked that I must've stolen it from oratorios around town!)—Made heart cookies, went to Elsa's for lunch…Afterwards, to Cordillera with Hilda & Francisco's [Cristina's brother's] micro, spent quiet evening at volleyball GO GO GO, the more energy I burn the more I seem to have. And all this while making progress in THE IDIOT: excellent book!

Journal entry 15 Feb—Perfect situation: Doing so much, measured in terms other than "hours spent"—keeping own hours.

*Now it's kaaru-eté and che ahá-ta hospitalpe. Che pochy ña Normande...
Ha'e oñe'emonguetá-vaera kuri la-socia-kuera ndi, pero ndajapói. Chembo-
ombo'é. [Now it's late afternoon and I'm going to the hospital. I'm mad at ña
Norma...She was going to talk to the socias but she didn't do it. I'm going to
do the teaching.]*

    *"I used to let the universe control me, I wished to remain with no resistance
but now I certainly do see that some resistance is quite beyond reproach."(DOST.
I THINK)...Ah how often have I felt precisely as dear Prince Myshkin...The
things those people do! It's an absolutely brilliant book...*

Everything was going great—and then along came Chayo.

14

MARTÍN

Doctors Gladys Meilinger de Sannemann and Jorge Canesse set up a clinic
in Emboscada, with support from the Committee of Churches and the
International Red Cross. Several prisoners worked as nurses. Dr. Roberto Vera
Grau (no relation to the colonel) set up a dental practice. In addition to providing medical services, the doctors gave talks on hygiene and first aid. These
activities helped improve health conditions in Emboscada and benefited the
conscripts and neighbors of the camp as well. There were also courses on agriculture taught by three prisoners who were *ingenieros agrónomos.*

    We got permission to hold our Minas-cué cultural gatherings on Saturdays.
These were mostly spontaneous performances by different artists who, with
very modest means, achieved prodigious results. We enjoyed outstanding
guitar playing and singing, mime and acting, poetry, speakers, folk dance, a
marionette theater, and a chorus of fifty voices that sang exiled musician José
Asunción Flores's "Ñemity" ("Cultivate"), an homage to the land, with its profound and emotional verses. We also had soccer games, chess tournaments, and
classes in folk art.

Even though the authorities had removed me from the literacy project, for a time they let me participate in these gatherings. One fine day, sometime in March of 1977, I decided to recite a parody I'd written called "To the Guy in the Gray Suit," which I dedicated to the donkey who carried water from the Piribebuy River.

That was at 5:30 p.m. An hour later, an officer approached to inform me that, by orders from above, I was under arrest. I asked why, and he responded, "For publicly ridiculing the glorious uniform of the armed forces."

I was taken to Colonel Grau's office. He reprimanded me, saying his patience had run out and I was completely mad. I tried to explain that the "guy in the gray suit" represented the donkey and not the officials under his charge, but there was no way I could convince him. Grau had been wanting to get rid of me for some time, and the parody was the excuse he needed to have me taken back to the Tomb of the Living. Alfonso Silva, being punished for some other "lack of discipline," was also ordered to be moved, and shortly thereafter we were both shoved into a *perrera* and taken away to the Third Precinct. The van in which we were transported had been sitting in the sun all morning with its doors and windows closed, so getting in it was like being put into an oven at its highest setting. Silva and I felt terribly ill. I fainted several times (he later told me) because of my extreme weakness and being enclosed in the stifling heat for several hours. Silva banged so hard on the walls of the van that the driver finally stopped, and the two of them pulled me out. I was very thirsty—my throat dry, my mouth bitter, without saliva—but at least I was still breathing.

At the Third Precinct, Ananías Maidana and a few comrades greeted us. Next to us in cell number two was the Argentine Amílcar Latino Santucho, who had to inhale cement dust all day because the superintendent had converted Santucho's cell into a depository for construction materials.

A week later, two new "guests" from Emboscada arrived. They had committed the grave offense of asking the camp chaplain why Silva and I had been transferred to the Tomb.

One day the cells were being inspected, and we were ordered into the hallway. The operation took about forty minutes, which allowed me my first confidential conversation with Santucho. He told me he had been detained since May 1975. The traces of the terrible torture he had suffered were still visible; he said high-level military officials from Argentina, Uruguay, and Chile had taken part in his torture sessions.

Santucho fondly remembered Jorge Fuentes Alarcón, a Chilean he had shared a cell with at Investigations, who was later turned over to the Chilean government.[96] As we walked up and down the hallway, Santucho discreetly told me, "I am very fond of your country. It is worthy, it has suffered, and in prison I have learned to value its qualities even more. In Argentina we have thousands of exiled Paraguayans sharing our struggles; our jails are full of your countrymen. There are also many disappeared. The fight for liberation should not be on a national level, but rather like in the times of independence, on a continental scale." We embraced and went back to our respective tombs, as ordered by the police.

Nevertheless, although my body was imprisoned in that small, five-by-five-meter space, I felt my spirit grow and pass through the bars of our cage. The torturers never broke my confidence or suppressed my faith in the justice of our cause.

In Emboscada we had been hungry and thirsty and plagued by a lack of hygiene, but at least we had the sun. In contrast, the dungeons of the Third Precinct were cold, damp, and dark, which further undermined my health and damaged my vision.

I was finally returned to Emboscada, the lesser of two evils.

Through conversations with Dr. Sannemann in Emboscada, I became aware of how police cooperation in the Southern Cone functioned within the framework of the Inter-American Defense Treaty. Under the treaty's title—Plan Cóndor—collaboration among the repressive governments of Argentina, Uruguay, Chile, Brazil, Bolivia, and Paraguay was established

96 Arrested as they entered Paraguay together, Santucho and Fuentes were both high-level members of armed revolutionary movements from Argentina and Chile, respectively. They had been en route to a meeting in Paris as part of the Revolutionary Coordinating Body, a group comprising movements from Argentina, Chile, Uruguay, and Bolivia to fight the Southern Cone's military dictatorships. The arrests likely led to the formalization of Operation Condor in Santiago six months later. Fuentes disappeared after being transferred to Chile in January 1976.

Amílcar Santucho survived prison and served as secretary general of the Workers' Revolutionary Party until his death in July 1995. A heartbreaking article on the persecution of the Santucho family and the growth of state terrorism in Argentina can be found in "The General and the Children," by Mark Dowie, *Mother Jones Magazine* (July 1978, pp. 37–48).

with the support of the CIA and Secretary of State Henry Kissinger. Prisoner exchange was the order of the day, as was the swift circulation of information obtained from political prisoners in the torture chambers. The "Center for Information" was in Argentina, run by the army.

Dr. Sannemann came from a traditional and authentic Colorado family. Her anti-Stroessner beliefs stemmed from 1957, the year she graduated from medical school and began to practice medicine at the Rigoberto Caballero Police Hospital. In 1958 a young labor leader was tortured by an army officer, and it was Dr. Sannemann's job to fill out the death certificate. The officer insisted that the record state the death was caused by a heart attack, but Dr. Sannemann refused. She ordered an autopsy instead, which revealed lesions of the brain, trauma, and more. That was when her torment really began.

This was Dr. Sannemann's introduction to the systematic persecution carried out by the regime. Her situation worsened when she committed the "crime" of marrying a well-known Stroessner opponent and leader of the Colorado youth movement, Jorge Rodolfo Sannemann. Following their incarceration and release within Paraguay, in 1960 the couple left on an odyssey around the bordering countries.

The Sannemanns owned a clinic in Candelaria, province of Misiones, Argentina, where they and their family had lived for a decade as political refugees. Her current torment began on March 24, 1976, hours after the military coup establishing dictator Jorge Videla as president—and unleashing one of the bloodiest dictatorships in South America. The combined forces of the army, gendarmerie, and federal and provincial police broke open the door of her clinic (her husband was away at the time) and, at machine-gun point, evacuated the patients. They then searched every corner of the premises. They banged on the floors, walls, and ceilings in search of weapons and, upon finding none, grabbed typewriters, cameras, fishing gear, and household appliances. They also confiscated the week's earnings in Argentine pesos and a small stash of dollars the doctor was saving.

Dr. Sannemann was interrogated in a police station in Posadas. Her cell was small and damp, water leaked through the walls, and a bright light bulb shone day and night. Among her cellmates she remembered many women and girls. One morning several of the women were covered with hoods, removed from the cell, and transferred to an undisclosed location.

A week later, Dr. Sannemann was placed in a van and taken to the port of Posadas, where an Argentine naval boat was waiting. The chief inspector of the Paraguayan police received her on the other side of the border, in Encarnación, and transported her to the Office of Investigations in Asunción.

After seventeen years of forced exile, Gladys was re-arrested and came to be imprisoned with us at Emboscada, her morale as strong as the stones surrounding the prison. Her optimism was contagious, and her confidence in the triumph of the people over the military nightmare spread to us. According to information gathered by the family, her husband was alive somewhere in a Buenos Aires jail after being tortured by Argentine and Paraguayan police, in accordance with the terms of police cooperation in the Southern Cone abetted by the Pentagon.

In addition to Dr. Sannemann, dozens more Paraguayan citizens had been arrested in Argentina and transported to Paraguay under Operation Condor. There are many unknown names of the disappeared who were arrested, humiliated, tortured, and killed, the product of a horrific collaboration among dictators against the peoples of Latin America. The day will come when, through the efforts of all, Latin American countries will unite in movements for progress and integrated community development—activities that nurture life, not death.

15

EMILY

I met Chayo at one of the bake sales held by our commission to raise funds for the Club de Madres. People here had to raise their own money for everything, it seemed.

"You must be the Peace Corps volunteer," I heard a young man say. I gritted my teeth: *Here we go again.* But when I turned around and saw this cute guy about my height with dark, wavy hair wearing a blue University of Michigan T-shirt (from a friend in Ann Arbor, he said), my attitude evaporated. His smile took up half his face and had an ironic twist I found engaging.

"I'm Cesáreo, but they call me Chayo. Please come to my house tonight for an *asado*. My mother is a midwife here in town, and I'm home on break from medical school in Argentina. I'd love it if you came."

Midwife? That's what *I* wanted to be! I loved my work with the obstetrician here. How could I say no?

At the party I discovered that Chayo played guitar and sang, quite well in fact, and when he sang "Sabor a Mí," I felt my resolve slipping a little.

That night he walked me home and gave me the requisite air kiss on each cheek, then came back the next day. He taught me the popular tune "An Old Love Song,"[97] in which the guy is madly—pathetically, I would have said—in love with a girl but is too bashful to tell her. That rang true for me as well, of course, but my question was always *How do you know love when you find it?* Maybe the only thing I was capable of loving was the thrill of falling in love itself, as Steve Goodman sang in that sad but true song about "the findin'" being tamer than "the lookin' for," and the gambler who's lovin' the game.[98]

You could say I never knew what I was looking for but always knew when I hadn't found it. But the truth was, I didn't have to worry about it with Chayo—I just liked being around him. He wanted to learn English, so we started hanging out. He was kind, not at all overbearing, and treated me as an equal. We talked about everything—he knew more than I did about what was happening around the world—and he thought what I had to say was important. When I told him I was determined to go to Catamarca someday, he said it was only 440 kilometers (273 miles) from Córdoba!

Was this relationship "meant to be"? Was Chayo "the one"? My imagination started running away with me, my heart in hot pursuit—despite the pesky little voice in my head that kept saying *This can't be happening...all I wanted was to get back to where I once belonged!*

Journal entry 23 Feb—Ash Wednesday. By returning to this my book of revelations I enter another realm of awareness. Beguiling—that's my atmosphere at the moment. Not confusing: but intriguing. I'm involved in the swing of the universe,

---

97 Raúl Abramzon, "Una Vieja Canción de Amor," 1975.

98 Victoria Armstrong and Pat Garvey, "The Loving of the Game," 1965.

a great Force has gathered me up and hurled me into the giant mechanism, at a speed not likely to diminish...in time, perhaps a very lifetime.

What palabras dulces [sweet words] I write to Chayo...

The things Chayo said to me: love an art; the river talks; sex education needed in developed countries; all information on birth, etc. (the technical stuff I found so useful); the commission, etc.; the improvised songs in English, Spanish, Guaraní.

My vision: working in campo, barefoot doctors. Later, in Arizona, southern, near Mexico (could be in Chiricahuas, anywhere—FLAGSTAFF) doing natural births.

Journal entry 25 Feb—Selling cake today—and doing charlas?!—at centro de salud. For vaccinations...there won't be many people, but we'll sell all the torta, methinks. I was "elected" president of the commission. At first I was opposed to the idea but now I realize I can set a good example (if I can figure out what I'm doing)...

My relationship with the ladies on the street—in the entire neighborhood—has changed, now that we're involved in this comisión. At first I think they really didn't want anything to do with it, and only came because they couldn't turn me down. But after yesterday, and the cake baking, and my visiting everyone to chat and keep up...we've entered into new areas of communication, they appreciate me more (know me better) and vice versa. This is a good thing, I'm positively glowing, and the energy abounds. But still planning to terminate, probably end of May, go to Córdoba. See what happens...One step at a time, lady.

Journal entry 6 March—Saw my first birth last night in health center, with Norma. I loved it, scientifically and poetically. Birth is such a marvelous phenomenon. This one was without complications of any sort, and happened so fast I have almost no impressions...except constant comparisons of Norma's style with what I know intuitively (and from what he's told me) to be Chayo's; also comparing with how births are done in America...the difference is staggering. This is what having a baby is! Not being interned in a hospital with a white gown, lying down, being fed drugs to speed the process and lessen the pain, doctors and stainless steel, incubators and babies two rooms down, being wheeled to the operating room, semi-conscious from (———). NO NO NO !!!

This lady's 4th baby. She's walking around all afternoon, evening. Full moon. Calls for Norma, too early (only open 4 cm—6 to go). The suspense is invigorating. We prepare the delivery room: snips, scissors, vitamins, pañuelitos [little cloths]. Finally it's time. She's in pain now: "Mamita!" The head begins to appear. After the head comes out it's easy: the live thing, kicking, demanding a right to existence. The lady's still in her own dress! Afterwards comes the umbilical cord and placenta (Norma dumps them). Sacred objects!

I do sincerely love this work.

I loved talking to Chayo about birthing babies. One Saturday when we were out hiking, I said, "It baffles me how pregnant women here refuse to eat peanuts or eggs because they think they'll have a dry birth, or molasses because they'll have a dark baby…just the foods they *should* be eating. It's frustrating."

"You're right," he said. "Old ways die hard. To this day nobody wants a *morochito* like me." I stopped and turned around, relieved to see him grinning as he walked right into me—he wasn't one to play the victim. I myself loved dark skin, as he well knew. I kissed him and continued up the path.

"Furthermore," I went on, "I refuse to believe that the babies I watch being delivered are born with so-called 'original sin.'"

He laughed. "I agree, that's ridiculous. Another thing, women here want to use birth control, but their husbands—and the church, naturally—don't approve. Of course there's no real social security and the infant-mortality rate is high, so people have as many kids as they can so they'll be taken care of in old age." He paused as we rock-hopped over a stream. "And speaking of infant mortality…I wish our government—goaded by those villains at Nestlé—would stop pushing baby formula so much. There are too many health risks associated with it. Breast milk is by far the better alternative."

That's what *I* always said! I could see Chayo would make an excellent doctor. He *understood.*

We spent his remaining days in Piribebuy cooking, playing guitar, singing, writing down Javier Solís lyrics together—and making the sweetest love I'd ever made in my life. I finally got it: sex was not only sacred, it was supposed to be *fun*. Satori! Never had I felt so complete. Surely Chayo was the answer to my dreams. I was sad to see him return to Córdoba.

I wrote to my grandmother on March 11:

In my house we're celebrating progress: yesterday we installed our faucet, and now have running water! Isn't that marvelous?...

Thank you so much for your letter, you know how much I do love them...

I get up every morning before 6:00. These nights of such heat I sleep outside, beneath the stars. In the mornings I go to the health center, where I'm learning an incredible amount of useful things. Tomorrow I'm going to apply my first injection, God-willing (providing I find myself a willing victim). Once a week we have our Mother's Club, which is about to end. On March 31 we have the "graduation" ceremonies, and we'll award diplomas...

I plan a short trip to Argentina for Easter...

Journal entry 15 March—*Events certainly have a way of presenting themselves, and regardless of what one is living mentally, outside circumstances are a slap in the face because one realizes that one is really in no position of control...*

My future suddenly became my present, with Chayo's unexpected arrival, telephone call. "DON'T SAY MY NAME" [in English], my trip to Caacupé (Sánchez, then camión de carga [freight truck]), Asunción, confusion. Clarity at first, pure expression, freedom in love and sheer joy. The demands being made on me—I'm making on myself—are tremendous, luckily my pace prior to all this switching of tables was swift and sure. I do love Chayo; I do plan to make every effort to overcome childish hesitation and make a life together, because it could be such a good life, karmically. Do I really envision myself studying nursing in Argentina? Well... sure would be nice if he transfers to Asunción...

I'm so involved in the Here and Now, as never before. Yet Argüelles' book[99] is helping me achieve an illuminating perspective not only on the history of art and expression, with the conflict beween TECHNE and PSYCHE, but also of course into myself. He reinforces many of my beliefs about the beauty of oriental thought:

"The oriental tradition of nature painting is based on a philosophical and spiritual tradition that emphasizes man's being at one or fully engaged with the processes of nature... The oriental view of nature assumes an inherent correspondence between mind and nature; the object of nature painting is to express through whatever image the indissoluble union of mind and nature, which is spirit itself. Wilderness, the lofty mountains, the changing seasons, the varied life of plants are valued because through them is revealed the self-same breath that gives man his duration and sustenance. Wilderness becomes a metaphor for mind in its original state, and vice versa." p. 104

"For the wisdom of the East is not necessarily in the symbols themselves but in knowing that it is still possible to become whole and pure, singing the joy of creation endlessly and fabulously as it unfolds itself through us." p. 131

Civilization: what has literally been citified—"A highly evolved state of social/technical refinement and development. If human existence poses the problem of suffering and death, civilization compounds the problem by pretending that it has been solved, or even worse, that it never existed in the first place. The author of this deception is man's own cleverness..." pp. 169–70

Quoting Wassily Kandinsky: "The artist must have something to communicate, since mastery over form is not the end, but, instead, the adopting of form to internal significance." p. 187 (FULL CIRCLE)

Before dawn, Saturday, 19 March 1977, Dearest Mom,

I had a dream last night that you came to visit me again. What say we take in Bolivia and Peru this time? It's raining, and the lights are out—I'm writing by kerosene lamplight, as I used to do in Caazapá... I'm also having <u>mate</u>, as you might have guessed...

---

99 José Argüelles, *The Transformative Vision: Reflections on the Nature and History of Human Expression* (Boston: Shambhala Publications, 1975).

One characteristic I've developed here in Peace Corps is a desire to teach things. For example, when I'm assisting the lady obstetrician I work with, anything from pap smears to vaccinations to interviews, I can't help but be turned off to her method, so typically Paraguayan (and worse yet for women professionals): a magnification of the "military," "sit down here, pull up your dress, pull down your pants, I'm the one who knows it all so you just do what I say and everything will be all right..."While I'm DYING to say: "Now, this is a test to see if you might show signs of developing cancer," etc. And, during the birth I saw, when the kid came out it was whisked away, wrapped in cloths and put in its crib...When I begin performing births, I'm going to slap that kid right down on the mother's abdomen before cutting the umbilical cord...Perhaps some women wouldn't like it, but to me it's a very intimate gesture, mother and child.

In another instance, when first aid is administered at the hospital, the patients are never counseled in how they might have treated their own cut, for example, or insect bite, before it became infected and abscessed. Why keep these people in their ignorant fog? Why not let some light shine in? It drives me crazy, the entire boss patron/peon system. It's so medieval.

Yesterday a lady came with her baby boy to the hospital, his head cut and infected, his eyes swollen shut. It had happened two days before, and she hadn't even washed it! Many times it's not only ignorance that prevents proper action, but ancient beliefs and special plant-based remedial practices, that stand in the way. But: If they only knew that the cut must be washed and protected from dirt...that's not an impossible goal. I find great satisfaction in treating people, no stomach problems—so far—at seeing pus or blood. When you're thinking about curing someone, those things lose their power to make you squeamish.

I'm very happy now, happier than I've ever been in my life, or at least since I learned what happiness and wretchedness (which I am much more familiar with) are. Perhaps before reaching such desperation I could never appreciate and honor happiness. Now the suffering seems worthwhile—looking back—because it's such a radical change, what I'm feeling these days. Everything is under control, I have a motive for every action I take, yet it's all being created every moment anew. There is no routine that I'm succumbing to. I'm glad I decided to extend, I couldn't bear to think about leaving yet.

My roommate will have her baby in July, around the 12th. That should be exciting. Our club's graduation takes place the 31st of March...We'll donate baby clothes and gowns to the hospital ("we" being my commission that I've formed of ladies in my neighborhood... we have nearly 30,000 guaranies [$240] in the treasury). My big project before I leave will be to get the running water system going in the health center. Six months isn't much time, so we'll all have to do some pretty positive thinking...

In closing, I just want to tell you, Mom, that one of the factors in my present situation that makes me joyful is Chayo, my Paraguayan sweetheart...

Much love always, E

I made the decision to extend my Peace Corps service for two months, to pay back the time I'd lost being...well, lost. It seemed like the right thing to do, and I felt good signing the papers in Todd's office.

Chayo had returned to Córdoba and then, the evening of March 15, surprised me with the phone call. As in Caazapá, no one in Piribebuy had home phones, so a messenger was sent to fetch me and I'd had to walk the eight blocks to the ANTELCO office to answer it, having no idea who it could be. To fool the eavesdropping operator, Chayo had started speaking in English, confusing the hell out of me as well. I ended up "escaping" to Asunción for two days, which we spent together. Then for some reason he was back in Piribebuy.

My life consisted only of work and Chayo. I was trying to memorize a song in Guaraní he had taught me called "Mboraijhú Jhasy"[100] [mboh-rye-HOO hah-SÜH] (painful or difficult love). The song was sad, but it turned out singing

---

100 Rosalía Díaz León and Juan Escobar, date unknown.

in Guaraní was a blast! I was able to express things I couldn't in conversation, really fast, and actually understand what I was saying. I could even feel the ache in the lyrics "I cannot go on living without you."

Learning songs in another language was still the best way to become fluent—and know the culture better.

Journal entry 26 March—A score of potentially disrupting events: health conference, letters from Ellyn, Mom, John Smartt: Yet I've held steadfast to my course, can it be?

Chayo has been in town for over two weeks now, and my love and respect for him have grown in depth since we first met. We've spent many moments together, difficult ones, intimate ones, analytical ones, high artistic/mystical ones. I've found in him what I've not found in anyone before: a purity and reverence before Nature. Little "ritual," that is, he does not use any philosophical "system" through which to interpret what he sees and feels...He merely listens to the rivers, and the birds, watching their courses and uniting with them in spirit and soul. He denies the existence of soul, but it's merely semantics. I've remained strong, straightforward, lucid, with faith in my feelings. I don't know what's to become of it all...

My senses have become so sharp here, and this is of course heightened by Chayo—he's so sensitive, can always interpret what I'm doing, saying, thinking—I simply cannot return to live in the States, only to pollute my senses once again with industrialism's malignant capitalist tumor...I can have everything I need here in Paraguay, can realize my dream of building my own house, having a garden, animals—and not to forget the barefoot doctors! A full life indeed. Back to "cornbread and beans in the hills"...

Saw another birth, Thurs. 24. This time paid more attention to technical aspect. I LOVE IT!!!

Journal entry 27 March—I feel unsettled and don't know why...Chayo left today, I feel alone but don't want to admit it...Last night I told Chayo, "I'm tired of being a stranger." It's true. Of course I can't deny I felt a stranger in the US. Always "in a strange land"...

Ourobouros biting his own tail—the circle completed...

Journal entry 28 March—Monday. Thinking more about Chayo, and what he is to me...I must hold on to my own system of thought, and express it through him—He listens to me, and takes me to Nature...

How I love the mornings here: Arise, head out to latrine, return to wash hands and splash face, exercises, heat up water for mate, prepare yerba, dress, sit and drink mate while planning, musing, pensando lejos [thinking far away]...

Journal entry 31 March—[I Ching] Reading: 16YU Enthusiasm (thunder over earth, child riding an elephant joyously), Celebration

Thunderstorm clears air, removes oppression.

Danger of self-deception if enthusiasm is ungrounded.

I had time off for Easter—a spring holiday celebrating life back home, but here the opposite, a cold foreshadowing of wintry death—so on April Fool's Day I went to see Chayo in Córdoba, a stately old city founded by the Jesuits in the seventeenth century. After the butt-numbing twenty-four-hour bus ride, we escaped to his single bed—slaves to the hunger that consumed us—and later grilled some meat on the roof of his twelve-story apartment building so we could watch the glorious *puesto del sol*.

"Look at that luscious pink hue, like the inside of a conch shell," he said, pointing to the cathedral with one arm and holding me close with the other. He looked at me and smiled. "It makes that old bell tower blush."

I smiled back, but all I could think of was the alpenglow on the Catalina Mountains back home. I shivered in the chill.

"I wait for this moment every night." Chayo sighed. He kissed me on the forehead and turned back toward the sun, his face now the same deep coral. "At some point you realize the sunset is the most important thing in the world, just to be able to enjoy the moment and carry that happiness with you into the next day."

I couldn't disagree, but was it really that simple? Especially now, with the way things were around here? I was trying my best to believe it was.

Chayo said he wanted to take me places and he did...to record stores—where I bought the Cafrune and Sosa albums I'd fallen in love with at Steve's—and restaurants, parks, even the zoo...though of course I paid for everything. The zoo was pitiful, especially the Andean condors, who sat bone idle in their cages. They looked like creepy clerics, even their white "collars" failing to charm, mangy as they were.

Chayo was somber. "Look at these shameful specimens. It hurts to see them like this. The condor, Emilia, is the national symbol of six countries in South America, the 'magnificent bird of life,' the epitome of power and freedom. But all that has been stripped from these poor souls. They no longer have a reason for being and they know it, you can tell."

I couldn't help thinking about Paul Simon's song "El Cóndor Pasa" and wasn't sure what was more haunting, the melody or the narrator longing to be free. To me, though, condors may have symbolized power and freedom, but they were hardly *magnificent*—they were vultures, for crissakes, and preyed only on that which couldn't fend for itself.

Valiant Chayo even took me to Catamarca! But I was already worn out, and the six-hour bus ride—each way—only made me wish I'd never gone. I realized that making the "pilgrimage," as it were, hadn't made me happy the way I thought it would.

The truth was, I was afraid.

"Catamarca and Córdoba have both been centers of resistance," Chayo had said after assuring me he was sympathetic to the cause but had never been involved in any guerrilla movements. "Skirmishes still happen here from time to time. Just a year ago, several hundred people suspected of collaborating with the ERP were rounded up, and many were killed."

Jesus, all you had to do was be suspected!

Chayo also said a famous insurrection known as the "Cordobazo" had taken place in May 1969 after students and auto workers—Córdoba was apparently the "Detroit of Argentina"—marched together in solidarity, and sixty people lost their lives. The event had sparked protests throughout the country.

"Naturally," he said, grinning in his endearing way, "the government called it a 'conspiracy of international communism.'" I smiled back, no doubt a sort of dazed expression on my face, because in that moment I finally comprehended the gravity of the situation here.

And in Paraguay. Chayo said that some of his relatives had disappeared. How awful, I thought, to not know if your family member was dead or alive. Then he told me about the "rebaptism" that took place in Piribebuy in 1965, when he was eleven. Around seventy campesinos, mostly young men, had been accused by people in their communities of being communists, taken to *estancias* (ranches) in the area, and tortured. Those lucky enough not to end up in Asunción in the Office of Investigations—the place Diego had shown us!—were brought to Piribebuy on September 13, to the main plaza in front of the cathedral, and trapped inside by Stroessner's thugs. Forced to declare publicly that they were not communists, the young men were then "rebaptized."

"Because of the ostracism that resulted from the *rebautismo*," Chayo said, "many of the guys became outcasts in their communities." We were sitting on a park bench where no one could hear us. He glanced down at our interlaced fingers, paused, and then looked unsmiling at me. "But that's Stroessner's plan, isn't it—to undermine Paraguayan society by creating fear and mistrust among the people."

Where would it all end? Would it end, period? I realized I would never be able to look at anyone in Piribebuy or Caazapá the same way again: Who had done what to whom? Who was hiding what? Who was hiding, period?

It made me sad. How would the Paraguayans ever be able to trust one another again? I remembered Alan Watts saying freedom was the ability to trust—what did that mean for the future of my dear adopted country?

Clearly nothing I could do would ever change things.

Of course Chayo and I attracted attention wherever we went, which didn't help my nerves any, what with all the prepubescent boys in uniform standing on every corner, their fingers lightly touching the triggers of their automatic weapons. One little twitch and...

It was starting to dawn on me—*I had to get out of here!* A twist of fate had brought me to Latin America, but it wasn't my destiny to stay. How did I know, you may ask? I didn't. It was just a feeling I had, deep down in my gut: *Time for this one to come home.*

I was thankful I had a choice, something most people here didn't have.

When I kissed Chayo good-bye at the terminal, I couldn't see his face through my tears. We held each other a long time, and I finally grasped what those sad Paraguayan songs were really about: You didn't know if you would ever see someone again. Even "Bésame Mucho" had that element of permanent loss. I wished I was a stronger person and could take Chayo home with me, like some of the other PCVs, but I wasn't, and I couldn't. It was bad timing, plain and simple. I had to face the fact that I still wasn't ready to grow up and settle down.

Truth be told, I felt unworthy of Chayo.

His voice rang clear in my head: *"Solamente una vez,"*[101] a bolero he'd sung every night before we fell asleep. I sat back for the trip to Asunción and sighed. It hurt. *Chayo.* "Only once did I love in life."

Was he that one I would never forget?

Journal entry 16 April—Home again at last, after two-week absence—It feels so good to be here, I knew it would. Can't begin to describe my time spent in Córdoba with Chayo, except to say that on the whole the venture was "successful," I did doubt though at times, and wanted to escape. I love Chayo purely and simply. All I fear is…commitment. (Obligación?) In-phase says YES, out-phase NO. What is involved in the decision? But it's not immediate now…

I'm afraid. Still. Yet: When I'm with him it seems right. I made it plain to him that I couldn't commit myself. Had felt strangled. We have such a rapport!

My philosophy, etc. coming together. I know how I feel about my life, what it is, in relation to God. Still confused about my own particular destiny. Wanna travel. Chayo, too. Wouldn't it be nice? It will probably come about. I feel it.

People like us right away, the tall blonde with the short morocho [the term everyone used], figure what we have is pretty special.

Is.

[Tarot] Reading: "Illusion"

---

101 Agustín Lara, "Solamente Una Vez," 1941.

*Journal entry 18 April—Eye-opening Sunday, clarity of vision, a glimpse of…
freedom? ("Just another word…?"[102]) Read my cards…a move back to religion,
purity? I feel so contaminated, not lucid, this sedentary life I'm leading is
beginning to drag me down.*

*Yesterday, with [new acquaintances in Asunción] DeeDee and Tewfik, both on
the road, Tewfik a guru of sorts…A day of deep relating, massage, talk, laughter.
Rain, no lights…I realize what it is I'm looking for—don't I always?—I'm
weary of this, I knew sooner or later I'd have to let go. I want to explore my artistic
abilities, I want to be vegetarian and dance!…I go about my duties here but it
seems empty. I must face the fact that I'm an unconstant person, and not try to be
constant.*

My spirit is clean! It's my body that I want to work on.

*At this point I don't have the energy to carry on as I have been. It will hurt
to leave, to leave Chayo. O Lord, give me something to hold onto!*

Journal entry 19 April—I CHING
11 T'AI—PEACE, grass pulled up
"There is no going away so that there shall not be a return…"
9 HSIAO CH'U—LESSER NOURISHER (SMALL RESTRAINT)
Returns & pursues own path—returns to own course
*I'm certain now about what I must do. I must set out on my own. Alone, I must
pursue the answers to my questions. If at times I'm guilty of self-deceit it's because I
harbor certain instincts within, am a slave to my passions…I want to overcome this.*

*Journal entry 26 April—The times they are a'changin…I'm terminating 6
June, feel so good! Spent weekend in park with DeeDee. Thanks to her I've
realized I must go.*

*Journal entry 28 April—Today club reunion, I'm lacking in visual aids but can
get by. I'm bothered because I'm solely in charge, Norma didn't even make an
appearance last time. So POOF! It disappears when I do…*

---

102   Kris Kristofferson and Fred Foster, "Me and Bobby McGee," 1969.

Later—Saw another birth today, the first boy (I had a presentiment that it would be a boy)...Amazing how kids cry when they're born, as if lamenting the fact they've been brought into this world only to suffer, grow old, die.

Quote from Gin's herb book: "Life is a constant struggle against oxygen deficiency..." IVAN PETROVICH PAVLOV

Journal entry 1 May—Labor Day. Overcast a bit, cool, lovely Sunday.

Yesterday I stopped by ña Victoria's [Chayo's mother]. She threw her arms around me, told me Chayo had asked her to help me in any way she could, that she wants to have a course for empiricas [lay midwives], as she's heard many children and mothers have been dying of late in the campo...I just couldn't tell her! Now the day arrives that I must write Chayo, the thing I've most lamented...

It's Sunday a.m., and before long I'll be with my mom, drinking coffee, reading the Sunday papers.

God, I don't want kids. (Jesus María is being a special bratty crybaby at the moment.)...

Journal entry 9 May—Back home, after weekend in Asunción...

Today went and visited the Hospital de Clínicas [Teaching Hospital] with [PC doctor], pretty dismal place, all right. Grew out of one unit into many, all separate, no central design at all, split-level (no way to get a patient from one "ward" to another). And all run by different department heads, so there's no coordination...In addition, the rooms themselves are ghastly, plaster peeling off walls, stench of urine, even! And that ever-present smell of burning gas...The maternal ward was also absolutely joyless. What a paradise is the USA! I now take my hat off to St. Joseph's Hospital (but you'll never catch me working there).

Getting ready to leave for good, and feeling so excited!

Journal entry 20 May—After several days in Asunción, doing darkroom work, termination procedures, never once doubting that I must go. Got real cold lately, mornings and nights are almost freezing (got down to 6° [43°F])...

Saw 5th birth yesterday, a boy, 4 kilos (that's 8.8 lbs)! Was huge. The mother was neat, totally present throughout, telling me where more rags are, etc.

Didn't want suero [saline solution]. I think the woman must go into temporary shock when the head pops out. Amazing how Norma grabs the head then pulls the rest of the kid out.

Almost all Americans I have spoken to express grave doubts as to my plans to become a midwife. I sometimes wonder if the hearty Paraguayan women really are better built, or better prepared, to have babies—because we've never had a problem (except the kid who was born dead), and only once that I've known about has a woman with high blood pressure been sent to Caacupé to have twins. No, I think many of the problems can be directly caused by the hospital...and if a woman is prepared mentally and physically she won't have any problems. That's only my opinion.

Journal entry 23 May—Spent weekend at Diego's...Did my TAROT with him...Most symbolic combination was Wheel of Fortune for cover and Lovers for cross...It certainly outlines my entire life's strife, that of knowing when to listen to divine messages and when to take the reins myself...I give the appearance of letting things ride—don't I?—Sometimes too much so; yet my force of Will is tremendous, and that force is inevitably misdirected. In more concrete terms, I act when I should let other forces take over, and kick back when perhaps I should take a stand. It's most frustrating, especially where men are concerned. I never intend to hurt any of them, I simply make mistakes is all...

Journal entry 26 May—Another Thursday, Mothers' Club, this time overcast and wet, probably few will come...

Yesterday: A VISION of myself as the Kerouac of our group (the chronicler), the maker of legends...

My life will be changing so...This is my life, then—a gas stove, electric refrigerator, blue and white painted (by me) fiambrera [cupboard] with Arizona Highways photos lining top and Time, Inc. covers lining bottom, shelf that's made by me using stacked bricks (rather clever of me), spice rack and magazine picture of young boy eating peanut butter and banana sandwich.

Sun's going down. Chickens starting to roost, roosters crowing, crickets. Evening sounds: talking, radio, cow, bird. Jesus María and Antola che ama.

Hummingbird!
Bogs darking [sic].
Mate time, at ña Fernanda's.

It was time to leave, dreaded as much as desired. Ellyn said she would travel with me through Brazil, Uruguay, and Argentina. I wasn't sure what I would do when I got home. Perhaps it was time to fulfill another childhood dream—working in a different jungle, New York City, with the United Nations.

The stillbirth had of course made me sad. I didn't get to watch the delivery—Norma made me leave when she realized what was happening. I sat outside the door but could hear only muffled voices. Would things have turned out better if the lady had been in a more up-to-date facility? *Claro que sí.*

Midwifery did have its downside.

Our commission held a ceremony and awarded the health center around $350 to buy new beds and other necessary items—far short of the running water it so desperately needed. I was jazzed because commission members promised they would keep working together after I left; I could only hope they meant it.

I embroidered a banner that said "Three Cheers for María Auxiliadora" and gave it to Cristina, along with the Snoopy doll Mom had brought me. Cristina of course organized a *despedida*, and I cried as I said good-bye for the last time to my friends in Piribebuy. I swapped my guitar for a cheap Paraguayan model (bad trade on my part) and practically gave my tape player away.

Kristi's mother was devastated to see me go. As in the Yucatán, I had to wonder if it was really fair to become part of people's lives and then just up and leave them—what I'd done all my life, I realized. But what was I to do? I couldn't stay. I had my whole life ahead of me, and it wasn't in Paraguay.

You see, I never did swim in the Río Tebicuary.

But damn if the guys in our group didn't build their raft, "Kururú Tuyú" [koo-roo-ROO too-JOO] (mud toad), after all and float it down the Río Paraguay, starting more than five hundred miles up north in Brazil. They were full of stories, like the time during a storm when everything turned pitch black, including the raging water that threatened to overwhelm them, and Alonzo got so scared he yelled, "God, if you're out there, please just take me now!" He was eventually able to grab a rope and tie the raft to a tree, "like in the movies," he said. Unfortunately, Gino got stung by a stingray (I had no idea such monsters lurked in the rivers here!) and they had to hold over in Concepción for a few days. Ellyn of course played housemother to them all even though she was trying to terminate. Guys could be so pathetic. Still, their retention rate was better than the girls'—out of nineteen original candidates, eight finished, nearly half to our measly quarter.

Back in Piribebuy for the last time, I started packing a box that I would ship home. Lying on the bed was the white *ñandutí* I'd finally bought, which had eight different motifs around a center. I dug out my *Lace and Legend* book to see if I could identify any of them but nearly went cross-eyed before recognizing only a vase and a guava flower (there were thirty samples on each page, and the print was microscopic). The motifs had colorful names that told stories of their own, everything from "anthill in a corn field" to "groups of spiders," "cattle ticks" to "frog's backside"—and two different designs for "legend about the kidnapping of children."

I chuckled. Paraguay. Nothing like it.

[Final entry]
Journal entry 27 May—24 hours is such a pitifully short time...

Last night, the last supper at twins', [with] their three boyfriends...I'm talking to the parents by the brasero [brazier], or rather ña Olinda is talking to me about her two months in the Hospital de Clínicas (that terrible rat's nest of alcohol smell and mold and rusty needles). Actually she's talking in mixed Spanish and Guaraní. I'm understanding very little, mostly because I can NO LONGER make an effort (as we've seen).Well I am understanding the "gist" as am able to drift in and out enough to ask the appropriate questions, and it wasn't of course for lack of respect or anything that my thoughts were thousands of miles away, it's simply that...my thoughts were thousands of miles away.

So, if my novel about Peace Corps TWO YEARS OF SOLITUDE ever gets written, the zany times in that house will of course have to be included. (Also the tragedy of my having sold my guitar to Balbi, where it will pickle away in some ropero somewhere. No serenades or wild guitar jam sessions for that one.)...

Finished the Kerouac book, it ended very sadly ("massive abdominal hemorrhaging"—he died in an operation). I wonder when he was last conscious. The book stresses that he himself was not the beat generation...His later tragedy as a "success" was that he was rarely taken seriously as a writer. And he was incredulous at the generation he'd fathered. (Not truly "beat" in the religious sense of the word.) For me he'll always remain "King of the Beats."

My travel sketches will change much from these inner reflections, I want mostly descriptions and an occasional comment. Plus much napkin haiku.

Asunción, 4 June 1977, Dearest Nanny,

It's Saturday morning, and as I sit over my <u>mate</u> (house-sitting for a friend) I'm imagining what life will be like for me back in the States. I doubt if conditions there have really changed much, even probably less than I have. I've become very tolerant (or so I think) of those things that I found difficult to accept in the States before, e.g., the wastefulness in general; the materialistic needs created by industry and advertising, and how people seem to go along being manipulated without realizing what's happening and fighting back.

(This I've come to understand happens anywhere and everywhere. I think it has to do more with individuals and their reaching a state of self-assurance with things that develop according to a well-known pattern, and the security that results from this, and the ease of life thereafter, etc. etc. instead of always questioning, questioning, questioning, trying to get to the source and/or truth—this can be most painful.)

Relatively speaking, people in the USA <u>do</u> have more of a choice and <u>do</u> exercise their rights to create a life for themselves, apart from the norm if need be...This happens <u>very</u> seldom in Paraguay. What "being Paraguayan" is is <u>so</u> well defined here...

More later—Love you always...E

On June 6 I sat in the PC office and typed my final site report, in which I described the physical, social, and political features of my beloved town:

The arroyo running through Piribebuy (which incidentally means "soft breeze" or "gentle shiver," the name stemming from the claim that even summer nights are cool) is the main source of life for the people. The two dams provide excellent swimming holes which are filled with people on hot summer afternoons; women look forward to mass clothes-washing happenings in the mornings; even water is sometimes brought from the arroyo for drinking (there are few wells in town, due to its altitude). Thanks to the respite offered by the water and the sensational views as well, there is an overwhelming feeling in Piribebuy that life isn't all that painful. People are gay and full of energy…

I was always treated very warmly by the people, who have had good luck with PCVs (two before me). There are many young people in town. The two athletic/social clubs 12 de Agosto and Club Atlético Independiente, who are long-time rivals, provide for much entertainment. Spring nights resound with either music from the one or the other—sometimes both!—parlantes, announcing a coming dance or cóctel, or else the air is alive with shouts from the volleyball, fútbol de salón and handball games that are held every Sunday, Tuesday and Thursday nights. You're often in the public eye in Piribebuy.

The several distinct barrios in town allow one to live one's entire life completely immersed in one's own immediate surroundings, without ever knowing what life is like anywhere else, not even in another barrio. Each has its own leaders, its own activities. The athletic clubs do much to bring people together…

Politically, Piribebuy is a disaster. Intra-party strife, manifesting itself primarily in disputes between the Colorado Party headquarters and the municipality, have stymied many projects that people have tried to initiate. The new intendente [police chief], Rehnfeldt, is basically open to change. The municipality helped the SENASA inspector and me in a "Beautify Piribebuy" campaign, paying for small trash cans (32) that were installed throughout the city. However, I would hesitate to ask the municipality for much. When I asked them to help out the health center they wouldn't budge; much hostility is felt for the directora/doctora, who refuses to organize her own commission. As I mentioned, there is a history of quarrels with SENASA. Piribebuy was SENASA's choice for its first water project. For the second one, the municipality didn't want to go through SENASA to finance, claiming that SENASA creams too much off the top. Although, however, there is basic anti-SENASA sentiment, the inspector is working with the municipality in various projects. That is, it's not hopeless…

Basically, there is much work to be done in the health center. The place needs money and basic repairs desperately. Termination of the running-water project would be ideal. The main obstacle is the doctor herself. She feels it's the community's responsibility to care for its health center, while her duty is caring for the community. The community feels it's her responsibility to communicate the health center's problems to the town and set the wheels in motion, but she won't listen. However, she liked me and had faith in me as a hard-working volunteer. If I hadn't left so soon, we could have worked together, I had her to that point. I think that if another conscientious PCV who wanted to work in community development were to go to Piribebuy and work in the health center, then much could be accomplished…

I feel that if a program can be worked out to fit Piribebuy, then by all means the town is ready for another PCV.

17 June 1977, Dearest Mom,

Hello from Río! Ellyn and I arrived last night, are staying in the apartment of a friend…Feels so magnificent to be on the road… Departure date was pretty sad, that is, the day I left Piribebuy. Got a little choked up with Elsa, and bawled like a baby in duet with ña Fernanda. It's different to be saying goodbye when you doubt you'll ever see anyone again, I've never been good in that position. Can't say I thrive on it. Will be so good to be home to stay…

Thanks for all the nice things you wrote me in your letter…

Love you!…E

15

MARTÍN

The fact that torturers and their victims were face-to-face made me think it would lead to the formation of two antagonistic blocks in the Emboscada prison camp. However, in practice I saw that the issue was more complex.

I noticed how some inmates tried to win over the officials, arguing that we should confuse the enemy by appearing to be common delinquents and not political prisoners, that it was more important to be free and continue the struggle than to be confined in prison. In short, the price of freedom was cooperation with the police. If not, then one should simply avoid conversations about the country's problems and pass the time making folk art and patronizing the police cafeteria.

I had observed some contradictions among the torturers as well. The torture team at Investigations had shown pride in taking orders directly from the president of the republic and not from the minister of the interior, their immediate superior in the hierarchy. Similarly, the new generation of police officers did not hide their displeasure at the fact that a military person was head of administration. And those belonging to the security guard barely tolerated their superiors, the high-level police officers. Plus, there was notable friction among the career officers and those who had been drafted, who were pejoratively called "Sergeant Cookie," "Captain Cookie," and the like.

One would think savagery could be measured with different measuring sticks, according to each individual and his line of service. Some officers showed support by passing us a page of the newspaper or a glass of water, or by giving us news of our families. We could tell what kind of person an officer was just by the way he opened and closed the doors to our cells.

I should mention that we prisoners chose not to take advantage of the contradictions among the torturers. They, however, took maximum and scientific advantage of our main weakness—the divisions among us, which seemed to be getting more and more acute. It was hard for me to understand how a political prisoner could see his fellow political prisoner as his true enemy. The persecution complex would go to intolerable extremes. Everyone mistrusted everyone else—I think we even got to the point of hating one another.

The pro-Muscovite communists trusted only their comrades, and the rest were suspected of being allies of the police or agitators sent specifically to their cells by the dictatorship and US imperialism.

For the pro-Chinese communists, the problems of Stroessner's dictatorship and US imperialism were secondary. It seemed that for them, the fundamental problem was imperialist, bourgeois Russia under Brezhnev. They considered Marxist-Leninist revolutionaries (connected to ERP and the Montoneros) "leftist terrorists" and "petit bourgeois Trotskyites."

There was also tension among the Febrerista militants, who could be easily classified according to their tendencies, whether they be social democrat, conservative, or Marxist-Leninist revolutionary. The Colorados, Liberals, and Febreristas alike felt the communists and revolutionaries were a true social plague and avoided contact with them, trying above all to keep from being seen with them by the guards. If they shared a cell, they would avoid conversation.

I remember a Colorado leader who once asked me to request that the authorities provide cells exclusively for Colorados, in order to avoid Marxist "contamination" and thereby enjoy some of the privileges granted to informants, such as special family visits or decent drinking water. My answer was a categorical no, and from that moment my relationship with my fellow Colorados began to deteriorate.

My openness to dialogue with the Marxists worried the Colorados so much that one day they told me to declare my ideology. I told them I was a Colorado, like them, and the only difference was that I was progressive. I specified that my Colorado beliefs were along the agrarian lines of Blas Garay, Juan León Mallorquín, and Roberto L. Petit. On the spot they accused me of being a Bolshevik trying to pass as a Colorado.

I was in prison for many reasons, one of which was my teachers' union militancy—so the police thought I was a dangerous bomb-thrower. The communists thought I was a Colorado in disgrace, unworthy of their trust. For my fellow party members, I was a communist. For the

Marxist-Leninist revolutionaries, I was an anarchist. Communist, anarchist, Maoist, and Trotskyite were titles given me by the torturers and the tortured. They couldn't understand me—and it was difficult for me to understand them.

I demanded justice, and because of that I was against Stroessner and imperialism. It's true that I lacked knowledge of political theory, but in spite of being around leftist organizations during my stay in La Plata (as were all students there at the time), I had not joined any of them. The injustices committed by the dictatorship in the educational arena were the true motives behind my actions—that is, distancing myself from the Stroessner Colorado beliefs and embracing the authentic, progressive Colorado system.

I had suffered and rebelled because Paraguayan teachers went to work hungry and lived in fear. I had frequently confronted the president of the Stroessner Colorado faction in San Lorenzo about the injustices he committed against the teachers' interests, as I could not tolerate people who claimed the right to appoint and dismiss teachers. I was equally distressed by students who went to school hungry and lived in fear. My ideological position was confirmed when I proved through my pedagogical research that education in Stroessner's Paraguay did not serve the people at large.

In spite of the aforementioned contradictions within the army and police who guarded us, they were solidly united, or at least appeared to be, under the absolute, top-down control of General Stroessner…whereas at the same time the inmates, who said they represented the revolutionary avant-garde, devoured each other under a similar top-down structure, without any possible dialogue. At that moment I thought I understood why the dictatorship had no difficulty inserting its agents into the center of the Paraguayan communist parties and destroying them from within.

The prison underworld reflected what was going on in the country. On the one hand was Stroessner, complacent with his friends and allies yet implacable with his enemies. On the other was the forbidden opposition in exile (mostly in Buenos Aires) and the permitted opposition in Asunción, complacent with the dictatorship yet implacable with their party members and allies.

I had also realized that the regime was supported not only by institution-alized fear—in other words, the direct manipulation of public opinion—but also by divisions within the opposition. It was evident that most leaders of the allowed opposition in Asunción were corrupt and, consequently, manipulated at will. It should also be acknowledged that the dictatorship had defeated this opposition by cleverly exploiting fear, chaos, and the communist threat. As far as the regime was concerned, political prisoners did not present a problem because there was not enough pressure from within the country. And from abroad, only Amnesty International and the few committees of solidarity for the Paraguayan cause were concerned for everyone indiscriminately (the vari-ous political parties generally demanded freedom for their own members only).

However, this dynamic changed completely when farmers started stream-ing into Emboscada. Philosophical theorizing decreased and spirits were calmed. A great majority of the campesinos, even though they knew little about political theory, had acquired valuable revolutionary experience in the Agrarian Leagues, which they had put into practice as a result of the struggle. Leaders of the political factions within the prison—whose speeches declared and pro-claimed the need to unite closely with the popular classes, in whose name we protesters were eating the stale bread of prison—finally had the opportunity to grasp the enormous potential of the farmworkers' movement and discover the depths of the Paraguayan tragedy.

At first the political types and the farmers were like vinegar and oil. The arrogance of the theoreticians didn't go with the humility—and especially the prudence—of the farmers. The revolutionary avant-garde of Paraguay was in the rear guard of the process of struggle, which was why small revolutionary move-ments tended to develop in urban and rural centers, with no interest whatsoever in establishing contact with organized, resolutely antidictatorial political parties.

When I would voice my impression that there was a political vacuum, the theoreticians responded with sentimental speeches. They mentioned their party's long history of struggle and, above all, its martyrs. They com-pletely neglected to acknowledge the dead and tortured of the other parties.

My attention was also drawn to their tendency to deny that there was a crisis in the different political groupings. Those "forward-thinking" comrades could not accept reality, and that seemed absurd to me. It was true, though, that none of them had forgotten to repeat the little catchphrase: "The only way to overturn the dictatorship is by a broad, popular mobilization of workers, farmers, students, and soldiers."

I constantly had to censor myself because I realized I risked the penalty of isolation. Until then I had censored myself because I was afraid of Stroessner, and now I had to do it because I was afraid of my fellow inmates, who were bothered by my remarks and, above all, my questions.

But the presence of the farmers became a uniting element, to the extent that the political "closed shops" finally opened up to dialogue and agreed that the political powers in opposition to the regime should commit to an agreement, without exclusions, to sustain *together* the power to build a democracy and throw out all forms of violence among Paraguayans. Only in this way could we move toward freedom.

As Dr. Sannemann said, the biggest mistake Stroessner made was to put us all together in the same place: communists, atheists, Liberals, Colorados, Febreristas, independents, anarchists, socialists, Catholics of liberation theology, leaders of the Agrarian Leagues. We "contaminated" each other there, and we left that hell with a revolutionary spirit—men and women made anew.[103]

---

103   Rodolfo and Gladys Sannemann survived prison; Gladys wrote books about her experience under Operation Condor. She died in Asunción on January 29, 2014, at age eighty-four, shortly after Rodolfo's passing.

PART X

MARGARITAVILLE
JULY–AUGUST 1977

—⚇—

EMILY

We shall not cease from exploration, and the end of all our exploring will be to arrive where we started and know the place for the first time.

T. S. Eliot

I'm in Manhattan Beach at my brother's bungalow two blocks from the Pacific—flew in a week ago from Buenos Aires after watching *Rocky* three tearful times in a row—and I must say it feels good to be back in the good ol' U S of A. But talk about culture shock! California is decadence incarnate. They have machines here where you can withdraw cash any time of night or day, even weekends. I mean, bankers' hours were a pain, but is nothing sacred? Americans' "needs" are *way* out of control.

Sam's writing for a magazine here in LA. He's always been the best brother, but I'm concerned about his lifestyle. When he's home he keeps the TV on with the volume off so he can blast the Grateful Dead through his stereo...though I have to admit listening to "Truckin'" at high decibels does a body good. He does turn up the TV sometimes...to watch this ridiculous show called *Saturday Night Live*. The one time I saw it, everybody was laughing at a joke I couldn't see the humor in—something about a scientific study proving rats get cancer from wearing leisure suits. What in the hell is a leisure suit, anyway? And why would a rat be wearing one in the first place? Is this what passes for comedy these days?

We've been playing a little guitar together, which is cool. What song, you might ask? A decadent one I keep hearing on the radio about some loser wasting away in a drunken margarita fog with a broken flip-flop, a cut heel, and a "Mexican cutie" tattoo.[104] Is that all people here have to worry about? At least the guy admits at the end it's his own damn fault. And to think the song shares the same name as my dear friend in Paraguay! Gino had taught me a couple other Buffett tunes, "Peanut Butter Conspiracy" and "Door Number Three." Now, I agree Jimmy Buffett is great...but is he not the best-paid *slacker* in the world?

Most decadent of all is the current issue of *Hustler* magazine sitting on my brother's table, which believe it or not has a page where you can "scratch and sniff" a woman's, you know, *tatú*. Imbeciles! Though I confess I am curious to see if they got it right, there's no way I could stoop that low.

Sometimes I'm afraid I've made a huge mistake by leaving Chayo for all this...madness. What if I don't fit in here, either? Everything disappoints, even crossing the street—drivers stop before you even step off the damn curb.

---

104 Jimmy Buffett, "Margaritaville," 1977.

Come on, people, don't deny me my favorite game, dodge traffic! One night Sam and I stood in line around the block like everyone else to see the new film *Star Wars*, a futuristic Western of sorts, which I liked (the special effects were mind boggling)—but all I could think about was how many millions of dollars had been wasted on it...for what? "Entertainment"?

I reflect on the protest I saw at the Plaza de Mayo before I left Buenos Aires, dozens of mothers in mourning wearing white scarves and carrying signs with pictures of their "disappeared" children, their *desaparecidos*, valiantly defying the authorities and marching in front of the Casa Rosada.[105] I take out the wood carving I bought on Calle Palma before I left Asunción, made of *quebracho* they said, and run my fingers over the figure of a woman with huge hands and feet, naked from the waist up, bending backward over a wall and in obvious agony. Whose hands have created this exquisite work, have touched it lovingly as I'm doing now, and why? Here in California I want to shout, "THIS IS WHAT'S IMPORTANT, PEOPLE, this is what's happening in Paraguay, in most of Latin America, RIGHT NOW!"

But people here have their own concerns, don't they? And not necessarily trivial ones...not for them, anyway. The bottom line is, I didn't change the stinkin' world. I didn't even make it a better place, except perhaps for the tiniest impact I may have had on a few communities through my friendships there—which I must admit is part of the PC's mission. Still, the only thing really different is me, and now I have to get on with my life. Here. In the United States.

I'll continue to do what I can to end injustice, starting with treating people fairly and advocating for those less fortunate. I plan to live simply and consume only my fair share of natural resources—skills I learned from the Paraguayans. I think about Chayo and Margarita and Olimpia and Cristi and the others every day and can only hope they'll be all right.

---

105   Since their first march on April 30, 1977, the Mothers of the Plaza de Mayo have continued to push for information on their children (now grandchildren) and raise global awareness of human rights abuses perpetrated by Argentina and surrounding countries. Since 2011, the United Nations, Amnesty International, and other organizations have observed the International Day of the Victims of Enforced Disappearances (International Day of the Disappeared) on August 30.

I feel as though I've passed through a membrane from one time to another, one "me" to another, the same yet different. But I don't cry over Dad anymore, and I can roll with the punches better now. I feel I have more to offer the world overall. It has indeed been a long, strange trip, but I am proud of my service and honored to be a "veteran of foreign peace"—if you can call it that.

I survived the Peace Corps! Yes, it *was* the toughest job I ever loved…and at times hated, of course. But who would I be if I hadn't done it? I can't imagine *not* having had this profound experience. I was honored to have met some courageous and remarkable people along the way, everyday heroes whose stories need to be told. It's true I was often critical of Paraguay and Paraguayans, but it was only because I wanted more for them—wanted them to want more for themselves—not consumer goods, necessarily, but things like autonomy and freedom from fear.

One thing is certain: world peace will never come about until we learn to recognize ourselves in one another and see that we have more in common than not.

I'm just relieved the burden of saving the world is not on me anymore… for now, anyway. The torch has been passed to current and future generations of Peace Corps volunteers. Do we simply tilt at windmills? I guess it depends on your perspective.

"Sufro al pensar…" I'm sitting in Chip Curry's living room playing some Paraguayan songs for him and a few of his bandmates, who have a "bluegrass experience, mariachi and swing ensemble" called Summerdog. I don't mean to be—I'm just following orders from my new boss, Michelle, who dragged me over here (why did I have to tell her I played guitar, anyway?)—but I am charming the pants off them.

I've been back in monsoon-soaked Tucson for a few weeks, and the Sonoran Desert never smelled so sweet. Mesquite branches hang low with ripe golden pods whose seeds practically beg to be ground into a delicious, tangy flour. I'm renting a house within biking distance of the university, where I've enrolled as a graduate student…in teaching English as a second language, not nursing, as originally planned. Midwifery is not the career for me, I've realized; as much as I fear overpopulation, there's no way I could bring babies into the world and feel good about it. Education, on the other hand—especially for girls—is clearly the means to alleviating poverty and making the world a better place.

Thanks to Peace Corps–Paraguay, I have a plan now, a calling even. They say nothing worthwhile comes easy...perhaps that should be the PC's motto. If value is in inverse proportion to ease, then I have benefited greatly!

I'm still a seeker but have known contentment. I've learned that the only meaning in life is what we give it. If we "celebrate" sorrow or weakness we will yield to it, and if we feel helpless, we probably will be. Life itself is to be celebrated...even still being single. As Emily Dickinson wrote, if we can "ease one life the aching" or help but one "fainting robin" return to its nest, our life will not have been in vain. My hope is to learn to see everything around me as inspiration.

I now understand what Margarita meant when she said happiness doesn't come from what "happens" to us, from outside—rather, *true joy* comes from within. And if anything comes between us and our joy, it's because we allow it to be there or we put it there ourselves. As long as I'm in "pursuit" of happiness, I'll never reach it; I simply need to embrace it. I will always be grateful to the PC—and the Paraguayan people—for helping me realize that I can reliably access the light within my own soul.

Painful memories still force their way in sometimes, of course, though I now realize they're like waves and will pass—even as I'm kept awake at night by the pounding in my heart. But I can't let the past hold me back.

I've just started working at the Unicorn Coffeehouse, across the street from Chip's, where Summerdog plays Monday nights for supper and tips. This is where I belong, where I will begin the next chapter of my life, a newly liberated, fuller person. The prodigal daughter has come home at last...well, for now, anyway. I'll see how it feels. After all, my new goal is to go everywhere and learn every language—still restless, I guess. Life is a journey, after all...you never know where it might take you.

But I will never forget Paraguay. *¡Ro jhai jhú, che retä!*

[The author finally put down roots in her hometown and never left again, after discovering that roots aren't so bad after all—they may tie you down, but you can't grow without them.]

PART XI

THE PRICE OF FREEDOM
AUGUST–SEPTEMBER 1977

—◊—

MARTÍN

Freedom, Sancho, is one of the most precious gifts the heavens gave to man, unequaled by any treasure within the earth or beneath the sea. For freedom, as for honor, one can and should risk one's life.

Miguel de Cervantes
Don Quixote de la Mancha

After careful reflection, I resolved to go on a hunger strike. It was to pro-test my detention and the humiliations I had endured, demand my imme-diate freedom, and affirm my position as a Christian and a militant, authentic Colorado. I explained my idea to my cellmates in the Third Precinct—where I had been transferred yet again—and then, through the mediation of the cap-tain, made my decision known to the chief of police, clearly establishing my ideological position and demands.

The ordeal was extremely difficult, but my cellmates' solidarity helped me overcome the obstacles I encountered. On the fifth day, I felt the first painful cramps that caused me to faint. I had trouble with my heart and vision, and could barely sip water. I became exhausted very quickly, my body weakened as a result of my torture and poor diet.

Fellow inmates constantly raised protests and demanded the presence of the police doctor at critical moments. But the superintendent systematically turned down these requests and ridiculed us and my "subversive activity," trying to demoralize us. The verbal provocations I received from this official and some of his underlings were so unbearable that I could feel their effects in my heart and lungs—my heart would throb uncontrollably and seem about to burst. Finally I would suffer a general contraction that left me prostrate.

If I so much as glanced at the container of drinking water, my whole di-gestive system would shut down and my stomach would rebel. And no matter what my cellmates talked about, it always seemed the topic was food, and they were describing varieties of delectable dishes.

Fifteen days into the strike, I became delirious. The black and white tiles of the cell floor became birthday cakes with several layers. Every bar of the prison looked like a big loaf of french bread. Instead of swords, I saw sausages hang-ing from the guards' waists. The old shoes under my bed were not footwear but pieces of meat; the smell of the soles brought back the delicious barbeques we had at the Teachers' Village during the days of our community service.

Mealtimes were particularly wretched. We were in that five-by-five-meter room, and I could obviously see and smell the food. In my mental state I even glorified it. Out of respect, my cellmates ate very discreetly, almost with em-barrassment. The only time I broke my fast was when I chewed my nails. My mouth was dry but I couldn't drink, and my taste buds felt as though they were hardening and coming off. My gums bled, and the taste of it nauseated me.

The days of agony passed slowly. I lost track of time. No one received visitors. We were all isolated from the outside world from the moment I began the hunger strike. As the twentieth day approached, I was like a vegetable. In my moments of lucidity, I became conscious of myself through my senses. I seemed to give off a smell of death. I looked at myself in a mirror and had the impression of a mummy embedded in its sarcophagus.

There would be a change of guard and I would see, on the other side of the grille, the potbellied officials and sergeants who looked like pigs in uniform, walking, heads down. Yes, their heads were down because they were witnessing the death of an innocent man, whose only crime had been writing a book with the purpose of improving the Paraguayan educational system and proposing a new pedagogical order. But oddly enough, despite my hunger, I didn't feel the least desire to consume those strange beasts.

I was so weak I couldn't stand up, so when I needed to urinate, I had to turn to my cellmates for help. Our foul-smelling toilet was right in our cell, one meter from my bed.

The days passed, and I was becoming a human rag. Nevertheless, my morale remained intact. It's true I was a skeleton, but with my head held high. My energy was running out, but so were the authorities' resources. Not one of their procedures had worked—not threats, blackmail, or persuasion. Finally, they made my mother intervene, allowing her a special visit. She was terrified to see me in such condition. We began a new conversation.

"My son, you are nothing but bones, you are on the verge of death. Don't you think of your children, who need you so much, and of me, who will die too? Why are you playing with your life like this?"

The head guard intervened and, turning to the other officers, said to them, "Look, typical communist behavior, insensitive to the suffering of a desperate mother. Communists are heartless."

My poor mother held me in her arms and gave me drops of salted water. Between sobs she told me my freedom was near, and spoke of the intervention of the Committee of Churches of Paraguay, of Monsignor Juan Bockwinkel of

Amnesty International, of the Paraguayan Lawyers' Association, and of national and international solidarity.

In spite of all the encouragement, I could barely hear her. A moment later I lost consciousness, and the guard took me back to my cell. Operation "persuasion" had not yielded the expected result. I remember that as I was approaching my cell, Amílcar Santucho raised his voice from the cell next door: "Leave that man in peace, you imbeciles."

During a moment of lucidity, I thought of my mother's suffering and my children's future. I realized I was committing suicide, which went against my Christian beliefs. And finally, I thought of something a cellmate had said: "A living patriot is more useful to the Paraguayan cause than a dead patriot." And I decided to end my hunger strike.

It had lasted thirty days.

On September 21, 1977, I was ordered back to Emboscada. Upon my arrival I was taken to the infirmary, where I received attentive care from the prisoner Dr. Jorge Canesse and other sympathetic inmates.

I threatened Colonel Grau that I would renew my hunger strike if the authorities did not set me free. Grau was condescending and declared that my freedom depended on my physical recovery. He advised me to eat well and go out into the sun and walk. But I was now afflicted with photophobia and could not tolerate sunlight; it burned my eyes and forced me to seek shade. And I had another physical ailment—from the waist up I felt a suffocating heat, but from the waist down intense cold.

Then, on September 24, an officer notified me that the president of the republic had ordered my freedom at the request of Amnesty International, which had launched an "Urgent Action" campaign, and the Committee of Churches of Paraguay. I looked at him in disbelief, but moments later Father Sosa and Sister Blasa confirmed the news. The president had finally acceded to the petition for my freedom that Monsignor Bockwinkel had carried out on behalf of the Committee of Churches.

Four days later, I was taken to the Office of Investigations and shortly thereafter to the Adventist Hospital of Asunción, where I stayed the entire month of October. There, between lucid and delirious moments, I had my first visitors.

Among others, I received a visit of solidarity and a sum of money from the Lions Club of San Lorenzo.

In mid-November I sent a letter to the Ministry of Education requesting that they reverse the takeover of the Juan Bautista Alberdi Institute, which was my property, because the reason for the takeover—"abandonment by the director of his position"—no longer existed. Nowhere had the order explained that it was because I had been imprisoned. This letter caused me new problems.

In the early hours of December 5, an official showed up at the house where I was staying to tell me I was under arrest. He took me to the Third Precinct.

I was again subjected to painstaking interrogation, this time at the hands of Campos Alum himself, now chief of the department. There were four charges against me. The first was having used, in the letter I sent to the Ministry of Education, the letterhead we used for our correspondence at the Alberdi Institute, which featured the following caption taken from the message of Medellín: "Education at all levels should be creative and anticipate the new kind of society to which we aspire in Latin America."

The second charge was provoking unrest at the institute, where, as a result of my liberation, the students had rebelled against my successor and accused her of being complicit in my detention.

The third charge was creating a climate of unrest on the university campus in San Lorenzo. At several meetings the students (the majority of whom were upper middle class) had openly demonstrated their indignation over the humiliations I had been subjected to.

The final charge: confusing public opinion by making improper comments about what I had experienced, seen, and heard during nearly three years in prison.

The political police claimed to have irrefutable proof of the above, furnished by the authorities of the pro-Stroessner Colorado Party local headquarters in San Lorenzo and the Education Ministry. The minister of education personally felt that I hadn't learned my lesson yet and recommended that I be sent to the Chaco.

After a grueling ten-hour interrogation that I could hardly bear in my poor health, they let me go home, with strict orders to return the following day. For the next two months, a *caperucita roja* picked me up every day and took me to the Third Precinct, where I was questioned about my political ideology, my connections with national and international communism, my links with certain members of the clergy—because of the intervention of Monsignor Bockwinkel—and countless other issues.

On my way home one night I met a friend, a prominent lawyer. He asked me where I was coming from and I said the Anticommunist Office of the Ministry of the Interior.

"Be careful," he warned, "one of these days they might get rid of you once and for all. Repression in this country is getting worse and worse. Yesterday they killed a well-known militant. This week the leg of a mutilated person turned up in the Mburicaó River."

As I entered my house, my head was spinning. What was I going to do in this country, infirm and unemployed? Should I continue to show up for these interrogations that were wearing me out? Was I right in continuing to burden my mother and children with the presence of police and sinister vehicles patrolling the house day and night? Was it fair to risk being killed and abandoning those who had struggled with me, who had repeatedly shown proof of their loyalty in my worst moments?

After long reflection, I decided to begin the paper work to leave Paraguay. Two arguments convinced me: fear, and the conviction that my survival would contribute to the cause of the liberation of my country.

I am not embarrassed to admit it: I—who had borne the worst tortures, who had undertaken a hunger strike that brought me close to death, who could resist my mother's tears, who had never let myself be intimidated by the officials' sadistic provocations—was afraid. Any noise, any person who walked behind me, any relatively ambiguous gesture threw me into a state of indescribable tension. If I remained in Paraguay, I would soon end up in the psychiatric ward—or the cemetery.

At the same time I was sure that, wherever I was, I would never forget my "humiliated and offended" country. Leaving Paraguay in no way meant giving up my commitment to my people, but rather continuing to fight for them under more favorable conditions. I remembered José Martí's words: "The fighter should place himself where he can be the most useful."

Professors Nelly Barrios Frutos and Lilian López discreetly put me in contact with the Panamanian Embassy in Asunción, run by Colonel Alejandro

Arauz. I entered the embassy at midnight on December 31, 1977, and asked for asylum. Colonel Arauz said he had nowhere to put me at the moment, but he would do everything possible to get me out of the country.

Together with the Apostolic Nunciature, the Committee of Churches, and the Paraguayan Episcopal Conference, and with the help of Humberto Rubín (director of Radio Ñandutí), Colonel Arauz organized my departure from Paraguay. On February 28, 1978, I set out for Panama, accompanied by my three children, Ricardo, Lincoln, and Celeste. The government of Panama declared me a guest of honor by merit of my dissertation, which had been inspired by the country's educational model. The Office of the United Nations High Commissioner for Refugees immediately granted us refugee status.

From the moment we reached Panamanian soil, we had the support of the authorities, the archdiocese, and various teaching organizations. Their solidarity came in the form of food, lodging, medical attention, and more. The Ministry of Foreign Affairs had appointed the Hotel Central to lodge and feed the many Latin American political refugees—mostly Nicaraguans, Chileans, Argentines, Uruguayans, Bolivians, and Paraguayans. The Hotel Central was opened around 1900, during construction of the Panama Canal. In the beginning, its guests were Europeans and North Americans who financed the canal's construction. On the threshold of the year 1978, however, this same hotel had as its clients the victims of fascism in Latin America.

Despite everyone's generosity, our first weeks in Panama were not easy. The transition from terror to freedom, from the status of object to that of human being, from a gloomy environment to one in which people smiled at us and shook our hands, was a complex process. It isn't strange, then, that I was surprised every time people spoke to me kindly, showed me consideration, invited me to their homes, or valued my family. I had the impression that I had landed on another planet.

I was in Panama physically, but spiritually I remained in Paraguay. It wasn't easy convincing myself that there was no danger and I was free and, even better, I was in Panama, a democratic country with no political prisoners. People opened their doors to me, especially when they found out I was the author of a book inspired by the Panamanian educational system.

I noticed there were no places in Panama named after Torrijos. In Paraguay everything is named "Stroessner," a constant reminder not only of the dictator but of his father, mother, wife, and children as well.

In Panama I tirelessly denounced the dictatorship in Paraguay—in churches, the university, the Ministry of Education, labor unions, every meeting, interview, or forum. That was my job. In meetings with the Educators' Reformist Front and United Panamanian Teachers, the cases of Virgilio Bareiro and Ananías Maidana were considered.

It soothed me to know that I was fulfilling my obligation.

The mortal remains of my beloved wife, Celestina, were currently resting in a mausoleum vault belonging to a personal friend, a man who'd had the courage to do me such a great favor considering he could have been persecuted for it. After recovering my freedom in Panama, I wanted to make sure Celestina would be buried in a Christian cemetery.

I began paperwork for the construction of a modest mausoleum so that I could proceed to transfer her body. I wrote to the town of San Lorenzo, requesting to purchase a plot in the cemetery. As the days passed and there was no response, I repeated the request. I then discovered the reason for the delay: the document had been forwarded to the interior minister for his consideration. For the officials of my town, it was a special burial that lay beyond local authority.

Stroessner, who had claimed to be Catholic and a defender of Western and Christian values, was placing obstacles in the way of my wife's Christian burial. Her "terrible crime" was having been the wife of a "subversive" teacher. She had died as a result of the psychological tortures to which the political police of Asunción and San Lorenzo subjected her. From Panama, I wrote to my mother in Buenos Aires, begging her to insist to the local authorities of my town that they put an end to such terrible political persecution.

I finally received news that neighbors and friends in San Lorenzo had mobilized and succeeded in obtaining a promise that the burial would take place. The minister of the interior set one condition: neither my name nor the name of any person allied with the political opposition would appear as the owner of the plot in the municipal cemetery.

This book is part of an effort to ensure that Paraguay ceases to be the no-man's-land of Latin America and overcomes the pessimistic image of a nation resigned to its fate. It is a denial of the ill-intentioned statement that "In Paraguay nothing happens," and an attempt to demonstrate that, on the contrary, below the seemingly calm surface and behind the official appearance of "peace and progress," violent tension and dramatic confrontations are rising, a truly explosive oppression, a cauldron that has begun to boil over.

This memoir is the testimony of an educator who was a political prisoner for 1,038 days and then became one of the millions of Paraguayans in exile. It is my testimony, the testimony of a Colorado open to new ideas—and it is my intention, through this book, to help raise the awareness of all those interested in forging a unified movement, to begin a process that will bring together the most diverse efforts. It is my fervent desire to collaborate in the unification of all Paraguayans, to overcome obstacles in order to proceed more securely and with more strength in the upcoming revolutionary times.

My attempt at evaluation is with the purpose of stimulating a search for the points of intersection, emphasizing all that unites us, creating a great national call to fight against the enemy that has made terror, dominance, and authoritarianism the supreme law in Paraguay. I hope it encourages analysis and reflection and helps show that what is revolutionary is to identify and address major social issues so that we can become a democratic society in which human rights are strictly observed, a society with social justice whose members are connected by ties of solidarity and not of oppression, a society in which we can develop ourselves integrally together, as Paraguayans, and become united fraternally to the other peoples of Latin America.

What I lived, saw, and heard in the prisons of Paraguay tempered my character, and in my spirit was born a passionate hatred of fascism and imperialism. Yet the vigor of the struggle of the Paraguayan people and the militant solidarity in Panama and abroad allow me to view the future with optimism, to work for the destruction of the dictatorship and the creation of a truly democratic system, and, finally, to repeat with profound emotion these verses by Osvaldo Chaves:

Por ese día abierto, florecido
con pan, con libertad, sin llantos,
prisiones rotas y pueblo redimido,
por ese día inevitable, canto...

[For that open, flowering day
with bread, with liberty, without cries,
prisons broken open and a nation redeemed,
for that inevitable day, I sing...]

[The author remained in exile for the next fourteen years, living one year in Panama and the rest in France and Switzerland, while working for UNESCO. During that time, in 1989, Alfredo Stroessner was ousted in a coup after thirty-five years of dictatorship; he died at age ninety-three without being brought to justice. In September 2015, at age seventy-eight, Dr. Almada testified at the International Human Rights Tribunal in Rome and met privately with Pope Francis to discuss Operation Condor.]

GLOSSARY

SPANISH

NOTE: Paraguayans love to drink an infusion made from yerba *mate*. *Mate* is pronounced "MAH-tay." The word *mate* in English, however, is incorrectly spelled "maté" with an accent mark and mispronounced "mah-TAY." To retain authenticity, we have treated *mate* as a foreign word and italicized it: "MAH-tay."

a diez—At ten (guaranies) each.
absolutamente nada—Absolutely nothing.
adiós—Good-bye.
al pelo—Far out, cool (lit. "to the hair").
alegría—Joy.
almacén—Store.
almácigo—Seed bed.
almidón—Starch from mandioca.
amante—Lover.
amor(es)—Love(s).
Antola, che ama—Antola, my dear lady (housewife).
argel—Angry; disagreeable; not inspiring sympathy.
argentino/a—Argentine.
arriero—Muleteer; a genial, resourceful person.
asado/a—Barbecue(d).
avenida—Avenue.
baile—Dance.
barriga—Belly.
barrio—Neighborhood.
beso(s)—Kiss(es).
bicho(s)—Bug(s).
bicicleta (bici)—Bicycle.
bombilla—Metal "straw" used to drink yerba *mate*.

bonita(s)/o(s)—Pretty.

borracha/o—Drunk.

brasero—Brazier.

budín—Pudding.

cabeza—Head.

cabrón (cabrones)—Billy goat(s); scoundrel(s).

camión de carga—Freight ("cargo") truck.

campesina/o—Someone who lives in the countryside; farmer.

campo—Countryside.

cancha—Court (as in volleyball); field (as in soccer).

canción—Song.

caña—Sugarcane; cane liquor.

capacidad—Capacity.

caperucita roja—Little red riding hood; name given to Chevy vans used to transport prisoners.

carnicera/o—Butcher.

cartulinas—Charts, posters.

casita rosada—Little pink house.

castrista—Supporter of Fidel Castro.

cataratas—Cataracts, waterfalls.

cena—Supper.

centro de salud—Health center.

cerro—Hill; the hills.

chacra—Cultivated garden plot for home consumption.

charla—Talk.

che—Friend.

chofer—Chauffeur; driver.

chicas/os—Girls/boys; little ones.

chiquititas/os—Little tiny ones.

chusky—Made up, pretty.

cigarillo—Cigarette; small cigar.

cigarro—Cigar.

circular—Shuttle bus.

ciudad—City.

claro que sí—Of course.

clausura—Closing; graduation.

cobertura—Coverage.

cocido—Sweet *mate* drink (lit. "cooked").

cocina a gas—Gas stove.

cóctel—Cocktail party.

cojones—Slang for testicles.

comadre—Co-mother; close friend.

comida—Food; meal.

comité—Committee.

con cariño—With affection.

cooperación—Cooperation.

corazón—Heart.

crema—Custard.

criatura—Creature; young child.

croquetas—Croquettes (fried dough).

cursillo—Short course.

dale—Take it; it's yours; that's it.

dar a luz—Birth (v.) (lit. "give to light").

de todo un poco y de nada mucho—Of everything a little and of nothing a lot.

despedida—Going-away event.

despedida de soltero—Bachelor party.

despensa—Small store.

Día de los Enamorados—Day of the Enamored (Valentine's Day).

día feriado—Holiday.

dictadura—Dictatorship (lit. "hard rule").

dios mío—My God.

director/a—Director; principal.

dulce—Sweet.

educadora del hogar—Home educator.

el cóndor pasa—The condor passes.

elaboración de informe—Preparation of report.

empanadas—Meat or fruit turnovers.

empíricas—Lay midwives.

enamorada(s)/o(s)—Enamored one(s).

escuelitas campesinas—Small rural schools.

estados unidos—United States.

estancia—Ranch.

estofado—Stew(ed).

estrella—Star.

fiambrera—Cupboard.

ficha—Record, file.

fogón (fogones)—Raised brick stove(s).

formulario—Form.

frialdad—Pain in belly; coldness; lack of enthusiasm.

fútbol—Soccer (term used only in the United States).

fútbol de salón—Indoor soccer.

galleta—Cracker; cookie.

ganga—Deal, bargain (slang in Mexico).

generalísimo—Very much general.

gente—People.

gracias a dios—Thank God (lit. "thanks to God").

gringa/o—Female/male foreigner in a Spanish-speaking country.

guampa—Cow's horn or gourd used for drinking *yerba mate*.

güera/o—Blond, light-skinned.

heladera—Freezer.

hombre—Man.

hormiga(s)—Ant(s).

hospital de clínicas—Teaching hospital.

huerta (familiar)—(Family) garden.

increíble—Incredible.

informe mensual—Monthly report.

ingeniero agrónomo—Agronomic engineer.

jefe—Chief; boss.

jugo de pomelo—Grapefruit juice.

La Técnica—Alternate name for the Third Precinct, also known as the "Tomb of the Living."

La Voz del Coloradismo—"The Voice of Coloradism," a radio program from the time.

lechuga—Lettuce.

limpieza—Cleaning.

lluvia—Rain.

maestro/a, profesor/a—Teacher, professor.

Malacara—Emily's horse in Caazapá (lit. "Bad Face" for his crooked blaze).

manejo—Management.

manualidades—Handicrafts.

mañana—Tomorrow.

mariposa—Butterfly.

más vale tarde que nunca—Better late than never.

mate—Yerba *mate*, leaves of the *Ilex paraguariensis* tree smoked and ground; the beverage made with yerba *mate*.

matero—Generic term for a vessel used to drink *yerba mate*.

médico—Doctor.

mentirosa/o—Liar.

merienda—Afternoon snack; picnic.

Militarismo mata mi patria...qué tristeza me cobra—Militarism kills my homeland...what sadness it costs me.

Ministerio de Agricultura y Ganadería—Ministry of Agriculture and Livestock.

mira un poco—Look at this (lit. "Look a little.")

mis noches sin ti—My nights without you.

misa(s)—Catholic mass(es).

monte—Mountains; forest.

morocha/o—Person with dark hair and skin.

moto—Motorcycle.

municipalidad—Municipality.

nada—Nothing.

naranja lima—Lemony orange.

nata—Cream.

no da gusto—It's no fun (lit. "it doesn't give pleasure").

no hay vehículo—There's no vehicle.

nomás—No more; is all.

no me digas—You don't say (lit. "don't tell me").

nogal(es)—Walnut(s); walnut tree(s).

novia/o—Girlfriend/boyfriend.

obstetra—Female obstetrician.

oficina—Office.

oliva—Olive.

oratorios—Oratories, chapels.

palabras dulces—Sweet words.

palma—Palm.

pañuelitos—Little cloths.

pariente(s)—Relative(s).

parlante—Loudspeaker (often attached to a car).

parrillada—Grilled; restaurant serving grilled meat.

patria—Homeland (fatherland); country.

patrón—Boss; patron.

pensando lejos—Thinking far away.

perejil—Parsley.

perrera—Dog-catcher; name given to windowless red van used to transport prisoners.

perrita/o—Little female/male dog.

perros locos—Crazy (male) dogs.

pileta—Tub; pool.

plancha—Metal plate with holes that sits on top of a fogón (stove) for cooking; iron (for pressing clothes).

plata—Slang for money (lit. "silver").

por fin—At last.

pundonoroso—Honorable man.

purgante—Purgative, laxative.

¡qué curvas, y yo sin freno!—What curves, and I with no brakes!

que me ha dado tanto—That has given me so much.

quebracho—A hardwood.

rabanito—Little radish; penis.

recuerdo—Memory; souvenir.

refrescante—Refreshing.

remedio—Remedy. *remolacha*—Beet(s).

repollo—Cabbage.

reunión—Meeting; reunion.

ropero—Armoire, wardrobe.

ruta abierta—Open road (route).

ruta clausurada—Closed road (route).

sabor—Flavor; taste.

saneamiento ambiental—Environmental health.

señora—Married woman; "Mrs."

Sepulcro de los Vivos—Tomb of the Living, epithet for the Third Precinct (also called "La Técnica").

servicio agrícola—Agricultural extension.

siembra—Sowing; sowing season.

simpática / o—Nice (lit. "sympathetic").

socia / o—Club member; partner; associate.

soja—Soy.

sueltas / os—Loose; free; unattached.

suero—Serum; saline solution.

tablón (tablones)—Plot(s), bed(s) (as in garden).

taxista—Taxi driver.

técnica—Technique; technology; skill.

tía—Aunt.

todo el mundo—The whole world.

tomasita—Chaperone (lit. "little Tomasa").

torta—Cake (in South America).

trago—Swig, sip, shot.

tranquila / o, nomás—Tranquil, is all.

un ratito, nomás—A little while, is all.

vamos—Let's go.

vieja / o—Old; old person.

vitamina(s)—Vitamin(s); smoothie(s).

yerba (hierba)—Herb, specifically *mate* (in Paraguay).

yo he dicho—I have spoken (lit. "I have said").

yuyo(s)—Medicinal plant(s).

GUARANÍ

acä-në—Having no intelligence (lit. "smelly head").

araí—Cloud.

ara-tirí—Lightning.

cabajú—Horse (*caballo*).

caraí—Mr.

che—I; me; my.

che añó—Only me, by myself.

che retä—My homeland.

chipa guazú—Similar to sopa paraguaya but made with meat.

chipa paraguaya—Baked, cheese-flavored roll made with mandioca starch and anise.

chipera(s)—Maker(s) and/or vendor(s) of chipa.

cunu-ú—Tenderness; affection.

cuñataï—Señorita (young, unmarried woman).

etereí—Very; too much.

guá—From.

guaraní—Native people of South America; indigenous language spoken in Paraguay; currency of Paraguay.

guazú—Large.

í (mí)—Small.

i porä—Good, pretty.

kamby—Milk.

kupi-í—Termite.

mba-eichapá?—How's it going?

mbaracá-jhape—Guitar "happening" (lit. "where guitar is played").[106]

mburicá—Mule.

minga—Work of mutual cooperation.

---

106 Coincidentally, *mbaracá ováma* (sounds like "Barack Obama") means "the guitar has been moved already."

ndaikuaai—I don't know.

ndaipori problema—No problem.

nde—You; your.

ñandutí—Spiderweb; Paraguayan folk art.

pa-í—Priest.

pyragüé—Hairy foot; a spy or informant for the political police.

retä—Homeland, nation.

ro jhai jhú—I love you.

saporó—Boiled beans.

sevo-í—Hookworm (lit. "little worm").

tambo verá—Kitchen help (lit. "sparkling-clean milking stall").

tatá—Fire.

tatacuá—Beehive-shaped outdoor oven made of clay.

tatú—Vulva.

tavy—Crazy; ignorant.

tayy—Lapacho.

tranquilopá—Very tranquil.

tukaé—Tag (children's game).

ura—A worm that grows under the skin and in wounds.

yguazú—Big water.

yvapurü—A large, grape-like fruit with white flesh that grows on the trunk and branches of the jabuticabeira tree.

Martín and Emily discussing their book in the studios of Ecocultura Community Television of Paraguay in Asunción, January 2015.

Although attempting to bring about world peace through the internal transformation of individuals is difficult, it is the only way.

His Holiness the Dalai Lama

61957382R00252

Made in the USA
Charleston, SC
28 September 2016